Lecture Notes in Computer Science 15600

Founding Editors

Gerhard Goos
Juris Hartmanis

Editorial Board Members

Elisa Bertino, *Purdue University, West Lafayette, IN, USA*
Wen Gao, *Peking University, Beijing, China*
Bernhard Steffen , *TU Dortmund University, Dortmund, Germany*
Gerhard Woeginger, *RWTH Aachen, Aachen, Germany*
Moti Yung, *Columbia University, New York, NY, USA*

The series Lecture Notes in Computer Science (LNCS), including its subseries Lecture Notes in Artificial Intelligence (LNAI) and Lecture Notes in Bioinformatics (LNBI), has established itself as a medium for the publication of new developments in computer science and information technology research, teaching, and education.

LNCS enjoys close cooperation with the computer science R & D community, the series counts many renowned academics among its volume editors and paper authors, and collaborates with prestigious societies. Its mission is to serve this international community by providing an invaluable service, mainly focused on the publication of conference and workshop proceedings and postproceedings. LNCS commenced publication in 1973.

Colin Boyd · Reihaneh Safavi-Naini ·
Leonie Simpson
Editors

Information Security
in a Connected World

Celebrating the Life and Work of Ed Dawson

 Springer

Editors
Colin Boyd
Norwegian University of Science
and Technology
Trondheim, Norway

Reihaneh Safavi-Naini 🆔
University of Calgary
Calgary, AB, Canada

Leonie Simpson 🆔
Queensland University of Technology
Brisbane, QLD, Australia

ISSN 0302-9743   ISSN 1611-3349 (electronic)
Lecture Notes in Computer Science
ISBN 978-3-031-83489-9   ISBN 978-3-031-83490-5 (eBook)
https://doi.org/10.1007/978-3-031-83490-5

© The Editor(s) (if applicable) and The Author(s), under exclusive license
to Springer Nature Switzerland AG 2025

This work is subject to copyright. All rights are solely and exclusively licensed by the Publisher, whether the whole or part of the material is concerned, specifically the rights of translation, reprinting, reuse of illustrations, recitation, broadcasting, reproduction on microfilms or in any other physical way, and transmission or information storage and retrieval, electronic adaptation, computer software, or by similar or dissimilar methodology now known or hereafter developed.
The use of general descriptive names, registered names, trademarks, service marks, etc. in this publication does not imply, even in the absence of a specific statement, that such names are exempt from the relevant protective laws and regulations and therefore free for general use.
The publisher, the authors and the editors are safe to assume that the advice and information in this book are believed to be true and accurate at the date of publication. Neither the publisher nor the authors or the editors give a warranty, expressed or implied, with respect to the material contained herein or for any errors or omissions that may have been made. The publisher remains neutral with regard to jurisdictional claims in published maps and institutional affiliations.

The cover figure is based on a diagram by Ed Dawson and illustrates a general stream cipher.

This Springer imprint is published by the registered company Springer Nature Switzerland AG
The registered company address is: Gewerbestrasse 11, 6330 Cham, Switzerland

If disposing of this product, please recycle the paper.

Fig. 1. Professor Ed Dawson, 1946–2023

Preface

This volume contains papers dedicated to the memory of Ed Dawson. All of the papers are concerned in some way with information security, with the majority focussing on cryptography. In today's connected world cryptography forms the technical foundation for protecting data against malicious adversaries. The technical solutions are only useful if they support the needs of society.

The contents of this book include 11 original technical papers and an initial chapter of personal memories of Ed. All of the technical papers were blind reviewed by two independent reviewers. The volume contains the full revised papers. We are very grateful to all of the reviewers named below for their invaluable help. It is a pleasure to thank Springer for making this volume possible.

Ed Dawson was originally trained as a mathematician and first worked as a schoolteacher before joining Queensland Institute of Technology (later Queensland University of Technology). Like many of us (including the three undersigned) he was attracted by the exciting developments in the emerging academic field of cryptology and made the shift from pure mathematics into a new applied world. As his career developed his interests broadened further. At the start of his research career he concentrated on symmetric key cryptology, analysing randomness, searching for new building blocks and designing cryptographic engines. Later he expanded his interest to public key cryptography with a particular focus on the implementation aspects of elliptic curves. As he became more senior, Ed oversaw the formation of a multidisciplinary Information Security Institute at QUT, involving researchers from across the spectrum including mathematics, computer science, engineering, business and law. This allowed him to broaden his expertise still further to incorporate human aspects, often called socio-technical security.

Ed's breadth of interests is reflected in the diverse topics of the papers in this volume. We have divided the technical papers into sections on: symmetric key cryptology, public key cryptography, and socio-technical systems.

Symmetric Key Cryptography. The first two papers connect cryptography with coding. Coding was one of Ed's first research interests and this connection is explored in the paper *From Block Designs to Codes to Crypto and Back Again*. The paper *Cryptographic Applications of the ANS Compression* explores how the features of a relatively new compression algorithm can provide cryptographic properties. The second pair of papers are concerned with cryptanalysis. *Differential Fault Analysis of TinyJAMBU* uses techniques which would have been familiar to Ed to analyse the security of a recent lightweight encryption algorithm. *Integrity-Protecting Block Cipher Modes — Untangling a Tangled Web* connects with a paper co-authored by Ed that showed a proposed attack on a certain block cipher mode of operation known as EPBC did not work in practice. This paper looks more deeply into a class of block cipher modes for integrity protection that includes EPBC, and finds a new forgery attack approach that applies with high probability.

Public Key Cryptography. Ed had a particular interest in elliptic curve cryptography. This section has two papers on this topic. In p261: *A Karatsuba-Friendly Prime for Fast Elliptic Curve Arithmetic*, co-authored by one of Ed's PhD students, a new curve with exceptionally good implementation properties is investigated. The selection of elliptic curves with good security and implementation properties is comprehensively surveyed in *Safe Curves for Elliptic-Curve Cryptography*. Another paper with a focus on implementation efficiency is *Asymptotic Complexity and Performance Comparison of* FALCON *and* SOLMAE *Using Their C Implementation* which compares a standardised quantumsecure signature with a variant proposed for standardisation in South Korea. The final paper in the section is *Falsifiability, Composability, and Comparability of Game-Based Security Models for Key Exchange Protocols* which establishes and justifies a way to make cryptographic security models for key exchange more comparable.

Socio-technical Aspects. Papers in this section are concerned with the intersection of humans and the world of information security. These are difficult areas of interdisciplinary research which Ed took a big interest in during his later research career. Risk modelling for small businesses is an important real-world problem which is explored in *Structuring the Chaos: Enabling Small Business Cyber-Security Risks & Assets Modelling with a UML Class Model*. The next paper, *Data Processing Displacements: The Use of CHERI Fat Pointers and the GDPR*, takes a legal view on an emerging technology and how it will influence privacy laws. The final paper in the volume looks to the future of information security in the emerging world where digital artefacts are increasingly constructed by AI agents. *The Mis/Dis-information Problem Is Hard to Solve* considers to what extent the technology used in the past to keep society safe will be effective in the future digital world.

We believe that Ed would have appreciated all of the papers in this volume. All of the diverse topics explored were firmly within the range of his research interests. We are grateful to all of the authors for their major efforts in building a fitting research memorial for Ed.

October 2024

Colin Boyd
Reihaneh Safavi-Naini
Leonie Simpson

Organization

Reviewers

Harry Bartlett	Queensland University of Technology, Australia
Colin Boyd	NTNU, Norway & QUT, Australia
Gary Carter	Queensland University of Technology, Australia
Craig Costello	Microsoft, USA
Bor de Kock	NTNU, Norway
Kai Gellert	University of Wuppertal, Germany
Gregory Hagen	University of Calgary, Canada
Huseyin Hisil	University of Wollongong, Australia
Michael Jacobson	University of Calgary, Canada
Håvard Raddum	Simula UiB, Norway
Tjerand Silde	NTNU, Norway
Leonie Simpson	Queensland University of Technology, Australia
Reihaneh Safavi-Naini	University of Calgary, Canada
Kenneth Radke	Griffith University, Australia
Kenneth Wong	Queensland University of Technology, Australia

Contents

Socio-technical Aspects

Personal Reflections

Remembering Ed Dawson

Colin Boyd[1,3(✉)], Reihaneh Safavi-Naini[2], and Leonie Simpson[3]

[1] Norwegian University of Science and Technology, Trondheim, Norway
[2] University of Calgary, Calgary, Canada
[3] Queensland University of Technology, Brisbane, Australia

Like a lot of people, Ed Dawson had many roles in life: a researcher, a teacher, a husband, a father and grandfather, a friend, a traveller, a sports fan, a nature lover, even a poet. Yet unlike some people, Ed's life cannot be easily partitioned according to these roles. His research collaborators and students often became his friends, he frequently invited his colleagues into his family, and he shared his enthusiasm for bushwalking, cricket, mathematics or cryptology with anyone who was interested.

In this chapter we have collected some snapshots of Ed Dawson's life as seen by several of his friends and colleagues. We have made a number of headings to try to organise the memories, but these are not precise and they overlap in various ways. We start with an overview of Ed's professional life and then turn to his achievements as a researcher, a teacher, an international ambassador and a friend and mentor.

1 Ed's Professional Roles and Leadership

Ed and his wife Ana moved from USA to Australia in 1971. Initially Ed worked as a high school mathematics teacher in Sydney for a couple of years. In 1974 Ed successfully applied for a job at the Queensland Institute of Technology (QIT), and he and Ana moved to Brisbane where they put down permanent roots. The move went well, and in the same year Ed became a lecturer at QIT. During the 1980s Ed took some sabbaticals and developed his research interests in mathematics and coding theory.

1.1 Ed's Career at QUT

When QIT became QUT (Queensland University of Technology) in 1989, Ed took the opportunity to enrol in the new PhD program, with Bill Caelli as his supervisor. By 1991 Ed was one of the first PhD graduates from QUT, and he also received a promotion to Senior Lecturer. The expansion of research at QUT led to the formation of the Information Security Research Centre (ISRC) at QUT under the direction of Bill Caelli. In 1993, when Bill formed a new academic school (Software Engineering and Data Communications), Ed took over the position of

Includes contributions from: Mark Burdon, Diane Donovan, Gary Gaskell, Kwangjo Kim, Paul Montague, Winfried B. Müller, Tony Pettitt, Josef Pieprzyk, Jennifer Seberry, Jason Smith, Willy Susilo, Kenneth Koon-Ho Wong and Moti Yung.

© The Author(s), under exclusive license to Springer Nature Switzerland AG 2025
C. Boyd et al. (Eds.): Ed Dawson Festschrift 2024, LNCS 15600, pp. 3–22, 2025.
https://doi.org/10.1007/978-3-031-83490-5_1

Director of the ISRC; a position he held for over 10 years. This coincided with Ed's move from the School of Mathematics to the School of Software Engineering and Data Communications in the new Faculty of Information Technology. Over these years, the ISRC flourished and expanded; Ed became a full Professor of Cryptology and Its Applications in 2000.

In 2005 the ISRC evolved into the Information Security Institute (ISI); one of four cross-faculty research institutes at QUT. Ed became Director of the ISI. Having established its success, he retired as Emeritus Professor in 2007, but continued to work part-time for many more years as a project leader, PhD supervisor, and adviser.

Tony writes: My personal memories of Ed start when I first met Ed in 1989 when I joined QUT in November of that year. I was his nominal boss as head of department of Mathematics. He spent 1990 on leave to concentrate on finishing his PhD in the Faculty of Information Technology's (FIT) Information Security Research Centre (ISRC) working on cryptology.

In the 1980s he'd been on various sabbaticals from QIT. After visiting University of Waterloo in 1983, Ed published a couple of papers with Professor Ron Mullin on mathematical error control coding theory. This contributed to a research masters from the University of Queensland. Another outcome from the Waterloo sabbatical was Ed's introduction of the Cooperative Education program for maths degree students at QIT. Later the QIT Faculty of Information Technology took it up with much success.

From January-June 1987, Ed had a six-month sabbatical within the Digital Communications Group at the South Australia Institute of Technology (SAIT) in South Australia. Ed decided to focus his research on cryptology instead of error correcting codes. Ed started collaborating with Bill Caelli in 1988. Bill was the Director of the new Information Security Research Centre (ISRC) within the QIT Faculty of Information Technology.

In 1990 Ed spent most of his sabbatical in Brisbane, coming in to QUT from his home. I met him mostly for social occasions and working with Helen Gustafson in maths and Nev Davies, my visitor from Nottingham. We collaborated on the CRYPT-X Statistical Package which covered material I had worked on in the early 1970s as part of my Nottingham PhD. There were a few social occasions too, in Ed's inimitable style! With BBQs and the Irish Club featuring. In August 1990 Ed attended his first Crypto conference in Santa Barbara.

In April 1991, Ed was the first person to be awarded a PhD by QUT, a fledgling organisation in the world of research. However, he was technically the second to graduate as the Faculty of Science graduation ceremony took place a few hours before Faculty of IT's (FIT) with Nancy Spencer (Science Faculty) being the only other graduating PhD of QUT at that time. In August 1991 Ed was promoted to Senior Lecturer on the basis of his new PhD. He left maths to join the ISRC and FIT. What a loss to maths!

Ed was making up for lost time during 1990 to 2010, developing an academic research career of 20 years rather than 40 or 50 years. Ed was promoted to Associate Professor in 1992 and to Professor in 2000. In 2007 he officially retired from QUT and received the title of Emeritus Professor (see Fig. 1). However, Ed maintained a full academic involvement, being appointed a QUT Adjunct Professor. He maintained he was far better off financially "retired" than working—a quirk of the Australian tax system.

Professor Ed Dawson has worked for QUT for 34 years. During that time, he has become one of the University's most distinguished researchers, with a long history of ARC, Government and industry-funded research in the area of Information Security. Highlights of his outstanding career at QUT include:

- *launched the cooperative education (industry experience) program in the Faculty of Science in 1984; adopted by FIT in 1986*
- *director of the Information Security Research Centre from 1993-2004*
- *research director of the ISI from 2004-present*
- *node leader, ARC Research Network for a Secure Australia*
- *engagements in many ARC grants, CRC smart internet, CRC smart services, etc*
- *significant and ongoing successful production of HDR students.*

Professor Dawson has been the single most outstanding research contributor to the Faculty of Information Technology for at least the past 15 years, and has built a national and international reputation for impact and excellence in the information security area. His contributions to the Faculty and the ISI are highly regarded, and a continued association with Professor Dawson would be valued. The award of an Emeritus Professorship would appropriately recognize one of the University's most outstanding and influential scholars.

Fig. 1. QUT Council citation for Ed Dawson appointment as Emeritus Professor, 7 December 2007

1.2 Ed's Influence in Australia

Rei writes: I first met Ed at a symposium on symmetric-key cryptography that he had organized in Sydney, Australia, in 1989. I was presenting at the symposium, and he was one of the main organizers. Over the next 20 years, Ed became a colleague and a friend whom I respected as one of the key people in Australasia in promoting, founding, and organizing events and leading initiatives related to cryptology and information security. Ed had a key role in shaping ACISP (Australasian Conference on Information Security and Privacy), Auscrypt, and finally Asiacrypt (International

Conference on the Theory and Application of Cryptology and Information Security). He was also a driving figure behind large nationwide initiatives such as the Cybersecurity CRC (Cooperative Research Centre).

Ed was understanding of people's diverse backgrounds and respectful of the cultural sensitivities and nuances of meeting and discussing with delegates from different countries. This was crucial in building trust and strong relationships that led to the formation of Asiacrypt.

It is hard to overstate the wisdom, positive energy, laughter, and joy that Ed brought to meetings, whether a casual chat during a coffee break or dinner at a conference with Ana by his side, or a formal Steering Committee meeting of Asiacrypt with him leading the Australian delegation (of which I was a member for some time). He was, and will be, an exemplary figure on how to bridge differences and build relationships with others as equals.

Josef writes: If my memory serves me right, my first encounter with Ed was at the 5th IFIP International Conference on Computer Security, organized by William Caelli on the Gold Coast in May 1988. Ed was part of the organizing committee. Our next meeting was at Auscrypt 1990 in Sydney, where Ed presented his work. One of his presentations was delivered at the Rump Session, which I organized. At that time, we were both deeply interested in the design of symmetric-key cryptosystems. The subsequent Auscrypt conference was held on the Gold Coast in December 1992, with Ed again contributing to the organizing committee. This collaboration led to the creation of our local and highly successful series of ACISP conferences. These conferences generally alternate between New South Wales (Sydney/Wollongong) and Queensland (QUT). Ed played significant roles in many of them, serving as General Chair and/or Program Chair. However, his most memorable role was as the chair of the Rump Sessions. His terrific sense of humour, contagious laugh, and easygoing nature made these sessions enjoyable for both presenters and the audience.

Probably my most intense interactions with Ed were after 2014, when I joined QUT. Upon my arrival in Brisbane to take up a professorial position at QUT, Ed and Ana graciously offered me accommodation at their home while they were visiting friends in New Zealand. During my stay in Brisbane, we often spent weekends together, climbing the Glass House Mountains and bushwalking in national parks surrounding Brisbane. I fondly remember our overnight stay at a cottage in Bunya Mountains National Park, the picturesque views of the Gold Coast from Lamington National Park, and barbecues on the beaches along Moreton Bay. Professionally, we co-supervised Iftekhar Salam, whose research focused on the analysis of symmetric ciphers. We met fortnightly to discuss potential research directions and evaluate student progress.

Apart from being an exemplary researcher and teacher, Ed was a paragon of reliability, friendship, and mentorship. His legacy is, without exaggeration, the robust and flourishing cryptographic community in Australia and beyond. His PhD students and postdocs have become key figures in the Australian IT security industry and academia, testament to his profound influence and enduring contributions.

Rest in peace, Ed. I miss you.

Jason writes: Ed has been a tremendous influence on, and supporter of, my career. I first encountered Ed in the early 2000s when he agreed to have me join a PKI project as a research assistant while I was completing my undergraduate studies at QUT. Following this work and my completion of a degree, Ed was instrumental in securing a scholarship for my PhD studies under the CRC for Railway Engineering and Technologies. During my PhD studies and in a number of post-doctoral research roles, Ed was tremendously supportive in the work we were proposing around critical information infrastructure protection. Notably, his leadership in the ARC Research Network for a Secure Australia, the Australia-India sponsored research under the Department of Broadband Communications and the Digital Economy and work we undertook on behalf of the Attorney-General's Department working with critical infrastructure utilities in performing computer network vulnerability assessments. These experiences all laid the foundation for the current work I do securing energy infrastructure across Australia.

Ed was a boss like none other that I had before or since. With Ed, what you saw was what you got, he was incredibly transparent and personable and really knew how to bring a team together. The friendships I established during my time at the ISRC and ISI have endured and the Kelly pool and taco nights at Ed's place were a key part in that.

Diane writes: Ed's career exemplifies an unwavering commitment to his discipline, his students, and his colleagues, both nationally and internationally. By establishing personal connections with others, he forged strong working relationships that often evolved into lasting friendships. A key principle of his working ethos was fostering an inclusive atmosphere that nurtured outstanding research with global impact, allowing Ed to influence research environments throughout Australia and beyond.

Through his extensive personal network of over 140 co-authors, Ed attracted talented researchers to Australia, hosting many distinguished visitors who were leaders in their fields. His efforts were crucial in organizing seminal conferences that featured impressive lineups of invited speakers and attracted participants from Australasia and beyond.

Dedicated to supporting early-career researchers, Ed provided vital financial assistance, including Postdoctoral Fellowships within the ISRC and ISI. Beyond securing funding, he actively fostered a culture of collegiality and collaboration, offering opportunities for personal development and participation in research projects alongside international experts. This commitment is reflected in the success of many students and early-career researchers who have advanced to prominent roles in both industry and academia.

In his roles as Director of the Information Security Research Centre (ISRC), the Information Security Institute, and Head of the School of Data Communication at QUT, Ed had a significant impact on research environments throughout Australia by prioritizing collaboration and assembling strong teams with the right expertise to tackle significant challenges. By promoting equality among team members and valuing everyone's contributions, he instilled these principles in others.

Ed's influence extended beyond QUT as he established fruitful partnerships with collaborators at the University of Queensland, the University of Wollongong, and Deakin University, effectively spreading his principles throughout Australia. In Brisbane, he played a pivotal role in joint activities with the University of Queensland, facilitating collaborative courses, graduate student supervision, and research projects. Beyond academia, Ed actively engaged in industrial research projects with organizations such as Australian Telecom, Korea Telecom, the Australian Government, the Queensland Government, Austraclear (the Australian banking fund clearing organization), the Hong Kong Jockey Club, the Commonwealth Bank, Advance Bank, Motorola, and the Japanese Government. He also worked on significant projects with various Australian airports and government agencies, including the Federal Police, Customs, and Immigration, addressing critical issues regarding the future operations of airports.

Overall, Ed's career is characterized by a dedication to inclusivity and collaboration, resulting in a lasting impact across Australia and beyond.

1.3   Ed's Influence Internationally

Kwangjo writes: The IACR (International Association for Cryptologic Research), which was formed in the 1980s by the cryptography community in the United States and Europe, held the first annual international academic conferences on the science and practice of cryptology and its related fields, Crypto 1981 and Eurocrypt 1982, at UCSB in the United States and a European country, respectively.

Inspired by the growing global interest in cryptography, Japanese and Australian cryptographers took the initiative to host international academic conferences on cryptology in their respective countries. In 1990, the first Auscrypt conference was held in Sydney, Australia, with prominent figures such as Professor Jennifer Seberry playing a key role in its organization. This event marked a significant step for Australia in contributing to the global cryptographic research community.

Following Australia's lead, Japanese cryptographers launched Asiacrypt in 1991, the first crypto conference in Asia. Held in Fujiyoshida, this conference was organized by Professor Hideki Imai and other notable Japanese cryptographers. Asiacrypt aimed to foster regional collaboration and advance cryptographic research in Asia. This effort marked significant milestones in the field's development and collaboration across the Asia-Pacific region.

After the second Auscrypt conference in 1992 at the Gold Coast, Australian and Japanese cryptographers decided to consolidate their efforts. To manage the growing influence and responsibilities of Asiacrypt, the Asiacrypt Steering Committee (ASC) was formed in 1993, with Professor Hideki Imai serving as its first chair. The initial ASC member countries included Australia, China, Japan, Korea, and Singapore, each represented by 2 to 3 delegates. The ASC's primary role is to decide the hosting country for future Asiacrypt conferences through majority voting, with each member country having one vote. Ed served as ASC chair from 1997 to 2000 following Professor Hideki Imai.

In 1994, Asiacrypt was hosted in Wollongong, Australia, under an agreement between the leading cryptographic researchers from Japan and Australia. This merger symbolized a unified effort to strengthen and streamline cryptographic research across the Asia-Pacific region. No more Auscrypt.

Over the years, the ASC has expanded to include additional countries such as New Zealand, India, Taiwan, Malaysia, Pakistan, and the UAE. This expansion reflects the growing interest and involvement in cryptographic research across a broader range of nations, further enhancing the collaborative spirit and impact of the Asiacrypt conferences.

The first bi-annual Asiacrypt was held in 1996 in Kyoungju, Korea. The program co-chairs for this conference were Professor Kwangjo Kim and Professor Tsutomu Matsumoto. Ed, known for his outgoing personality, served as the rump session chair, making the informal gathering enjoyable and engaging for the attendees. During his visit to Korea, Ed explored Korean food and culture, enhancing his understanding of Korean behavior and thinking, as recalled by Professor Min Surb Rhee who spent a one-year sabbatical leave at QUT in 1993. The establishment and evolution of these conferences and committees have significantly contributed to the advancement of cryptographic research and collaboration across the Asia-Pacific region, fostering a robust international cryptographic community [1].

China hosted Asiacrypt for the first time in 1998 in Beijing. Recognizing the growing importance and popularity of the conference, the ASC decided to hold the conference annually starting from 1999 in Singapore. This change was further solidified by a strong suggestion to the IACR, making Asiacrypt an annual flagship conference for the Asian region from 2000 onwards. It now holds the same prestige as other major cryptographic conferences like Crypto and Eurocrypt.

Asiacrypt has seen substantial growth over the years. More than 200 papers are submitted annually, with approximately one-third being selected for publication after rigorous peer review. The proceedings are published in the Lecture Notes in Computer Science (LNCS) series by Springer. Attendance has also increased, averaging over 250 participants and reaching nearly 400 in recent years. Asiacrypt, a prominent conference in the field of cryptography, has evolved significantly since its inception, contributing greatly to the global cryptographic research community.

Ed, a key figure in the Australian cryptographic community, was a familiar face at Asiacrypt conferences, often seen enjoying social gatherings with colleagues like Professor Kwangjo Kim from Korea and Professor Eiji Okamoto from Japan. In 2017, Ed became the second Australian cryptographer to be elected as an IACR Fellow. His citation highlights his "visionary service to the IACR and fostering the Asian-Pacific cryptographic community, and for important scientific contributions".

Ed's sociable personality and academic excellence have been widely recognized. His significant contributions to the development and exchange of cryptology and information security research in Australia and Asia have left a lasting impact on the global cryptographic community.

Jennifer writes: The HBED Cryptosystem. As I was returning from my early morning swim at the Asiacrypt 1996 Conference Hotel in Kyongju, Korea, I ran into Ed Dawson and in our conversation he told me that it was his birthday. I mentioned this to a fellow Australian later and he said to me "yes he's 50 today and he's doing it hard". So I decided to do something for him.

I went to Tom Berson, a newly appointed Fellow of the IACR, who was the leading IACR representative at the conference and suggested to him that we could do something at the rump session to highlight Ed. Tom was in agreement and so we decided to use the birthday paradox to allow me to talk about what we called the HBED Cryptosystem. (Happy Birthday Ed Dawson). I asked the hotel to provide a cake. Tom, who was the chairman for the rump session, scheduled my talk to just before the break. The room which was used held about 200 people. I made sure everyone knew that the demonstration presented had been helped greatly by the local hotel.

I then pointed that the birthday paradox is crucial to understand the security of cryptosystems as in any collection of instances of an event there will be a coincidence: for example, if we have 30 people in a room there will be two people with the same birthday. I asked the audience if they agreed about the importance and got no response. I looked to Tom in panic and he suggested we vote on it. I then said "as the audience didn't seem convinced we would vote by month". I asked "How many of you were born in January?", some people put up their hands. I went on "okay let's try February", more people put up their hands, "how about March, April, ..., September, October?". I then paused and said "as this is November, we will go through November one day at a time."

"Who had a birthday on the first of November?" no one volunteered. "Who had a birthday on the second of November?" Again no one volunteered. I tried the third of November and again there we no takers. So I called out "But Ed you said your birthday was today", he replied "it is but this is the fifth November." There were two people who had birthdays that day, Ed Dawson and a man from Singapore (whose name I have forgotten).

I then invited the two of them to come down to the front of the room to congratulate them on their birthday. Everyone now noticed that an area at the front of the room had been screened off. The hotel staff then removed the screen and displayed on a pedestal about 40 cm high was a beautiful birthday cake. The staff presented the two with a very big original Japanese sword so they would be able to cut the cake. Everybody cheered loudly. Then all the people who knew this song *Happy Birthday to You* now sang it spontaneously. Then after that they sang the acclamation Hip Hip Hurray. Everybody was thrilled. As we went into the break a young cryptographer came up to me and said "we have known the tradition of the cake but we didn't know about the song".

Ed, I believe you have been instrumental in giving the happy birthday song to the Asian cryptography community. Well Done!

2   Ed the Researcher

Coming from a mathematics background, it is not surprising that Ed's research focus started off with the mathematics of coding and speech scrambling. However, he quickly identified cryptology as an exciting new field and moved into such topics as boolean functions and non-linearity. Later he diversified into public key cryptography and protocols and, later still, applications of information security in a range of scenarios. However, it is fair to say that cryptology remained his home game right through until his final years.

2.1   Symmetric-Key Cryptology

Leonie writes: Ed was the Principal Supervisor for my doctoral studies at QUT in the late 1990s. My research was on the security of stream ciphers, specifically the stream cipher designs that used keystream generators based on feedback shift registers. This was a popular design choice at that time.

One of the benefits of working with Ed was that the research was not performed in isolation. At the time, Ed was the director of the Information Security Research Centre, with academic staff, post-doctoral researchers and other PhD students working in related areas. We formed a community of interest. There was always someone to discuss ideas with, and we collaborated on various aspects of cryptanalysis and cipher design, from the properties of Boolean functions that provided resistance to correlation attacks to exploring equivalent representations of cipher designs that were more readily analysed using particular mathematical tools or techniques. The CRYPT-X package developed at QUT by a team including

Helen Gustafson, Ed, Lauren Nielson (May) and Bill Caelli was used for statistical analysis of components of many designs.

Alongside our doctoral research, Ed encouraged our participation in the development of designs intended for international projects, such as the LILI-128 stream cipher submitted to NESSIE, and the DRAGON stream cipher submitted to eSTREAM, the ECRYPT stream cipher project. Ed was a people person, and enjoyed putting diverse teams together to tackle problems. He loved discussing the projects, and exploring options for analysis, design and implementation in both software and hardware. If Ed did not know the answer to a research related question, he generally knew who might be of assistance and would facilitate introductions.

Research with Ed was always collaborative, and he was generous with both time and ideas. We continued to collaborate on symmetric-key cryptographic research after I completed my PhD, and co-supervised multiple PhD students at QUT. Long after Ed had officially retired from QUT, he continued attending supervisory meetings on campus and remained actively involved in symmetric-key cryptographic research at QUT. Ed's support and encouragement have been invaluable in my own academic career.

Kenneth writes: Ed supervised many students in symmetric-key cryptology, including my own supervisor Dr. Gary Carter, who worked on the Advanced Encryption Standard candidates. During my time at QUT, both as a student and a co-supervisor with Ed, we investigated many symmetric cipher candidates to the eSTREAM stream cipher project, the CAESAR authenticated stream cipher competition, and more recently the NIST lightweight cryptography standard.

Ed had always kept pace with the latest developments in symmetric cipher design and analysis, and would share with us new research ideas he had gathered from his conference travels and also his vast network of academic and industry partners around the world. Ed certainly helped many of us stay up-to-date and relevant with our work in the rapidly changing field of symmetric cryptology.

2.2   Public-Key Cryptography and Elliptic Curves

Kenneth writes: Before I began my studies, one of Ed's students, Yvonne Cliff, née Hitchcock, had already begun elliptic curve cryptography research at the Information Security Institute at QUT. Through Ed's connections with industry, Dr. Paul Montague, then from Motorola, whom I had the opportunity to work briefly with as well, was also in her supervisory team.

After completing my studies, I joined Ed in supervising my first postgraduate student Hüseyin Hışıl, who worked on efficient elliptic curve cryptographic algorithms. Shortly after, Ed introduced Craig Costello, who went through his undergraduate studies at the QUT School of Mathematics, to study with Prof. Colin Boyd on efficient elliptic curve cryptographic protocols, building on the experience we have already gathered on elliptic curves.

As students, Hüseyin and Craig crossed paths briefly at the Information Security Institute. Ed encouraged them to exchange ideas in their similar research interests and work together on publications. Both of them went on to establish successful cryptology careers, and have since intermittently collaborated on more current research topics in elliptic curve cryptography.

Paul writes: Ed, together with Andrew Clark, presented a four day long intensive Crypto Training Course in 1998 at Motorola Australia Software Centre in Adelaide, with a focus on DES, RSA and some simple authentication and key agreement protocols. As well as being invaluable for Motorola's software engineers, who were developing cryptographic libraries for support of smart cards and mobile devices and trying to come to grips with the underlying theory, this training course for me was personally significant as it introduced me to Ed and his team, and led to the establishment of a collaboration over the next years. This collaborative work was funded by the Australian government as well as Motorola Australia, under the SPIRT/Linkage scheme.

Ed's enthusiasm and knowledge made this collaboration both fruitful and immensely enjoyable, and it led to a number of papers, largely in the area of elliptic curves (and three with Ed as co-author, considering the discrete log problem in the elliptic curve context, issues of security with fixed vs randomly chosen curves, and implementation of elliptic curve cryptography on smart cards), as well as a successfully co-supervised PhD student, Yvonne Hitchcock. I fondly remember trips from Adelaide to Brisbane during this time to visit Ed and his team, and the great hospitality he and his team showed me.

Willy writes: My personal recollections of Ed begin with our first meeting at the ACISP 1998 conference, which was held at QUT. At the time, I was a student attending the conference, sharing accommodation with several other students. We drove from Wollongong to Queensland, and, as students with minimal budgets, we participated in a group registration. I distinctly remember that we were not initially entitled to attend the conference dinner. However, Ed, who was serving as the General Chair of the conference, kindly extended an invitation for us to join the dinner. This gesture left a lasting impression on me as a PhD student.

Later, I had the opportunity to attend Asiacrypt 2001 in Gold Coast, where Ed again served as the General Chair. The conference was exceptionally well-attended, and any event where Ed chaired the rump session was guaranteed to be both enjoyable and memorable.

From that point onward, I encountered Ed numerous times at various conferences. Ed was a regular attendee at ACISP conferences. His simplicity particularly struck me; he often traveled with just a backpack, and when I inquired about his accommodation, I was surprised to learn that he always chose modest places to stay, such as an Airbnb. It was remarkable that such a distinguished professor opted for such humble arrangements wherever he went.

Ed was always extremely supportive of younger academics. Early in my career, I vividly recall how he consistently encouraged everyone he met, including myself. His support extended to his peers as well. I particularly remember when he took the initiative to establish the IACR fellowship for Professors Josef Pieprzyk and Rei Safavi-Naini, meticulously coordinating every detail to ensure a smooth process.

Ed's influential and outstanding research contributions to the community, especially to the Australasian cryptography family, will be remembered by all of us.

2.3 Interdisciplinary Research

Mark writes: Ed interviewed me for my first academic post, and my first job in Australia, back in 2005. I wasn't an academic at that stage and had a work history predominantly in the UK public sector, so I came from a legal policy background. I started work at QUT's ISI as a senior research assistant developing research on information protection strategies for electronic courts. It was an area I had previous experience in from my UK work, so I was well suited for the position.

Ed, of course, was not from a legal/policy background. If you look at his distinguished publication record and the many achievements he had in his career, you would not be wrong in thinking that he was a hard-core maths and cryptography scholar –a background that does not necessarily lend itself to the uncertain complexities of law in action and in theory. In the many meetings I had with Ed, and the large-scale teams of interdisciplinary scholars working on a range of diverse projects, Ed always demonstrated a genuine openness to different disciplinary perspectives, logics and general ways of doing things. Ed did not believe our legal and policy input was an adjunct to technical projects. Instead, entwining the complexities of legal, technical and policy requirement was at the heart of everything we did together in those ISI projects. That is a testament to Ed, who was a genuinely curious scholar and one who was open to learning new ways of thinking. If he didn't like something, he would tell you. But he would always give you the opportunity of explaining why you believed something was important and worth considering.

I eventually started my PhD through the ISI and QUT Law in 2007 on data breach notification law. It was a newly developing field back then and many people wondered out loud why I was studying that area and was it really necessary to study privacy law, given that it was such a niche field. Seventeen years later, it turned out to be a good call, but it was a call that somehow chose me rather than me choosing it. I now contribute to this book as a professor, and I think Ed would have liked the chapter with my colleagues. It's a complex tale of how existing law can apply to new technology. A tale that was explored many times over during my ISI days.

A professorial career is never built on the back of one person. There are numerous collections of sage advice and active advocates who help guide paths for you to walk down. It seems fitting then to conclude by honouring Ed and acknowledging that I would not be here now if it was not for his support and his interdisciplinary spirit. I am always grateful.

Kenneth writes: At QUT, Ed began with the School of Mathematics, and his interest in cryptology eventually brought him to the Faculty of Information Technology, and subsequently the Information Security Institute, where he was Director. Ed maintained a close relationship with the School of Mathematics, and often introduced both staff and students across the two areas, myself being one of them. While I was studying in the School of Mathematics, Ed offered me the opportunity to complete my postgraduate studies in cryptology along with Dr. Gary Carter from the School of Mathematics. The year was 2003.

Perhaps due to Ed's background in mathematics, he valued the importance of a having a strong mathematical foundation for cryptology research, as mathematics forms the basis of many aspects of cryptology, such as in cipher design, implementation, and cryptanalysis. In particular, a working understanding of abstract algebra, in particular finite fields, would be fundamental to working in the more mathematically-inclined topics in cryptology. One of Ed's go-to books was Lidl and Niederreiter's *Introduction to Finite Fields and Their Applications*, which he recommended as background reading for many of his students.

Indeed, equipped with this background, I found myself being able to move across various research topics in both symmetric key and public key cryptology, drawing upon a common set of mathematical knowledge and skills. This was especially possible under Ed's supervision, as he was well-versed across all these topics.

Ed was keen on computing technologies, which has over the years opened new doors to many cryptological advancements. The early 2000's saw Computer Algebra System (CAS) and High-Performance Computing (HPC) becoming more accessible as research tools. The Magma computational algebra system is one of the few examples of a CAS that has advanced capabilities in discrete mathematics such as abstract algebra and number theory, upon which most of cryptology is based on. It was with Ed's introduction of Magma to QUT, together with another popular general-purpose CAS, Maple, which Ed helped bring over from the School of Mathematics, that our research in both symmetric and public key cryptology began to benefit from this new wave of computing revolution.

Around the same time, the QUT HPC facility was also starting to take shape. Through Ed's connection to Prof. John Cannon, the founder of

Magma at the University of Sydney, QUT acquired Magma for use on the QUT HPC facility, so that we could have Magma perform for large-scale computations, which was often required for resource-intensive cryptanalysis experiments. This also marked the beginning of the use of HPC for cryptology research at QUT.

Ed's constant reminder to us that our theoretical results should be accompanied by experimentation has added to the credibility of our research, and in turn the quality of our publications. His influence continued after his retirement, with the latest computing technologies still being actively used by our students to test ideas, confirm correctness of results and assess effectiveness of algorithms that they have developed.

The mathematical and computing skills I have gathered during my time with Ed and at QUT has also enabled me to contribute positively to other scientific fields that have similarly benefitted from the use of computer algebra, high performance computing and modern analysis tools. This further highlights the well-established idea that cryptology is a truly multidisciplinary field.

3   Ed the Teacher

Teaching was important to Ed. Even after he took on more management roles he continued to be active in the classroom. He developed the first courses in cryptology at QUT and taught both the introductory and advanced classes for many years.

Leonie writes: I first met Ed in the classroom – I was a student in the Cryptography class he taught at QUT. At the time, I was working as a high school mathematics teacher, and studying part-time. This was in the era of face-to-face classes – there was no online learning then, so I always chose university subjects that were offered in the evening. Cryptography was a wonderful discovery, and the lectures kept my attention and focus, even at the end of a workday. So many different types of mathematics applied in various ways – either to provide security for information, or to break the security of existing schemes. I was captivated.

In Ed's cryptography class, the theory was closely connected to real-world examples. Some of the assessment tasks in Ed's cryptography classes involved being given ciphertexts, and having to analyse them and recover the underlying plaintexts. This seemed more like a fun exercise than an assessment task. The thrill of successfully recovering a message was very motivating, and I happily applied myself to the tasks.

As the semester progressed, I talked with Ed about cryptography and mathematics. It was such a fun class, I wanted to continue learning more about cryptography. I took the Advanced Cryptography class in the following semester. Ed was interested in my progress and kept in touch. When I asked about cryptographic research, Ed was quick to suggest a

PhD research project. Eventually, I left my high school teaching job and returned to university as a PhD student, with Ed as my supervisor, to investigate stream ciphers. In a way, this was similar to Ed's own pathway from high school mathematics teacher to cryptographic researcher, and a common pathway for several of Ed's PhD students.

I'm grateful to Ed for introducing me to cryptography. It was a subject area that I did not even know existed prior to taking that first class with Ed. That was a change point in my working life, and opened the door to a new career as an academic, cryptographer and security researcher. What a wonderful opportunity – I thank Ed for that.

Tony writes: Ed joined Queensland Institute of Technology (QIT) maths department in February 1974 as a Senior Tutor and soon was promoted to a Lecturer. Ed demonstrated his commitment to the students and his high teaching quality.

Ed was a great joy to be with, he always had 110% enthusiasm and energy for any venture he decided to pursue. His introduction at QIT of Cooperative Education for maths students is an example, the program he learned about at the University of Waterloo. There was much university opposition from management. Later QUT would be *The university for the real world*, as exemplified by cooperative education introduced by Ed.

Ed was always taking our bright maths students to do PhDs in information security. Of course, we used the maths in code breaking as a draw for students to study maths as Ed himself had been attracted in the 1970s. And the maths department gained some valuable service teaching of FIT students. A relationship of mutual benefit. We were united in our desire to see QUT research dollars directed towards the maths and IT areas and not to other softer disciplines. Certain QUT DVCs of research were more sympathetic than others and this had to be exploited.

Professor Ian Turner, QUT, was studying for a B.AppSci. QIT in the 1980s. Ian recalled Ed's high quality teaching, and great enthusiasm for cryptology and life in general. Some other testaments include the following.

Nancy Spencer, studying for a QIT B.AppSci. in the early 1980s, says:

"[Ed]was the first lecturer I met when I transferred from Engineering, making me feel like I had come home. I had intended to go back to Engineering but his kindness made me stay on [in Maths]. He was the most brilliant teacher and always waited for me to fall through the door after driving like a maniac from Northgate. He was also a great friend and we had many great times with him both here and in the UK."

Robert Fox was a QIT maths student in the 1970s. He was a part-time student coming into QIT for evening lectures; he writes:

"Ed would always wait 5 min for us to arrive late for the algebra class [starting at 6pm]. And then greet us in a very friendly way. We struck up quite a friendship. He took us rock climbing on Kangaroo Cliffs, initially he led. Then we went on more difficult climbs in the Scenic Rim and NSW from 1977 to 1991. By the early 1980s I was leading."

Winfried writes: Ed's passion for mathematics but also administrative matters was always present. The interdisciplinary orientation of Ed and the strict organization of his working group were exemplary. He was an excellent mentor and under his supervision many scientific papers and projects were established and successfully finished. Ed's high sensibility concerning data protection was a true role model for me.

From my point of view, the following points summarize the most important things of Ed's impact to the international crypto community:

- Founder of ISI at QUT as an interdisciplinary approach bringing together researchers of Mathematics, Computer Science, Law, Economy and Social Sciences in order to cooperate on problems of data security.
- Strict organization of Ed's working group at QUT, every talk had to be presented and discussed internally before it was allowed to be presented outside (content and timeliness were strictly observed).
- Ed's international orientation. He established contacts and cooperations with researchers interested in cryptography in all parts of the world. Ed welcomed young researchers of many parts of the world at QUT.
- Broad interest in all aspects of cryptology (public-key cryptography, symmetric-key cryptography, protocols, applications and practical solutions).
- Ed's high sensibility with respect to data protection.
- Ed made Asiacrypt one of the most important crypto conferences. Ed was an excellent organizer of scientific conferences.

4   Ed's Travel Adventures

Ed had friends all over the world. Ed liked the adventure and this included new places and experiences and was always up for a new adventure on short notice. While he somehow developed an uncanny habit of getting his luggage lost, the trips always seemed to turn out well in the end.

Tony writes: I was very envious of Ed's QUT travel budget. He was always off to some interesting part of the world. I would tell him I'd had an attractive trip to northern Norway, Trondheim, visiting the mountains, seeing the fjords; only for Ed to recount stories of several trips to Norway over the years, exciting rail trips to a research centre high in the Norwegian mountains. I was very envious. A few years ago Ed and his wife Ana wrote a 254-page memoir: "Adventure Travels with Ed and Ana". This describes his many trips to places all over the world and includes many of Ed's poems in the style of e.e. cummings which I had not read before.

Ed was a lover of train journeys and a lover of steam trains. He travelled on them in New Zealand, Scotland, but not, unfortunately, Stanthorpe in 2022. The scheduled steam train had broken down in Warwick and was replaced by a diesel engine instead. This also broke down just 5 min out of Stanthorpe and we returned to Stanthorpe disappointed.

Generally, Ed went on many rock climbing, hiking and mountaineering adventures in the 1970s and 1980s. Ed continued to be an enthusiastic bushwalker and we went on annual trips to the Scenic Rim which he organised and led. A couple of years ago we went walking the trails at the Bunya Mountains in winter, a favourite of his and a first for us. Ed showed great enthusiasm for the hiking although it was his 21st or 22nd visit.

Colin writes: Ed was well known as a tireless traveller. I was privileged to accompany him on many trips from the time that I joined QUT in 1995 until the time of his retirement. Here are some highlights of my most memorable adventures with him.

- In 1997 we made our first trip to China for the ICICS conference. China was still a slightly exotic place to visit; the streets of Beijing had huge numbers of bicycles and our main source of transport within the city was by small yellow taxi. There was almost no English spoken or written so we had to ensure that we kept the name of our hotel with us so that we could show it to the taxi drivers to get back home. One evening a group of us had dinner in a restaurant where the menu seemed to consist mostly of reptiles. Some of the dishes I remember (by sight, not taste) were bullfrog and tortoise but the main feature was snake, first shown to us in a live state and then served up alongside the bodily fluids. I went rather hungry that night but Ed characteristically tried everything, encouraged by glasses of the local firewater.
- Between 1997 and 2000 Ed was leading a project funded by Korea Telecom. This entailed regular visits to Seoul for partner meetings. We got to know Korean food quite well. Ed was very fond of the ubiquitous kimchi and the Korean barbecue.
- Asiacrypt 2000 took place in Kyoto. I almost missed the conference due to an injury I sustained on the basketball court a few days before travelling. However, I made it in the end. I chaired a session on one day and carelessly jumped out of my chair to help one of the presenters, setting off my injury again and thereby rendering me unable to move. When the session ended Ed came to my rescue. Somehow

he procured a wheelchair in which he drove me to the nearby hotel where he and Ana were staying and I spent the afternoon stretched out on their floor. You could always rely on Ed to be looking out for your welfare.

- Asiacrypt was in Bangalore in 2005. Afterwards Ed and Ana joined me and my family for a tour of South India. We each had a car with its own driver and had memorable trips involving a tea plantation, elephants, trains and Indian cuisine such as masala dosas and kulfi.

Moti writes: The event at the Hunan restaurant in 1997 in Beijing during ICICS (which Colin mentions) is very much what the description says it was, but let me add and say that to each reptile meat dish there were specifically two added alcoholic drinks, mixed, resp. with Bile and Blood ... Ed boldly ate and drank all, but, being the good natured guy that he was, he could not fight the snakes (which, according to stories, he feared!), and he vomited the meal upon the return to the famous "Friendship Hotel"...

The next day I went out for dinner with J.-J. Quisquater and, not surprisingly, we decided to get vegetarian food!

Since that dinner I have the following repeating story: People ask how does the bullfrog taste? I answer: like a chicken but more delicate! Then, they ask: How does the tortoise taste? I answer: like a bullfrog but more delicate! Then, they finally ask: How does the snake taste? I answer: Like a tortoise but a bit more delicate! Conclusion: By transitivity they are all just celebrated chickens!

I met Ed there and in many other places, but this is the most memorable (unique) event! He always took care of his colleagues and spoke very highly of them; advancing the field and people in the field (primarily at his home institute and in Australia) was always a priority to him.

Winfried writes: Beside several research visits from Ed in Klagenfurt and Vienna and numerous visits from me to QUT we attended together many Crypto, Eurocrypt and Asiacrypt Conferences. Beside his interest in the scientific programme of the conferences, Ed was always somehow restless and full of energy in exploring the region. So, we completed together a wonderful wine tasting tour in Santa Barbara, visited the Top of Europe (Jungfraujoch) and the North Face of the Eiger in Switzerland, made several mountain trips at the border between Austria and Slovenia and close to Vienna as well as visits to the Bunya Mountains National Park in Queensland.

Ed's special interest was always adventures. But he underestimated sometimes the requirements and dangers of such trips. But similar to Ed's tenacity and commitment in solving mathematical problems, Ed was physically very tough and we survived and managed all problems, having left wonderful memories. And last but not least, Ed was always strongly supported by his lovely wife Ana.

5 Ed's Community

One of Ed's greatest qualities was his support for the people he worked with, whether students, colleagues or people he knew around the world. He supervised more than 40 research students in his time at QUT in addition to many other junior researchers. He encouraged and facilitated connections wherever he could, independent of whether it concerned students or world-famous researchers.

Kenneth writes: It has been my great honour to share a small part of Ed's immense journey in cryptology. His deep and vast understanding of the field is reflected in his well-informed and timely advice to his many students on research topics, directions, and methodologies, which at times brought us onto the world stage and the forefront of cryptology research.

As I pursued other interests after my postgraduate studies, Ed offered me the opportunity to continue my cryptology journey as a part-time supervisor and mentor at QUT, along with A/Prof. Leonie Simpson, and later joined by Dr. Harold Bartlett from the School of Mathematics, for which I am forever grateful.

Ed's leadership, mentorship and friendship certainly added much to my fruitful and memorable time at QUT. Not to mention all the social events I enjoyed with Ed and also with his family and colleagues through the years.

Tony writes: Away from the classroom, Ed participated in the social life of QIT. There's a booklet "No class at all – a history of Fun Times at the Queensland Institute of Technology [QIT]" by Merrilyn [Burrows], 1990, which documents how Ed received, or earned, the nickname Cleanaway.

One year the [Christmas] party was held at Charlie Cheeses (which was a kids' playhouse) and a separate small function was held for the adults. One comment the next day was that 'He must have eaten 14 pizzas on his own'. Consequently, Ed Dawson was nicknamed 'Cleanaway'. Good one Ed, we promised that you would never be allowed to forget it!!

Over the years of our working at QUT, what was initially a working relationship between us soon became a deep friendship and admiration. After we retired we enjoyed our e-prof status. While at QUT we collaborated at a personal level and on a school/centre level in research into information security.

Gary writes: One can only think of so many positives when reflecting on Ed that it is hard to know where to start. These reflections are in no particular order of significance, as I'm sure that he meant different things to the different people in this life. It was the people in Ed's life that made life exciting for him - to share their company, but also to build them up. That's a core value of his that made him a great father, grandfather, teacher and professor.

Ed's own research focus was in cryptology. As for Ed's professional leadership, he was driven to see this science applied for the benefit of our society. He actively encouraged students and staff across both the IT and engineering disciplines to carefully integrate cryptography as they designed safe and secure systems. As a director of a research centre, he would monitor the progress of approximately 50 post graduate students. While others might have just focused on their own research, he cared about everyone.

6   The Last Word

We leave the last word with Tony, expressing sentiments which we know are shared by most of the people who knew Ed.

I remember Ed as a dear and loyal friend and a host of others do so. A birthday shared with Guy Fawkes (fireworks) and Ed's goodbye shared with Saint Patrick (ironically something to do with driving out snakes, snakes for which Ed had an irrational fear). We will badly miss Ed's company. A successful professional life of cracking codes but Ed successfully cracked the code of life and knew how to enjoy it and be generous and kind to his friends.

References

1. Phan, R.C., et al.: Advances in security research in the Asiacrypt region. Commun. ACM **63**(4), 76–81 (2020). https://doi.org/10.1145/3378428

Symmetric Key Cryptography

From Block Designs to Codes to Crypto and Back Again

Diane Donovan[1]([⊠])[iD], James Lefevre[1][iD], and E. Şule Yazıcı[2][iD]

[1] School of Mathematics and Physics, ARC Centre of Excellence, Plant Success in Nature and Agriculture, University of Queensland, Brisbane 4072, Australia
dmd@maths.uq.edu.au, j.lefevre@uq.edu.au
[2] Mathematics Department, Koç University, Istanbul, Turkey
eyazici@ku.edu.tr

Abstract. This article reviews Edward Dawson's contribution to research linking design theory to the study of codes and cryptosystems. We will briefly discuss Dawson's work on binary codes associated with biplanes and ternary codes associated with Hadamard matrices. Then the focus will be on applying Latin squares and balanced incomplete block designs in the study of s-boxes and secret sharing schemes. The article concludes with some open questions.

Keywords: Block designs · s-boxes · Secret sharing schemes

Dedicated to the memory of Edward Pyle Dawson, a friend and esteemed colleague.

1 Introduction and Preliminaries

A review of Ed Dawson's publications reveals a diversity of research interests and, more notably, a broad mathematical background underpinning a significant contribution to information security. Applications of mathematics are a recurring theme of Dawson's research. For instance, see Dawson's 1985 Master of Science dissertation titled *"Relations between codes and designs"* [12] and supervised by Anne Penfold Street at the University of Queensland (UQ). See also his 1991 Doctor of Philosophy dissertation titled *"Design and cryptanalysis of symmetric ciphers"* [13] with principal supervisor William Caelli at Queensland University of Technology (QUT).

Dawson's knowledge of design theory and more broadly combinatorial mathematics allowed him to take a novel approach to the analysis and solution of problems in both coding theory and cryptography. In the current article, we will

This work was funded by The Australian Research Council Centre of Excellence for Plant Success in Nature and Agriculture (CE200100015).

© The Author(s), under exclusive license to Springer Nature Switzerland AG 2025
C. Boyd et al. (Eds.): Ed Dawson Festschrift 2024, LNCS 15600, pp. 25–43, 2025.
https://doi.org/10.1007/978-3-031-83490-5_2

focus on Dawson's publications that use block designs to study codes and cryptosystems. At the same time, we review a few salient articles (applying design theory in cryptography) that demonstrate the impact of Dawson's approach.

This introduction will provide the relevant definitions from design theory with more details to be found in [9]. Subsequent sections on coding theory and information security go into the details of how Dawson applied these structures in his studies. Section 4 is devoted to conclusions and some open questions.

We begin with the definition of a block design, a structure that featured strongly in Dawson's research. A *block design* is a pair, $\mathcal{D} = (\mathcal{V}, \mathcal{B})$, where $\mathcal{V}$ is the point set and $\mathcal{B}$ is a set of subsets of $\mathcal{V}$ called *blocks*, with repetition retained, (let $v = |\mathcal{V}|$ and $b = |\mathcal{B}|$). Generally, constraints are placed on the incidence of points within blocks, for instance, the block size can be fixed (denoted k). The block design is said to be *balanced* if the number of blocks containing a pair x, y is constant over all pairs (denoted λ) and *incomplete* if $k < v$. A *balanced incomplete block design*, with constant block size $k < v$, may be denoted as a (v, k, λ)-design. The *incidence matrix* of a (v, k, λ)-design is a $v \times b$ matrix, $\mathcal{I}$, where cell (i, j) contains 1 if point i occurs in block j, and zero otherwise. A (v, k, λ)-design is said to be *symmetric* if $b = v$. If $\lambda = 1$ the block design is said to be a *Steiner system*. A *biplane*, denoted $(v, k, 2)$-biplane, is a symmetric balanced incomplete block design with $\lambda = 2$. *Collineations* are automorphisms of a biplane and the group of automorphisms is called the *collineation group* of the biplane. A *defining set* for a block design $\mathcal{D} = (\mathcal{V}, \mathcal{B})$ is a subset $D \subset \mathcal{B}$ which uniquely determines the remaining blocks of $\mathcal{B}$. Given two block designs, $\mathcal{D} = (\mathcal{V}, \mathcal{B})$ and $\mathcal{D}' = (\mathcal{V}, \mathcal{B}')$, on the same parameter set, the differences $(\mathcal{B} \setminus \mathcal{B}', \mathcal{B}' \setminus \mathcal{B})$ is said to be a *trade*.

Let $N = \{0, \ldots, n - 1\}$. A Latin square $L = [L(r, c)]$, of order n, is an $n \times n$ array containing entries of N in such a way that each entry occurs once in each row and once in each column. In our discussions, the rows and columns of L will be indexed by N.

A connection of Latin squares to block designs can be obtained by representing the Latin square $L = [L(r, c)]$ as a *group divisible design*, where the point set is the union of three groups $G_1 = \{0, 1, \ldots, n - 1\}$, $G_2 = \{n, \ldots, 2n - 1\}$, $G_3 = \{2n, \ldots, 3n - 1\}$ and blocks are subsets $\{r, n + c, 2n + L(r, c)\}$ corresponding to entry $L(r, c)$ in cell (r, c) of the Latin square. The Latin square properties ensure that pairs of points within groups do not occur in blocks, while all other pairs occur in precisely one block of size three.

An algebraic representation of a Latin square is obtained by adding a headline and sideline (indexed by N) to the $n \times n$ array to form a "multiplication table" with binary operation $\circ$, defined by $r \circ c = L(r, c)$, whenever symbol $L(r, c) \in N$ occurs in cell (r, c). This forms the Cayley table of a *quasigroup* $(N, \circ)$. It follows from the properties of a Latin square that, for $r, r', c, c' \in N$, if $r \circ c = r' \circ c$ then $r = r'$ and if $r \circ c = r \circ c'$ then $c = c'$.

A simple example of a quasigroup is $(\mathbb{F}_2, \oplus)$, with the binary operation $\oplus$ as addition modulo 2 (equivalently exclusive or, XOR). By contrast, $(\mathbb{F}_2, \otimes)$, with the binary operation $\otimes$ as multiplication modulo 2 (equivalently conjunction

AND), does not yield a quasigroup, see (1).

$$
\begin{array}{c|cc}
\oplus & 0 & 1 \\
\hline
0 & 0 & 1 \\
1 & 1 & 0
\end{array}
\qquad
\begin{array}{c|cc}
\otimes & 0 & 1 \\
\hline
0 & 0 & 0 \\
1 & 0 & 1
\end{array}
\tag{1}
$$

There is much freedom in the construction of quasigroups, with the binary operation not necessarily being associative, let alone commutative. Further, there is no requirement for identities or inverse elements.

Superimposing one Latin square $L = [L(r, c)]$ on top of the other $M = [M(r, c)]$, both of order n, yields an $n \times n$ array with cell (r, c) occupied by the ordered pair $(L(r, c), M(r, c))$. If no ordered pair is repeated across all n^2 cells, the two Latin squares L and M are said to be *orthogonal*. A set of m Latin squares, of order n, are said to be *mutually orthogonal* if they are pairwise orthogonal. Dawson also considered orthogonal arrays in his work [15]. An *orthogonal array*, $OA_1(t, m + 2, v)$, is a generalisation of a set of m mutually orthogonal Latin squares and may be thought of as a group divisible design (see [9] for more details) with point set partitioned into $m + 2$ groups of size v. The blocks, of size $m + 2$, are chosen in such a way that no block contains a pair of points from the same group, however each subset of t points chosen across groups occurs in precisely one block.

In the next two sections, we apply these definitions in the study of codes and cryptosystems.

2 Coding Theory

To understand Dawson's contribution to coding theory we first establish some notation. An $[n, k, d]$ *code*, C, is defined as a subspace of $\mathbb{F}^n$, where $\mathbb{F}$ denotes a finite field. The parameter n defines the *length* of the codewords/vectors in C, k the dimension of the code and d the minimum weight (number of nonzero entries) over all codewords. For *binary codes* we take $\mathbb{F}_2^n$ and $\mathbb{F}_3^n$ for *ternary codes*.

In [11] Dawson studied ternary codes with generating matrices of the form $[I_n : A]$, where, for weight κ, A is a weighing matrix over the set $\{-1, 0, 1\}$ such that $AA^T = \kappa I_n$. Dawson recognised that the well studied Hadamard matrices, H_n, (defined as $n \times n$ matrices with entries chosen from $\{-1, 0, 1\}$ such that $H_n H_n^T = nI_n$) provided good examples of weighing matrices. He showed that when $n \equiv -1 \pmod{3}$, $[I_n : H_n]$ can be used as a generating matrix for a selfdual ternary code with parameters $[2n, n, d]$. He thereby established the existence of self-dual ternary codes with minimum weight $\frac{n}{2} + 2$ for $n \in \{2, 8, 20, 32\}$ and systematically studied their properties.

Earlier in 1984, Dawson studied the relationship between binary codes and biplanes, see [10]. Dawson explored the possible structure of a $(191, 20, 2)$-biplane by representing it as a code. That is, assuming that a $(191, 20, 2)$-biplane, $\mathcal{D}$, exists with incidence matrix $\mathcal{I}_\mathcal{D}$, let $C_\mathcal{D}$ be the binary code spanned by the rows of $\mathcal{I}_\mathcal{D}$. Dawson determined that the dimension of such a code $C_\mathcal{D}$ is 95 and that any such code would be self-orthogonal. He also studied the *weight enumerator* of such a code, defined to be

$$W_C(x, y) = \sum_{i=0}^{n} A_i x^{n-i} y^i,$$

where A_i is the number of codewords of weight i and x and y are indeterminates. The set $\{A_0, \ldots, A_n\}$ defines the *weight distribution*. Dawson generalised biplane to symmetric $(v, 2k, 2\lambda)$-designs and, provided $\lambda(j-1) < k$, he showed that in the associated binary codes, $A_j = A_{v-j} = 0$. Then specifically for $(191, 20, 2)$-biplanes with collineation groups of orders 17 and 19, Dawson investigated the weight distribution of the codes $C_{\mathcal{D}}$.

The value of this work can be found not only in the light it shed on the structure of a possible $(191, 20, 2)$-biplane and the structure of the corresponding code, but also in the technique of using the different representations for the same object to illuminate relevant information.

3   Information Security

Through his PhD dissertation Dawson developed an interest and reputation for insightful research in information security. Some of his early articles (see [4,5,18]) explored the application of combinatorial mathematics to the design of s-boxes in block ciphers, particularly in DES, and authentication schemes. Of particular interest was the application of Latin squares.

3.1   A Straightforward Authentication Scheme

In 1992 Denes and Keedwell [20] proposed using quasigroups to authenticate signatures. Essentially, a given message was authenticated by dividing it into (message) blocks and computing a signature bit for each block, with the overall signature being the concatenation of these signature bits: given a secret quasigroup $(N, \circ)$ and message block $B = [m_1, \ldots, m_b]$, where $m_i \in N$, a signature bit s_B was obtained by computing

$$s_B = (((m_1 \circ m_2) \circ m_3) \circ \cdots \circ m_b). \tag{2}$$

In the article [18], Dawson, Donovan and Offer used the properties of the quasigroup to analyse the security of this scheme. Their results showed flaws with some block partitioning methods exposing the quasigroup and consequently enabling the forging of signatures by an eavesdropper. Further, certain selections of parameters (e.g. block size etc.) could lead to repeated authentication tags.

While these investigations highlighted possible security flaws, the broader use of quasigroups and their binary operations showed much merit and has been utilised over time. One salient example is the synchronous stream cipher

Edon80 which was proposed as a Phase 3 candidate for the eStream Project [28]. The associated algorithm incorporates quasigroups or Latin squares of order 4 and uses the binary operations of 80 quasigroups to progressively evaluate intermediate terms culminating in keystream bits.

3.2 Block Ciphers and S-Boxes

For block ciphers with fixed block length, the key principles of confusion and diffusion are often implemented through a two layer Substitution-Permutation Network (SPN): a substitution layer to introduce confusion and a permutation layer to achieve diffusion. A high degree of confusion is obtained if there is a complex relationship between the ciphertext and the secret key where the input to each ciphertext bit is taken across a range of key bits. High diffusion is achieved if a one bit change in either the plaintext or ciphertext propagates a 50% change in respectively the ciphertext or the plaintext.

Given $n, m \in \mathbb{N}$, a substitution layer can be constructed as an s-box, which is a mapping of the n-bit input vectors to m-bit output vectors, often implemented as *Boolean functions* $f : \mathbb{F}_2^n \to \mathbb{F}_2$, specifying the output bits of the s-box. Formally an *s-box* is an (n, m)-function of the form $F : \mathbb{F}_2^n \to \mathbb{F}_2^m$, defined by coordinate functions (Boolean functions), $f_i : \mathbb{F}_2^n \to \mathbb{F}_2$, for all $i \in \{1, \ldots, m\}$. Generally m is taken to equal n.

To facilitate decryption the substitution layers need to be bijective, and to adhere to the confusion principle they need to exhibit high nonlinearity. Indeed, Fuller, Millan and Dawson, [26] commented that *"Bijective s-boxes play an important role in the provision of security in many modern block ciphers."* and are *"... chosen to minimise the risk from linear and differential cryptanalysis ..."*. See also the 2023 article by Mariot and Manzoni [44].

Nonlinearity of an s-box may be defined through the *Walsh transform* of a Boolean function $f : \mathbb{F}_2^n \to \mathbb{F}_2$, which is a mapping

$$W_f : \mathbb{F}_2^n \to \mathbb{Z}$$
$$W_f(a) = \sum_{x \in \mathbb{F}_2^n} (-1)^{f(x) \oplus a \cdot x}, \ \forall a \in \mathbb{F}_2^n,$$

where $\cdot$ is the dot product. The nonlinearity nl of a Boolean function f can be calculated as

$$nl(f) = 2^{n-1} - 1/2 \max_{a \in \mathbb{F}_2^n} \{|W_f(a)|\}. \tag{3}$$

Intuitively, the nonlinearity of a Boolean function f is the minimum Hamming distance of f from the set of all n-variable affine functions.

In 1995 Carter, Dawson and Neilsen, [4,5], noted that the selection of s-boxes is critical in the design and analysis of block ciphers and investigated the use of Latin squares to construct the s-boxes in DES and DESV. This idea was raised again in a 2016 review of DES-like block ciphers compiled by Loebenberger and Nüsken [43], where a 1990 article by Brown and Seberry [2] is also referenced. Later Dawson et al. used knowledge of the bitwise "exclusive or (XOR)" operations of AES to expose weaknesses in the key schedule [48].

While the binary operation of quasigroups need not be associative, commutative or distributive and an identity element and inverses may not exist, quasigroups associated with finite fields satisfy these properties and have been used extensively. In 2004, Fuller, Millan and Dawson commented *"... many of the current crop of block cipher proposals have s-boxes that are directly constructed from finite field operations."* However, they went on to note that *"There are already signs that using finite field based s-boxes directly causes algebraic weaknesses and may lead to powerful new attacks."* [26]. Dawson et al. had been exploring alternate approaches for some time, for instance see the 1998 article titled *"Heuristic Design of cryptographically strong balanced Boolean functions"* [49], coauthored by Millan, Clark and Dawson (and featuring as one of Dawson's most highly cited papers). This paper moved away from specific constructions, supported by algebraic proofs, and presented a modification of the genetic algorithm (GA) to construct well balanced nonlinear Boolean functions.

Over the years Dawson continued to work in this area and in 2004 had achieved *"... the best known example of highly nonlinear s-boxes without linear redundancy."* [50]. See also the references listed in [50], including [26].

Recently (2018) Mariot revisited these ideas in the PhD dissertation titled *"Cellular automata, boolean functions and combinatorial designs"* [45]. Of particular interest to the current discussion is Mariot's heuristic approach (based on genetic programming), to constructing s-boxes from cellular automata that exhibit the desirable cryptographic properties of nonlinearity, especially the investigation of orthogonal Latin squares generated by nonlinear cellular automata. This work together with the 2023 article by Mariot and Manzoni [44] will be discussed in Subsect. 4.1 where we will propose possible new avenues of study.

Another important application of quasigroups is the study of elliptic curves in information security, where the associated algebraic stuctures are examples of a special class of quasigroups. While we will not go into details, Dawson et al. used their knowledge of affine laws and algebraic structures to study three forms of elliptic curves. They provide a complete description of the group law with respect to the affine coordinates and developed a toolbox using computer algebra to implement group laws and optimize computation. Later the results of this work were used in attacks, see for example Neves and Tibouchi, [51]. Relevant references for Dawson's work are [36–39], with [38] providing an application in smart card security.

3.3 Block Designs and Secret Sharing Schemes

The secret sharing scheme (SSS) is also a recurring theme of Dawson's research. To understand this contribution we will begin with the necessary definitions.

We will assume that a dealer Δ sets up a SSS by randomly choosing a secret or key from a set $\mathcal{K}$ and then distributes *shares* in the secret to a set of players P. We will use $\mathcal{S}_p$ to denote the set of possible shares distributed to player $p \in P$ and, for a given $Q \subseteq P$, $\mathcal{S}_Q$ to denote the possible assignment of shares to the players of Q. The aim is to design a scheme where any *designated subset* of players can recover the secret by combining their shares, and the remaining subsets of players obtain very little or ideally no information about the secret by combining their shares.

An access structure, A, may be used to define the collection of designated subsets of P that can combine their shares to reconstruct the secret, while the shares of any subset of players $Q' \notin A$ cannot recover the secret. We will assume all access structures are *monotone* in that, if Q is a designated subset in A, then all super sets of Q will also be designated subsets in A.

Of interest is the construction of secure and efficient perfect SSS, where a scheme is *perfect* if the shares of $Q' \notin A$ provide no information about the secret and efficiency is measured through the *information rate* (ratio of secret size to the size of the biggest share) and the *average information rate* (the ratio of the secret size to the arithmetic mean of the sizes of the shares). These parameters are important since they directly relate to the storage complexity, the communication complexity and the amount of secret information of the scheme. A SSS with information rate equal to one is referred to as *ideal*. It is well known that share sizes can not be smaller than the secret size and so an ideal SSS is the best possible.

A matrix $M = [M(i,j)]$ can provide a concise framework for specifying a general SSS (with $\mathcal{K}$, Δ, P, A, $\mathcal{S}_Q$ and $\mathcal{S}_p$, for $p \in P$ defined above). The columns of M are indexed by $\{\Delta\} \cup P$, with entries in column $p \in P$ chosen from $\mathcal{S}_p$ and entries in column Δ chosen from $\mathcal{K}$. A perfect SSS with access structure A is realised if the following conditions are satisfied.

1. If $Q \in A$ and $M(r,p) = M(r',p)$ for all $p \in Q$, then $M(r,\Delta) = M(r',\Delta)$.
2. If $Q' \notin A$, then for every possible assignment $\mathcal{S}_{Q'}$ of shares to the players in Q', there exists a non-negative integer $\lambda(\mathcal{S}_{Q'})$ such that $\forall K \in \mathcal{K}$, $|\{r : M(r,\Delta) = K$ and $M(r,p) \in \mathcal{S}_{Q'}, \forall p \in Q'\}| = \lambda(\mathcal{S}_{Q'})$.

A well known class of secret sharing schemes is a (t,n)-*threshold scheme* where the access structure consists of every t-subset of the n players, while no set of $t - 1$ or fewer players can determine the secret. Another well studied class of access structures is that consisting of some two element subsets of P and all supersets thereof. Such an access structure A can be modelled by a graph G_A. Studies have shown that graph decomposition techniques may be useful for the analysis of such schemes [1,58]. Essentially, G_A is decomposed into subgraphs with associated access structures for which the SSSs can be realised with optimal information rates. Then these can be combined into a SSS with "good" information rates. If the subgraphs can be realised as multipartite graphs that satisfy certain conditions then an ideal SSS with access structure A can be realised where each player receives one share for each incident subgraph. Stinson generalised this scheme beyond graph based access structures, see [57], and more recently work has appeared on relating SSS to decompositions of hypergraphs. This work will be briefly reviewed in Sect. 4.

While Dawson did not directly study SSS arising from graphs it is interesting that together with colleagues he used graphs to model the navigation of indoor space where access control is a necessary feature of building security, see [55].

The connection between SSS and combinatorial designs is well documented, see for instance [56] and [9]. Dawson's interest in SSS was first documented in 1992, with more recent articles appearing in 2016, see [3, 14–17, 31–35].

Stinson [59] credits Dawson, Mahmoodian and Rahilly, [15] and independently Martin, [47], with establishing the connection between threshold schemes and orthogonal arrays. These articles establish that a perfect (t, n)-threshold scheme (defined over an alphabet of size v) exists if and only if there exists an $OA_1(t, n+1, v)$, and the orthogonal array then provides a threshold scheme which is also ideal and gives the largest possible number of allowed keys for a given number of possible shares. The complexity of this result is in proving that the existence of a perfect (t, n)-threshold scheme implies the existence of an OA, see [15, 47].

An example of a matrix M constructed from a $OA_1(2, 4, 3)$ and realising a threshold scheme is provided below. Note one possible assignment of columns (rows of M^T) to the dealer and players is shown.

$$
M^T = \begin{bmatrix} 1\ 1\ 1\ 2\ 2\ 2\ 3\ 3\ 3 \\ 1\ 2\ 3\ 1\ 2\ 3\ 1\ 2\ 3 \\ 1\ 2\ 3\ 2\ 3\ 1\ 3\ 1\ 2 \\ 1\ 2\ 3\ 3\ 1\ 2\ 2\ 3\ 1 \end{bmatrix} \begin{matrix} \Delta \\ p_1 \\ p_2 \\ p_3 \end{matrix} \tag{4}
$$

Secret sharing schemes, as defined above, are *ordered* in the sense that for a given collection of shares, the value of the key depends on the player to which each share is allocated. For example, in M above share set $\{1, 2\}$ may correspond to either key 2 or key 3. If the scheme is unordered, and $S_p = S_q$ for any players p and q, then a more compact representation is possible. In 1990, Chen and Stinson [7] and later Jackson and Martin [40] developed a realisation of an unordered perfect (t, k)-threshold scheme as a block design. Specifically, we assume the existence of a block design $(\mathcal{V}, \mathcal{B})$ with block size k on $v = |\mathcal{V}|$ points, for which the blocks of $\mathcal{B}$ may be partitioned into m parts, say $\mathcal{B}_1, \ldots, \mathcal{B}_m$, in such a way that:

- for all $i \neq j$ and all pairs of blocks $B_1 \in \mathcal{B}_i$ and $B_2 \in \mathcal{B}_j$, then $|B_1 \cap B_2| < t$ (that is, if two blocks intersect in t or more points they belong to the same partition);
- for any subset Q' of $t' < t$ points, there exists a non-negative integer $\lambda(Q')$ such that for every i ($1 \leq i \leq m$) there are exactly $\lambda(Q')$ blocks $B \in \mathcal{B}_i$ with $Q' \subseteq B$ (that is, there are the same number of blocks in each partition containing each subset of $t - 1$ or fewer points).

Often the design is taken to be the full design covering all possible k-subsets of V, partitioned into designs with $t = k - 1$, providing a compact construction for $t = k$; a generalisation for $t < k$ is a partition of a $S(t, k, v)$ Steiner system into $S(t - 1, k, v)$ Steiner systems. In the ordered SSS each block B of $\mathcal{B}$ corresponds to $k!$ rows of M. Entries in the columns labelled by P are the points of B in every order, while the value in column Δ of each of these rows is i, where $B \in \mathcal{B}_i$.

The example below defines the matrix M for a $(3, 3)$-threshold scheme where the set of keys is $\mathcal{K} = \{0, 1, \ldots, 6\}$ and the partition of the blocks are denoted by the vertical bars. M_0^T provides one of the 6 possible permutations of each block; the additional 420 rows of M are given by permutations of p_1, p_2, p_3. Row 1 of the 4×84 matrix M_0^T provides the assignment of keys to each of the seven parts of the partition, with the blocks of partition $\mathcal{B}_1$ to $\mathcal{B}_6$ obtained by developing orbits of the blocks of $\mathcal{B}_0$ using the mapping $f_i(7) = 7$, $f_i(8) = 8$, $f_i(x) = x + i$ mod 7, for $x \in \mathbb{Z}_7$. That is, the first 12 columns are as written, then subsequent groups of 12 columns can be obtained by applying the mapping f_i to the entries in columns 1 to 12.

$$M_0^T =$$

$$\begin{bmatrix} 0\,0\,0\,0\,0\,0\,0\,0\,0\,0\,0\,0 & f_1(0) & f_2(0) & f_3(0) & f_4(0) & f_5(0) & f_6(0) \\ 7\,7\,7\,7\,8\,8\,8\,0\,0\,0\,1\,3 & f_1(\ldots) & f_2(\ldots) & f_3(\ldots) & f_4(\ldots) & f_5(\ldots) & f_6(\ldots) \\ 8\,1\,2\,4\,3\,6\,5\,1\,2\,3\,2\,5 & f_1(\ldots) & f_2(\ldots) & f_3(\ldots) & f_4(\ldots) & f_5(\ldots) & f_6(\ldots) \\ 0\,5\,3\,6\,1\,2\,4\,6\,5\,4\,4\,6 & f_1(\ldots) & f_2(\ldots) & f_3(\ldots) & f_4(\ldots) & f_5(\ldots) & f_6(\ldots) \end{bmatrix} \begin{matrix} \Delta \\ p_1 \\ p_2 \\ p_3 \end{matrix}$$

From the early 1990's onwards researchers were exploring the use of defining sets of block designs [27,54] and critical sets of Latin squares [8]. For example, Donovan et.al. [22] suggest methods that reduce the problem of finding the defining sets of a given simple design to finding defining sets of the related full design, see also [24,30,41]. These ideas provide a link with Chen and Stinson's earlier work and research shifted to exploring the connection with SSS.

For instance, one possible construction is to take the secret to be a block design or Latin square, with the dealer sharing blocks of the design (or Latin square) to the players in such a way that the players of the designated subsets together can obtain a defining set of the design (or a critical set of the Latin square). However, in 2006, Grannell, Griggs and Street [29] showed that the secret (design) could be recovered uniquely by exploiting knowledge of trades in the underlying design. To understand this work, assume that a designated subset of players is given the blocks of a defining set D and that players holding shares aligned with $D \setminus \{b\}$, $b \in \mathcal{B}$, wish to cheat and recover the secret without share b. Grannell, Griggs and Street were able to identify scenarios where all the distinct completions of $D \setminus \{b\}$ intersected in a non-empty subset of blocks. Further, this information could then be combined with $D \setminus \{b\}$ to recover the unique completion of D and hence the secret. Thus, the properties of the block design could be exploited by cheaters.

The ideas underpinning the research in [29] are related to the concept of the "fairness" or the contribution of a share in the reconstruction process of a SSS. Here *fairness* is defined by the concept that if any player has the ability to recover the secret then all players should have the ability to recover the same secret. Conversely, if any player has no knowledge of the secret then all players have no information. He and Dawson [33] extensively studied this problem. A particular interest was SSS incorporating multiple secrets (see for instance [35]) and probabilities were used to model various scenarios. He and Dawson's work showed that fairness does impact on security and established methods for achieving fair reconstruction processes. An interesting application of this work is in secure electronic first-bid sealed-bid auction protocols, see for instance the papers [52, 53].

4   Open Research Problems

This article addresses a broad range of mathematical topics and is a testament to the breadth and depth of Dawson's research, collaborating with many colleagues and supervising many students. His research was the catalyst for new ideas and in keeping with this we conclude this article with open questions and ideas for their investigation.

4.1   Latin Squares and S-Boxes

In 2023, Mariot and Manzoni [44] revisited the construction of s-boxes from Latin squares and associated cellular automata. We will briefly review this work, as it allows us to propose a possible research avenue.

A one-dimensional cellular automaton is a $1 \times d$ array where the state of cell i at time step $t + 1$ is obtained by applying a local rule with inputs the state of neighbouring cells at time step t. More formally, for $d, n \in \mathbb{N}$, $d \leq n$, $b = d - 1$, and local rule $f : \mathbb{F}_2^d \to \mathbb{F}_2$, a *one-dimensional no-boundary cellular automaton* (CA) is a *vectorial Boolean function* $F : \mathbb{F}_2^n \to \mathbb{F}_2^{n-b}$, where the i-th coordinate $(i = 1, \ldots, n - b)$ is $F_i(x_1, \ldots, x_n) = f(x_i, \ldots, x_{i+b})$. The *diameter* of the local rule is d and, generally, computation uses addition modulo 2, $\oplus$. Of specific interest are *bipermutive* local rules $f : \mathbb{F}_2^d \to \mathbb{F}_2$, for which there exists $h : \mathbb{F}_2^{d-2} \to \mathbb{F}_2$ such that $f(x_1, \ldots, x_d) = x_1 \oplus h(x_2, \ldots, x_{d-1}) \oplus x_d$. The linearity/nonlinearity of a CA is determined by the nonlinearity of its local rule.

Given a CA, $F : \mathbb{F}_2^{2b} \to \mathbb{F}_2^b$, with a bipermutive local rule and output denoted $F(\mathbf{x})$, where $[\mathbf{x}] = [r_1, \ldots, r_b, c_1, \ldots, c_b] \in \mathbb{F}_2^{2b}$, Mariot and Manzoni [44] define the binary operation $||$ to be concatenation. So for $\mathbf{x_r} = [r_1, \ldots, r_b] \in \mathbb{F}_2^b$ and $\mathbf{x_c} = [c_1, \ldots, c_b] \in \mathbb{F}_2^b$,

$$F(\mathbf{x}) = \mathbf{x_r} || \mathbf{x_c}.$$

The proof that $(\mathbb{F}_2^b, ||)$ forms a quasigroup can be found in [46] and the earlier paper [25]. The fact that the local rule is bipermutative is a key element of this proof. The quasigroup corresponds to a Latin square of order 2^b.

Mariot, [45], has identified pairs of CA that may be used to construct a pair of orthogonal Latin squares. Accordingly, a pair of *orthogonal CA* (OCA) is a pair of CA $F, G : \mathbb{F}_2^{2b} \to \mathbb{F}_2^b$ defined by bipermutive rules $f, g : \mathbb{F}_2^{b+1} \to \mathbb{F}_2$ such that the corresponding Latin squares, of order 2^b, are orthogonal.

To obtain the associated s-boxes assume the existence of two bipermutive local rules, $f, g : \mathbb{F}_2^b \to \mathbb{F}_2$ of diameter $d = b + 1$ that generate a pair of OCA $F, G : \mathbb{F}_2^{2b} \to \mathbb{F}_2^b$, respectively. Then the vectorial function $H : \mathbb{F}_2^{2b} \to \mathbb{F}_2^{2b}$

defined for all $\mathbf{x} \in \mathbb{F}_2^{2b}$ by

$$H(\mathbf{x}) = F(\mathbf{x})||G(\mathbf{x})$$
$$= (f(x_1, \ldots, x_{b+1}), \ldots, f(x_b, \ldots, x_{2b}), g(x_1, \ldots, x_{b+1}), \ldots, g(x_b, \ldots, x_{2b}))$$

gives a superposition s-box. It can be seen that these s-boxes align with the orthogonal Latin squares defined above.

Mariot and Manzoni argue that the OCA pair provides a good candidate for the construction of nonlinear s-boxes as they define a bijective transformation, and further the orthogonality property of the resulting Latin squares contributes through a minimum amount of diffusion, see [44] for more details.

Based on this analysis Mariot and Manzoni extended their results by exhaustively enumerating pairs of OCA of diameter $d = 4, 5, 6$. Their results showed that CA of diameter $d = 4$ or 5 with nonlinear local rules, all resulted in linear s-boxes. However, when $d = 6$, it was possible to generate s-boxes exhibiting a small degree of nonlinearity, unfortunately not enough for practical purposes. Despite this Mariot and Manzoni commented "... that OCA S-boxes might be of interest for the design of nonlinear diffusion layers, where the goal is not to reach the highest possible nonlinearity, but rather to add some extra confusion in the permutation layer.", recommending further investigations for higher values of d. One issue here is the increased computational load, suggesting an alternative approach may be worthwhile, one that systematically investigates structural difference in the orthogonal Latin squares associated with linear/nonlinear s-boxes. Also see Mariot's dissertation [45] for additional research questions based on a combinatorial approach.

Specifically with respect to research into the interplay between Latin squares, cellular automata and nonlinear s-boxes we raise two experimental approaches.

a) Use Mariot and Manzoni's [44] ideas to investigate the OCA, of diameter $d = 6$, and generate a dataset DS of the associated pairs of orthogonal Latin squares, of order 2^5, then investigate Latin bi-trades between these Latin squares. The difference $(L \setminus M, M \setminus L)$ between two Latin squares L and M, of the same order, is a *Latin bi-trade*. The partial Latin square $L \setminus M$ is said to be a *Latin trade* in L, which when removed can be replaced by $M \setminus L$ to give M. A Latin bi-trade is said to be minimal if it does not contain a smaller bi-trade. For more details on Latin bi-trades see [9], and for bi-trades in orthogonal Latin squares see [6, 19] and the references therein. The article [6] investigates families of three Latin squares L_1, L_2, M, of the same order, such that L_1 and M are a pair of orthogonal Latin squares, as are L_2 and M. The difference between L_1 and L_2 defines a Latin bi-trade $(L_1 \setminus L_2, L_2 \setminus L_1)$ that preserves orthogonality. While article [6] focuses on Latin squares of order an odd prime, with L_1 corresponding to the additive group of a finite field, those constructed by Mariot and Manzoni are of order a power of 2 and not aligned with the finite field. However, the ideas in [6] can be applied to the dataset. Specifically one could start with the orthogonal Latin squares of order 2^5 in DS that correspond to nonlinear s-boxes [44] and identify, if possible, two pairs of orthogonal Latin squares L_1 and M and L_2 and M and the associated minimal Latin bi-trades (ignoring those associated with permutations of symbols) which maintain orthogonality. Consider the following questions with respect to these Latin squares:

- How do the minimal Latin bi-trades manifest in the CA or local rules?
- Can a theory of bi-trades in CA or Boolean functions be developed and if so does it add to the discussion?
- Can a link between the bi-trades and nonlinearity be characterised? It might also be useful to consider orthogonal Latin squares associated with linear s-boxes. Here a good start would be to investigate the invariance properties of orthogonal Latin squares generated by CA, and given by Mariot in his dissertation [45]. Can this study add to the discussion?

The above ideas focus on Latin bi-trades in a single square of the pair of orthogonal Latin squares, whereas the article [19] studies pairs of orthogonal Latin squares, of order v, as orthogonal arrays $OA_1(2, 4, v)$ and defines a bi-trade as the difference between the orthogonal arrays, in canonical form, with the same parameters. Again one can focus on the orthogonal Latin squares of order $v = 2^5$ and investigate the questions given above.

If this research is fruitful it would also be worth investigating the nonlinear bipermutive CA with local rules of diameter $d = 7$, 8 given in Mariot dissertation [45].

b) A distinct experimental direction is to investigate the application of other pairs of Latin squares, for instance biembedded Latin squares.
  - Can a pair of biembedded Latin squares be constructed from CA?

The relevant definitions are as follows (see [42] and references therein for further details). Let L be an arbitrary Latin square of order n, with rows, columns and entries indexed by N and identified as $R = \{r_1, r_2, \ldots, r_n\}$, $C = \{c_1, c_2, \ldots, c_n\}$ and $E = \{e_1, e_2, \ldots, e_n\}$ respectively. Denote the associated quasigroup by $Q = (N, \circ)$. For each $i \in N$, row r_i of L can be defined by a bijection

$$\beta_{r,i}^L : C \to E, \text{ with}$$
$$\beta_{r,i}^L(c_j) = e_k \text{ if and only if } r_i \circ c_j = e_k.$$

Similarly, for each $i \in N$ column c_i and entry e_i define bijections

$$\beta_{c,i}^L : E \to R, \text{ by } \beta_{c,i}^L(e_j) = r_k \text{ if and only if } r_k \circ c_i = e_j \text{ and}$$
$$\beta_{e,i}^L : R \to C \text{ and } \beta_{e,i}^L(r_j) = c_k \text{ if and only if } r_j \circ c_k = e_i.$$

Next let A and B be a pair of Latin squares of order n, with common row, column and entry identifiers. The Latin squares A and B may be *biembedded* if, for $\alpha \in \{r, c, e\}$ and $i \in N$, the composite mappings

$$\beta_{\alpha,i}^A(\beta_{\alpha,i}^B)^{-1} \tag{5}$$

each form a single n-cycle.

4.2   Secret Sharing Schemes, Block Designs and Hypergraphs

Given a SSS, the associated matrix $M = [M(r,c)]$ may be regarded as a block design, $(\mathcal{V}, \mathcal{B})$, with point set $\mathcal{V} = \mathcal{K} \cup \bigcup_{p \in P} p \times \mathcal{S}_p$ and blocks of $\mathcal{B}$ corresponding to the rows of M. That is, block $B_r = \{M(r,c) \mid 1 \leq c \leq |P| + 1\}$, with each block of size $n + 1 = |P| + 1$. An equivalent representation can be obtained by partitioning the set of blocks $\mathcal{B}$ by the secret key, and removing all secret keys as points, thus reducing the block size to n. That is, we obtain $|\mathcal{K}|$ sub-collections, one for each $K \in \mathcal{K}$, and where block $B_r \setminus \mathcal{K} \in \mathcal{B}_K$ if $K \in B_r$. Note that for the orthogonal array construction specifically, this corresponds to the equivalence between an $OA_1(t, n + 1, v)$ and a collection of v distinct $OA_1(t - 1, n, v)$ such that no two blocks from different orthogonal arrays overlap in t or more points.

Using this partitioned block design representation, the conditions for a perfect (t, k)-threshold scheme are exactly the two conditions listed in Sect. 3.3 for the Chen and Stinson block design system for an unordered perfect (t, k)-threshold scheme. We see that an ordered scheme is obtained by using a distinct group of points for each participant, and preventing a block from containing two points from the same group; otherwise these systems are entirely equivalent. In fact, this provides a general representation for SSS, ordered or unordered, with the sole caveat that if we wish to represent an unordered scheme in which share values can be used more than once, the definition of a block must be generalised to a multi-set of points. This general block design representation holds for arbitrary access structures, but we focus here on threshold schemes, in which the conditions correspond to variations of design balance.

The use of collections of orthogonal arrays (ordered) or Steiner systems (unordered) to construct (t, k)-threshold systems is an attractive approach, using the maximum possible number of blocks while ensuring that each permissible t-set occurs in exactly one block in the entire collection, and each $(t - 1)$-set in exactly one block of each part. Intuitively, we can understand that this provides the maximum possible number of allowed keys for the number of possible shares. However, these structures do not always exist. Indeed, in the block design constructions given in [7], several of the examples require a "leave", a set of pairs which do not occur in any blocks. Conversely, the condition that each permissible t-set occurs in exactly one block is retained. This is a restriction of the general condition that each t-set occurs in the blocks of at most one partition, but it is consistent with known constructions and the objective of allowing the largest number of key values for a given number of share values. We therefore suggest that the investigation of (t, n)-threshold schemes should focus on block designs with block size n and a block set $\mathcal{B}$ partitioned into m parts, $\mathcal{B}_1, \ldots, \mathcal{B}_m$, such that

1. Any t-set of points occurs in at most one block of $\mathcal{B}$.
2. Any $(t - 1)$-subset occurs in the same number of blocks in each part $\mathcal{B}_i$, $1 \leq i \leq m$.

The SSS is ordered if we impose the additional condition that the point set $\mathcal{V}$ is partitioned into n groups, so that no block may contain more than one point from the same group.

We observe that if we relax the first condition to require only that each block occurs at most once in $\mathcal{B}$, then we have precisely the definition of an m-way $(v, n, t - 1)$-trade. Indeed, for $t = n$ the required design is exactly an m-way trade, while for $t < n$ the required design is a trade with an additional restriction. This connection prompts the following avenue of inquiry:

– Can a review of the block trade literature provide either restrictions or methods of construction for (t, n)-threshold schemes?

Many authors have extended the discussion of block designs and SSS to a discussion of matroids and SSS, see for instance the 1992 article by Stinson [57]. In recent years there has been an uptake in the study of hypergraphs which may be thought of as general block designs and are also generalisations of matroids. Given this connection we wanted to briefly review recent work on hypergraphs and SSS.

As explained in Sect. 3.3, graphs are used as models for the general access structure where the minimal authorized subsets all have size two. This idea has been generalized to hypergraphs. A simple hypergraph is a pair $(\mathcal{V}, \mathcal{E})$, where $\mathcal{V}$ is a nonempty set of vertices and $\mathcal{E} \subseteq 2^{\mathcal{V}}$. Specifically, a hyperstar is a hypergraph satisfying the following properties

i) There exists $v \in \mathcal{V}$ such that $v \in e$, for all $e \in \mathcal{E}$.
ii) For all $e \in \mathcal{E}$ there exists $v \in \mathcal{V}$ such that $v \notin f \in \mathcal{E}$, for all $f \neq e$.

In [21], the authors propose the decomposition of hypergraphs as a model general access structure, where the hypergraph is decomposed into hyperstars with efficient (best possible being ideal) access structures. First of all, they efficiently identify all hyperstars that represent ideal access structures, then proceeded to show that finding the optimal decomposition into ideal access structures is NP-Complete for general hypergraphs but can be solved efficiently for some classes like hyperpaths and hypercycles.

One possible avenue of research would be to investigate the following questions:

– Since hypergraphs are a generalisation of graphs is there benefit in representing this model in terms of the matrix representation M? Can we induce a trade like structure and does it allow us to generalise beyond hyperstars and hyperpaths? The discussion of the matrix representation with respect to graphs, given in [1], would be a good starting point for this problem.
– Can the efficiency or run time of the algorithms in [21] (Sect. 4.2.1. Partitioning the hypergraph in regions and Sect. 5.2.1. The case of hyperpaths and hypercycles) be improved by considering the eigencentrality of a vertex in the hypergraph, and in particular the influence of vertices on other vertices to direct the decomposition algorithm? So is it good to start with high eigencentrality or low and does it affect multi-stage protocols?

If the decomposition is driven by starting with vertices that are only in some subset of hyperedges then low eigencentrality would be a good starting point. In the paper, the authors focus on a star graph focus that will have a dichotomy of eigencentralities, and decompose the hypergraph into hyperstars, implying eigencentrality is worth considering, subject to the requirement that ideal hyperstars are the ultimate goal.

4.3 Autotopisms of Latin Square to Automorphisms of Block Designs

To resolve issues around the identified flaws in the SSS associated with defining sets in block designs and critical sets in Latin squares [23, 29], in 2016 Stones et al. [60] developed an SSS where the secret is an autotopism θ of a Latin square of order n, that is, an element of $S_n \times S_n \times S_n$. An autotopism of a Latin square L may be defined in terms of permutations between quasigroups. Let $(L, \circ)$ and $(L, *)$ be two quasigroups. They are said to be *isotopic* if there exists a triple of permutations (α, β, γ) on L such that, for all $x, y \in L$, $\alpha(x) \circ \beta(y) = \gamma(x * y)$. An isotopism (α, β, γ) that maps $(L, \circ)$ to itself, is said to be an *autotopism*, with the set of all autotopisms on $(L, \circ)$ forming the autotopism group of $(L, \circ)$ or the corresponding Latin square L. For an autotopism (α, β, γ) of $(L, \circ)$ and $i, j \in L$, the set of triples $(\alpha^k(i), \beta^k(j), \gamma^k(i \circ j))$, $k = 1, \ldots, |L|$, is said to be the *orbit* of $(i, j, i \circ j)$ under the *action* of (α, β, γ). We may think of an autotopism as partitioning the entries of the corresponding Latin square into orbits, and given the autotopism and an entry of each orbit, we may recover the entire Latin square.

The general idea for a (m, m)-threshold scheme is for the dealer to construct a (L, θ) pair at random where θ is an element of the autotopism group of Latin square L, with say m orbits. The Stone et.al. protocol only considers autotopisms where each component decomposes into two disjoint $n/2$ cycles, simplifying the cryptographic analysis. In this protocol, θ is the secret. The dealer identifies a subset, C, of m entries of L, one from each orbit of θ. Then the dealer chooses a set of m permutations $\sigma_1, \sigma_2 \ldots, \sigma_m$ such that $\sigma_1 \sigma_2 \ldots \sigma_m = \theta$. Each player $p \in P = \{p_1, \ldots, p_m\}$ is given σ_p as a share. The entries of C are made public after some masking operation. When the m players collaborate they can recover the secret θ and use it with the entries of C to recover L. If the secret they obtain and publicly available entries do not match to produce an array that satisfies the properties of a Latin square (in other words have repeated entries in one of the rows or columns) then the subset of players can conclude that one of the players in the subset is cheating or there is a transmission error while one of the shares is returned. In this way, Stones et.al. claim to use the underlying Latin square for verification purposes without jeopardizing the security. But as stated in the paper if somehow the underlying Latin square is discovered it jeopardizes the security of the protocol.

A generalisation of this scheme appeared in 2023, when Takeuti and Tomoko [61] proposed the scheme for general groups rather than autotopism groups of Latin squares.

For a possible avenue of research we suggest investigating the following questions:

– In the above SSS proposed by Stone et al. would replacing the autotopism group of the Latin square, by an automorphism of a block design, have an impact on the fairness of the SSS?

In studying this question it is worth noting the following taken from The Handbook of Combinatorial Design, Remark 9.7 [9] *"Automorphism groups of combinatorial structures form a rich source of permutation groups. Although most combinatorial objects admit only the trivial automorphism or have very small automorphism groups, objects with large automorphism groups are elegant and sought after. Designs, graphs, and geometries with large groups are often the easiest to construct, and the first to be discovered among members of specified families. Moreover, such objects can be presented efficiently, frequently in terms of generators of their automorphism groups and certain base blocks."* Suitable selection of parameters v, k and t may result in suitable designs for SSS. A promising family to investigate may be cyclic or 1-rotational designs. For an extensive discussion of automorphism groups of block designs see [9] Chap. 9.

5   Summary

In this article, we summarize Dawson's contribution to information security through applications of combinatorial mathematics, specifically combinatorial designs. We begin by introducing definitions and useful structures such as block designs and Latin squares. To emphasize the breadth and depth of Dawson's research we give examples that illustrate how he used these structures to construct efficient error-correcting codes and information security tools such as block ciphers, s-boxes and secret sharing schemes. We conclude this article with open questions and ideas for their investigation.

References

1. Blundo, C., De Santis, A., Stinson, D.R., Vaccaro, U.: Graph decompositions and secret sharing schemes. J. Cryptol. **8**, 39–64 (1995)
2. Brown, L. and Seberry, J.: On the design of permutation P in DES type cryptosystems. In: Quisquater, J.J, Vandewalle, J. (eds) Advances in Cryptology - EUROCRYPT '89. EUROCRYPT 1989. LNCS, vol. 434. Springer, Berlin, Heidelberg (1990)
3. Camtepe, S., Dawson, E., Boyen, X.: A combinatorial construct for keyless message dispersal, QUT ePrints (2016). https://eprints.qut.edu.au/94441/
4. Carter, G., Dawson, E., Nielsen, L.: A Latin square version of DES. In: Proceeding of Workshop of Selected Areas in Cryptography, Ottawa, Canada (1995)
5. Carter, G., Dawson, E., Nielsen, L.: DESV: a Latin square variation of DES. In: Proceedings of the Workshop on Selected Areas in Cryptography, Ottawa, Canada (1995)
6. Cavenagh, N., Demirkale, F., Donovan, D.: Orthogonal trades in complete sets of MOLS. Electron. J. Comb. **24**(3), P3.15 (2017)
7. Chen, D., Stinson, D.R.: Recent results on combinatorial constructions for threshold schemes. Australas. J. Comb. **1**, 29–48 (1990)

8. Cooper, J., Donovan, D., Seberry, J.: Secret Sharing schemes arising from Latin squares. Bull. Inst. Comb. Appl. **12**, 33–43 (1994)
9. Colbourn, C.J., Dinitz, J.H.: CRC Handbook of Combinatorial Designs. CRC Press, Boca Raton (2010)
10. Dawson, E.P.: The binary code of the [191,20,2] biplane. Ars Combin. **17**, 209–223 (1984)
11. Dawson, E.P.: Self-dual ternary codes and Hadamard matrices. ARS Comb. **19**(A), 303–308 (1985)
12. Dawson, E.P.: Relations between codes and designs, Dissertation, University of Queensland (1985)
13. Dawson, E.P.: Design and cryptanalysis of symmetric ciphers, Dissertation, Queensland University of Technology (1991)
14. Dawson, E., Donovan, D. and Rahilly, A.: Methods for sharing cryptographic keys. In: Communications' 92: Communications Technology, Services and Systems, pp. 135–139 (1992)
15. Dawson, E., Mahmoodian, E.S., Rahilly, A.: Orthogonal arrays and ordered threshold schemes. Australas. J. Comb. **8**, 27–44 (1993)
16. Dawson, E. and Donovan, D.: Shamir's scheme says it all. In: Proceedings of the IFIP TC11, Ninth International Conference on Information Security: 1993, Computer Security, pp. 91–102 (1993)
17. Dawson, E., Donovan, D.: The breadth of Shamir's secret-sharing scheme. Comput. Secur. **13**(1), 69–78 (1994)
18. Dawson, E., Donovan, D.M., Offer, A.: Quasigroups isotopisms and authentication schemes. Australas. J. Comb. **13**, 75–88 (1996)
19. Demirkale, F., Donovan, D., Küçükçifçi, S., Yazıcı, E.Ş: Orthogonal trades and the intersection problem for orthogonal arrays. Graph. Comb. **32**(3), 1–10 (2015)
20. Denes, J., Keedwell, A.D.: A new authentication scheme based on Latin squares. Discret. Math. **106**(107), 157–161 (1992)
21. Di Crescenzo, G., Galdi, C.: Hypergraph decomposition and secret sharing. Discret. Appl. Math. **157**(5), 928–946 (2009)
22. Donovan, D,M., Mahmoodian, E., Ramsay, C., Street, A.P.: Defining sets in combinatorics: a survey. Surv. Comb., 115–174 (2003)
23. Donovan, D.M., Lefevre, J.G., McCourt, T.A., Cavenagh, N.J., Khodkar, A.: Identifying flaws in the security of critical sets in Latin squares via triangulations. Australas. J. Comb. **52**, 243–268 (2012)
24. Donovan, D., Lefevre, J., Waterhouse, M., Yazıcı, E.Ş: On defining sets of full designs with block size three. Graph. Comb. **25**(6), 825–839 (2009)
25. Eloranta, K.: Partially permutive cellular automata. Nonlinearity **6**(6), 1009 (1993)
26. Fuller, F., Millan W. and Dawson, E.: Multi-objective optimisation of bijective s-boxes. Evol. Comput. CEC2004 **2**, 1525–1532 (2004)
27. Gamble, G., Maenhaut, B.M., Seberry, J., Street, A.P.: Further results on strong-box secured secret sharing schemes. Utilitas Math. **66**, 165–193 (2004)
28. Gligoroski, D., Markovski, S., Kocarev, L., Gusev, M.: Edon80. Candidate eStream Phase 3. https://www.ecrypt.eu.org/stream/edon80p3.html. Accessed 4 Jan 2024
29. Grannell, M.J., Griggs, T.S., Street, A.P.: A flaw in the use of minimal defining sets for secret sharing schemes. Des. Codes Cryptograph **40**, 225–236 (2006)
30. Havas, G., Lawrence, J.L., Ramsay, C., Street, A.P., Yazıcı, E.Ş: Defining set spectra for designs can have arbitrarily large gaps. Utilitas Math. **75**, 67–81 (2008)
31. He, J., Dawson, E.: Multistage secret sharing based on one-way function. Electron. Lett. **30**(19), 1591–1592 (1994)

32. He, J., Dawson, D.: Multisecret-sharing scheme based on one-way function. Electron. Lett. **31**(2), 93–95 (1995)
33. He, J., Dawson, E.: How to fairly reconstruct a shared secret. In: Cryptography: Policy and Algorithms, pp. 115–124 (1996)
34. He, J., Dawson, E.: On the reconstruction of shared secrets. In: Information Systems Security: Facing the Information Society of the 21st Century, pp. 209–218 (1996)
35. He, J., Dawson, E.: Shared secret reconstruction. Des. Codes Crypt. **14**(3), 221–237 (1998)
36. Hisil, H., Carter, G., Dawson, E: New formulae for efficient elliptic curve arithmetic. In: Progress in Cryptology-INDOCRYPT, pp. 138–151 (2007)
37. Hisil, H., Wong, K.K.H., Carter, G., Dawson, E.: An exploration of affine group laws for elliptic curves. J. Math. Cryptol. **5**(1), 1–50 (2011)
38. Hitchcock, Y., Dawson, E., Clark, A., Montague, P.: Implementing an efficient elliptic curve cryptosystem over $GF(p)$ on a smart card. ANZIAM J. **44**(E), C354–C377 (2003)
39. Hitchcock, Y., Montague, P., Carter, G., Dawson, E.: The efficiency of solving multiple discrete logarithm problems and the implications for the security of fixed elliptic curves. Int. J. Inf. Secur. **3**, 86–98 (2004)
40. Jackson, W.A., Martin, K.M.: A combinatorial interpretation of ramp schemes. Australas. J. Comb. **14**, 51–60 (1996)
41. Kolotoglu, E., Yazıcı, E.Ş: On minimal defining sets of full designs and self-complementary designs, and a new algorithm for finding defining sets of t-designs. Graph. Comb. **26**(2), 259–281 (2010)
42. Lefevre, J.G., Donovan, D.M., Grannell, M.J., Griggs, T.S.: A constraint on the biembedding of Latin squares. Eur. J. Comb. **30**(2), 380–386 (2009)
43. Loebenberger, D., Nüsken, M.: Design principles of DES-like ciphers: a historical overview. Cryptologia **40**(3), 221–239 (2016)
44. Mariot, L., Manzoni, L.A.: A classification of S-boxes generated by orthogonal cellular automata. Nat. Comput (2023). https://doi.org/10.1007/s11047-023-09956-z
45. Mariot, L.: Cellular automata, Boolean functions and combinatorial designs. d'Université Côte d'Azur (2018)
46. Mariot, L., Formenti, E., Leporati, A.: Constructing orthogonal Latin squares from linear cellular automata. arXiv preprint arXiv:1610.00139 (2016)
47. Martin, K.M.: Discrete structures in the theory of secret sharing, PhD Dissertation, University of London (1991)
48. May, L., Henricksen, M., Millan, W., Carter, G., Dawson, E.: Strengthening the key schedule of the AES. In: Information Security and Privacy, pp. 117–134 (2002)
49. Millan, W., Clark, A., Dawson, E.: Heuristic design of cryptographically strong balanced Boolean functions. In: Advances in Cryptology-EUROCRYPT'98: International Conference on the Theory and Application of Cryptographic Techniques Espoo, Finland, 1998, Proceedings 17, vol. 19. Springer, Berlin, Heidelberg (1998)
50. Millan, W., Fuller, J., Dawson, E.: New concepts in evolutionary search for Boolean functions in cryptology. Comput. Intell. **20**(3), 463–474 (2004)
51. Neves, S., Tibouchi, M.: Degenerate curve attacks: extending invalid curve attacks to Edwards curves and other models. IET Inf. Secur. **12**(3), 217–225 (2018)
52. Peng, K., Boyd, C., Dawson, E., Viswanathan, K.: Robust, privacy protecting and publicly verifiable sealed-bid auction. In 4th International Conference of Information and Communications Security, ICICS 2002, vol. 2513, pp. 147–159. LNCS, Springer, Berlin (2002)

53. Peng, K. Boyd. C., Dawson, E.: Optimization of electronic first-bid sealed-bid auction based on homomorphic secret sharing. Progress in Cryptology-Mycrypt, pp. 84–98 (2005)
54. Seberry, J., Street, A.P.: Strongbox secured secret sharing schemes. Utilitas Math. **57**, 147–163 (2000)
55. Skandhakumar, N., Salim, F., Reid, J., Drogemuller, R., Dawson, E.: Graph theory based representation of building information models for access control applications. Autom. Constr. **68**, 44–51 (2016)
56. Song, Y., Tsujii, S.: Secret sharing schemes and combinatorial designs. RIMS Kôkyûroku **853**, 80–87 (1993)
57. Stinson, D.R.: An explication of secret sharing schemes. Des. Codes Crypt. **2**, 357–390 (1992)
58. Stinson, D.R.: Decomposition constructions for secret-sharing schemes. IEEE Trans. Inf. Theory **40**, 118–125 (1994)
59. Stinson, D.R.: Combinatorial designs and cryptography, revisited, in 50 Years of combinatorics, graph theory, and computing. In: Chung, F., Graham, R., Hoffman, F., Hogben, F., Mullin, R.C., West, D.B.: Routledge Handbooks Online, Boca Raton. CRC Press (2019)
60. Stones, R., Su, M., Liu, X., Wang, G., Lin, S.: A Latin square autotopism secret sharing scheme. Des. Codes Crypt. **80**, 635–650 (2016)
61. Takeuti, I., Tomoko, A.: Secret sharing scheme with perfect concealment. Cryptology ePrint Archive (2023)

Cryptographic Applications of the ANS Compression

Josef Pieprzyk[1,2(✉)]

[1] Institute of Computer Science, Polish Academy of Sciences, Warsaw, Poland
josef.pieprzyk@csiro.au
[2] Data61, CSIRO, Sydney, Australia

Abstract. Much of the data transmitted and stored today is both highly redundant and sensitive in terms of security. This includes applications that manage legal documents, medical records, software code, and scientific data. The typical approach to handling such data involves compressing it first, followed by encryption. Among the various compression algorithms, the relatively new Asymmetric Numeral Systems (ANS) is becoming increasingly popular within the IT sector.

The paper explores possible applications of ANS in Cryptography. It presents the ANS algorithms and their properties that can be useful for security sensitive applications. The ANS with randomised states can be seen as the basic cryptographic tool that can be used to convert uniformly random sequences into an arbitrary probability distribution calibrated by appropriate selection of symbol spreads. The paper presents two generic joint compression and encryption (also called compcrypt). The first uses the sponge structure and the second follows the CBC mode. Security of the compcrypt algorithm is discussed. The main take away is that both the linear and differential analysis become less effective due to fact that the adversary needs to guess lengths of ANS encoding.

Keywords: Cryptography · Asymmetric Numeral Systems

1 Introduction

Cryptography is an essential toolset not just for offering various security features like confidentiality, integrity, and authentication (commonly known as the CIA triad), but also for creating complex security services such as electronic voting, digital payment systems, and multiparty protocols. Intriguingly, the effectiveness of cryptographic operations relies significantly on the quality of the randomness they use. Several natural sources provide randomness, including thermal noise, quantum events, pulsars, and Active Galactic Nuclei (AGN), among others. Regardless of the randomness source and its specific probability distribution, most cryptographic applications necessitate the generation of uniformly random bits. One practical method for deriving randomness from a sequence of symbols with a defined probability distribution is through compression.

© The Author(s), under exclusive license to Springer Nature Switzerland AG 2025
C. Boyd et al. (Eds.): Ed Dawson Festschrift 2024, LNCS 15600, pp. 44–67, 2025.
https://doi.org/10.1007/978-3-031-83490-5_3

Compression can be viewed as part of Shannon's information theory, where symbols are encoded into binary strings. The average length of these strings is either equal to or closely approximates the symbol's entropy, as noted by Shannon in 1948 [24]. The Huffman code, introduced in 1952 [13], is the earliest example of this concept. It enables optimal encoding when the symbol probability distribution is expressible by natural powers of $1/2$. Here, 'optimal' means that the average length of binary encodings is equal to the symbol entropy. Hence, compression is also known as source coding. There are two primary types of compression: lossy and lossless. Lossy compression does not allow the original symbols to be recovered, whereas lossless compression enables their exact recovery. This work focuses on the latter category, specifically lossless source encoding. Note that it is possible to obtain lossy compression from lossless one. This can be achieved by converting the source symbols by fixing (or ignoring) the less significant bits of the source symbols and then applying lossless compression to this modified source. Decompression involves two steps: first, performing lossless decompression, followed by a random selection of the less significant bits. Lossless source encoding encompasses several techniques, including the aforementioned Huffman code [13], arithmetic coding (AC) [15, 16, 21], Lempel-Ziv coding and its variants [26, 27, 29], prediction by partial matching (PPM) coding [6], run-length encoding (RLE) [22], and asymmetric numeral systems (ANS) coding [8].

In recent years, the ANS compression attracts a lot attention especially from the IT industry [9]. Facebook, Apple, Google, Dropbox, and Red Hat have integrated ANS into their systems and services, highlighting the widespread adoption and versatility of the ANS compression. Let us introduce it briefly (see [8,10]). ANS is a stateful compression algorithm that encodes a string of symbols over an alphabet $\mathbb{S}$ one by one. Consider a sequence over an alphabet $\mathbb{S}$ with a probability distribution $p : \mathbb{S} \to [0, 1]$. Given the algorithm is in a state x and we would like to encode a symbol s that occurs with probability p_s then s is encoded into $x' = C(x, s)$, where the function $C(x, s)$ is designed in such a way that $\log_2 x' \approx \log_2 x + \log_2 1/p_s$. In other words, the encoding of s increases the length of x by $\log_2 1/p_s$. Additionally, one would require the function $x' = C(x, s)$ to be reversible so knowing x', it is possible to recover (x, s) or there exists a decoding function $D(x') = (x, s)$. For example, consider a simple case of two symbols $\mathbb{S} = \{a, b\}$ both occurring with probability $1/2$. The encoding function is $x' = C(x, s) = 2x + s$. It is easy to find out its decoding function, which is $(x, s) = D(x') = (\lfloor x'/2 \rfloor, x' \pmod 2)$. For the case, when symbols occur with different probabilities p_a and p_b for a and b, respectively, the encoding function becomes $x' = C(x, s) = \lfloor x/p_s \rfloor + s$, where $s \in \mathbb{S}$. Note that when processing long sequences of symbols, the integer encodings grow fast and quickly reach the computer precision. To solve this problem, ANS deploys re-normalisation.

The primary objective of any compression algorithm is the reduction of redundancy from a sequence of symbols generated by its source. This sequence of symbols is alternatively called a symbol frame. Similarly, a sequence of symbol encodings is called a binary frame. In an ideal scenario, the content of a compressed frame should resemble the characteristics of truly random bits. However, this is not entirely accurate, as even the most advanced compression algorithms leave some residual redundancy in the compressed bit frames. This phenomenon can be explained by the fact that compression algorithms are typically designed for a specific probability distribution of symbols. Note that there is a separate class of universal compression algorithms, such as Ziv-Lempel, that can deal with symbols generated according to arbitrary probability distributions. In this model, each symbol is treated as an independent and identically distributed (iid) random variable. However, real-world sequences of symbols do not conform to such a simplistic probabilistic model. There are statistical correlations not only between pairs but also among larger groups of symbols. To address this, one could develop compression algorithms tailored to more complex probability distributions, considering pairs, triples, and so on, of elementary symbols. The downside of this approach is the exponential increase in the complexity of the algorithm.

Motivation. This work explores potential applications of the ANS compression in cryptography. ANS can function as a pseudorandom bit generator (PRBG), utilizing a variety of symbol sources. These sources can be any sufficiently long text file or other types of files, including audio and video files. Furthermore, decompression algorithms can transform a sequence of independent and identically distributed binary variables (a binary frame) into a frame, where the symbols adhere to a specific probability distribution. This distribution is defined by the internal parameters of ANS. It is noteworthy that ANS can also be employed to extract publicly available randomness from astronomical objects like pulsars or active galactic nuclei (AGN). This capability presents an opportunity to develop new key establishment and distribution protocols. In such protocols, multiple parties could observe a mutually agreed-upon astronomical object to derive the same randomness.

There are two characteristics of compression algorithms that make them appealing for use in encryption. The first characteristic is the ability to encode symbols into binary encodings whose lengths vary depending on their symbol probabilities. In other words, more probable symbols are encoded into shorter binary strings. This attribute complicates cryptanalysis, as an adversary must deduce the lengths of symbol encodings, which are merged into a single binary frame. This characteristic was noted in the context of the Huffman code by Gillman et al. [11]. The second characteristic is the inclusion of parameters in a compression algorithm that can be arbitrarily selected. These parameters can be manipulated by a secret cryptographic key known to both communicating parties. Integrating compression with encryption has the potential to significantly enhance the security of the combined system. However, the integration should be done with care as it may introduce a weakness – see the CRIME attack on TLS as demonstrated in Sect. 12.5 of [23]. This approach is referred to as 'compcrypt' in the paper. Furthermore, assuming an equivalent level of security, the compcrypt algorithm could be implemented with a reduced number of encryption rounds, making it much faster.

ANS can be conceptualized as a finite state machine (FSM). In this framework, the transition of states during compression is dictated by the sequence of symbols in a frame. This characteristic implies that ANS inherently possesses a mechanism for authentication. It enables the generation of a form of message authentication code (MAC), which could be represented either by the current state of ANS or by the XOR (exclusive OR) of a selected subset of states observed throughout the symbol frame processing.

Contributions. The main purpose of this paper is to discuss and demonstrate possible applications of compression in cryptography. Our focus is on ANS compression, which offers an interesting and elegant mathematical structure that can potentially be seamlessly incorporated into cryptographic systems. The paper builds on earlier works by the author [3,4,19]. It summarizes the ANS properties that are particularly interesting from a cryptographic point of view. It also provides a new perspective on ANS as an algorithm that can be used to translate one probability distribution into another. Some applications of custom-designed probability distributions are discussed, including a group sharing of symbol frames, which can be seen as a variant of secret sharing. The paper introduces a general framework for designing compcrypt algorithms that jointly compress and encrypt symbol frames. Unlike traditional encryption algorithms, where the input and output bits hold specific and well-defined positions, compcrypt generates binary frames whose encodings (bits) are concatenated and may vary in length. This increases the difficulty of cryptanalysis, as the adversary must guess the positions of the symbol encodings.

The rest of the paper is structured as follows. Section 2 introduces ANS compression. Section 3 explores the cryptographic properties of ANS. Section 4 investigates how to translate one probability distribution into a customised one with desired parameters. Section 5 describes a general framework for designing compcrypt algorithms. The security of compcrypt algorithms is discussed in Sect. 6. Section 7 concludes the work.

2 ANS Compression

The reader who is interested in alternative descriptions of ANS is directed to the original Duda's work [8] but also to works [3,4,10]. We first introduce notation that is used in the description of ANS.

- L^R is the number of all ANS states/integers, where R is a parameter.
- $\mathbb{I} = \{L, \ldots, 2L - 1\}$ is the set of ANS states.
- $L_s \approx Lp_s$ is the number of states assigned to a symbol s. Note that the bigger R the better the approximation.
- $\bar{s} : \mathbb{I} \to \mathbb{S}$ is a symbol spread function, which, for a given symbol s, assigns states from $\mathbb{I}$. This set is denoted by $\mathbb{L}_s$ and $L_s = |\mathbb{L}_s|$. The states from $\mathbb{L}_s$ are assigned in the increasing order.
- $C(y, s)$ is an ANS encoding function, which for an integer $y \in \{L_s, \ldots, 2L_s - 1\}$, assigns states $x \in \mathbb{L}_s$ according to the symbol spread function.

Example 1. We start from an example, where the set of ANS states covers the whole set of positive integers or $\mathbb{I} = \mathbb{N}^+$. Assume that we need to design an ANS instance for two symbols $s \in \{0,1\}$, which occur with the probabilities $p_s \in \{^1/_4, ^3/_4\}$, respectively. We need an encoding function that generates integers whose values increase inversely proportional to the symbol probabilities or $x' =$

Table 1. Encoding function $C(x, s)$ for binary symbols with probabilities $p_0 = 1/4$ and $p_1 = 3/4$

$x' \rightarrow$	0	1	2	3	4	5	6	7	8	9	$\cdots$
$s = 0$	0				1				2		$\cdots$
$s = 1$		0	1	2		3	4	5		6	$\cdots$

$C(x, s) = \lfloor x/p_s \rfloor + s$. This means that $x' = C(x, s = 0) = 4x$ and $x' = C(x, s = 1) = \lfloor \frac{4}{3}x \rfloor + 1$. Table 1 illustrates the encoding. Encoding the symbol frame $(1, 0, 1, 1)$ starting from an initial state $x = 0$ proceeds according to the following steps: $0 \xrightarrow{1} 1 \xrightarrow{0} 4 \xrightarrow{1} 6 \xrightarrow{1} 9$. The decoding process, however, proceeds in reverse order: $9 \rightarrow (6, 1) \rightarrow (4, 1) \rightarrow (1, 0) \rightarrow (0, 1)$, thereby reconstructing the original frame $(1, 0, 1, 1)$ in reverse order.

It is worth noting the following facts:

- In the context of lossless compression, the encoding function $x' = C(x, s)$ must indeed be reversible. This implies that for any given x', one should be able to accurately determine the original state/integer x and the symbol s. Thus, each column of Table 1 should contain a unique x to ensure that the decoding process is unambiguous.
- The number of non-empty entries in each symbol row is indicative of its probability. In Table 1, the row for $s = 0$ has one non-empty entry for every four entries. Similarly, for $s = 1$, there are three non-empty entries in every group of four.
- The encoding table can be split into intervals of the length 2^R, where each symbol row of an interval has $L_s = p_s 2^R$ non-empty entries and $\sum_s L_s = 2^R$. For our Table 1, $R = 2$ and each interval includes four columns.
- The ANS encoding can be adapted for cases involving an arbitrary number of symbols or $|\mathbb{S}| \geq 2$.
- There is flexibility in the selection of $C(x, s)$ as long as $L_s = p_s 2^R$ and $\sum_s L_s = 2^R$. Table 2 illustrates such an instance.

It is evident that the ANS described above can compress symbol frames of any length. Consequently, the final value of the integer x' increases rapidly, eventually reaching the value $\log_2(x') \approx \ell H(\mathbb{S})$, where $H(\mathbb{S})$ is an entropy of the symbol source and ℓ – the number of compressed symbols. This issue becomes significant when processing long frames. To tackle this, ANS implements a technique

Table 2. A different version of $C(x, s)$ for binary symbols with probabilities $p_0 = 1/4$ and $p_1 = 3/4$

$x' \rightarrow$	0	1	2	3	4	5	6	7	8	9	$\cdots$
$s = 0$		0				1				2	$\cdots$
$s = 1$	0		1	2	3		4	5	6		$\cdots$

known as *re-normalization*. The concept is straightforward: during compression, it utilises states/integers from two adjacent intervals, i.e. $\{1, \ldots, 2^R - 1\}$ and $\{2^R, \ldots, 2^{2R} - 1\}$. When a state x' is in the range $x' \in \{2^R, \ldots, 2^{2R} - 1\}$, it can be expressed as a pair $(x' \bmod 2^k, \lfloor \frac{x'}{2^k} \rfloor)$, where $k \geq 1$. It is important to note that this representation is bijective. While processing a symbol s, ANS extracts $x' \bmod 2^k$ as the binary encoding of the symbol and transitions to a new state $x = \lfloor \frac{x'}{2^k} \rfloor$ in the range $\{1, \ldots, 2^R - 1\}$. Next, it applies the encoding function to determine $x' = C(x, s)$ in the range $\{2^R, \ldots, 2^{2R} - 1\}$.

Example 2. Let us illustrate the re-normalisation on a simple example using the encoding from Table 1. This time our initial state $x' = 1$. Note that encoding starting from the state '0' ignores all consecutive symbols '$s = 1$' so the state must be avoided. We encode the frame $(1, 0, 1, 1)$ – see the table given below (Table 3). Finding the symbol frame from the output bits and the current state is possible by performing reverse operations, provided that the number of bits

Table 3. Re-normalisation of encoding the frame $(1, 0, 1, 1)$, where $\varnothing$ stands for an empty bit

Original Encoding	Encoding with Re-Normalization	Output Bits	Number of Output Bits
$1 \xrightarrow{s=1} 2$	$1 \xrightarrow{s=1} 2$	$\varnothing$	0
$2 \xrightarrow{s=0} 8$	$(2 \xrightarrow{s=0} 8); (8 \bmod 2^2, \lfloor \frac{8}{2^2} \rfloor) = (00, 2)$	00	2
$8 \xrightarrow{s=1} 11$	$2 \xrightarrow{s=1} 3$	$\varnothing$	0
$11 \xrightarrow{s=1} 15$	$(3 \xrightarrow{s=1} 5); (5 \bmod 2, \lfloor \frac{5}{2} \rfloor) = (1, 2)$	1	1

that need to be extracted from the binary frame is known. ANS implements this by assigning each state a unique symbol and the parameter k. A careful reader should note that ANS is fully determined by its encoding function $C(x, s)$ for the initial states and all possible symbols. In these circumstances, ANS becomes a finite state machine (FSM).

2.1 ANS Algorithms

ANS can be viewed as an encoding mechanism for pairs of (symbol, state/integer) into consecutive natural numbers from $\mathbb{N}^+$. For a given symbol s in the set $\mathbb{S}$, the number of encodings corresponds to the symbol probability p_s. To manage the growth of the encodings, ANS employs re-normalisation described above. Now, we are ready to detail the ANS suite of algorithms. ANS initialisation proceeds according to Algorithm 1.

Algorithm 1: ANS Initialisation

Input: Given a set of symbols $\mathbb{S}$, symbol probability distribution $p : \mathbb{S} \to [0, 1]$ and a parameter $R \in \mathbb{N}^+$.

Output: Instantiation of:
- functions $C(y, s)$ and $k_s(x)$;
- functions $D(x)$ and $k(y)$.

Steps:
- calculate $L = 2^R$ and determine a set $\mathbb{I}$;
- for each symbol $s \in \mathbb{S}$, compute integer $L_s \approx L p_s$;
- define the symbol spread function $\overline{s} : \mathbb{I} \to \mathbb{S}$, such that $|\{x \in \mathbb{I} : \overline{s}(x) = s\}| = L_s$. The selection of states is arbitrary as long as they appear in the increasing order in $\mathbb{L}_s$;
- establish the coding function $C(y, s) = x$ for an integer $y \in \{L_s, \dots, 2L_s - 1\}$, which assigns states $x \in \mathbb{L}_s$ according to the symbol spread function;
- compute $k_s(x) = \lfloor \log_2(x/L_s) \rfloor$ for $x \in \mathbb{I}$ and $s \in \mathbb{S}$. It gives the number of output bits per an encoding step;
- construct the decoding function $D(x) = (y, s)$, which for a state $x \in \mathbb{I}$ assigns the integer y and a matching symbol s. Note that $D(x) = C^{-1}(x)$;
- calculate $k(y) = R - \lfloor \log_2(y) \rfloor$, which gives the number of bits that need to be read out from the bitstream.

To initialise, ANS requires knowledge of the symbol probability distribution. This distribution may be known beforehand, but in most cases, it needs to be determined just before compression. Under these circumstances, ANS first computes the statistics for the symbol frame and places the frame in reverse order onto a stack. With these statistics, ANS initialises itself and processes the frame in reverse order, reading symbols from the stack – see Algorithm 2.

A binary frame **b** is processed step by step through a "while" loop until it becomes empty. For each step, ANS is in a state x and applies the decoding function $D(x)$, which identifies a distinct pair (y, s). The symbol s is outputted but the integer y is later used to determine the next state. To identify the state, ANS requires to determine the number k of bits that encode the symbol s. With

---

Algorithm 2: ANS Encoding

Input: Given a symbol frame $\mathbf{s} = (s_1, s_2, \ldots, s_\ell) \in \mathbb{S}^*$ and an initial state $x = x_\ell \in \mathbb{I}$.

Output: A binary frame $\mathbf{b} = (b_1|b_2|\ldots|b_\ell) \in \mathbb{B}^*$, where $|b_i| = k_{s_i}(x_i)$ and x_i is the state in the i-th step.

Steps: for $i = \ell, \ell - 1, \ldots, 2, 1$ do

$\quad | \quad s := s_i;$

$\quad | \quad k = k_s(x) = \lfloor \log_2(x/L_s) \rfloor;$ // *calculate the number of bits to be extracted*

$\quad | \quad b_i = x \bmod 2^k;$ $\qquad$ // *output the k_s least significant bits (LSB) of x*

$\quad | \quad x := C(\lfloor x/2^k \rfloor, s);$ $\quad$ // *update the state using the symbol spread function*

Store the final state $x_0 = x$;

---

the number k found, ANS extracts the binary string b from the binary frame $\mathbf{b}$. The string b consists of the k most significant bits of $\mathbf{b}$. The binary frame $\mathbf{b}$ is then updated by removing b, and the next state is reconstructed. The integer y gives the $(R - k)$ most significant bits, and b contributes the k least significant bits. The decoding process is detailed in Algorithm 3.

Algorithm 3: ANS Decoding

Input: Given a binary frame $\mathbf{b} \in \mathbb{B}^*$ and the final state $x = x_0 \in \mathbb{I}$.

Output: Symbol frame $\mathbf{s} \in \mathbb{S}^*$.

Steps: while $\mathbf{b} \neq \varnothing$ do

$\quad | \quad (y, s) = D(x);$ // *find (y, s) from the state x using the decoding function*

$\quad | \quad k = R - \lfloor \log_2 y \rfloor;$ $\qquad$ // *calculate the number of bits used to encode s*

$\quad | \quad b = MSB(\mathbf{b})_k;$ $\qquad$ // *extract the k most significant bits of $\mathbf{b}$*

$\quad | \quad \mathbf{b} := LSB(\mathbf{b})_{|\mathbf{b}|-k};$ $\qquad$ // *update $\mathbf{b}$ by removing k MSB of $\mathbf{b}$*

$\quad | \quad x := 2^k y + b;$ $\qquad$ // *calculate the next state*

Example 3. Let us illustrate the above ANS algorithms for a simple case, when a symbol source $\mathbb{S} = \{s_1, s_2\}$, where $p_1 = 3/4$, $p_2 = 1/4$ and the parameter $R = 2$. The number of states $L = 2^R = 4$ and the state set $\mathbb{I} = \{4, 5, 6, 7\}$. We follow the initialisation.

- Determine symbol spread function $\overline{s} : \mathbb{I} \to \mathbb{S}$ such that

$$\overline{s}(x) = \begin{cases} s_1 & \text{if } x \in \{4, 5, 7\} = \mathbb{L}_1 \\ s_2 & \text{if } x \in \{6\} = \mathbb{L}_2 \end{cases}$$

where $L_1 = |\mathbb{L}_1| = 3$ and $L_2 = |\mathbb{L}_2| = 1$.

- Write the coding function $C(y, s)$, which can be represented as

$s \backslash y$	1	2	3	4	5	6	7
s_1	$-$	$-$	4	5	7	$-$	$-$
s_2	6	$-$	$-$	$-$	$-$	$-$	$-$

- Design the following encoding table $\mathbb{E}(x, s) = (x', b) \stackrel{\text{def}}{\equiv} \binom{x'}{b}$ as follows:

$s \backslash x$	4	5	6	7
s_1	$\binom{5}{\varnothing}$	$\binom{7}{\varnothing}$	$\binom{4}{0}$	$\binom{4}{1}$;
s_2	$\binom{6}{00}$	$\binom{6}{01}$	$\binom{6}{10}$	$\binom{6}{11}$

where $\varnothing$ stands for empty bit (no encoding is sent to the output).
- Determine a decoding table/function $\mathbb{D}(x, b)$. For a given state x, it is convenient to find its unique integer y using the following table

x	4	5	6	7
y	3	4	1	5

The decoding table $\mathbb{D}(x, b)$ can be represented as follows

x	4	5	6	7
s	s_1	s_1	s_2	s_1
k	1	0	2	0
x'	$6 + b$	4	$4 + b$	5

Note that $x' = 2^k y + b$, where b is an integer that corresponds to the binary string b.

Given a symbol frame $(s_1, s_1, s_1, s_1, s_2, s_1)$ and assume that ANS is in the state $x = 6$. Then encoding progresses according to the following sequence:

$$6 \xrightarrow{s_1} \binom{4}{0} \xrightarrow{s_1} \binom{5}{\varnothing} \xrightarrow{s_1} \binom{7}{\varnothing} \xrightarrow{s_1} \binom{4}{1} \xrightarrow{s_2} \binom{6}{00} \xrightarrow{s_1} \binom{4}{0}.$$

This means that the symbol frame is compressed into its binary frame $\mathbf{b} = (01000)$ and ANS stops at $x = 4$. The decoding of the binary frame proceeds in reverse and is shown below:

$$6 \xleftarrow{k=1; \, b=0} \binom{4}{s_1} \xleftarrow{k=0} \binom{5}{s_1} \xleftarrow{k=0} \binom{7}{s_1} \xleftarrow{k=1; \, b=1} \binom{4}{s_1} \xleftarrow{k=2; \, b=00} \binom{6}{s_2} \xleftarrow{k=1; \, b=0} \binom{4}{s_1}.$$

$\square$

3   Properties of ANS

When evaluating the performance of ANS in source coding, a key question arises regarding its compression efficiency. Specifically, the focus is on the extent of the difference between the average length of the symbol encodings and the symbol entropy. ANS targets a particular probability distribution $\mathcal{Q} = \{q(s)|s \in \mathbb{S}\}$ aiming to approximate the actual symbol probability distribution $\mathcal{P} = \{p(s)|s \in \mathbb{S}\}$. This approximation becomes equality when a sufficiently large parameter R is chosen, ensuring that $p_s 2^R$ is an integer for every $s \in \mathbb{S}$.

In this context, the question of whether ANS achieves optimal encoding – meaning the average length of symbol encodings matches the symbol entropy – merits consideration. Dube and Yokoo affirmatively addressed this question, demonstrating ANS asymptotic optimality in their study [7]. However, this assertion of optimality does not extend to ANS instances with static parameters. The compression performance of ANS can be evaluated by analysing the probability distribution of ANS states through a Markov chain model.

Interestingly, this analysis reveals a tendency for ANS state probabilities to favour states represented by smaller integers. This characteristic is advantageous for compression, as states with lower numerical values are associated with shorter binary encodings. A significant factor impacting the ANS compression is its flexible symbol spread function, offering a variety of selection instances, each of which with a slightly different compression rate. Those interested in exploring this aspect of ANS further are encouraged to consult the work [19], which delves into the details of this aspect.

It turns out that variations in the probability distributions of ANS states, caused by different symbol spread functions, can facilitate a cryptographic attack. This vulnerability allows an adversary to determine the specific symbol spread function employed. The attack outlined in the work [4] assumes that the adversary is capable of altering the symbol probability distribution. By preparing a suitable symbol frame and observing the resulting number of bits in the binary frame, the adversary can exploit this information to identify the symbol spread function used.

Let us continue our discussion and take into account the lemma shown below proven in the work [4].

Lemma 1. *Given ANS described by Algorithm 2 and the parameter R is big enough so $L_s = p_s 2^R$. Then a symbol s is encoded into a binary string of the length k_s, where*

- $k_s = i$ *if* $p_s = 2^{-i}$, $i \in \mathbb{N}$;
- $k_s \in \{i, i+1\}$ *if* $2^{-(i+1)} < p_s < 2^{-i}$. *This includes the case when* $2^{-1} < p_s < 2^0$ *with* $k_s \in \{0, 1\}$, *i.e. some symbols are encoded into void bits* $\varnothing$.

We can draw the following conclusions:

C1 ANS compression achieves optimality when compressing symbols with a probability distribution represented by natural powers of $1/2$, effectively becoming equivalent to an instance of Huffman coding. In other words, a symbol with its probability $p_s = 2^{-i}$ are encoded into a i-bit string.

C2 For a symbol s occurring with a probability in the range $2^{-(i+1)} < p_s < 2^{-i}$, it is encoded into binary strings of length k_s, which is either i or $(i+1)$. The specific encoding length is determined by the current ANS state. Given any symbol and an ANS encoding table, the length k_s can be considered a random variable. Its probability distribution can be computed using Markov chains.

C3 Each row of the encoding table corresponding to a symbol s includes all consecutive binary strings from both $\{0, \ldots, 2^i - 1\}$ and $\{0, \ldots, 2^{i+1} - 1\}$ if $2^{-(i+1)} < p_s < 2^{-i}$. Moreover, if the row is "long", it must include multiple copies of $\{0, \ldots, 2^i - 1\}$ and/or $\{0, \ldots, 2^{i+1} - 1\}$, where integers are represented their binary equivalents.

Assume that an adversary can manipulate the symbol probability distribution and can observe the output (binary encodings). It means that the adversary can prepare symbol frames, where certain symbols are entirely absent (i.e., some symbols occur with zero probability). Consequently, the ANS encoding table can be reduced by removing both all rows for symbols that never occur and all columns/states that are never used (states that are assigned to absent symbols). It is possible to make the attack less effective by forcing ANS state to occur randomly and uniformly. This is to say that instead of normal state transitions

$$\cdots \xrightarrow{s_{i-1}} \mathbf{x}_{i-1} \xrightarrow{s_i} \mathbf{x}_i \xrightarrow{s_{i+1}} \mathbf{x}_{i+1} \xrightarrow{s_{i+2}} \cdots$$

we choose states using a pseudorandom bit generator (PrBG) so states are calculated as follows:

$$\cdots \xrightarrow{s_{i-1}} \underbrace{\mathbf{x}_{i-1} := \mathbf{x}_{i-1} \oplus \mathrm{PrBG(K)}}_{} \xrightarrow{s_i} \underbrace{\mathbf{x}_i := \mathbf{x}_i \oplus \mathrm{PrBG(K)}}_{} \xrightarrow{s_{i+1}}$$
$$\underbrace{\mathbf{x}_{i+1} := \mathbf{x}_{i+1} \oplus \mathrm{PrBG(K)}}_{} \xrightarrow{s_{i+2}} \cdots$$

where K is cryptographic key that controls PrBG. As a result, ANS states exhibit a uniform probability distribution, rendering the statistical attacks outlined in the work by Camtepe et al. [4] ineffective. The price to pay, however, is a minor reduction in the compression rate $\approx 0.5\%$.

The following fact can be proven (see [4]):

Fact 1. *Given an instance of ANS whose states are randomised according to Eq. 1 and PrBG generates binary strings uniformly at random for each K. Then ANS outputs binary encodings uniformly at random.*

The compression loss incurred by making state probabilities uniform can be mitigated by employing shorter PrBG strings. Let n be the number of bits of ANS states. Assume that PrBG modifies u least significant bits of ANS states ($u < n$). Then ANS states are updated by choosing at random the next state from a set of 2^u consecutive candidates.

To achieve a uniform probability distribution of ANS states, it is sufficient for PrBG to generate bits that are uniformly random. A basic PrBG implementation might utilise a linear feedback shift register (LFSR), with its initial state set by the cryptographic key K. For applications where security is paramount, employing a cryptographically secure PrBG, operated by its secret key K, is advisable.

There are two approaches to constructing such secure PrBGs. The first involves the use of a non-linear feedback shift register (NLFSR), which derives its security from its resistance against all known cryptographic attacks, offering heuristic security. The second approach entails using a PrBG constructed on the foundation of a problem believed to be intractable. The security of this PrBG is closely related to the complexity of solving a specific instance of the intractable problem (provable security).

4   Construction of Customised Probability Distributions

ANS can be seen as a mechanism for translating the probabilities of symbols into a uniform probability distribution of output bits. Intuitively, a compressed binary frame should not contain redundant bits. This means that the frame is a sequence of bits uniformly distributed at random. Consequently, inputting any uniformly random binary frame into the ANS decoding algorithm should convert the binary frame back into its symbol frame, adhering to the original probability distribution for which ANS has been designed.

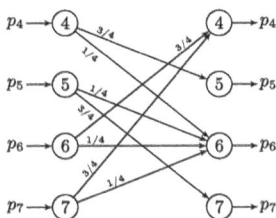

Fig. 1. Transition probabilities for ANS encoding

Consider the ANS example outlined in Example 3, which demonstrates the issue at hand. Figure 1 shows how state probabilities evolve when processing a single symbol. By employing Markov chains, it's possible to determine the equilibrium state probabilities as $(p_4, p_5, p_6, p_7) = (12/37, 9/37, 1/4, 27/148)$. This results in an average binary encoding length per symbol of $61/74 \approx 0.824$. It is important to note that the symbol entropy, $H(\mathbb{S}) = \sum_{i=1,2} p_i \log_2 p_i^{-1}$, is approximately 0.811. Furthermore, the bits in binary frames exhibit a bias towards "0", which is a result of states labeled by smaller integers occurring with higher probabilities.

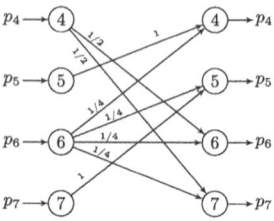

Fig. 2. Transition probabilities for ANS decoding

Suppose we utilise our ANS decoding algorithm, which receives input from bits generated by a truly random generator (TRG). This implies that each bit is an independent and identically distributed (i.i.d.) random variable. The state evolution during the decoding process of a single binary encoding is depicted in Fig. 2. The decoding of a large binary frame can be modeled by a Markov chain, which reaches equilibrium with state probabilities

$$(p_4, p_5, p_6, p_7) = (6/19, 5/19, 4/19, 4/19).$$

From this, we can deduce that the probability of symbol a, represented as $p(a) = \sum_{i=4,5,7} p_i = 15/19$, and the probability of symbol b, represented as $p(b) = p_6 = 4/19$. The symbol probability distribution significantly deviates from the original one that has been used in the design of our ANS. This observation highlights how the decoding process, when fed with truly random bits, results in symbol probabilities that do not align with the initial design parameters of the ANS system.

Given a target probability distribution $\mathcal{Q} = \{q_i; i = 1, \ldots, n\}$, we aim to design it using ANS and TRG. Such tasks are frequently encountered in various cryptographic applications and simulations, where a specific type of randomness is required.

- The probability distribution $\mathcal{Q}$ can be synthesised by initially configuring an ANS specifically for the target probability distribution and then processing a binary frame generated by a TRG through the ANS decoding algorithm. This method is likely to produce a frame with a symbol probability distribution that closely resembles $\mathcal{Q}$. However, there might be significant deviations from the anticipated distribution required for the specific application. To mitigate this issue, two basic options are available. The first involves identifying a symbol spread function that enhances the compression quality of ANS, bringing it closer to the optimal rate, as discussed in the study [19]. The second option entails choosing a sufficiently large parameter R, and thus the number 2^R of ANS states, to better emulate the randomness provided by the TRG. As a result, the ANS decoding process generates symbols with a probability distribution that aligns closely with $\mathcal{Q}$.
- According to Lemma 1, for each symbol, its encodings span multiple collections of all binary sequences from two sets $\{0, \ldots, 2^i - 1\}$ and $\{0, \ldots, 2^{i+1} - 1\}$,

where $2^{-(i+1)} < p_s < 2^{-i}$. This indicates that binary strings in the ANS encoding table are "balanced", meaning bits from $\{0, 1\}$ appear an equal number of times, as do 2-bit strings from $\{00, 01, 10, 11\}$, and so on. It is important to note that some i-bit encodings are absent if there is no symbol with a matching probability. If we employ a PrBG to ensure a uniform probability distribution of ANS states as outlined in Eq. 1, then Fact 1 confirms that the ANS encoding algorithm yields binary strings uniformly at random. As a result, the ANS decoding process generates symbol frames with a probability distribution of $\mathcal{Q}$, regardless of whether the binary frames originate from a TRG or the ANS encoding algorithm.

To summarise our discussion, it is important to acknowledge that the specific design of converting uniformly random binary frames into symbol frames with the desired probability distribution $\mathcal{Q}$ using ANS significantly depends on the application and its security requirements. Below is a list of potential scenarios for applications with:

- Low security requirements, such as simulations, where the symbol probability distribution $\mathcal{Q}$ does not need to be exact. In these cases, a linear feedback shift register (LFSR) can serve as an adequate substitute for a TRG. The binary frame produced by the LFSR can then be processed by an ANS decoding algorithm. To achieve a reasonable approximation of $\mathcal{Q}$, the ANS parameter RR should be chosen to be sufficiently large. In summary, LFSR $\rightarrow$ ANS$_D$ $\rightarrow$ $\approx \mathcal{Q}$, where ANS$_D$ denotes the ANS decoding algorithm.
- Low security requirements but with a necessity for the symbol probability distribution $\mathcal{Q}$ to be precise. It is feasible to use an LFSR to generate binary frames, however, the ANS states need to be uniformly randomised, potentially also using an LFSR. Therefore, LFSR $\rightarrow$ ANS(RS)$_D$ $\rightarrow$ $\mathcal{Q}$, where ANS(RS)$_D$ represents the ANS decoding algorithm with randomised states.
- High security requirements and a need for the exact probability distribution $\mathcal{Q}$. In such cases, the ANS decoding algorithm with randomised states should be fed binary frames generated by a cryptographically strong pseudo-random bit generator (CSPrBG). Thus, CSPrBG $\rightarrow$ ANS(RS)$_D$ $\rightarrow$ $\mathcal{Q}$.

4.1   Applications

Assume there is a streaming service (such as Netflix or Stan) offering a broad array of multimedia content, including movies, TV series, and sports events. In their business model, the service provides digital content at a significant discount or even for free, albeit at lower quality (both in terms of picture and sound). However, customers are charged additional fees based on the quality of the digital content (HD, 4K, or 8K). Let us explore some potential solutions to the challenges presented by this scenario. We start our discussion from the assumption that a multimedia stream is compressed and transmitted to a customer in the form of a series of ANS binary frames.

- **Solution 1.** A high-quality digital content symbol frame $\mathbf{s} = (s_1, \ldots, s_\ell)$ is divided into two frames: $\bar{\mathbf{s}} = (\bar{s}_1, \ldots, \bar{s}_\ell)$ for low-quality content, and $\underline{\mathbf{s}} = (\underline{s}_1, \ldots, \underline{s}_\ell)$ for the enhancement layer, with each $s_i = \bar{s}_i \oplus \underline{s}_i$ for $i = 1 \ldots, \ell$. The $\bar{\mathbf{s}}$ frame, containing enough information for low-quality content, might be generated by setting the least significant bits of $\mathbf{s}$ to zeros. On the other hand, $\underline{\mathbf{s}}$ comprises these least significant bits from $\mathbf{s}$. The service compresses the low-quality frame $\bar{\mathbf{s}}$ and broadcasts the resulting binary frame $\text{ANS}(\mathbf{s}) = \bar{\mathbf{b}}$ along with the ANS parameters, making it accessible to everyone. The enhancement layer $\underline{\mathbf{s}}$ is compressed using an ANS instance with randomized states, or $\text{ANS}(K, \underline{\mathbf{s}}) = \underline{\mathbf{b}}$, where the transitions between states are governed by an PrBG, which, in turn, is controlled by a secret key K. This binary frame $\underline{\mathbf{b}}$ is also broadcast. Customers desiring access to the detailed symbol frame $\underline{\mathbf{s}}$ (i.e., the least significant bits) must purchase the key K. With both symbol frames $\bar{\mathbf{s}}$, $\underline{\mathbf{s}}$ and the key K, customers can reconstruct the original high-quality frame $\mathbf{s}$.
- **Solution 2.** It is possible to condense the transmission into a single frame. For a high-quality symbol frame $\mathbf{s} = (s_1, \ldots, s_\ell)$, the service creates a masking frame $\boldsymbol{\varepsilon} = (\varepsilon_1, \ldots, \varepsilon_\ell)$ to alter the original frame $\mathbf{s}$. The distortion probability distribution $\mathcal{Q}$ can be determined experimentally by focusing on symbols representing the least significant bits. This masking frame $\boldsymbol{\varepsilon}(\mathcal{Q})$ can be produced using LFSR and ANS or LFSR $\rightarrow \text{ANS}(K)_D \rightarrow \boldsymbol{\varepsilon}(\mathcal{Q})$, where LFSR is public, however, ANS decoding state transitions are forced by a PrBG controlled by a secret key K and $\mathcal{Q}$ is the chosen distortion probability distribution. The service then compresses the combined frame $\tilde{\mathbf{s}} = \mathbf{s} \oplus \boldsymbol{\varepsilon}(\mathcal{Q})$ and broadcasts it to customers. All customers can decompress and view the modified frame $\tilde{\mathbf{s}}$. However, accessing the original, high-quality frame $\mathbf{s}$ requires purchasing the cryptographic key K. This key enables them to reconstruct $\boldsymbol{\varepsilon}(\mathcal{Q})$, thereby allowing the recovery of $\mathbf{s} = \tilde{\mathbf{s}} \oplus \boldsymbol{\varepsilon}(\mathcal{Q})$.

The primary security concern is ensuring that no customer or adversary can access the high-quality frames without purchasing the cryptographic key K. This implies that the adversary cannot deduce K, even if they have access to the encoding oracles that produce (encrypted) binary frames using K. The security objective is met when the PrBG used is cryptographically strong. It is argued that security is not compromised even if the PrBG is substituted with a LFSR, particularly for certain probability distributions $\mathcal{Q}$, where cryptanalysis depends on predicting the lengths of binary encodings. For readers interested in delving deeper into such cryptanalytic methods, they are directed to explore the study referenced as [3].

The discussion leads us to a method that enables a group of participants to share symbol frames. The approach is detailed in Algorithm 4, where it is noted that all parameters are public with the exception of cryptographic keys. This method bears a resemblance to the traditional (n, n) threshold secret sharing, but its distinctive characteristic lies in the flexibility to assign specific probability distributions to each participant. This allows an authority to finely tune

---

Algorithm 4: Group Sharing of Symbol Frames

Input: Given a trusted authority A, a group of participants $G = \{P_1 \ldots, P_n\}$ and a symbol frame $\mathbf{s} = (s_1, s_2, \ldots, s_\ell) \in \mathbb{S}^*$

Output: A collection of cryptographic keys $K = (K_1, \ldots, K_n)$, which allows G to recover $\mathbf{s}$

Authority(*Dealer*)

Steps:

1. Choose cryptographic keys $K = (K_1, \ldots, K_n)$;
2. **for** $i = 1, \ldots, n$ **do**

   generate symbol frame $\mathbf{s}_i \leftarrow \text{ANS}_{D_i} \leftarrow \text{LFSR}(K_i)$, where the initial state of LFSR is public and ANS_{D_i} is designed for a public symbol probability $\mathcal{P}_i$ chosen by A;

3. Calculate $\tilde{\mathbf{s}} = \mathbf{s} \oplus \sum_{i=1}^{n} \mathbf{s}_i$ and calculate its binary frame $\tilde{\mathbf{b}} \leftarrow ANS(\tilde{\mathbf{s}})$, where parameters of ANS are public;
4. Publish the binary frame $\tilde{\mathbf{b}}$ and send cryptographic keys the respective participants via secure channels.

Group(*Combiner*)

1. Knowing its secret key K_i, the participant P_i calculates its symbol frame $\mathbf{s}_i \leftarrow \text{ANS}_{D_i} \leftarrow \text{LFSR}(K_i)$;
2. The group recovers the masked symbol frame $\tilde{\mathbf{s}} \leftarrow ANS_D(\tilde{\mathbf{b}})$;
3. The group collectively reconstructs the original frame $\mathbf{s} = \tilde{\mathbf{s}} \oplus \sum_{i=1}^{n} \mathbf{s}_i$.

---

the probability distribution of the symbol frame and, consequently, balance its redundancy with security.

5   Joint Compression and Encryption – Compcrypt

As the Internet increasingly facilitates the exchange of data characterised by both high redundancy and sensitivity – encompassing voice, video, images, music, and streaming entertainment among others – the demand for both secure and efficient data transmission has intensified. A practical approach to meet this need involves the concurrent compression and encryption of data for Internet transmission. Typically, encryption targets either individual bits/words, as seen in stream ciphers, or operates on fixed-length bit blocks (e.g., 64/128/256 bits) as in block ciphers. However, when combining compression with encryption, the fundamental unit of processing becomes a symbol frame for plaintext and a binary frame for ciphertext. Probably the first work that dealt with the cryptographic application of Huffman compression is the paper [11]. Encryption based on arithmetic coding compression is studied in papers [1,28]. Joint compression and encryption has been studied by many authors using specific compression algorithms and targeting different applications (see works [5,12,17,20,25] for example).

For the sake of clarity, the terms "joint compression and encryption" and "compcrypt" are used interchangeably here. A straightforward method for compcrypt is explored in the work [3], which employs encryption through state jumps controlled by an LFSR, with its initial state acting as the cryptographic key. Despite its strengths, this approach is critiqued for failing to authenticate transmitted frames. The study [4] addresses this gap by proposing a framework for both joint compression and authenticated encryption, utilizing a sponge structure for encryption. This model can serve as a template for compcrypt design, as depicted in Fig. 3. A symbol frame is compressed by ANS, which randomises its states according to an LFSR controlled by a cryptographic key. The ANS then generates a binary frame that is segmented into blocks of r bits, in alignment with the defined sponge structure. These blocks are XOR-ed with the upper part of the sponge, forming ciphertext blocks. Consequently, the sponge extracts these blocks and ensemble the ciphertext frame. A notable benefit of this compcrypt approach is the substantial decrease in the number of Keccak permutations required in P, attributable to the ANS effective randomisation of the binary frame. The following corollary, proven in [4], formalizes this advantage:

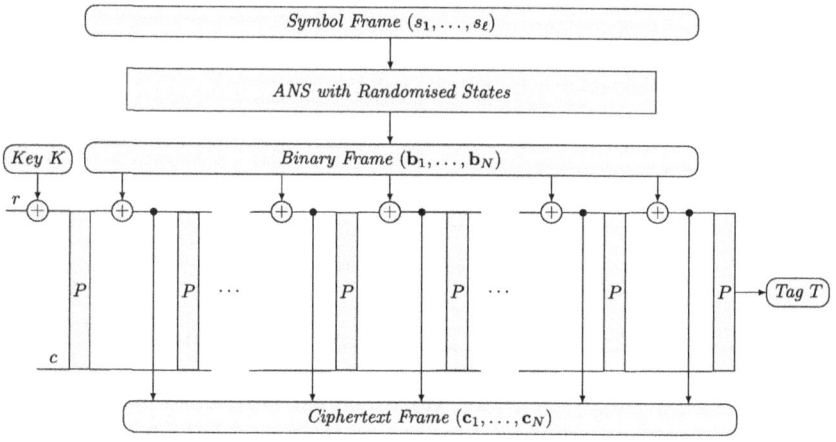

Fig. 3. Compcrypt based on ANS and the sponge structure

Corollary 1. *Consider the ANS as outlined in Sect. 2, where the ANS algorithm selects the next states in a manner that is uniformly random (i.e., $x_i \leftarrow x_i \oplus RBG$, with RBG representing a truly random bit generator). Assume an adversary $\mathcal{A}$ manipulates the symbol frames, injecting a sequence of ℓ symbols, denoted by $(s_1, s_2, \ldots, s_\ell)$, and records the number k of resulting bits. Under these conditions, the likelihood of $\mathcal{A}$ successfully guessing the bits is 2^{-k}.*

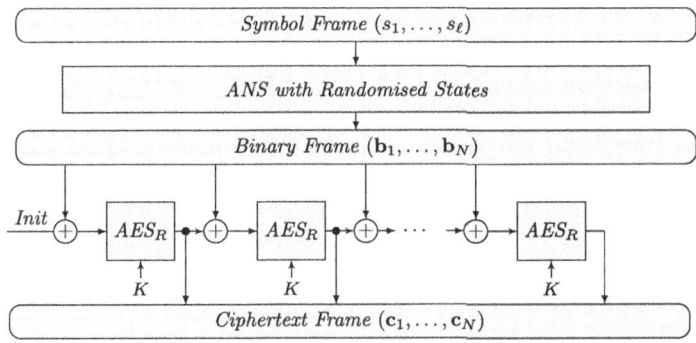

Fig. 4. Compcrypt with ANS and AES, where AES_R stands for round-reduced AES

It is important to note that this corollary remains valid even if the adversary $\mathcal{A}$ inputs a sequence of identical symbols to ANS. Consequently, combined compression and encryption (compcrypt) allows much more efficient compression and encryption than performing compression followed by encryption separately. Assuming that ANS are perfectly randomised, the blocks of binary frames create a one-time pad (OTP). This means that the sponge requires a minimal number of Keccak permutations without reducing the security level of compcrypt. A similar argument can be made when designing compcrypt using ANS and AES, as illustrated in Fig. 4. The encryption layer is created by AES operating in cipher block chaining (CBC) mode. Using the same arguments, we can claim that it is possible to reduce the number of AES rounds to just a few, thus making compcrypt faster without sacrificing its security level.

6   Security of Compcrypt

We investigate the properties of ANS that determine the security of compcrypt algorithms. We consider two basic scenarios: (1) where an adversary $\mathcal{A}$ has access to a plain ANS and attempts to find its symbol distribution, and (2) where $\mathcal{A}$ interacts with an ANS with randomized states, knows the symbol distribution of the ANS, and attempts to uncover the randomness used to induce state transitions.

6.1   ANS with Secret Symbol Spread

We begin with the straightforward scenario where a compcrypt algorithm utilizes ANS with a secret symbol spread function (refer to Fig. 5). We assume that our adversary $\mathcal{A}$ fully controls the symbol frames and can observe the corresponding binary frames. $\mathcal{A}$ can create symbol frames that do not necessarily follow the symbol statistics designed for the ANS. The objective is to reconstruct the symbol spread or, equivalently, to determine the encoding table. This attack is referred to as the *chosen symbol frame attack*. Note that the attack is equivalent to the well-known chosen plaintext attack. A variant of the chosen symbol frame attack has been described in the work [4]. In this variant, the adversary selects different pairs of symbols and employs them to create symbol frames with varying probabilities for the chosen symbols. Consequently, $\mathcal{A}$ can determine the symbol spread for each pair of chosen symbols through exhaustive search. By selecting pairs of symbols ranging from the least to most probable, the attack facilitates the recovery of the ANS symbol spread with a complexity given by:

$$\binom{L}{L_{s_1}}\binom{L - L_{s_1}}{L_{s_2}} + \sum_{j=3}^{n-1}\binom{L - \sum_{i=1}^{j-1} L_i}{L_{s_j}}, \tag{1}$$

where $n = |\mathbb{S}|$ and L_s is the number of states assigned by the symbol spread function for the symbol s.

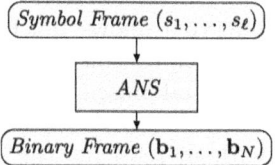

Fig. 5. ANS with secret symbol spread

6.2   ANS with Randomised States

This time our adversary $\mathcal{A}$ knows the ANS encoding table (and ANS symbol spread) and fully controls symbol frames. The goal of $\mathcal{A}$ is to collect enough information about binary strings generated by PRBG so it can launch a direct attack against PRBG and recover its secret key. Let us consider the following possible cases:

- There is a symbol s whose probability $p_s = 1/2^R$ and consequently $L_s = 1$. It means that encodings of s cover the full range of R-bit strings (their length is always R). Consequently, for a frame that consists of a large number of the symbol s, $\mathcal{A}$ is able to uniquely determine R-bit strings generated by PRBG (assuming $\mathcal{A}$ knows the initial state of ANS). This case is illustrated in Example 3. If symbol frame consists of all s_2, $\mathcal{A}$ can uniquely identify state transitions and corresponding strings generated by PRBG.
- There is a symbol s whose probability p_s is a natural power of $1/2$ and $L_s \geq 2$. Note that the row s of the encoding table consists of L_s copies of encodings. This means that $\mathcal{A}$ observing the corresponding binary frame has to consider L_s possibilities for strings generated by PRBG. In other words, there are

L_s ANS state jumps that generate the same binary encodings. This analysis can be improved by the selection of some bits where all possible PRBG strings agree. Note that this allows to recover the secret key if ANS state randomisation uses LFSR.

- All symbols occur with probabilities that are not natural powers of $1/2$ and their $L_s \geq 2$. In such circumstances, $\mathcal{A}$ needs to deal with L_s possible PRBG candidates but also with two lengths of encodings. As the binary frame is accessed as a single block, $\mathcal{A}$ must guess encoding lengths.

The above discussion leads us to the following conclusion.

Corollary 2. *Given ANS with randomised states, where none of symbol probabilities is a natural power of $1/2$. Assume further a chosen symbol frame adversary $\mathcal{A}$ whose goal is to collect PRBG binary strings generated during symbol frame processing. Then for each symbol s, $\mathcal{A}$ has to choose one from L_s possible PRBG binary strings and identify the correct position and length of binary encoding b_s, which is a part of the binary frame.*

Note that it is relatively easy to increase L_s for all symbols by choosing a big enough parameter R. If we increase R by one then all parameters L_s, $s \in \mathbb{S}$, are multiplied by two and the number of ANS states doubles.

The adversary $\mathcal{A}$ has a significant advantage in case when there are symbols whose probabilities are natural powers of $1/2$. If, however, security is our main concern, we can design ANS for symbol probabilities different from natural powers of $1/2$. There are the following options:

- If there are some single symbols whose probabilities are natural powers of $1/2$ but statistics of symbol pairs are not, then we can design ANS for symbol pairs (or triplets, quartets, etc.). This increases complexity of ANS but can improve its compression ratio.
- Given probability distribution of symbols $\mathcal{P} = \{p_s | s \in \mathbb{S}\}$, where some $p_s = (1/2)^i$. Then we can design ANS for its symbol probability $\mathcal{Q} = \{q_s | s \in \mathbb{S}\}$ such that all $q_s \neq (1/2)^i$. However, the ANS produces binary frames with a bigger redundancy (i.e. a worse compression ratio). We can apply the Kullback-Leibler [14] relative entropy to approximate the compression loss as

$$\Delta H = \sum_{s \in \mathbb{S}} p_s \lg \frac{p_s}{q_s} \approx \frac{1}{\ln(4)} \sum_{s \in \mathbb{S}} \frac{(p_s - q_s)^2}{p_s}$$

In order to calculate the loss precisely, one can compute equilibrium probabilities of ANS states for the appropriate Markov chain and then it is easy to calculate the ANS compression loss. The calculations are easy when ANS states are randomised as state probabilities are uniformly random.

6.3 Linear and Differential Cryptanalysis

Linear cryptanalysis [18] allows an adversary to create linear characteristics by concatenating the best linear approximations of cipher rounds (S-boxes). These characteristics reveal an observable probability bias for correctly guessed round keys. The probability of such bias can be calculated using Matsui's piling-up lemma. Differential cryptanalysis [2], on the other hand, explores the differential profile of a cipher's single round (S-boxes). This profile is then used to construct a differential characteristic for the entire cipher. This allows the adversary to select specific input differences and observe the corresponding output differences. A careful analysis of input/output differences for the last cipher round reveals that some round keys are more probable than others. After enough observations, the adversary can determine some bits of the last round key. By targeting specific bits of the last round key with appropriate differential characteristics, the adversary can discover all the round key bits. Once this is accomplished, the entire round can be "peeled off" by adding the inverse round to the cipher. The attack can be repeated as many times as there are rounds in the cipher.

Note that our compcrypt algorithm can be analysed using both linear and differential cryptanalysis. Let us consider components of ANS. We assume that they are public. Suppose further that the adversary wishes to find their best linear approximations. The most challenging task would be finding a collection of (good) linear approximations of the ANS symbol spread or equivalently its encoding function $C(y, s)$. It can be looked at as a big S-box, where the input includes $R + \log_2 |\mathbb{S}|$ bits. In practice, $R = 10$ and the number of bits for symbols is usually bigger than 8. Searching for best linear approximations of such big S-box seems to be a daunting problem. Unlike for the case of static S-boxes for block ciphers, ANS chooses its encoding function $C(y, s)$ depending on symbol statistics and the parameter R. It means that ANS uses dynamic S-boxes.

The most crucial feature of ANS that significantly reduces efficiency of linear and differential cryptanalysis is its irregular length of symbol encodings. In a case of differential cryptanalysis, to create differential characteristics, the adversary needs to prepare a differential (XOR) profile of the function $C(y, s)$, which needs to deal with two different lengths of encodings per a symbol (this always happens when p_s is not a natural power of $1/2$). Moreover, to create differential characteristics for more than a single symbol, the adversary needs to create a concatenation of simple characteristics that involves guessing both the lengths of symbol encodings and their positions in the binary frame. A similar situation happens in the case of linear cryptanalysis.

To make both differential and linear cryptanalysis less effective, one can trade compression rate with security. Note that adversary guesses about encoding lengths and consequently also about their positions in the binary frame depend on symbol probabilities. If a symbol probability is a natural power of $1/2$, then there is a single encoding length. The best case from a security point of view is when all symbol probabilities are in the middle between $1/2^{i+1}$ and $1/2^i$, where $i = 0, 1, 2, \cdots$. This means that we design ANS for symbol probabilities $q_s = 3/2^{i+2}$ when $1/2^{i+1} \leq p_s \leq 1/2^i$. Clearly, the ANS compression rate drops but for each symbol, our adversary has to choose one from two equally probable encoding lengths.

The above considerations lead us to the following conclusions:

- To find good linear approximations and differential profiles, the adversary needs to treat ANS as a big S-box, whose structure changes depending on the parameter R and the symbol probability distribution. This task becomes much harder when the adversary does not know the symbol spread function chosen by the ANS designer.
- To derive linear and differential characteristics, the adversary needs to guess the positions of output bits in the binary frame observed on the output. The guesses are not needed when symbol probabilities are natural powers of $1/2$.
- To trade compression rate with security, it is possible to design ANS in such a way that any symbol is encoded into two equally probable encodings of different lengths. This can be done by designing ANS for symbol probabilities that are in the middle between two consecutive natural powers of $1/2$.

7 Conclusions and Further Research Directions

There is a growing need to make Internet communication (such as teleconferences, entertainment streaming for example) more efficient and secure. To achieve these goals, one can use concatenation of compression and encryption. This work investigates how to merge compression and encryption into a single algorithm called compcrypt. For compression we use a relatively recent ANS algorithm. It exhibits an interesting mathematical structure that makes it an ideal tool for producing an arbitrary probability distribution from a uniform one provided by LFSR or CSPrBG. We illustrate applications of ANS-designed probability distributions to deliver digital contents with variable quality, which depends whether or not user is a streaming subscriber. ANS can be also used to symbol frame sharing among a group of participants.

We present two possible generic constructions for compcrypt. The first uses the sponge structure (see [3]). The second follows the well-known CBC mode, which can be applied for any block cipher with a reduced number of rounds. How many rounds can be dropped is a matter of a careful analysis, which depends on the particular encryption algorithm and an instance of ANS. Security aspect seems to be the most important but yet not fully explored. Compcrypt based on ANS only with secret symbol spread seems to be an excellent choice for environments with limited computing resources (such as IoT). Note that any instance of symbol spread gives a specific compression rate, which, in general, is different from the best/optimal one. Work [19] describes a randomised selection of symbol spread that achieves a local optimality, which trades compression rate with security. In case of compcrypt with randomised ANS, security analysis is done under assumption that the adversary knows symbol spread and wishes to recover strings generated by PRBG. It is clear that such analysis becomes more difficult, where symbol probabilities are different from natural powers of $1/2$ as the adversary needs to guess encoding lengths.

Linear and differential cryptanalysis for compcrypt is still possible but they become less effective due to the fact that ANS assigns encoding of two different lengths for symbols that are not natural powers of $1/2$. It is possible to trade compression rate with security by designing ANS whose symbol probability distribution enforces two lengths for each symbol. This is interesting problem how to maximise security while minimising compression rate losses.

References

1. Bergen, H.A., Hogan, J.M.: A chosen plaintext attack on an adaptive arithmetic coding compression algorithm. Comput. Secur. **12**(2), 157–167 (1993)
2. Biham, E., Shamir, A.: Differential cryptanalysis of DES-like cryptosystems. J. Cryptol. **4**(1), 3–72 (1991)
3. Camtepe, S., et al.: Compcrypt - lightweight ANS-based compression and encryption. IEEE Trans. Inf. Forensics Secur. **16**, 3859–3873 (2021)
4. Camtepe, S., et al.: ANS-based compression and encryption with 128-bit security. Int. J. Inf. Secur. (2022)
5. Cao, W., Leng, X., Tao, Yu., Xingfa, G., Liu, Q.: A joint encryption and compression algorithm for multiband remote sensing image transmission. Sensors **23**(17), 7600 (2023)
6. Cleary, J., Witten, I.: Data compression using adaptive coding and partial string matching. IEEE Trans. Commun. **32**(4), 396–402 (1984)
7. Dube, D., Yokoo, H.: Fast construction of almost optimal symbol distributions for asymmetric numeral systems. In: 2019 IEEE International Symposium on Information Theory (ISIT). IEEE (2019)
8. Duda, J.: Asymmetric Numeral Systems. Internet Archive, arxiv-0902.0271:1–47 (2009)
9. Duda, J.: Asymmetric numeral systems: entropy coding combining speed of Huffman coding with compression rate of arithmetic coding (2013). https://arxiv.org/pdf/1311.2540.pdf
10. Gibbons, J.: Coding with asymmetric numeral systems. In: Hutton, G. (ed.) MPC 2019. LNCS, vol. 11825, pp. 444–465. Springer, Cham (2019). https://doi.org/10.1007/978-3-030-33636-3_16
11. Gillman, D.W., Mohtashemi, M., Rivest, R.L.: On breaking a Huffman code. IEEE Trans. Inf. Theory **42**(3), 972–976 (1996)
12. Huang, X., Dong, Y., Ye, G., Shi, Y.: Meaningful image encryption algorithm based on compressive sensing and integer wavelet transform. Front. Comput. Sci. **17**(3), 173804 (2022)
13. Huffman, D.A.: A method for the construction of minimum-redundancy codes. Proc. IRE **40**(9), 1098–1101 (1952)
14. Kullback, S., Leibler, R.A.: On information and sufficiency. Ann. Math. Stat. **22**(1), 79–86 (1951)
15. Langdon, G., Rissanen, J.: A simple general binary source code (corresp.). IEEE Trans. Inf. Theory, **28**(5), 800–803 (1982)
16. Langdon, G.G.: An introduction to arithmetic coding. IBM J. Res. Dev. **28**, 135–149 (1984)

17. Lei, B.Y., Lo, K.T., Lei, H.: A new h.264 video encryption scheme based on chaotic cipher. In: 2010 International Conference on Communications, Circuits and Systems (ICCCAS), pp. 373–377 (2010)
18. Matsui, M.: Linear cryptanalysis method for DES cipher. In: Helleseth, T. (ed.) EUROCRYPT 1993. LNCS, vol. 765, pp. 386–397. Springer, Heidelberg (1994). https://doi.org/10.1007/3-540-48285-7_33
19. Pieprzyk, J., Duda, J., Pawłowski, M., Camtepe, S., Mahboubi, A., Morawiecki, P.: The compression optimality of Asymmetric Numeral Systems. Entropy **25**(4), 672 (2023)
20. Priyanka, N.B., Singh, K.N., Singh, A.K.: YOLO-based ROI selection for joint encryption and compression of medical images with reconstruction through super-resolution network. Fut. Gen. Comput. Syst., **150**, 1–9 (2024)
21. Rissanen, J.J.: Generalized Kraft inequality and arithmetic coding. IBM J. Res. Dev. **20**(3), 198–203 (1976)
22. Robinson, A.H., Cherry, C.: Results of a prototype television bandwidth compression scheme. Proc. IEEE **55**(3), 356–364 (1967)
23. Schwenk, J.: Guide to Internet Cryptography: Security Protocols and Real-World Attack Implications. Springer (2022)
24. Shannon, C.E.: A mathematical theory of communication. Bell Sys. Tech. J. **27**, 623–656 (1948)
25. Shi, M., Guo, S., Song, X., Zhou, Y., Wang, E.: Visual secure image encryption scheme based on compressed sensing and regional energy. Entropy **23**(5), 570 (2021)
26. Storer, J.A., Szymanski, T.G.: Data compression via textual substitution. J. ACM **29**(4), 928–951 (1982)
27. Welch. A technique for high-performance data compression. Computer **17**(6), 8–19 (1984)
28. Witten, I.H., Cleary, J.G.: On the privacy afforded by adaptive text compression. Comput. Secur. **7**(4), 397–408 (1988)
29. Ziv, J., Lempel, A.: Compression of individual sequences via variable-rate coding. IEEE Trans. Inf. Theory **24**(5), 530–536 (1978)

Differential Fault Analysis of TinyJAMBU

Samuel Russell Prajasantosa[1] and Iftekhar Salam[1,2(✉)] (iD)

[1] School of Computing and Data Science, Xiamen University Malaysia,
Sepang 43900, Selangor, Malaysia
{swe1809941,iftekhar.salam}@xmu.edu.my
[2] Department of Software Engineering, Daffodil International University,
Daffodil Smart City, Dhaka 1216, Bangladesh

Abstract. We applied bit-flipping and random fault attacks to Tiny-JAMBUv2. These attacks are investigated using three precision controls: precise, moderate and no control. To the best of our knowledge, this is the first application of these fault models to TinyJAMBU. Our research indicates that the bit-flipping fault attacks using precise control and moderate control require an average of 128 faults and 456 faults, respectively. For the random fault attacks using the precise control and moderate control model, an average of 256 faults and 850 faults are required, respectively. These bit-flipping and random fault attacks can recover 58 internal state bits and 15 key bits of the cipher. For the no-control model, we conducted a preliminary investigation that shows one cannot conclusively determine which target register is injected with the fault. All the attacks are experimentally verified. Based on our analyses, TinyJAMBU has a large security margin against the selected approaches of the differential fault attack.

Keywords: Differential fault attack · TinyJAMBU · NIST LWC

1 Introduction

The Lightweight Cryptography (LWC) Project was launched by the National Institute of Standards and Technology (NIST) to standardize cryptographic algorithms for use in restricted environments [1]. Among the finalist algorithms of the NIST LWC project, TinyJAMBU is the only stream cipher based on a sponge permutation scheme. To the best of our knowledge, only a few cryptanalyses exist against the TinyJAMBU cipher. The bit-flipping and random fault attacks presented by Salam et al. [10], Bartlett et al. [3], and Wong et al. [17] have not been investigated on the TinyJAMBU cipher. These approaches were extended and shown to be effective against various other NIST LWC submissions [9,11,12]. In this work, we adopt and apply these fault attacks to the TinyJAMBU cipher.

A fault attack is a physical attack in which an adversary injects errors during the computation of the cryptographic operation to extract information about the secret key or state bits by observing faulty and fault-free outputs. Boneh et al. [5] demonstrated fault attacks against several cryptographic schemes in 1997,

© The Author(s), under exclusive license to Springer Nature Switzerland AG 2025
C. Boyd et al. (Eds.): Ed Dawson Festschrift 2024, LNCS 15600, pp. 68–88, 2025.
https://doi.org/10.1007/978-3-031-83490-5_4

including the RSA algorithms and Rabin signatures. In the same year, Biham and Shamir introduced [4] differential fault attack (DFA) to symmetric cryptosystems [4]. In recent years, fault attacks have proven to be a powerful technique against many modern cryptographic algorithms. Dey et al. [7] demonstrated a fault attack on the CAESAR candidate Tiaoxin-346 with a bit-flipping fault model. This attack is based on a particular structure of the cipher output where the target register contents are combined using a bit-wise AND operation. Later, Salam et al. [10] and Bartlett et al. [3] extended this attack with a random fault model on Tiaoxin-346 and AEGIS-128L. In these attacks, the bit-flipping and random fault models complement the content of the target register with a probability of 1 and 0.5, respectively. In addition to the condition of the bit-flipping fault, these random fault attacks observe cipher output function where the target register contents are combined using a bit-wise XOR operation. All these attacks are based on the assumption that an adversary can precisely target the fault location. Wong et al. [17] and Salam et al. [9,12] improved the fault precision models where an adversary does not need to inject fault in a precise location. We adopt these models in this work and compare the bit-flipping and random fault attacks on TinyJAMBU with different precision controls.

2   Fault Attack

Fault attacks can be classified as invasive, semi-invasive and non-invasive. The invasive process is usually costly and necessitates high-end equipment like probing stations. The semi-invasive procedure necessitates minor physical changes to the device and does not alter its internal structure. This is inexpensive and simpler to duplicate compared to the invasive process. Both invasive and semi-invasive methods directly access the chip surface, but the latter injects a fault without making electrical contact with the chip surface [13]. The non-invasive method is the least expensive and does not physically interfere with the device. For example, non-invasive faults may be injected using clock and voltage glitches, electromagnetic pulse, and overheating without de-packaging the device.

2.1   Fault Model Characteristics

The fault models can be categorized based on the characteristics of faults [2]. These are discussed below.

Nature of Fault. The impact on the target device and the precision of the location are used to describe the nature of the fault. This refers to the number of bits that may be influenced and the specific bit(s) the adversary can target.

  i Number of bits: This refers to the number of bits impacted by the fault attack. The fault may influence a single bit, single byte or multiple bytes.

ii Fault precision: This refers to how precise the adversary can control the location and timing of the fault. In precise control, the target location and timing can be controlled precisely by the adversary. For moderate control, the adversary only has limited controls for inducing faults. In the no-control model, the faults induced are at a random location but at a precise timing.

iii Fault duration: The duration of the fault can either be permanent or transient. Permanent refers to the case where the bit(s) are modified permanently, and data content can be damaged. Transient refers to bit(s) that are modified only for a certain duration of time.

Efficiency of the Fault. Efficiency indicates how precisely the adversary can manipulate fault values. A fault may cause the target register's content to become zero or one, flipped, or randomly complemented. The adversary has complete control for the first two cases and is able to set the faulty register's content to zero or one. The adversary is able to complement the target register content for bit flipping fault (e.g., from 0 to 1 or from 1 to 0). The adversary cannot control the fault impact for a random fault, and the probability of the target register bit getting flipped is the same as the probability of the target register content remaining unchanged.

Feasibility of the Fault. The feasibility of the fault refers to the practical aspects of the fault implementation, such as the time required, equipment required, equipment cost, etc. There are various models or characteristics that can be observed for an adversary to model fault attacks. It is to be noted that, generally, a more restrictive/precise model is less practical in the real-life scenario compared to the moderate/no-control model.

2.2 Our Contribution

We applied bit-flipping and random fault attacks to TinyJAMBU using different precision models. The three precision models include precise control, moderate control and no control model. Each fault is assumed to be transient in nature and affects a single bit of the target registers. Based on the results obtained from the bit-flipping fault attack and random fault attack with precise control and moderate control models, we can recover 58 state bits and 15 key bits at most. Table 1 summarizes our DFA results against TinyJAMBUv2 cipher.

Table 1. Summary of fault attacks applied to TinyJAMBUv2

Fault model	Fault precision	No. of faults	No. of keystreams	Data complexity	Recovered bits
Bit-Flipping	Precise	128	517	$2^{9.014}$	58 state bits & 15 key bits
	Moderate	456	4196	$2^{12.034}$	
Random	Precise	256	1034	$2^{10.014}$	58 state bits & 15 key bits
	Moderate	850	7706	$2^{12.911}$	

Existing studies demonstrate that precise fault injection is achievable through laser beams and focused flashlights [14–16]. For moderate control, the fault may be induced with an optical flashgun or a voltage glitch. The cost of these attacks with moderate control varies from low to 500 EUR, where a low cost refers to only a standard desktop PC (and in some cases, connection wires) to apply the attack [6]. Therefore, the attack methodologies discussed in this paper are deemed to be practically viable.

3   Fault Attacks on TinyJAMBU

TinyJAMBU is a keyed-permutation based stream cipher proposed by Wu and Huang [19], which is a variant of the JAMBU [18]. The cipher is a sponge construction-based authenticated encryption scheme. TinyJAMBU was one of the NIST LWC finalists. On May 17, 2021, the designers re-submitted the second version of TinyJAMBU with increased permutation rounds [20].

3.1   Specifications of TinyJAMBU

TinyJAMBU supports three key sizes of 128, 192 and 256 bits and the structure of the cipher is based on a 128-bit non-linear feedback shift register (NFSR). All members of the TinyJAMBU use a 96-bit nonce (IV) and a 64-bit tag. The main member of TinyJAMBU, TinyJAMBU-128, adopts a 128-bit keyed permutation, a 128-bit state, and a 32-bit message block, and is the main focus of this paper. The 128-bit state, 128-bit key, and the output keystream bits are defined as $S = \{s_0, s_1, \ldots, s_{127}\}$, $K = \{k_0, k_1, \ldots, k_{127}\}$, and $Z = \{z_0, z_1, \ldots, z_{mlen-1}\}$, respectively. The length of the keystream is the same as the plaintext length, $mlen$. The keystream bits are divided into blocks, where each block is 32 bits.

The encryption and TAG generation steps consist of four stages: initialization, processing the associated data, encryption and finalization. All of these stages use a keyed permutation as the cipher's main component. In this paper, the fault attack is applied during the encryption; hence, we discuss the details of the encryption and the keyed permutation. Interested readers are referred to the specification of TinyJAMBU for the details of the other stages.

Keyed Permutation. The keyed permutation function is cycled for n rounds of permutation, as indicated by the permutation P_n. In the ith round of the permutation, a 128-bit NFSR is used to update the state as shown in Algorithm 1, where the input S refers to the 128-bit internal state, K refers to the 128-bit key, and i refers to the ith round. As shown in Algorithm 1, the NFSR state bit s_{127} is updated by the non-linear feedback, whereas all the rest of the state bits are updated by shifting the contents from the previous clock.

Algorithm 1. State update function of TinyJAMBU

---

procedure STATEUPDATE(S, K, i)
   feedback $= s_0 \oplus s_{47} \oplus \overline{(s_{70}s_{85})} \oplus s_{91} \oplus k_{i \bmod klen}$
   for $j = 0$ to 126 **do**
      $s_j = s_{j+1}$
   end for
   $s_{127} = $ feedback
end procedure

Algorithm 2. Encryption stage of TinyJAMBU

---

procedure ENCRYPTION(S)
   for $i = 0$ to $\lfloor \frac{mlen}{32} \rfloor$ **do**
      $s_{36...38} = s_{36...38} \oplus FrameBits_{0...2}$
      Update S using keyed permutation P_{1024}
      $s_{96...127} = s_{96...127} \oplus m_{32i...32i+31}$
      $c_{32i...32i+31} = s_{64...95} \oplus m_{32i...32i+31}$
   end for
end procedure

Encryption. The encryption stage comes after the associated data has been processed. In this stage, plaintext $M = \{m_0, m_1, \ldots, m_{mlen-1}\}$ is encrypted 32-bits at a time. Firstly, the Framebits of plaintext with a value of 5 are XOR-ed with the state bits $\{s_{36}, s_{37}, s_{38}\}$ in each round. Then, the state is updated using the keyed permutation P_{1024} and the 32 bits of plaintext M are XOR-ed with the state bits $\{s_{96}, \ldots, s_{127}\}$. At the end of each step, the 32-bits of the ciphertext $C = \{c_0, c_1, \ldots, c_{mlen-1}\}$ is obtained by XOR-ing the plaintext with the state bits $\{s_{64}, s_{65}, \ldots, s_{95}\}$. These steps are done according to the length of the message, $mlen$, which is processed in a block of 32 bits. The overall process of the encryption is summarized in Algorithm 2, in which c_i refers to the ith bit of the ciphertext. The keystream block $\{z_0, z_1, \ldots, z_{31}\}$ refers to the content of bits $\{s_{64}, s_{65}, \ldots, s_{95}\}$ after the keyed permutation P_{1024} of the encryption.

3.2   Attack Process

The general workflow of the experiments conducted in this paper consists of six main phases to implement the differential fault attacks. These are briefly discussed below.

i Implementation of the TinyJAMBU cipher: The TinyJAMBUv2 is implemented using SageMath based on the specification of the cipher. The output bits of the cipher are generated in terms of symbolic expressions using the SageMath implementation.
ii Differentiation of the keystream equations with respect to the initial state bits: Based on the implementation of the first phase, each output keystream equations $\{z_0, z_1, \ldots, z_{31}\} = \{s_{64}, s_{65}, \ldots, s_{95}\}$ after the last n-rounds will

result in a long, complex algebraic equation. These output keystream bits are differentiated with respect to each initial state bit. All the generated equations resulting from the differentiation process are stored.

iii Identification of the fault targets and model: In this phase, the fault targets are identified based on the differentiation results from the previous phase. The fault model introduced in this work is the bit-flipping and the random fault attack. Three precision controls are applied on each fault attack: precise control, moderate control, and no control. Figure 1 summarizes fault models along with their respective precision controls.

iv Implementation of the fault attack: The fault injections of the two models, the bit-flipping fault attack and the random fault attack, are implemented in this phase. Besides the fault injection, the three fault precision controls are also implemented for each fault model. After the fault attacks are implemented, the number of bits (internal state bits and key bits) that can be recovered are identified. This is done by solving the output equations using the Gröbner basis. Furthermore, the number of faults needed to recover the state/key bits is also identified in this phase.

v Verification of attacks: In the final phase, the experiment is re-conducted using a random key and initialization vector. This allows us to apply the attacks to determine and verify the recovered state and key bits.

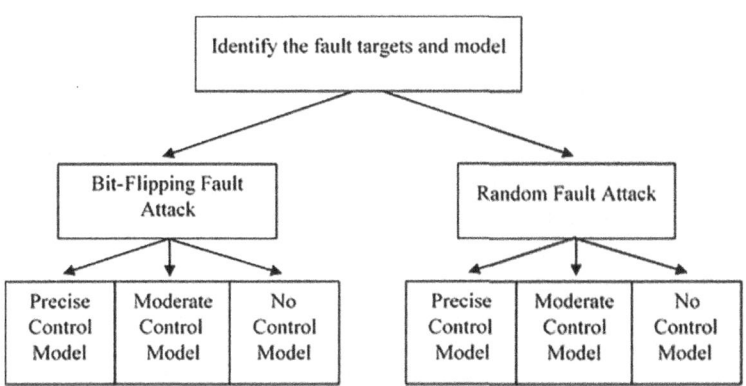

Fig. 1. Fault models and precision controls of the experiments

4   Implementation and Experimental Results of DFA

Before the attacks are modelled, implementing TinyJAMBU stages, initialization, associated data processing and encryption are completed using SageMath. Furthermore, the assumption of this attack is a known plaintext attack where the output keystreams are assumed to be observable. The following sections discuss and analyze the differential fault attacks applied to TinyJAMBU.

We implemented the experiments from a state that has gone through 864 permutation rounds. Let, $S^{864} = \{s_0^{864}, s_1^{864}, ..., s_{127}^{864}\} = \{s_0, s_1, ..., s_{127}\}$ denote the starting state at time $t = 864$. Note that in the following sections, whenever time instances are not indicated, $\{s_0, s_1, ..., s_{127}\}$ refers to the NFSR state S at time $t = 864$.

4.1   Bit-Flipping Fault Attack on TinyJAMBUv2

The bit-flipping fault flips the content of the target register. We first generated the Algebraic Normal Form (ANF) of the output bits to determine the target registers. The internal state of the cipher is updated by P_{1024} (1024 state update rounds) before the generation of the ciphertext. As a result, the ANF of the output will be of a very complex algebraic form with a high algebraic degree. Due to the constraint of the SageMath software, it is assumed that the state of the cipher has already iterated through a major portion of the permutation rounds. That is, we start from a high enough clock for which we can generate the ANF of the output function using SageMath. The experiments conducted show that we can generate the ANF of the TinyJAMBU output function for 160 rounds from a given starting state. We also managed to generate some ANF of the output for 192 rounds; however, the software cannot generate the last seven output keystream equations s_i, where $89 \leq i \leq 95$. Therefore, we limit our experiments by generating the ANFs for 160 rounds of permutations, as it allows us to observe the complete 32 keystream bits. The encryption of the message is done 32 bits at a time by using the keystream bits $\{z_0, z_1, ..., z_{31}\} = \{s_{64}, s_{65}, ..., s_{95}\}$, which are the only observable state bits after the permutation P_{1024}.

Let us assume that our starting state bits consist of variables from the state S^{864}. Thus, we have designed the experiments to go through the last 160 permutation rounds P_{160} before the output keystream equations are calculated. To identify the unique quadratic terms in the keystream equations, we conducted an experiment where the first order derivative of all output keystream z_i, where $0 \leq i \leq 31$, which refers to state bit s_i^{1024}, where $64 \leq i \leq 95$, are calculated with respect to s_j, where $0 \leq j \leq 127$. In this initial experiment, only linear equations are included and stored in an array. The results of the experiment are shown in Table 2. The result shows that 23 out of 128 bits of the NFSR state bits s_i, where $70 \leq i \leq 75$ and $85 \leq i \leq 101$ can be recovered. Assuming the fault injection is of a precise control model where the adversary is able to precisely target the fault location, 21 faults are required to recover the 23 state bits. As shown in Table 2, not all the output keystream equations consist of unique quadratic terms; thus, the set of linear equations generated is small.

Next, we conducted another similar experiment; however, we considered equations of any degree, including equations with degrees 2, 3, 4, 5, and up to the maximum possible degree of equations resulting from the first-order derivative. Following this, the resultant equations are solved using Gröbner Basis. Table 3 summarizes the number of state bits or register contents that can be recovered according to the degree of the observed first-order derivative equations. The

Table 2. Faulty registers that result in linear equations for TinyJAMBUv2

Target register	Output index	Linear equation	Target register	Output index	Linear equation
s_{70}	79	s_{85}	s_{82}	91	s_{97}
s_{71}	80	s_{86}	s_{83}	92	s_{98}
s_{72}	81	s_{87}	s_{84}	93	s_{99}
s_{73}	82	s_{88}	s_{85}	79	s_{70}
s_{74}	83	s_{89}	s_{85}	94	s_{100}
s_{75}	84	s_{90}	s_{86}	80	s_{71}
s_{76}	85	s_{91}	s_{86}	95	s_{101}
s_{77}	86	s_{92}	s_{87}	81	s_{72}
s_{78}	87	s_{93}	s_{88}	82	s_{73}
s_{79}	88	s_{94}	s_{89}	83	s_{74}
s_{80}	89	s_{95}	s_{90}	84	s_{75}
s_{81}	90	s_{96}	-	-	-

number of equations in Table 3 refers to the total number of observable first-order derivative equations in each experiment. Take note that all the equations may not be independent; that is, duplicates of the equation may exist and be included in the number of equations.

It is shown in Table 3 that certain key bits are recoverable when the first-order derivative results of degree three or more are added to the equation system. For instance, ten key bits are recoverable when including up to cubic equations of the first-order derivative. Furthermore, 15 key bits are recoverable when first-order derivative equations of degree 4 are observed. It can be concluded from Table 3 that the highest degree of the first-order derivative equation is of the degree 5. Despite having more equations to be observed when including all differentiated equations, the number of recoverable state bits and key bits is identical to that of observing up to first-order derivative quartic equations. This means that no additional information is gathered when including quintic or all equations in this case.

Overall, the best scenario that the bit-flipping attack could perform is to recover 58 registers and 15 key bits. In Table 3, there are some equations that appear more than once. We excluded the repeated or duplicated equations to reduce the required keystream bits. Excluding the duplicates, the number of keystreams required to generate the quartic equations is reduced from 722 to 517. Assuming a *precise control* model of the bit-flipping fault attack, 128 faults are required to recover these 58 registers and 15 key bits using these 517 low-degree equations.

4.2   Random Fault Attack on TinyJAMBUv2

The random fault model aims to calculate the value of the fault. To compute the random fault value, we first need to identify the keystream equations in which the target register variable appears only as a linear term and does not appear in any other monomials of that equation. For instance, register s_{15} is a unique linear term in output $z_0 = s_{64}^{1024}$. That is, the keystream equation $z_0 = s_{15} \oplus x$, where the remaining part of the equation, x, does not involve the variable s_{15}. When a random fault e is injected to s_{15}, we can describe the faulty keystream as $z_0' = (s_{15} \oplus e) \oplus x$. Note that the complete output equation is of a very long and complex ANF; thus, x in the above equations represents the remaining parts of the equation. Then, the value of e can be computed as the output differential, δ_{64}, of the fault-free and faulty output bits.

Table 3. Number of recoverable registers and/or key bits

Degree	No of equations	Recovered state bits	Recovered key bits	Recovered registers and/or key bits
1 (Linear)	23	23	0	$\{s_{70}, \ldots, s_{75}\}$ $\{s_{85}, \ldots, s_{101}\}$
≤ 2 (Quadratic)	52	23	0	$\{s_{70}, \ldots, s_{75}\}$ $\{s_{85}, \ldots, s_{101}\}$
≤ 3 (Cubic)	364	58	10	$\{s_{70}, \ldots, s_{127}\}$ $\{k_{38}, \ldots, k_{47}\}$
≤ 4 (Quartic)	722	58	15	$\{s_{70}, \ldots, s_{127}\}$ $\{k_{38}, \ldots, k_{52}\}$
≤ 5 (Quintiq)	772	58	15	$\{s_{70}, \ldots, s_{127}\}$ $\{k_{38}, \ldots, k_{52}\}$
All	772	58	15	$\{s_{70}, \ldots, s_{127}\}$ $\{k_{38}, \ldots, k_{52}\}$

This fault attack model targets output functions with such unique linear terms. The presence of the linear terms in the output keystream equations can be identified by calculating the first-order derivative of the equations with respect to the NFSR state bits s_i, where $0 \leq i \leq 127$. In particular, if $(dz_j)/(ds_i) = 1$, where $0 \leq j \leq 31$, then the corresponding output differentials of z_j can be used to identify the random fault value at target s_i.

By calculating the first-order derivative of the keystream equations, the influence of the random fault e can be determined in all the required fault locations of the NFSR. Table 4 lists the output bits using which the random fault value in a specific target register can be computed. The index j in Table 4 refers to the respective index of the state bit s_j^{1024}.

For instance, to compute a random fault e injected in target location s_{15}, the keystream bits z_0 and z_{30} shall be observed to calculate the corresponding output differentials, $\delta_{64} = z_0 \oplus z_0'$ and $\delta_{94} = z_{30} \oplus z_{30}'$, respectively. Take note that z_0 and z_{30} refer to s_{64}^{1024} and s_{94}^{1024}, respectively. Given that the corresponding output differential results in one, the random fault $e = 1$ can be deduced, i.e., it has complemented the target register s_{15}. Accordingly, once the required target register content is confirmed to be complemented, the corresponding faulty and fault-free keystreams can be used to recover the linear equations obtained in Table 2 and quadratic, cubic and quartic equations in Table 3.

Let us assume that $s_r s_t$ is a unique quadratic term in an output keystream equation. Next, a random fault e is injected at s_t, where s_t is assumed to appear as a unique linear term in another keystream equation. Then, the approach discussed above is applied and if it is observed that $e = 1$, it can be determined

Table 4. List of indices to compute the random fault value

Target register	Output indices, j (respective state bit)	Target register	Output indices, j (respective state bit)
s_0	79	s_{69}	64, 71, 74
s_1	80	s_{70}	65, 72, 75
$\vdots$	$\vdots$	$\vdots$	$\vdots$
s_{14}	93	s_{90}	85, 92, 95
s_{15}	64, 94	s_{91}	79, 86, 93
s_{16}	65, 95	s_{92}	80, 87, 94
s_{17}	66	s_{93}	81, 88, 95
$\vdots$	$\vdots$	s_{94}	82, 89
		s_{95}	83, 90
s_{21}	70	s_{96}	64, 84, 91
s_{22}	64, 71	s_{97}	65, 85, 92
$\vdots$	$\vdots$	$\vdots$	$\vdots$
s_{53}	85, 95	s_{100}	68, 88, 95
s_{54}	86	s_{101}	69, 89
$\vdots$	$\vdots$	$\vdots$	$\vdots$
s_{58}	90	s_{107}	75, 95
s_{59}	64, 91	s_{108}	76
s_{60}	65, 92	$\vdots$	$\vdots$
s_{61}	66, 93		
s_{62}	64, 67, 94	s_{112}	80
s_{63}	65, 68, 95	s_{113}	64, 81
s_{64}	66, 69	s_{114}	65, 82
$\vdots$	$\vdots$	$\vdots$	$\vdots$
s_{68}	70, 73	s_{127}	78, 95

that the content of s_t has been flipped. Consequently, we can then use the corresponding fault-free keystream z_i and faulty keystream z_i' to recover the content of register s_r using the bit-flipping attack discussed in Sect. 4.1. This process is then repeated until all the possible target registers are recovered. Algorithm 3 shows the process of the random fault attack applied on TinyJAMBUv2, where z_i refers to the keystream output equation after the last 160 permutation rounds and z_j refers to the keystream bits using which the random fault value is computed as per Table 4.

When considering linear up to quartic differentiated equations, s_r in Algorithm 3 may be of linear, quadratic, cubic or quartic equations. These are solved using the Gröbner Basis to recover the 58 state bits and 15 key bits shown in Table 3. We conducted experiments with random K, IV to verify the recovered state and key bits. The experimental results verify the expected outcomes.

For the random fault attack with precise control, we assume the capability to inject fault precisely to the target register s_t. The random fault e is induced to the same target register repetitively until $z_j \oplus z_j' = 1$. We simulated the scenario

---

Algorithm 3. Random fault attack on TinyJAMBUv2

Declare S as the internal state in terms of symbolic expression

Update S using P_{160} and output fault-free keystream bits z_j

while all possible state bits s_r are not traversed **do**

    for each target register s_t **do**

        Re-initialize state bits with the same K and IV

        Inject a random fault e in s_t

        Update the faulty state using P_{160} and output faulty keystream bits z_j'

        Compute $e = z_j \oplus z_j'$

        if $e = 1$ **then**

            recovered register, $s_r \leftarrow z_i \oplus z_i'$

        end if

    end for

end while

---

to determine the number of faults needed to flip all the target state bits, s_i, where $0 \leq i \leq 127$. The experiment shows that $128 \times 2 = 256$ faults are needed to flip all the target state bits as per Table 4. This is because e is 0 or 1 with equal probability, so on average, two random faults are required to complement one target bit. The data complexity of the random fault with *precise control* model is $2^{10.014}$ since, on average, a total of $517 \times 2 = 1034$ keystream equations are observed to recover the 58 state bits and 15 key bits.

4.3 Relaxing the Fault Precision

Next, we apply a more relaxed approach to the attack model than the precise control model. In the moderate control, it is assumed that the adversary is not able to precisely target a specific bit for fault injection; however, the adversary is able to target a specific byte array. The fault may affect any state bits in that particular byte array. Since the NFSR of TinyJAMBU consists of 128 state bits, the NFSR is divided into 16 byte arrays, S_{byte_i}, where $0 \leq i \leq 15$. Each byte array consists of 8 state bits, where S_{byte_0} consists of the first 8 bits $\{s_0, s_1, ..., s_7\}$, S_{byte_1} consists of the next 8 bits $\{s_8, s_9, ..., s_{15}\}$, and so on.

For instance, as shown in Table 4, when a fault is injected in S_{byte_0}, the output keystreams z_i, where $15 \leq i \leq 22$, and their corresponding output differentials δ_j, where $j = \{79, 80, 81, 82, 83, 84, 85, 86\}$, shall be observed to determine which of the particular state bit in S_{byte_0} had been complemented. If it is found that $\delta_{81} = 1$, it can be determined that the fault had successfully complemented the state bit s_2 based on Table 4. This can be deduced since no other state bits in S_{byte_0} affect the output keystream z_{81}.

However, in some cases, the fault location cannot be determined by only observing a single output differential δ_j for each target state bit. For instance, when a fault is injected in S_{byte_2} (consisting of target registers $\{s_{15}, s_{16}, ..., s_{23}\}$), the output keystreams z_j and their corresponding output differentials δ_j, where $j = \{65, 66, 67, 68, 69, 70, 71, 72, 95\}$, are observable to determine which of the particular state bit in S_{byte_2} had been complemented. If it is found that when the output difference $\delta_{65} = 1$, based on Table 5, it cannot be concluded whether the fault was injected at s_{16} or s_{23}. In order to confirm that s_{16} is complemented, both output differentials δ_{65} and δ_{95} shall be equal to one; thus, multiple output differentials may need to be observed for such target bit.

Table 5. Keystream bits required to identify the target registers in S_{byte_2}

Target register	Output indices, j
s_{16}	65, 95
s_{17}	66
s_{18}	67
s_{19}	68
s_{20}	69
s_{21}	70
s_{22}	64, 71
s_{23}	65, 72

Let us assume that a fault is injected at state bit s_{20} in the byte array S_{byte_2}. Its corresponding output differential δ_{69} shall definitely equal one. However, it is not guaranteed that other particular output differentials δ_j are not equal to one. Thus, we conducted an experiment to verify the feasibility of recovering the fault location by only relying on the output keystream indices as per Table 4 for each byte array. For all the 128 state bits, we calculated the output differentials between faulty and fault-free keystreams δ_j, where $64 \leq j \leq 95$, when injected with a fault $e = 1$. Then, we computed the number of times each output differential $\delta_j = 1$. The process is conducted 1000 times with different combinations of inputs. Figure 2 shows the result of the first-byte array, S_{byte_0}, obtained using the experiment described in Algorithm 4. For better data representation, the table cells are coloured as follows: values equal to 1000 are coloured in green, values larger than 0 and smaller than 1000 are coloured in red, and values equal to 0 are left uncoloured. As shown in Table 4, a single output differential $\delta_j = 1$ might be enough to determine which target register, $\{s_0, s_1, ..., s_7\}$ contained in S_{byte_0}, had been injected with fault. However, we further discovered that this is not always true as there are several cases where an output differential $\delta_j = 1$ may not precisely conclude which state bit had been injected with the fault (as per Table 4). For instance, as shown in Fig. 2, when $\delta_{85} = 1$, fault might have been induced at either s_0, s_1 or s_6. This is because, after the 1000 tests, it is observed that fault injection at s_0, s_1 and s_6 generates $\delta_{85} = 1$ for 508, 218 and 1000 times, respectively. Thus, the experiment result indicates that it is not always possible to conclusively identify the target register in the NFSR bytes using a single output differential.

Algorithm 4. Determine the no. of times $\delta_j = 1$ for each state bit

---

Declare a 2-dimensional array to store the final result of each state bit
for 1000 tests **do**
    Initialize TinyJAMBU with a random K and IV
    Update the state using P_{1024} and record the fault-free state bits s_j
    for $i = 0$ to 127 **do**
        Declare array to store the number of $\delta_j = 1$
        Re-initialize faulty state bits with the same K and IV
        Inject fault e into s_i^{864}
        Update the state using P_{1024} and record the faulty state bits s_j'
        for $j = 64$ to 95 **do**
            $\delta_j = s_j \oplus s_j'$
            if $\delta_j = 1$ **then**
                array[j] = array[j] + 1
            end if
        end for
        Add the results from the array to 2D-array accordingly
    end for
end for

Target State Bit	Output Differential							
	δ_{79}	δ_{80}	δ_{81}	δ_{82}	δ_{83}	δ_{84}	δ_{85}	δ_{86}
s_0	1000	0	0	0	0	267	508	0
s_1	0	1000	0	0	0	0	218	479
s_2	0	0	1000	0	0	0	0	246
s_3	0	0	0	1000	0	0	0	0
s_4	0	0	0	0	1000	0	0	0
s_5	0	0	0	0	0	1000	0	0
s_6	0	0	0	0	0	0	1000	0
s_7	0	0	0	0	0	0	0	1000

Fig. 2. No. of times $\delta_j = 1$ for each registers in S_{byte_0} in 1000 tests ($79 \leq j \leq 86$)

Determining Conditions to Confirm the Target State Bit. Despite being unable to determine the fault location in the NFSR bytes by observing just a single output differential, it is possible to determine the fault location by satisfying a few or more conditions. Based on Fig. 2, when $\delta_{85} = 1$, fault might have been induced at either at s_0, s_1 or s_6. However, it is possible to create or identify conditions to determine which of these three state bits had been injected with fault. For instance, in order to determine that s_0 had been injected with fault, we can compute the output differential δ_{79}, since there are no other state bits in S_{byte_0} that affects output keystream z_{15}, i.e., NFSR state s_{79}^{1024}. Next, in order to determine that s_1 had been injected with fault, we can compute the output differential δ_{80}, since there are no other state bits in S_{byte_0} that affects output keystream z_{16}, i.e., NFSR state s_{80}^{1024}. Nevertheless, additional conditions are needed to determine that s_6 had been injected with fault. Its only unique output differential is of δ_{85}, whereas there are chances where s_0 or s_1 are the one complemented when $\delta_{85} = 1$. Since δ_{85} is its only unique output differential, the unique output differentials of both s_0 and s_1 can be used as the condition to determine that s_6 had been the fault location. Thus, by observing the output differentials where $(\delta_{85} = 1 \wedge \delta_{79} \neq 1 \wedge \delta_{80} \neq 1)$, it can be determined that s_6 is the fault target location. Similar conditions can also be derived for the cases of s_5 and s_7. The conditions for all target registers in S_{byte_0} are shown in Table 6.

Table 6. Conditions to confirm that all the state bits in S_{byte_0} are complemented

Target register	Required keystream indices and condition	Remarks/ comments
0	$\delta_{79} = 1$	-
1	$\delta_{80} = 1$	-
2	$\delta_{81} = 1$	-
3	$\delta_{82} = 1$	-
4	$\delta_{83} = 1$	-
5	$\delta_{84} = 1 \wedge \delta_{79} \neq 1$	Does not satisfy for s_0 and $\delta_{84} = 1$
6	$\delta_{85} = 1 \wedge \delta_{79 \neq 1} \wedge \delta_{80 \neq 1}$	Does not satisfy for s_0, s_1 and $\delta_{85} = 1$
7	$\delta_{86} = 1 \wedge \delta_{80} \neq 1 \wedge \delta_{81} \neq 1$	Does not satisfy for s_1, s_2 and $\delta_{86} = 1$

By implementing a similar technique to all 16 bytes, we observed that one particular byte, $S_{byte_{13}}$, requires further analysis. Meanwhile, the conditions identified in the other 15 bytes, except for $S_{byte_{13}}$, can confirm the fault influence in all target state bits from Table 4. For the case of $S_{byte_{13}}$, we provide further analyses below.

Figure 3 and Table 7 show the number of times $\delta_j = 1$ in $S_{byte_{13}}$ for the 1000 instances of the experiment and the conditions generated for $S_{byte_{13}}$ to determine which state bit is complemented, respectively. For instance, the unique output differentials of s_{104} may coincide with that of s_{108} and vice versa. Let the output differentials $\delta_{72} = 1$ and $\delta_{92} = 1$, in which our expected target state bit location is of s_{104}. Based on Fig. 3, there is a possibility that when these output differentials are equal to one, the target state bit that had been complemented is s_{108} instead of s_{104}. Thus, the best condition to determine that s_{104} had been injected with fault is that $(\delta_{72} = 1 \wedge \delta_{92} = 1 \wedge \delta_{76} \neq 1)$, since the output differential δ_{76} is the only unique output differential of the target state bit s_{108}.

On the contrary, let our expected target state bit location be s_{108}. The output differential δ_{76} shall equal one. However, there is a possibility that either s_{107} or s_{104} will be injected with fault instead. The conditions to determine s_{107} exist and can be conclusively determined such that the unique output differential of s_{107} is satisfied, i.e., $\delta_{75} \neq 1$. However, there are no single output differentials such that we can conclusively determine either s_{104} or s_{108} is the fault target state bit. Thus, the best condition to determine that s_{108} had been injected with fault is that $\{(\delta_{76} = 1 \wedge \delta_{75} \neq 1) \wedge (\delta_{72} \neq 1 \vee \delta_{92} \neq 1)\}$. Nonetheless,

Target State Bit	Output Differential											
	δ_{72}	δ_{73}	δ_{74}	δ_{75}	δ_{76}	δ_{77}	δ_{78}	δ_{79}	δ_{92}	δ_{93}	δ_{94}	δ_{95}
s_{104}	1000	126	0	0	491	0	0	0	1000	0	0	0
s_{105}	0	1000	129	0	0	484	0	0	0	1000	0	0
s_{106}	0	0	1000	134	0	0	496	0	0	0	1000	0
s_{107}	0	0	0	1000	106	0	0	484	0	0	0	1000
s_{108}	502	0	0	0	1000	115	0	0	230	0	0	0
s_{109}	382	519	0	0	0	1000	127	0	0	244	0	0
s_{110}	0	359	540	0	0	0	1000	120	0	0	245	0
s_{111}	0	0	346	535	0	0	0	1000	0	0	0	233

Fig. 3. No. of times $\delta_j = 1$ for each registers in $S_{byte_{13}}$ in 1000 tests

Table 7. Conditions to confirm that all the state bits in $S_{byte_{13}}$ are complemented

Target register	Required keystream indices and condition	Remarks/ comments
104	$\delta_{72} = 1 \wedge \delta_{92} = 1 \wedge \delta_{76} \neq 1$	may coincide with target s_{108}
105	$\delta_{73} = 1 \wedge \delta_{93} = 1 \wedge \delta_{77} \neq 1$	may coincide with target s_{109}
106	$\delta_{74} = 1 \wedge \delta_{94} = 1 \wedge \delta_{78} \neq 1$	may coincide with target s_{110}
107	$\delta_{75} = 1 \wedge \delta_{95} = 1 \wedge \delta_{79} \neq 1$	may coincide with target s_{111}
108	$\delta_{76} = 1 \wedge \delta_{75} \neq 1 \wedge (\delta_{72} \neq 1 \vee \delta_{92} \neq 1)$	may coincide with target s_{104}
109	$\delta_{77} = 1 \wedge \delta_{76} \neq 1 \wedge (\delta_{73} \neq 1 \vee \delta_{93} \neq 1)$	may coincide with target s_{105}
110	$\delta_{78} = 1 \wedge \delta_{77} \neq 1 \wedge (\delta_{74} \neq 1 \vee \delta_{94} \neq 1)$	may coincide with target s_{106}
111	$\delta_{79} = 1 \wedge \delta_{78} \neq 1 \wedge (\delta_{75} \neq 1 \vee \delta_{95} \neq 1)$	may coincide with target s_{107}

there is a chance that the output differentials $\delta_{72} = 1$, $\delta_{76} = 1$, and $\delta_{92} = 1$, which makes it undeterminable, as shown in Fig. 3. We propose a solution to address this issue when $\delta_{72} = 1$, $\delta_{76} = 1$, and $\delta_{92} = 1$. In our solution, we re-initialize the cipher and re-compute the output differentials until the conditions of s_{104} or s_{108} are satisfied. The same technique is applicable for the other pairs (s_{105}, s_{109}), (s_{106}, s_{110}), (s_{107}, s_{111}), as shown in Table 7. Note that using this approach, it is possible to conclusively determine which state bits had been injected with a fault; however, this technique may also require more faults.

Optimizing the Output Indices to be Observed. In terms of moderate control, there might be cases in which we would have to observe multiple output differentials in order to confirm that all the target state bits in a byte array had been complemented. We analyzed each byte array to determine the minimum number of output keystream bits required for the above fault attacks. An example using S_{byte_2} is discussed below.

As shown in Table 5 and Fig. 4, ten output keystream indices δ_{64}, δ_{65}, δ_{66}, δ_{67}, δ_{68}, δ_{69}, δ_{70}, δ_{71}, δ_{72}, δ_{95}, need to be observed to determine that all the

Target State Bit	Output Differentials									
	δ_{64}	δ_{65}	δ_{66}	δ_{67}	δ_{68}	δ_{69}	δ_{70}	δ_{71}	δ_{72}	δ_{95}
s_{16}	481	1000	0	0	0	0	256	0	0	1000
s_{17}	0	496	1000	0	0	0	0	240	0	0
s_{18}	0	0	529	1000	0	0	0	0	267	0
s_{19}	0	0	0	482	1000	0	0	0	0	0
s_{20}	0	0	0	0	500	1000	0	0	0	0
s_{21}	0	0	0	0	0	524	1000	0	0	0
s_{22}	1000	0	0	0	0	0	501	1000	0	0
s_{23}	0	1000	0	0	0	0	0	511	1000	0

Fig. 4. No. of times $\delta_j = 1$ for each registers in S_{byte_2} in 1000 tests

Table 8. Conditions to confirm that all the state bits in S_{byte_2} are complemented

Target register	Required keystream indices and condition
16	$(\delta_{65} = 1 \wedge \delta_{66} \neq 1 \wedge \delta_{72} \neq 1) \vee (\delta_{65} = 1 \wedge \delta_{95} = 1)$
17	$\delta_{66} = 1 \wedge \delta_{67} \neq 1$
18	$\delta_{67} = 1 \wedge \delta_{68} \neq 1$
19	$\delta_{68} = 1 \wedge \delta_{69} \neq 1$
20	$\delta_{69} = 1 \wedge \delta_{70} \neq 1$
21	$\delta_{70} = 1 \wedge \delta_{65} \neq 1 \wedge (\delta_{64} \neq 1 \vee \delta_{71} \neq 1)$
22	$[\delta_{71} = 1 \wedge \delta_{66} \neq 1 \wedge (\delta_{65} \neq 1 \vee \delta_{72} \neq 1)] \vee (\delta_{64} = 1 \wedge \delta_{71} = 1)$
23	$\delta_{65} = 1 \wedge \delta_{72} = 1$

state bits in S_{byte_2} had been injected with fault. Now, let us assume that the fault is injected at state bit s_{16}. Instead of observing its two unique output differentials, δ_{65} and δ_{95}, we can observe the output differentials δ_{65}, δ_{66} and δ_{72} instead. The reason is that these output indices, δ_{66} and δ_{72}, are all unique output differential of a particular state bit in S_{byte_2} and these output keystream indices will be traversed. It can be concluded that s_{16} had been injected with fault if the output differential conditions do not satisfy for target state bit s_{17} and s_{23}, and $\delta_{65} = 1$. Thus, the output keystream index 95 is not necessary to be observed even though it is guaranteed that if the fault is injected at s_{16}, then $\delta_{95} = 1$. When continuing this experiment to all the other state bits in S_{byte_2}, we deduced that it is possible to conclude that all the state bits had been injected with fault by observing 8 output keystreams indices $\delta_{65}, \delta_{66}, \delta_{67}, \delta_{68}, \delta_{69}, \delta_{70}, \delta_{71}, \delta_{72}$ instead of observing 10 output keystream indices. Take note that the conditions coloured red in Table 8 mean that it is not necessary to observe that particular condition, i.e., excluding the red-coloured conditions will help to minimize the required number of output keystream bits. The minimum number of output keystream bits required in a particular byte is 8 since there are 8 state bits in an array, assuming they each have a unique output differential.

We identified the conditions for each of the 16 S_{byte} with the reduced number of keystream indices to be observed. The detailed conditions are available from the Github repository [8]. By applying this approach to the other bytes, the reduced number and the corresponding output keystream indices to be observed are summarized in Table 9. The number of faults needed to ensure that all state bits in a particular byte array have been complemented is discussed in the following sections based on the two different fault models: bit-flipping fault attack and random fault attack.

Table 9. Number of keystream for each byte

Target byte	Output keystream indices (minimized)	No. of keystream
S_{byte_0}	79, 80, 81, 82, 83, 84, 85, 86	8
S_{byte_1}	87, 88, 89, 90, 91, 92, 93, 94	8
S_{byte_2}	65, 66, 67, 68, 69, 70, 71, 72	8
S_{byte_3}	66, 67, 68, 69, 70, 71, 72, 73	8
S_{byte_4}	74, 75, 76, 77, 78, 79, 80, 81	8
S_{byte_5}	82, 83, 84, 85, 86, 87, 88, 89	8
S_{byte_6}	80, 81, 82, 83, 84, 85, 86, 87, 90, 91	10
S_{byte_7}	64, 65, 66, 67, 68, 88, 89, 90	8
S_{byte_8}	65, 66, 67, 68, 69, 70, 71, 72	8
S_{byte_9}	67, 68, 69, 70, 71, 72, 73, 74	8
$S_{byte_{10}}$	75, 76, 77, 78, 79, 80, 81, 82	8
$S_{byte_{11}}$	86, 87, 88, 89, 90, 91, 92, 93	8
$S_{byte_{12}}$	84, 85, 86, 87, 88, 89, 90, 91	8
$S_{byte_{13}}$	72, 73, 74, 75, 76, 77, 78, 79, 92, 93, 94, 95	12
$S_{byte_{14}}$	64, 66, 67, 68, 69, 70, 80, 85	8
$S_{byte_{15}}$	71, 72, 73, 74, 75, 76, 77, 78	8

Bit-Flipping Fault Attack with Moderate Control Model. In this attack model, we assumed that each injected fault in a byte would always complement one of the eight state bits (registers) in a targeted byte. The adversary is able to precisely target a specific byte. Furthermore, the injected fault will always affect any of the 8 state bits in the target byte. For each target byte in Table 9, we repeatedly inject fault $e = 1$ until all the required target registers in the respective target bytes are affected. For instance, we repeatedly inject fault $e = 1$ into S_{byte_0} until all the state bits s_0, s_1, s_2, s_3, s_4, s_5, s_6 and s_7 are confirmed to be complemented. We conducted our experiment 1000 times for each of the target bytes S_{byte_i}, where $0 \leq i \leq 15$. We verified our experiment using 1000 different combinations of random inputs (key, IV). Our experiment indicates that it takes an average of 22 fault injections to affect all the state bits in a particular byte. Meanwhile, for the case of $S_{byte_{13}}$, it takes an average of 126 faults to conclusively determine which state bits had been affected by faults. Overall, $(22 \times 15 + 126) = 456$ faults are required to determine all the state bits of the NFSR that had been injected with faults in the bit-flipping fault attack with a moderate control model. The data complexity of the bit-flipping fault attack with a moderate control model is $2^{12.034}$.

Random Fault Attack with Moderate Control Model. In this attack model, we assumed that each injected random fault e in a byte might complement one of any of the eight state bits in a targeted byte. The adversary is able to precisely target a specific byte; however, the fault may or may not affect any of the 8 state bits in the particular target byte. That is, the injected fault e may complement the target register bit for a given byte with a probability of 0.5. For each target byte in Table 9, we repeatedly inject random fault e, until all the target state bits in the respective target bytes are affected with faults. Similar to the bit-flipping attack fault model, we performed our experiment 1000 times for each of the target bytes separately. Our experiment indicates that it takes an average of 43 fault injections to affect all the state bits in a particular byte. Meanwhile, for the case of $S_{byte_{13}}$, it takes an average of 205 faults to conclusively determine which state bit had been affected. Overall, $(43 \times 15 + 205) = 850$ faults are required to determine all the state bits of the NFSR that had been injected with faults in the random fault attack with a moderate control model. The data complexity of the random fault attack with a moderate control model is $2^{12.911}$.

Fault Attacks Based on No Control Model. In this section, we further investigate applying the two fault attacks with no control model against Tiny-JAMBUv2. Under this model, the fault may be induced in any of the 128 state bits. Now let us assume that we expected s_0 to be the target state bit. Based on Table 4, the output differential δ_{79} will always equal one when the content of state bit s_0 has been complemented. However, this is the same case when the content of state bit s_{111} had been flipped. The output differential δ_{79} is the only unique term for both s_0 and s_{111}, thus making it undeterminable to conclude which states had been complemented. This is observable from the differential signatures of s_0 and s_{111} illustrated in Fig. 5. We conducted preliminary research in terms of the no-control precision model for the other target registers and noticed a similar observation.

Target State Bit	Output Differential														
	δ_{67}	δ_{68}	δ_{69}	δ_{74}	δ_{75}	δ_{79}	δ_{80}	δ_{83}	δ_{84}	δ_{85}	δ_{89}	δ_{90}	δ_{91}	δ_{92}	δ_{95}
s_0	0	0	355	0	0	1000	0	0	267	508	0	0	406	507	0
s_{111}	251	501	0	346	535	1000	112	492	0	0	468	505	0	0	233

Fig. 5. Number of Times $\delta_j = 1$ in 1000 tests for target registers s_0 and s_{111}

5 Conclusion

This paper applies the bit-flipping and random fault attacks to TinyJAMBUv2. The bit-flipping fault model uses cipher output functions where the target register contents are combined using a bit-wise AND operation. The random fault model identifies these fault values by using cipher output functions where the target register contents are combined using a bit-wise XOR operation. We showed that these attacks can recover 58 state bits and 15 key bits on TinyJAMBUv2. The application of these fault models to TinyJAMBUv2 is less successful than the previous applications that demonstrate state recovery or key recovery against Tiaoxin-346 [3,7,10,17], AEGIS-128L [3,17], Grain-128AEAD [11], CLX-128 [12]. This is because TinyJAMBU outputs 32 keystream bits at a time that contain limited cipher output functions of the above nature. Additionally, in between the processing of two keystream blocks, a large permutation P_{1024} is applied, preventing the generation of successive low-degree keystream equation blocks. Note that CLX-128 has a similar construction to TinyJAMBU and outputs a 32-bit keystream block at a time (separated by intermediate updates of large permutation rounds). However, unlike TinyJAMBU, similar fault analyses applied to the CLX-128 output function can generate enough differential signatures to recover the majority of the state bits. Therefore, the output structure of TinyJAMBU also plays a crucial role in making these fault attacks less successful.

The fault injections in this work are applied at the same clock. Future research may investigate fault injections by combining differentials from different clock instances. This may result in the recovery of additional key bits. Furthermore, future research may further investigate the no control model. During our preliminary investigation of the no-control model, we found many cases in which one cannot conclusively determine the fault targets. The reason is that the conditions to determine the fault target coincide with that of another target register. Further analysis of the no-control model can be conducted with a probabilistic approach or by combining multiple output differential signatures, if applicable.

Acknowledgements. This work is supported by the Ministry of Higher Education Malaysia through the Fundamental Research Grant Scheme (FRGS), project no. FRGS/1/2021/ICT07/XMU/02/1 and Xiamen University Malaysia Research Fund under Grant XMUMRF/2022-C9/IECE/0032.

References

1. Lightweight cryptography. https://csrc.nist.gov/Projects/lightweight-cryptography. Accessed 29 Mar 2024
2. Baksi, A., Bhasin, S., Breier, J., Jap, D., Saha, D.: A survey on fault attacks on symmetric key cryptosystems. ACM Comput. Surv. **55**(4), 1–34 (2022). https://doi.org/10.1145/3530054

3. Bartlett, H., Dawson, E., Qahur Al Mahri, H., Salam, M., Simpson, L., Wong, K.K.H.: Random fault attacks on a class of stream ciphers. Security and Commun. Netw. **2019** (2019). https://doi.org/10.1155/2019/1680263D

4. Biham, E., Shamir, A.: Differential fault analysis of secret key cryptosystems. In: Kaliski, B.S. (ed.) Advances in Cryptology — CRYPTO '97, pp. 513–525. Springer Berlin Heidelberg, Berlin, Heidelberg (1997). https://doi.org/10.1007/BFb0052259

5. Boneh, D., DeMillo, R.A., Lipton, R.J.: On the importance of checking cryptographic protocols for faults. In: Fumy, W. (ed.) Advances in Cryptology — EUROCRYPT '97, pp. 37–51. Springer Berlin Heidelberg, Berlin, Heidelberg (1997). https://doi.org/10.1007/3-540-69053-0_4

6. Breier, J., Hou, X.: How practical are fault injection attacks, really? IEEE Access **10**, 113122–113130 (2022). https://doi.org/10.1109/ACCESS.2022.3217212

7. Dey, P., Rohit, R.S., Sarkar, S., Adhikari, A.: Differential fault analysis on tiaoxin and aegis family of ciphers. In: Mueller, P., Thampi, S.M., Alam Bhuiyan, M.Z., Ko, R., Doss, R., Alcaraz Calero, J.M. (eds.) Security in Computing and Communications: 4th International Symposium, SSCC 2016, Jaipur, India, September 21-24, 2016, Proceedings, pp. 74–86. Springer Singapore, Singapore (2016). https://doi.org/10.1007/978-981-10-2738-3_7

8. Prajasantosa, S.R., Salam, I.: Differential fault analysis of TinyJAMBU. https://github.com/SamuelRussellP/TinyJambuDFAExperiments. Accessed 21 June 2024

9. Salam, I., Law, K.Y., Xue, L., Yau, W.C.: Differential fault based key recovery attacks on TRIAD. In: International Conference on Information Security and Cryptology, pp. 273–287. Springer (2020). https://doi.org/10.1007/978-3-030-68890-5_15

10. Salam, I., Mahri, H.Q.A., Simpson, L., Bartlett, H., Dawson, E., Wong, K.K.H.: Fault attacks on Tiaoxin-346. In: Proceedings of the Australasian Computer Science Week Multiconference, pp. 1–9. ACM (2018). https://doi.org/10.1145/3167918.3167940

11. Salam, I., Ooi, T.H., Xue, L., Yau, W.C., Pieprzyk, J., Phan, R.C.W.: Random differential fault attacks on the lightweight authenticated encryption stream cipher Grain-128AEAD. IEEE Access **9**, 72568–72586 (2021). https://doi.org/10.1109/ACCESS.2021.3078845

12. Salam, I., Yau, W.C., Phan, R.C.W., Pieprzyk, J.: Differential fault attacks on the lightweight authenticated encryption algorithm CLX-128. J. Cryptogr. Eng. **13**(3), 265–281 (2023). https://doi.org/10.1007/s13389-023-00326-0

13. Schmidt, J.M., Herbst, C.: A practical fault attack on square and multiply. In: 2008 5th Workshop on Fault Diagnosis and Tolerance in Cryptography, pp. 53–58. IEEE (2008). https://doi.org/10.1109/FDTC.2008.10

14. Selmke, B., Heyszl, J., Sigl, G.: Attack on a DFA protected AES by simultaneous laser fault injections. In: 2016 Workshop on Fault Diagnosis and Tolerance in Cryptography (FDTC), pp. 36–46. IEEE (2016). https://doi.org/10.1109/FDTC.2016.16

15. Skorobogatov, S.: Optical fault masking attacks. In: 2010 Workshop on Fault Diagnosis and Tolerance in Cryptography, pp. 23–29. IEEE (2010). https://doi.org/10.1109/FDTC.2010.18

16. Trichina, E., Korkikyan, R.: Multi fault laser attacks on protected CRT-RSA. In: 2010 Workshop on Fault Diagnosis and Tolerance in Cryptography, pp. 75–86. IEEE (2010). https://doi.org/10.1109/FDTC.2010.14

17. Wong, K.K.H., Bartlett, H., Simpson, L., Dawson, E.: Differential random fault attacks on certain caesar stream ciphers. In: International Conference on Information Security and Cryptology, pp. 297–315. Springer (2019). https://doi.org/10.1007/978-3-030-40921-0_18
18. Wu, H., Huang, T.: JAMBU lightweight authenticated encryption mode and AES-JAMBU. Submission to the CAESAR Competition (2014)
19. Wu, H., Huang, T.: TinyJAMBU: A family of lightweight authenticated encryption algorithms. Submission to the NIST Lightweight Cryptography Standardization Process (2019)
20. Wu, H., Huang, T.: TinyJAMBU: A family of lightweight authenticated encryption algorithms (version 2). Submission to the NIST Lightweight Cryptography Standardization Process (2021)

Integrity-Protecting Block Cipher Modes—Untangling a Tangled Web

Chris J. Mitchell$^{(\boxtimes)}$

Royal Holloway, University of London, Egham TW20 0EX, Egham, UK
c.mitchell@rhul.ac.uk
https://www.chrismitchell.net

Abstract. This paper re-examines the security of three related block cipher modes of operation designed to provide authenticated encryption. These modes, known as PES-PCBC, IOBC and EPBC, were all proposed in the mid-1990s. However, analyses of security of the latter two modes were published more recently. In each case one or more papers describing security issues with the schemes were eventually published, although a flaw in one of these analyses (of EPBC) was subsequently discovered; this means that until now EPBC had no known major issues. This paper establishes that, despite this, all three schemes possess defects which should prevent their use, especially as there are a number of efficient alternative schemes possessing proofs of security.

Keywords: authenticated encryption · cryptanalysis · mode of operation

1 Introduction

This paper is a somewhat tangled story of three different, albeit very closely related, proposals for a block cipher mode of operation providing authenticated encryption. Sadly, all of the schemes have been shown to be insecure—often in quite different ways. This is, to the author's knowledge, the first paper to bring together the three strands of research; at the same time errors in previous cryptanalysis are acknowledged and further attacks described.

All three of the schemes we examine are examples of a 'special' mode of operation for block ciphers, designed to offer 'low cost' combined integrity and confidentiality protection by combining encryption with the addition of simple (or fixed) redundancy to the plaintext. The underlying idea is to design the mode so that modifying the ciphertext without invalidating the added redundancy is impossible without knowledge of the encryption key. Such modes are the theme of Sect. 9.6.5 of Menezes, van Oorschot and Vanstone's landmark book [6]. Two main methods for adding redundancy have been proposed:

- add a fixed block (or blocks) at the end of the plaintext, which may be public or secret (in the latter case the block acts as an auxiliary key);

© The Author(s), under exclusive license to Springer Nature Switzerland AG 2025
C. Boyd et al. (Eds.): Ed Dawson Festschrift 2024, LNCS 15600, pp. 89–106, 2025.
https://doi.org/10.1007/978-3-031-83490-5_5

– append to the plaintext some easily computed and simple (public) function of the plaintext.

In either case we refer to the block added to the end of the plaintext as a *Manipulation Detection Code (MDC)*. Whichever approach is adopted, the method for computing the MDC needs to be simple, or it offers no advantage over the more conventional 'encrypt then MAC' approach. In all the modes we examine, the MDV (also known as an *Integrity Control Value* (ICV)) is defined to be a fixed, possibly secret, final plaintext block.

The first of the three schemes we examine is known as PES-PCBC. The name derives from it being a version of PCBC mode designed specifically for use in a Privacy Enhanced Socket (PES) protocol. There are actually a number of modes known as PCBC (Plaintext-Ciphertext Block Chaining); the version on which PES-PCBC was based is the one incorporated in Kerberos version 4. This mode was shown to be insecure for the purposes of integrity protection by Kohl, [3]. For a discussion of the weaknesses of other variants of PCBC see [7]. The design goal for PES-PCBC was to enhance the security of PCBC by preventing the known attacks. This scheme and its properties are discussed in Sect. 3.

The second scheme, known as IOBC (short for *Input and Output Block Chaining*) was published in 1996 by Rechacha [10]. IOBC is a straightforward variant of PES-PCBC. The paper describing IOBC was originally published in Spanish, and it wasn't until an English language translation was kindly provided by the author in around 2013[1] that any further discussion of the scheme appeared. This scheme and its properties are discussed in Sect. 4.

The last of the three schemes, known as EPBC (short for *Efficient Error-Propagating Block Chaining*) was published in 1997 by Zúquete and Gudes [16]. It is very similar to IOBC, and is designed to be used in exactly the same way. The design goal was to address issues in IOBC which restricted its use to relatively short messages. A possible method of cryptanalysis allowing certificational forgeries was published in 2007 [8], although Di et al. [2] showed in 2015 that the attack does not work as claimed. The scheme and its level of security are discussed in Sect. 5.

In Sect. 6 we examine other more general attacks which apply to all, or at least large classes of, schemes sharing the same underlying structure as PES-PCBC, IOBC and EPBC. In doing so we establish that all three modes suffer from attacks, and so they should not be adopted. We conclude the paper in Sects. 7 and 8 by first briefly mentioning two other related modes (and their analyses), and then summarising the main conclusions that can be drawn from the analyses given.

2   Preliminaries

We start by introducing some notation and assumptions. All three modes operate using a block cipher. We write:

---

[1] See https://inputoutputblockchaining.blogspot.com/.

- n for the plaintext/ciphertext block length of this cipher;
- $e_K(P)$ for the result of block cipher encrypting the n-bit block P using the secret key K;
- $d_K(C)$ for the result of block cipher decrypting the n-bit block C using the key K; and
- $\oplus$ for bit-wise exclusive-or.

Finally we suppose the plaintext to be protected using the mode of operation is divided into a sequence of n-bit blocks (if necessary, having first been padded): $P_1, P_2, \ldots, P_t$, where P_t is equal to the MDC.

3 PES-PCBC

The description follows Zúquete and Guedes [15], although we use the notation of [16]. The scheme uses two secret n-bit Initialisation Vectors (IVs), denoted by F_0 and G_0. The nature of their intended use is not described in [15]; however it is stated in [16] that the 'initial values of F_{i-1} and G_{i-1} are distinct, secret initialisation vectors', which is what we assume below.

3.1 PES-PCBC Operation

The PES-PCBC encryption of the plaintext $P_1, P_2, \ldots, P_t$ operates as follows:

$$G_i = P_i \oplus F_{i-1}, \quad (1 \leq i \leq t),$$
$$F_i = e_K(G_i), \quad (1 \leq i \leq t),$$
$$C_i = F_i \oplus G_{i-1}, \quad (1 \leq i \leq t).$$

The resulting ciphertext is $C_1, C_2, \ldots, C_t$.

The operation of the mode (when used for encryption) is shown in Fig. 1. Note that we refer to the values F_i and G_i as 'internal' values, as they are computed during encryption, but they do not constitute part of the ciphertext.

3.2 Cryptanalysis

It is clear that weaknesses in PES-PCBC when applied for integrity protection were discovered soon after its publication in 1996. The 1997 paper by Zúquete and Guedes, [16], briefly outlines a known-plaintext attack allowing simple forgeries. We next describe a slightly simplified variant of this attack, requiring just one known plaintext block instead of two.

First observe that, using the same notation as before, PES-PCBC decryption operates as follows:

$$F_i = C_i \oplus G_{i-1}, \quad (1 \leq i \leq t),$$
$$G_i = d_K(F_i), \quad (1 \leq i \leq t),$$
$$P_i = G_i \oplus F_{i-1}, \quad (1 \leq i \leq t),,$$

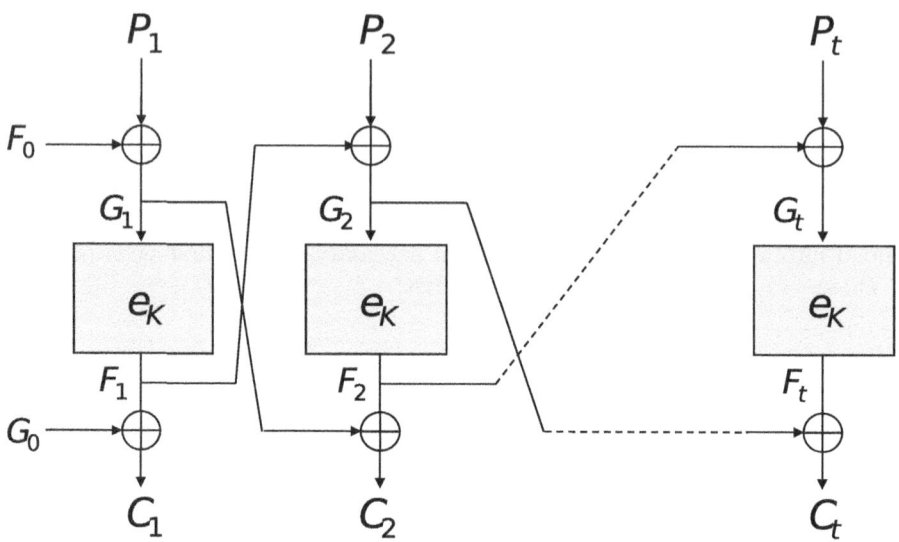

Fig. 1. PES-PCBC encryption

and the receiver of an encrypted message will accept it as genuine if the final recovered plaintext block P_t equals the expected MDC.

The following result captures the attack.

Theorem 1. *Suppose the ciphertext $C_1, C_2, \ldots, C_t$ was constructed using PES-PCBC from the plaintext $P_1, P_2, \ldots, P_t$, and that j satisfies $1 < j < t$. Suppose the $(t + 2)$-block ciphertext $C'_1, C'_2, \ldots, C'_{t+2}$ is constructed as follows:*

$$C'_i = C_i, \quad (1 \le i \le j),$$
$$C'_{j+1} = P_j,$$
$$C'_i = C_{i-2}, \quad (j + 2 \le i \le t + 2).$$

When decrypted to yield $P'_1, P'_2, \ldots, P'_{t+2}$, the value of the final plaintext block P'_{t+2} will equal P_t for the original (untampered) message, and hence will pass the integrity check.

Proof. In the discussion below we refer to the 'internal values' generated during decryption of $C'_1, C'_2, \ldots, C'_{t+2}$ as F'_i and G'_i. First note that, trivially: $F'_i = F_i$, $G'_i = G_i$, and $P'_i = P_i$, $(1 \le i \le j)$. Next observe that

$$F'_{j+1} = C'_{j+1} \oplus G'_j$$
$$= P_j \oplus G_j$$
$$= F_{j-1}.$$

Hence $G'_{j+1} = d_K(F'_{j+1}) = d_K(F_{j-1}) = G_{j-1}$. Finally, we have $P'_{j+1} = G'_{j+1} \oplus F'_j = G_{j-1} \oplus F_j = C_j$. Since $C'_{j+2} = C_j$, $F'_{j+1} = F_{j-1}$ and $G'_{j+1} = G_{j-1}$, it is immediate that $F'_{j+2} = F_j$, $G'_{j+2} = G_j$, and $P'_{j+2} = P_j$, and the desired result follows.   □

3.3 Impact

The above attack shows that, given just one PES-PCBC-encrypted message and knowledge of only a single plaintext block for this encrypted message, a 'fake' message can be constructed that will be guaranteed to pass the integrity checks. This fact meant that it has been recognised since 1996/97 that PES-PCBC should not be used.

Before proceeding note that the originally proposed context of use for PES-PCBC, as described in [15], involved including an encoded version of the message length in the first plaintext block. In such a case the attack described in Theorem 1 will not work since it involves lengthening the message by two blocks. However, a slightly more involved version of the Theorem 1 attack (outlined in [16]) avoids changing the message length and hence works even if the message length is encoded in the plaintext—at the cost of requiring knowledge of two plaintext blocks instead of one.

4 IOBC

The IOBC mode was published in 1996 by Recacha [10], the same year as the publication of PES-PCBC. One might reasonably conclude that the design of IOBC, as a modification to PES-PCBC, was motivated by the weaknesses in PES-PCBC, but curiously the Recacha paper does not even mention PES-PCBC. Certainly, the inclusion of the function g in the feedback stops the attack on PES-PCBC working—at least in a naive way.

4.1 IOBC Operation

We start by describing the operation of the IOBC mode of operation. We base the description on Recacha's 1996 paper [10], although we use the same notation as in the description of PES-PCBC. We suppose that the cipher block length n is a multiple of four (as is the case for almost all commonly used schemes), and put $n = 2m$ where m is even. The scheme uses two secret n-bit IVs, denoted by F_0 and G_0. The nature of the intended restrictions on their use is not altogether clear; one suggestion in the original Recacha paper [10] is that they should be generated as follows.

Suppose K' is an auxiliary key used solely for generating the IVs. Suppose also that S is a sequence number, managed so that different values are used for every message. Then $F_0 = e_{K'}(S)$ and $G_0 = e_{K'}(F_0)$. For the purposes of this paper we assume that F_0 and G_0 are always generated this way, and thus the scheme can be thought of as employing a pair of block cipher keys and a non-secret, non-repeating, sequence number (which must be carefully managed to prevent accidental re-use of sequence number values). Note that special measures will need to be taken if the same key is to be used to encrypt communications in both directions between a pair of parties. Avoiding sequence number re-use in such a case could be achieved by requiring one party to start the sequence number they use for encryption at a large value, perhaps halfway through the range.

The IOBC encryption of the plaintext $P_1, P_2, \ldots, P_t$ operates as follows:

$$G_i = P_i \oplus F_{i-1}, \quad (1 \le i \le t),$$
$$F_i = e_K(G_i), \quad (1 \le i \le t),$$
$$C_i = F_i \oplus g(G_{i-1}), \quad (2 \le i \le t),$$

where $C_1 = F_1 \oplus G_0$ and g is a function that maps an n-bit block to an n-bit block, defined below. The operation of the mode (when used for encryption) is shown in Fig. 2.

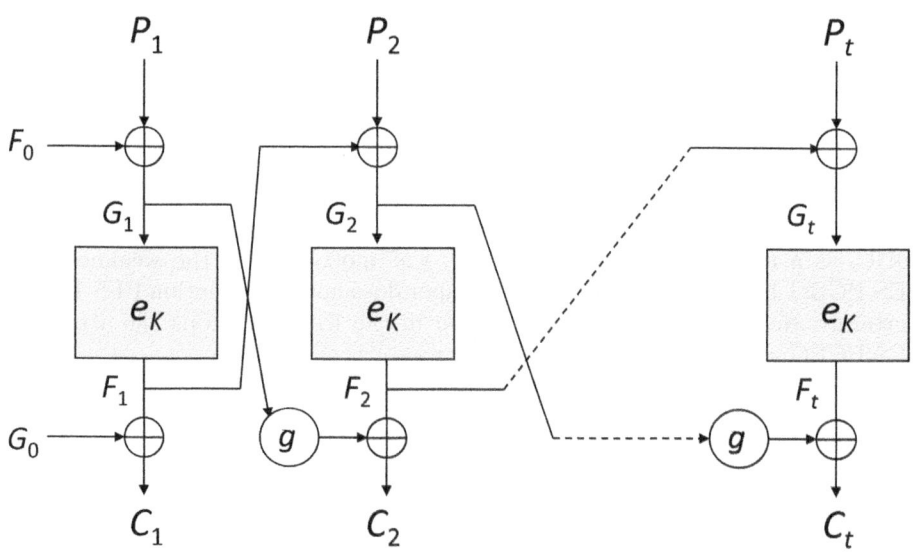

Fig. 2. IOBC encryption

The function g is defined as follows. Suppose X is an n-bit block, where $n = 2m$. Suppose also that $X = L \| R$ where L is the leftmost $m - 1$ bits of X and R is the rightmost $m + 1$ bits of X (and, as throughout, $\|$ denotes concatenation). Then

$$g(X) = (>_1 (L)) \| (>_1 (R))$$

where $>_i$ denotes a rightwards (cyclic) shift by i bit positions.

Decryption operates similarly. We have:

$$F_i = C_i \oplus g(G_{i-1}), \quad (2 \leq i \leq t),$$
$$G_i = d_K(F_i), \quad (1 \leq i \leq t),$$
$$P_i = G_i \oplus F_{i-1}, \quad (1 \leq i \leq t).$$

and $F_1 = C_1 \oplus G_0$, where d denotes block cipher decryption.

It should be clear that PES-PCBC is the same as IOBC with the exception that in PES-PCBC the function g is the identity function.

4.2 Remarks on Use

As described above, we assume throughout that the IVs F_0 and G_0 are derived by ECB-mode-encrypting a sequence number using a secondary key. Thus the ciphertext blocks will be a function of this serial number (as well as the pair of keys used). We thus write $[S], C_1, C_2, \ldots, C_t$ for a sequence of ciphertext blocks, meaning that $C_1, C_2, \ldots, C_t$ were encrypted using the sequence number S. This is logical, since the sequence number will need to be sent or stored with the ciphertext to enable correct decryption.

IOBC should only be used with relatively short messages. As specified by Recacha [10] (and for reasons which become clear below), a message to be encrypted using IOBC shall contain at most $n^2/2 - 1$ plaintext blocks, where n is the plaintext block length. Thus for $n = 64$ and $n = 128$, the two most commonly used block lengths, a message shall contain at most 2047 and 8191 blocks, respectively.

As with all modes we discuss here, data integrity is achieved by adding an MDC to the end of the plaintext.

4.3 Cryptanalysis

We start by giving a simple result that is implicit in Recacha [10]. It is interesting to note that this result applies regardless of the choice of function g, i.e. to any mode operating as in Fig. 2.

Lemma 1 (Mitchell, [9]). *Suppose* $[S], C_1, C_2, \ldots, C_t$ *and* $[S'], C_1', C_2', \ldots, C_{t'}'$ *are IOBC-encrypted versions of the plaintext block sequences* $P_1, P_2, \ldots, P_t$ *and* $P_1', P_2', \ldots, P_{t'}'$, *respectively. If the ciphertext:*

$$[S'], C_1^*, C_2^*, \ldots, C_{t-v+u}^* =$$
$$[S'], C_1', C_2', \ldots, C_{u-1}', C_v \oplus g(G_{u-1}') \oplus g(G_{v-1}), C_{v+1}, \ldots, C_t$$

is submitted for IOBC decryption (where $1 < u < t'$ *and* $1 < v < t$, *and* G_{v-1} *and* G_{u-1}' *are values computed during the encryption of the respective sequences of blocks), then the resulting sequence of plaintext blocks* $P_1^*, P_2^*, \ldots, P_{t-v+u}^*$ *will be equal to*

$$P_1', P_2', \ldots, P_{u-1}', P_v \oplus F_{u-1}' \oplus F_{v-1}, P_{v+1}, P_{v+2}, \ldots, P_t.$$

Lemma 1 suggests a way of forging an IOBC-encrypted message so that the final block will contain the correct MDC. However, the problem remains of discovering $g(G'_{u-1}) \oplus g(G_{v-1})$, as this is used in constructing the forged ciphertext in the statement of the lemma. Recacha [10] discusses this very point, and explains that making this difficult motivates the inclusion of the function g in the design of IOBC—that is, if g was not included (as is the case for PES-PCBC), then simple forgeries could be achieved.

We also have the following, also implicit in Recacha's 1996 paper.

Lemma 2 (Mitchell, [9]). *Suppose $[S], C_1, C_2, \ldots, C_t$ is the encryption of the plaintext $P_1, P_2, \ldots, P_t$ using IOBC, and that F_i and G_i are as defined in Sect. 4.1. Then:*

(i) $C_{j+1} \oplus P_{j+2} = g(G_j) \oplus G_{j+2}, \ 1 \leq j \leq t - 2;$
(ii) $\bigoplus_{i=1}^{k} g^{k-i}(C_{j+2i-1} \oplus P_{j+2i}) = g^k(G_j) \oplus G_{j+2k}, \ 1 \leq j \leq t - 2,$
    $1 \leq k \leq (t - j)/2.$

It is not hard to see that if $g^k(G_j) = G_j$ for some k, then Lemma 2(ii) could be combined with Lemma 1 to yield a forgery attack (given a ciphertext message with corresponding known plaintext). This point is made by Recacha [10], who explains that the bit permutation g has been chosen so that the smallest integer $i > 1$ such that g^i is the identity permutation is $(n/2 - 1)(n/2 + 1) = n^2/4 - 1$ (since $m = n/2$ is even). The restriction that the maximum length of messages encrypted using IOBC is $n^2/2 - 1$, as defined in Sect. 4.2, prevents this problem arising in practice.

However, in some cases g^k is 'close' to the identity permutation for somewhat smaller values of k. The following result highlights this for two practically important values of n. Observe that analogous results can be achieved for any n.

Lemma 3 (Mitchell, [9]). *Suppose X is a randomly selected n-bit block.*

(i) If $n = 64$ then $\Pr(X = g^{341}(X)) = 2^{-22}$; and
(ii) if $n = 128$ then $\Pr(X = g^{1365}(X)) = 2^{-42}$.

The above result can now be used in a straightforward way to enable message forgeries. As described in detail in [9], if $n = 64$, given an IOBC ciphertext containing at least 685 blocks and some of the corresponding plaintext, then it is possible to create a forged ciphertext that will pass integrity checks with probability 2^{-22}. 685 is clearly much less than the defined message length limit of 2047 blocks. A precisely analogous attack works for $n = 128$, although the success probability is only 2^{-42}.

4.4   Impact

The attack outlined immediately above could be prevented by further curtailing the maximum length for messages, but this would in turn further limit the applicability of the scheme. Moreover, the lack of a formal proof of security means that other attacks are possible. Indeed, a simple chosen plaintext forgery attack was outlined in [9], although it requires approaching $2^{n/2}$ ciphertexts for chosen plaintexts (this attack is discussed further in Sect. 6.1 below). These points strongly argue against adoption of this scheme.

5   EPBC

The EPBC scheme was proposed by Zúquete and Guedes [16] the year after the publication of IOBC. The primary design goal was to remove the message length restriction inherent in the design of IOBC; it also enables a small efficiency improvement. It was further claimed by its authors to be more secure than IOBC.

5.1   EPBC Operation

The scheme operates in a very similar way to IOBC, exactly as shown in Fig. 2, and (like IOBC) requires that n is even. The only significant difference is in the choice of the function g. The function g for EPBC is not bijective, unlike in IOBC, and operates as follows. Suppose X is an n-bit block, where $X = L || R$ and L and R are m-bit blocks (and, as throughout, $||$ denotes concatenation). Then

$$g(X) = (L \vee \overline{R}) || (L \wedge \overline{R})$$

where $\vee$ denotes the bit-wise inclusive or operation, $\wedge$ denotes the bit-wise logical and operation, and $\overline{X}$ denotes the logical negation of X (i.e. changing every zero to a one and vice versa).

Much like with PES-PCBC, the IVs F_0, G_0 are required to be distinct, secret initialisation values.

5.2   A Flawed Cryptanalysis

We first give some simple results on g.

Lemma 4 (Mitchell, [8]). *Suppose $g(X) = L' || R'$, where X is an n-bit block and we let $L' = (\ell'_1, \ell'_2, \ldots, \ell'_m)$ and $R' = (r'_1, r'_2, \ldots, r'_m)$ be m-bit blocks. Then, for every i ($1 \leq i \leq m$), if $\ell'_i = 0$ then $r'_i = 0$.*

The above Lemma implies that output bit pairs (ℓ'_i, r'_i) can never be equal to $(0,1)$. In fact, we can obtain the following more general result which gives Lemma 4 as a special case.

Lemma 5 (Mitchell, [8]). *Suppose that, as above, $X = L || R$ where $L = (\ell_1, \ell_2, \ldots, \ell_m)$ and $R = (r_1, r_2, \ldots, r_m)$. Suppose also that $g(X) = L' || R'$ where $L' = (\ell'_1, \ell'_2, \ldots, \ell'_m)$ and $R' = (r'_1, r'_2, \ldots, r'_m)$. Then if $(\ell_i, r_i) \in A$ then $(\ell'_i, r'_i) \in B$, where all possibilities for A and B are given in Table 1. Note that, for simplicity, in this table we write xy instad of (x, y).*

Table 1. Input/output possibilities for g

A (set of input pairs)	B (set of output pairs)
$\{00, 01, 10, 11\}$	$\{00, 10, 11\}$
$\{01, 10, 11\}$	$\{00, 10, 11\}$
$\{00, 10, 11\}$	$\{10, 11\}$
$\{00, 01, 11\}$	$\{00, 10\}$
$\{00, 01, 10\}$	$\{00, 10, 11\}$
$\{10, 11\}$	$\{10, 11\}$
$\{01, 11\}$	$\{00, 10\}$
$\{01, 10\}$	$\{00, 11\}$
$\{00, 11\}$	$\{10\}$
$\{00, 10\}$	$\{10, 11\}$
$\{00, 01\}$	$\{00, 10\}$
$\{11\}$	$\{10\}$
$\{10\}$	$\{11\}$
$\{01\}$	$\{00\}$
$\{00\}$	$\{10\}$

We next summarise the key part of the known-plaintext attack described in [8]. The primary objective is to use knowledge of known plaintext/ciphertext pairs (P_i, C_i) to learn the values of corresponding 'internal pairs' (F_i, G_i). These can then be used in a fairly straightforward way (as detailed in [8]) to construct a forged ciphertext which will pass the integrity checks.

It is claimed in [8] that, assuming that we have sufficiently many known plaintext and ciphertext pairs, for sufficiently large w there will only be one possibility for F_{j+2w}. Using knowledge of P_{j+2w+1}, this immediately gives certain knowledge of G_{j+2w+1}. I.e., for all sufficiently large values of w, complete knowledge can be obtained of F_{j+2w} and G_{j+2w+1}.

However, more recently, Di et al. [2] pointed out that the above analysis has a major flaw. The issue arises in the argument that, since $G_{j+1} = P_{j+1} \oplus F_j$, information about forbidden bit pairs in F_j, combined with knowledge of P_{j+1}, gives information about forbidden bit pairs in G_{j+1}. Di et al. [2] point out that if there are two possibilities for a bit pair in F_j then there will always still be two possibilities for the corresponding bit pair in $g(G_{j+1})$—as opposed to the analysis in [8] which suggests that the number of possibilities will be reduced to one with probability $1/6$. That is, the number of possibilities for a bit pair in $g(G_{j+1})$ will never go below two, preventing the attack strategy working.

5.3   Impact

Di et al. [2] were not able to suggest any further attacks apart from a brute force approach. This suggests that EPBC may, after all, be secure. However, in the next section we show otherwise.

6   Other Attacks

We now consider other possible attacks. Given that all three modes we have considered share the same underlying structure, as shown in Fig. 2, we focus on attacks that apply to large classes of possibilities for the function g.

6.1   A Chosen Plaintext Forgery Attack

We start by giving an attack which will work for any function g, using a method outlined in [9]—and presented here in greater detail. This certificational chosen-plaintext-based forgery attack limits the security of any scheme using the design shown in Fig. 2 (including IOBC and EPBC), regardless of length limits for plaintexts and the choice of g.

Lemma 6. *Suppose that $C'_1, C'_2, \ldots, C'_{t'}$ and $C_1, C_2, \ldots, C_t$ are encrypted versions of the plaintext sequences $P'_1, P'_2, \ldots, P'_{t'}$ and $P_1, P_2, \ldots, P_t$, respectively, using the same key K (although the IVs may be different). Suppose also that $P'_j = P_i$ and $C'_j = C_i$ for some $j < t'$ and $i < t$. As previously we refer to the 'internal values' computed during encryption of these two messages as F'_i, F_i, G'_i and G_i.*

Then (under reasonable assumptions about the random behaviour of the block cipher) with probability approximately 0.5 it will hold that $F'_{j-1} = F_{i-1}$, $G'_{j-1} = G_{i-1}$, $F'_j = F_i$ and $G'_j = G_i$.

Proof. Let the event E_Δ be that $\Delta = F'_{j-1} \oplus F_{i-1}$. Then, under reasonable assumptions about randomness, $Pr(E_\Delta)$ is 2^{-n} for any given Δ.

In the case E_0, we immediately have $G'_{j-1} = G_{i-1}$. Also, since $P'_j = P_i$, it follows immediately that $F'_j = F_i$, $G'_j = G_i$ and $C'_j = C_i$ with probability 1.

Now consider the event E_Δ for $\Delta \neq 0$, i.e. $F'_{j-1} \neq F_{i-1}$. Since $P'_j = P_i$ this immediately implies that $G'_j \neq G_i$, and hence $F'_j \neq F_i$. Now, since $C'_j = g(G'_{j-1}) \oplus F'_j$ and $C_i = g(G_{i-1}) \oplus F_i$, we have

$$C'_j = C_i \text{ if and only if } g(G'_{j-1}) \oplus g(G_{i-1}) = F'_j \oplus F_i.$$

Under reasonable assumptions about the random behaviour of the encryption function, this will occur with probability 2^{-n}. Hence, as Δ ranges over its 2^n possible values, the expected number of times that $C'_j = C_j$ will hold is approximately 2, one of which will occur when $F'_j = F_i$. The result follows. □

We can now give the following simple result that uses the same notation as Lemma 6. Note that it uses Lemma 1, which we already observed holds regardless of the choice of g.

Lemma 7. *Suppose that $C_1', C_2', \ldots, C_{t'}'$ and $C_1, C_2, \ldots, C_t$ are as in the statement of Lemma 6, and suppose also that $P_j' = P_i$ and $C_j' = C_i$ for some $j < t'$ and $i < t$. Then, with probability approximately 0.5, the constructed ciphertext message*

$$C_1', C_2', \ldots, C_{j-1}', C_i, C_{i+1}, \ldots, C_t$$

will decrypt to $P_1', P_2', \ldots, P_{j-1}', P_j, P_{j+1}, \ldots, P_t$.

Proof. The result follows immediately from Lemma 1, putting $u = j$, $v = i$ and observing that:

$$C_v \oplus g(G_{u-1}') \oplus g(G_{v-1}) = C_i \oplus g(G_{j-1}') \oplus g(G_{i-1})$$

which equals C_i with probability approximately 0.5, since, by Lemma 6 we know that $G_{j-1}' = G_{i-1}$ with probability approximately 0.5. □

That is, we can construct a forged message that will pass integrity checks with probability 0.5 if we can find a pair of messages $C_1', C_2', \ldots, C_{t'}'$ and $C_1, C_2, \ldots, C_t$ for which $P_j' = P_i$ and $C_j' = C_i$ for some $j < t'$ and $i < t$. If the attacker can arrange for $2^{n/2}$ messages to be encrypted, all containing the same plaintext block (at a known position in each case), then by the usual 'birthday paradox' probabilistic arguments, such a pair is likely to arise. In fact, as observed in [9], the number of required message encryptions can be reduced to somewhat less than $2^{n/2}$ by including many occurrences of the fixed plaintext block in each chosen message.

Of course, this is not likely to be a realistic attack in practice; the importance of the above discussion is that it limits the level of security provided by any scheme using the general construction of Fig. 2, regardless of the choice of g. In the remainder of this section we consider two attack strategies that work for two different general classes of possible functions g.

6.2   A New Attack Approach with Implications for EPBC

We start by giving a simple generalisation of Theorem 1.

Theorem 2. *Suppose the ciphertext $C_1, C_2, \ldots, C_t$ was constructed using a scheme of the type shown in Fig. 2, and that P_j is a plaintext block for some j satisfying $1 < j < t$. Suppose the $(t+2)$-block ciphertext $C_1', C_2', \ldots, C_{t+2}'$ is constructed as follows:*

$$\begin{aligned} C_i' &= C_i, \quad (1 \le i \le j), \\ C_{j+1}' &= P_j \oplus G_j \oplus g(G_j), \\ C_i' &= C_{i-2}, \quad (j+2 \le i \le t+2). \end{aligned}$$

When decrypted to yield $P_1', P_2', \ldots, P_{t+2}'$, the value of the final plaintext block P_{t+2}' will equal P_t for the original (untampered) message, and hence will pass the integrity check.

Remark 1. In the case where g is the identity function, as is the case for PES-PCBC, then the above result reduces to Theorem 1.

Proof. We need only examine the decryption of C'_{j+1}; the rest of the proof is exactly as in the proof of Theorem 1. Now:

$$\begin{aligned} F'_{j+1} &= C'_{j+1} \oplus G'_j \\ &= (P_j \oplus G_j \oplus g(G_j)) \oplus G_j \\ &= P_j \oplus g(G_j) \\ &= F_{j-1}. \end{aligned}$$

Hence $G'_{j+1} = d_K(F'_{j+1}) = d_K(F_{j-1}) = G_{j-1}$. Finally, we have

$$P'_{j+1} = G'_{j+1} \oplus F'_j = G_{j-1} \oplus F_j = C_j \oplus G_{j-1} \oplus g(G_{j-1}),$$

although the precise value of P'_{j+1} is unimportant. The result follows trivially. $\square$

Of course, the degree to which Theorem 2 is likely to enable a forgery attack depends very much on the properties of the function g. However, we have the following simple result for the function g used in EPBC.

Lemma 8. *Suppose g is as defined for EPBC, and (using the notation of Lemma 4) suppose also that $g(L||R) = L'||R'$. Then:*

(i) For all inputs $L||R$, we have $L \oplus L' = R \oplus R'$;
(ii) If $L||R$ is chosen at random, then each bit of $L \oplus L'$ is equal to 1 with probability 0.25.

Proof. Suppose ℓ is a bit in L, and r is the corresponding bit in R. Suppose also that (ℓ', r') are the bits in the same positions in $L'||R'$. Then

$$\ell' = (\ell \vee r) \oplus \ell = \neg \ell \wedge r.$$

Also

$$r' = (\ell \wedge r) \oplus r = \neg \ell \wedge r.$$

Claim (i) follows immediately, and claim (ii) follows from observing that $\neg \ell \wedge r = 1$ if and only if $r = 1$ and $\ell = 0$. $\square$

From Theorem 2, we can construct a possible forgery by guessing the value of $G_j \oplus g(G_j)$. If g is as defined for EPBC, then, from Lemma 8(i), we simply need to guess the first $n/2$ bits of $G_j \oplus g(G_j)$. Moreover, if we restrict our guesses for this 'first half' to $n/2$-bit strings containing at most $n/8$ ones (where we assume that n is a multiple of 8), then from Lemma 8(ii) we will have a better than evens chance of making a correct guess. The number of such strings is simply:

$$\sum_{i=0}^{n/8} \binom{n/2}{i}.$$

There are many ways of estimating this sum, but the following well known result is helpful.

Lemma 9. *Suppose $m \geq 1$ and $0 \leq k < m/2$. Then*

$$\sum_{i=0}^{k} \binom{m}{i} < \binom{m}{k} \frac{m-k+1}{m-2k+1}.$$

If $n = 64$ or $n = 128$ then the above sum is $1.50 \times 10^7 \simeq 2^{23.8}$ or $7.13 \times 10^{14} \simeq 2^{49.3}$, respectively. That is, for $n = 64$, after $2^{23.8}$ trials, there is a good chance one fake message will pass the integrity check, and for $n = 128$, $2^{49.3}$ trials will suffice.

Of course, these are large numbers, but they are significantly less than the certificational attack with complexity $2^{n/2}$ described in Sect. 6.1.

6.3   Issues with the Use of Initialisation Vectors (IVs)

We next show how to construct a forgery in any scheme of the type shown in Fig. 2 if the IVs (i.e. F_0 and G_0) are not different for every encrypted message and g is linear.

Before discussing the attack we briefly recap what the authors of the three schemes considered here say about the choice of IVs.

-   In the paper introducing PES-PCBC, [15], there is no mention of how F_0 and G_0 are chosen—indeed, the need for them to be selected does not even appear to be mentioned. However, in the subsequent paper introducing EPBC [16], which also points out an attack on PES-PCBC, it is stated that the 'initial values of F_{i-1} and G_{i-1} are distinct, secret initialisation vectors'.
-   In the paper introducing EPBC, exactly the same statement, i.e. that the 'initial values of F_{i-1} and G_{i-1} are distinct, secret initialisation vectors' is made twice, with no further guidance.
-   In the IOBC paper [10], the issue is discussed in slightly greater detail. It is stated that it 'is a design requirement for IOBC that the initialising vectors ... shall be changed for each encrypted message'.

Of course, changing the values of F_0 and G_0 for each encrypted message, as required for IOBC, is clearly good practice. Indeed, if the same values are used to encrypt two messages which contain the same initial plaintext block, then the resulting ciphertexts will share the same ciphertext block. That is, the mode would leak information about plaintext, which is clearly a highly undesirable property for any mode of operation intended to provide confidentiality. Nonetheless, the designers of EPBC and PES-PCBC did not impose any requirement for the values to be changed.

We can state the following result, which is essentially a special case of Lemma 1, and applies to all modes adhering to the design of Fig. 2 and for which g is linear (as is the case for IOBC and, trivially, PES-PCBC). In such a case, as observed in [9], the distributivity property $g(X \oplus Y) = g(X) \oplus g(Y)$ for any X and Y holds.

Lemma 10. *Suppose $C_1, C_2, \ldots, C_t$ and $C'_1, C'_2, \ldots, C'_{t'}$ are encrypted versions of the plaintext sequences $P_1, P_2, \ldots, P_t$ and $P'_1, P'_2, \ldots, P'_{t'}$, respectively, where the method of encryption is as shown in Fig. 2. Suppose also that the two messages are encrypted using identical IVs, i.e. $F_0 = F'_0$ and $G_0 = G'_0$.*

If the ciphertext

$$C_1^*, C_2^*, \ldots, C_t^* = C'_1, C'_2, C_3 \oplus g(C_1 \oplus C'_1 \oplus P_2 \oplus P'_2), C_4, \ldots, C_t$$

is submitted for IOBC decryption (where $1 < u$ and $1 < v < t$, and G_{v-1} and G'_{u-1} are values computed during the encryption of the respective sequences of blocks), then the resulting sequence of plaintext blocks $P_1^*, P_2^*, \ldots, P_t^*$ will be equal to

$$P'_1, P'_2, P_3 \oplus F'_2 \oplus F_2, P_4, P_5, \ldots, P_t.$$

Proof. First observe that, by definition, we know that

$$G_2 \oplus g(G_0) = P_2 \oplus C_1, \quad \text{and} \quad G'_2 \oplus g(G'_0) = P'_2 \oplus C'_1.$$

Hence, since we assume that $G_0 = G'_0$, we immediately have:

$$G_2 \oplus G'_2 = C_1 \oplus C'_1 \oplus P_2 \oplus P'_2,$$

and thus (using the distributive property of g):

$$g(G_2) \oplus g(G'_2) = g(C_1 \oplus C'_1 \oplus P_2 \oplus P'_2).$$

The result follows from Lemma 1, setting $u = v = 3$.   □

Thus if two ciphertexts are encrypted using the same IV, and a single plaintext block is known for each message, then a forgery can be constructed. Observe that this attack can be extended using Lemma 2(ii).

It may well be the case that other forgery strategies can be devised building on the distributive property when g is linear, but we do not explore this further here.

7   Other Related Modes

We conclude this discussion of modes by briefly mentioning two further modes 'from the same stable'.

There was a gap of some 16 years before the first of these two additional schemes was made public—IOC (short for *Input and Output Chaining*) was made public by Recacha in 2013 [11]. IOC is clearly closely related to IOBC and EPBC, but was designed to avoid the known issues with these schemes. IOC was made public at a time when there was a renewed interest in the area, at least partly prompted by a NIST initiative on lightweight cryptography[2]. A

---

[2] As discussed at https://csrc.nist.gov/Projects/Lightweight-Cryptography, NIST began investigating cryptography for constrained environments in 2013, and one of the goals was to find lightweight methods for authenticated encryption.

slightly revised version was made public in early 2014, [14]. Cryptanalyses of both versions of the scheme first appeared in 2014 [1].

The second additional scheme, known as ++AE, is a further evolution of the previous schemes, again designed with the intention of addressing the known issues. Like IOC, this scheme exists in two slightly different versions, v1.0 [12] and v1.1 [13], both promulgated in 2014. Both versions were cryptanalysed in a pair of papers published in 2016 and 2018 [4,5].

8   Summary and Conclusions

In this paper we have re-examined the security of three closely related block cipher modes of operation designed to provide authenticated encryption, namely PES-PCBC, IOBC and EPBC. Whilst cryptanalysis of all three schemes has previously been published, the attack on EPBC has subsequently been shown to be incorrect and hence until now no effective attack was known against this mode.

In this paper we have both elaborated on and enhanced existing cryptanalysis, and we have also demonstrated new attacks which show that none of the three schemes can be considered secure. The main findings of the paper are as follows.

- There exists a forgery attack on any scheme of the type shown in Fig. 2 which requires of the order of $2^{n/2}$ chosen plaintexts—see Sect. 6.1.
- It was already known (see [16]) that simple forgeries against PES-PCBC could be devised requiring a single ciphertext message and two known plaintext blocks for this ciphertext—a variant of this attack was described (see Sect. 3.2 requiring only a single known plaintext block. Another simple forgery attack against PES-PCBC was described in Sect. 6.3, which is realisable if IVs are ever re-used.
- Di et al. [2] showed that the only known attack on EPBC mode did not work. However, in Sect. 6.2 we described a new attack strategy which yields a successful forgery with high probability with significantly fewer than $2^{n/2}$ trials (e.g. $2^{23.8}$ trials for $n = 64$).
- Forgery attacks on IOBC were already known (see [9]). A further simple forgery attack was described in Sect. 6.3, which is realisable if IVs are ever re-used (although it is important to note that IV reuse is specifically prohibited in [10]).

Existing cryptanalysis, when combined with the new attacks described in this paper, suggests very strongly than none of the three modes considered in this paper are sufficiently robust against forgery attacks to be used in practice.

Dedication

This paper is dedicated to the memory of Ed Dawson.

References

1. Bottinelli, P., Reyhanitabar, R., Vaudenay, S.: Breaking the IOC authenticated encryption mode. In: Pointcheval, D., Vergnaud, D. (eds.) Progress in Cryptology — AFRICACRYPT 2014 — 7th International Conference on Cryptology in Africa, Marrakesh, Morocco, May 28–30, 2014. Proceedings. Lecture Notes in Computer Science, vol. 8469, pp. 126–135. Springer (2014). https://doi.org/10.1007/978-3-319-06734-6_8, https://doi.org/10.1007/978-3-319-06734-6_8

2. Di, B., Simpson, L., Bartlett, H., Dawson, E., Wong, K.K.: Correcting flaws in Mitchell's analysis of EPBC. In: Welch, I., Yi, X. (eds.) 13th Australasian Information Security Conference, AISC 2015, Sydney, Australia, January 2015. CRPIT, vol. 161, pp. 57–60. Australian Computer Society (2015). http://crpit.scem.westernsydney.edu.au/abstracts/CRPITV161Di.html

3. Kohl, J.T.: The use of Encryption in Kerberos for Network Authentication. In: Brassard, G. (ed.) CRYPTO 1989. LNCS, vol. 435, pp. 35–43. Springer, New York (1990). https://doi.org/10.1007/0-387-34805-0_5

4. Mahri, H.Q.A., Simpson, L., Bartlett, H., Dawson, E., Wong, K.K.: A fundamental flaw in the ++AE authenticated encryption mode. J. Math. Cryptol. **12**(1), 37–42 (2018). https://doi.org/10.1515/JMC-2016-0037

5. Mahri, H.Q.A., Simpson, L.R., Bartlett, H., Dawson, E., Wong, K.K.: Forgery attacks on ++AE authenticated encryption mode. In: ACSW '16: Proceedings of the Australasian Computer Science Week Multiconference, Canberra, Australia, February 2–5, 2016, pp. 1–9. ACM (2016). https://doi.org/10.1145/2843043.2843355

6. Menezes, A.J., van Oorschot, P.C., Vanstone, S.A.: Handbook of Applied Cryptography. CRC Press, Boca Raton (1997)

7. Mitchell, C.J.: Cryptanalysis of two variants of PCBC mode when used for message integrity. In: Boyd, C., González Nieto, J.M. (eds.) ACISP 2005. LNCS, vol. 3574, pp. 560–571. Springer, Heidelberg (2005). https://doi.org/10.1007/11506157_47

8. Mitchell, C.J.: Cryptanalysis of the EPBC authenticated encryption mode. In: Galbraith, S.D. (ed.) Cryptography and Coding, 11th IMA International Conference, Cirencester, UK, December 18–20, 2007, Proceedings. Lecture Notes in Computer Science, vol. 4887, pp. 118–128. Springer-Verlag, Berlin (2007)

9. Mitchell, C.J.: Analysing the IOBC authenticated encryption mode. In: Boyd, C., Simpson, L. (eds.) Information Security and Privacy — 18th Australasian Conference, ACISP 2013, Brisbane, Australia, July 1–3, 2013. Proceedings. Lecture Notes in Computer Science, vol. 7959, pp. 1–12. Springer (2013). https://doi.org/10.1007/978-3-642-39059-3_1

10. Recacha, F.: IOBC: Un nuevo modo de encadenamiento para cifrado en bloque. In: Proceedings: IV Reunion Espanola de Criptologia, Valladolid, September 1996, pp. 85–92 (1996)

11. Recacha, F.: IOC: The most lightweight authenticated encryption mode? (March 2013). https://csrc.nist.rip/groups/ST/toolkit/BCM/documents/proposedmodes/ioc/ioc-spec.pdf

12. Recacha, F.: ++AE v1.0 (March 2014). https://competitions.cr.yp.to/round1/aev10.pdf

13. Recacha, F.: ++AE v1.1 (April 2014). https://competitions.cr.yp.to/round1/aev11.pdf

14. Recacha, F.: Input output chaining (IOC) AE mode revisited (January 2014). https://inputoutputblockchaining.blogspot.com/

15. Zuquete, A., Guedes, P.: Transparent authentication and confidentiality for stream sockets. IEEE Micro **16**(3), 34–41 (May/June 1996)
16. Zuquete, A., Guedes, P.: Efficient error-propagating block chaining. In: Darnell, M. (ed.) Cryptography and Coding, 6th IMA International Conference, Cirencester, UK, December 17–19, 1997, Proceedings, pp. 323–334. No. 1355 in Lecture Notes in Computer Science, Springer-Verlag, Berlin (1997)

Public Key Cryptography

p261: A Karatsuba-Friendly Prime for Fast Elliptic Curve Arithmetic

Berkan Egrice[1] and Huseyin Hisil[2]

[1] Paylocity, Plzen, Czechia
begrice@paylocity.com
[2] University of Wollongong, Wollongong, Australia
hhisil@uow.edu.au

Abstract. We point to the cryptographic significance of the overlooked prime $p261 = 2^{261} - 2^{131} - 1$. We explain our motivation behind searching for such a prime. We present cryptographically secure elliptic curves over $GF(p261)$. We provide our speed oriented implementation of variable-base variable-scalar elliptic curve scalar multiplication using the Montgomery ladder. In this setting, a single scalar multiplication implemented with AVX2 instructions takes 85738 cycles on a Skylake 6500U processor.

1 Elliptic Curves and Cryptography

Cryptography is the science of securing information. Typical applications of modern cryptography are encryption/decryption of data, signing/verification of documents, checking the integrity of files, and secret sharing between parties. Higher level demands such as crypto currencies, e-voting, group signatures, smart contracts are satisfied by cryptographic protocols which are built upon such applications.

The use of elliptic curves in cryptographic applications was independently proposed by Miller [24] and Koblitz [20]. Since then, there has been a vast amount of development in elliptic curve cryptography (ECC). Today, elliptic curves are an indispensable component of secure communication and financial activities. For instance, elliptic curves are employed in TLS (Transport Layer Security) 1.3[1] which is supported by modern web browsers. Two important crypto-suits in TLS 1.3 are ECDHE[2]-ECDSA[3] and ECDHE-EdDSA[4]; both crypto-suits providing secure secret sharing and signing functionality with forward secrecy [13].

Many other applications of elliptic curves exist in the relevant literature. In particular, elliptic curves are central to Lenstra's integer factorization algorithm [22], Goldwasser & Kilian's primality proving algorithm [12], isogeny based post-quantum cryptosystems [18], and identity base cryptography with pairings [5,33].

---

[1] IETF RFC 8446, https://datatracker.ietf.org/doc/html/rfc8446 .

[2] NIST SP 800-56A, Rev. 3, https://csrc.nist.gov/publications/detail/sp/800-56a/rev-3/final .

[3] NIST FIPS 186-4, https://csrc.nist.gov/publications/detail/fips/186/4/final .

[4] IETF RFC 8032, https://datatracker.ietf.org/doc/html/rfc8032 .

© The Author(s), under exclusive license to Springer Nature Switzerland AG 2025
C. Boyd et al. (Eds.): Ed Dawson Festschrift 2024, LNCS 15600, pp. 109–123, 2025.
https://doi.org/10.1007/978-3-031-83490-5_6

In this work, we outline the cryptographic significance of the prime $2^{261} - 2^{131} - 1$. The structure of this prime allows application of fast Karatsuba multiplication and modular reduction. As a consequence, we show that this prime leads to extremely fast arithmetic for elliptic curve operations on AVX2 supported processors.

1.1   Elliptic Curves and the Group Law

We start with preliminary information on elliptic curves. Let k be a field. For algorithms presented in this work, we assume that $\text{char}(k) > 3$. For practical and efficient implementations on computers, we always require k to be a finite field with q elements.

An elliptic curve over k is algebraic smooth projective curve of genus one with a k-rational point, [34, Chapter III]. Such a curve can always be represented by the set of points satisfying the equation over k given in short Weierstrass form

$$E : y^2 = x^3 + a_4 x + a_6$$

for some $a_4, a_6 \in k$ with $\Delta = -16(4a_4^3 + 27a_6^2) \neq 0$, together with the inclusion of the point at infinity denoted ∞. The function field of E is written in the form $k(E)$. We denote the set of k-rational points by $E(k)$. We denote the cardinality of $E(k)$ by $\#E(k)$ which satisfies the Hasse bound

$$|\#E(k) - (q + 1)| \leq 2\sqrt{q}.$$

The points (x, y) form a commutative group with the selection of a distinguished point $\mathcal{O}$ as the identity, under an explicitly defined additive group law. E is usually denoted $(E, \mathcal{O})$ in order to emphasize the unique identity. It is a typical choice for Weierstrass form to fix $\mathcal{O} = \infty$. Two points P and Q on (E, ∞) can be added to form a third point $R = P + Q$ on (E, ∞). If P is not equal to ∞, then P is identified uniquely with its coordinates x_P, y_P and we write $P = (x_P, y_P)$. The negative of (x_P, y_P) is $(x_P, -y_P)$.

The addition law given explicitly in Algorithm 1 has several logical checks due to exceptional cases arising from the denominators $2y_P$ and $x_P - x_Q$. These logical checks can be eliminated

- if $E(k)$ does not have a point of order two, we embed E in the projective space $\mathbb{P}^2$, and use the complete formulas in [31], see also [7,21].
- if we the choice of a_4 and a_6 allows to work on a curve which is birationally equivalent over k to E, having complete point addition formulas, see [3,4,10,17].

Even in such scenarios, the coordinates x and y (or maybe more coordinates) are involved in computations.

Algorithm 1: Addition for short Weierstrass form

---

input : $P, Q \in E(k)$

output: $P + Q \in E(k)$

if $P = \infty$ then return Q

else if $Q = \infty$ then return P

else if $x_P = x_Q$ then

    if $y_P \neq y_Q$ then return ∞

    else if $y_P = 0$ then return ∞

    else

        $\lambda \leftarrow (3x_P^2 + a_4)/(2y_P)$

        $x_R \leftarrow \lambda^2 - 2x_P$

        $y_R \leftarrow \lambda(x_P - x_R) - y_P$

        return (x_R, y_R)

    end

else

    $\lambda \leftarrow (y_P - y_Q)/(x_P - x_Q)$

    $x_R \leftarrow \lambda^2 - x_P - x_Q$

    $y_R \leftarrow \lambda(x_P - x_R) - y_P$

    return (x_R, y_R)

end

One can work alternatively on $(E, \infty)/\{\pm 1\}$ which eliminates the y coordinate from computations. $(E, \infty)/\{\pm 1\}$ is called the x-line of E. The following addition and doubling formulas for $(E, \infty)/\{\pm 1\}$ are derived in [8]:

$$x([2]P) = \frac{(x_P^2 - a_4)^2 - 8a_6 x_P}{4(x_P^3 + a x_P + a_6)}, \tag{1}$$

$$x(P + Q)x(P - Q) = \frac{(x_P x_Q - a_4)^2 - 4a_6(x_P + x_Q)}{(x_P - x_Q)^2}. \tag{2}$$

Both (1) and (2) can be put into a more symmetric form for some elliptic curves over k. For instance, Gaudry and Lubicz [11, Section 6.2] put forward efficient formulas on Kummer lines associated to a Legendre form elliptic curve. Karati and Sarkar [19] provided the "squared" version of the formulas in [11, Section 6.2], namely squared Kummer lines, analogous its genus 2 counterpart in Bernstein's talk[5]. Hisil and Renes [16] showed that the squared Kummer line is the x-line of a Montgomery curve [26] translated by a point of order two. Below, we provide the connection between a squared Kummer line and a short Weierstrass curve to keep the text concise and self-contained. Now, if

---

[5] "Elliptic vs. hyperelliptic, part I". Talk at ECC, 2006.
https://cr.yp.to/talks/2006.09.20/slides.pdf .

$$a_4 = 27\left(1 - \frac{a^4}{b^4} - \frac{b^4}{a^4}\right)$$

and

$$a_6 = 27\left(\frac{a^2}{b^2} + \frac{b^2}{a^2}\right)\left(\frac{a^2}{b^2} - \frac{2b^2}{a^2}\right)\left(\frac{b^2}{a^2} - \frac{2a^2}{b^2}\right)$$

for some $a^2, b^2 \in k$ with $a^2 b^2 (a^2 - b^2) \neq 0$, then we can define the isomorphism γ over k,

$$\gamma : (E, \infty) \to (M, \mathcal{O}),$$

$$(x, y) \mapsto \left(3\frac{2(a^2 x - b^2) - \dfrac{b^6 x - a^6}{a^2 b^2}}{b^2 x - a^2}, \pm\frac{27(b^4 - a^4)}{(b^2 x - a^2)^2}y\right)$$

where $\mathcal{O} = (a^2/b^2, 0)$ and M is defined in the form

$$M : y^2 = x^3 + \left(-\frac{a^2}{b^2} - \frac{b^2}{a^2}\right)x^2 + x.$$

$(M, \mathcal{O})$ is a Montgomery curve with the extra condition of having three rational points of order two, namely the points $(0, 0)$, $(b^2/a^2, 0)$, and ∞, see [16]. The sign choice in the second coordinate of γ does not affect our computations since we work on the x-line. We note that a^2 and b^2 are required to be in k and a, b are permitted to be defined in an extension of k. The following Magma[6] script proves that γ is stated correctly.

```
k<a,b>:=RationalFunctionField(Rationals(),2); AS<x,y>:=AffineSpace(k,2);
a4:=27*(1-a^4/b^4-b^4/a^4);
a6:=27*(a^2/b^2+b^2/a^2)*(a^2/b^2-2*b^2/a^2)*(b^2/a^2-2*a^2/b^2);
K:=ProjectiveClosure(Curve(AS,[y^2-(x^3+(-a^2/b^2-b^2/a^2)*x^2+x)]));
E1,KtoE1:=EllipticCurve(K,K![a^2/b^2,0,1]); E1toK:=Inverse(KtoE1);
W:=ProjectiveClosure(Curve(AS,[y^2-(x^3+a4*x+a6)]));
E2,WtoE2:=EllipticCurve(W,W![0,1,0]); E2toW:=Inverse(WtoE2);
res,E1toE2:=IsIsomorphic(E1,E2); assert res; E2toE1:=Inverse(E1toE2);
KtoW:=KtoE1*E1toE2*E2toW; WtoK:=WtoE2*E2toE1*E1toK;
KtoW eq map<K->W|[3*(2*(a^2*x-b^2)-(b^6*x-a^6)/(a^2*b^2))/(b^2*x-a^2),
               +27*y*(b^4-a^4)/(b^2*x-a^2)^2,1]> or
KtoW eq map<K->W|[3*(2*(a^2*x-b^2)-(b^6*x-a^6)/(a^2*b^2))/(b^2*x-a^2),
               -27*y*(b^4-a^4)/(b^2*x-a^2)^2,1]>;
WtoK*KtoW eq IdentityMap(W); KtoW*WtoK eq IdentityMap(K);
```

The x-only doubling and addition formulas for points P and Q on $(M, \mathcal{O})/\{\pm 1\}$ then reads

---

[6] The script can be run on the free-to-use online Magma. http://magma.maths.usyd.edu.au/calc/.

$$x([2]P) = \frac{b^2}{a^2} \times \left(\frac{\dfrac{(x_P+1)^2}{(x_P-1)^2} + \dfrac{a^2+b^2}{a^2-b^2}}{\dfrac{(x_P+1)^2}{(x_P-1)^2} - \dfrac{a^2+b^2}{a^2-b^2}} \right)^2, \tag{3}$$

$$x(P+Q) \times x(P-Q) = \left(\frac{\dfrac{(x_P+1)(x_Q+1)}{(x_P-1)(x_Q-1)} + \dfrac{a^2+b^2}{a^2-b^2}}{\dfrac{(x_P+1)(x_Q+1)}{(x_P-1)(x_Q-1)} - \dfrac{a^2+b^2}{a^2-b^2}} \right)^2. \tag{4}$$

The projective version of these formulas are presented in [19, Section 2.4]. It is readily checked that (3) is a special case of (4). At the first glance, formulas (3) and (4) may look overly involved. However, there are several common subexpressions shared in computations. Moreover, these formulas are known to be 4-way SIMD-friendly, see [19]. These formulas are preferred in speed recording implementations with AVX2 instruction set, see [28]. Similarly, we provide our implementation in Sect. 3 using a squared Kummer-line over $GF(2^{261} - 2^{131} - 1)$ with "small" constants a^2, b^2, $a^2 + b^2$, and $a^2 - b^2$.

1.2   Scalar Multiplication

A scalar multiple of a point P is defined as

$$R = [m]P = \underbrace{P + P + \ldots + P}_{m \text{ times}}.$$

Finding m when only P and R are known is called the elliptic curve discrete logarithm problem (ECDLP) which is believed to be intractable for carefully selected k, a_4, a_6, P, and R. On the other hand, finding R when only m and P are known is efficiently computable. Algorithm 2 is called the Montgomery ladder [26] which can be used to compute $[k]P$.

Algorithm 2: Left-to-right Montgomery ladder

---
input : $P \in E(k)$
input : $m = (m_{n-1}, \ldots, m_1, m_0)_2$
output: $[m]\mathrm{P}, [m+1]P$
$(Q, P) \leftarrow (\mathcal{O}, P)$
for $i = n - 1$ **to** 0 **by** -1 **do**
  if $m_i = 0$ **then** $(Q, P) \leftarrow ([2]Q, P + Q)$
  else $(Q, P) \leftarrow (P + Q, [2]P)$
end
return Q, P

We use the formulas (3) and (4) in the place of $(P, Q) \leftarrow ([2]P, P + Q)$ in Algorithm 2. Therefore, the inputs are m and x_P while the output is $x_{[m]P}$.

Algorithm 2 can be implemented in a way to yield a constant running time and consequently become resistant to side channel attacks, see [2].

Following López and Dahab's construction in [23] (also see [30]), Algorithm 2 can be used to compute not only $x_{[m]P}$ but also $x_{[m+1]P}$. So, if $P = (x_1, y_1)$ then

$$
2y_1 y_{[m]P} = (x_1 x_{[m]P} + 1)(x_1 + x_{[m]P}) - \frac{a^2}{b^2}(x_1 + x_{[m]P})^2 +
$$
$$
\left(\frac{a^2}{b^2} - \frac{b^2}{a^2} \right) \left(2x_1 x_{[m]P} + \frac{a^2 (x_1 - x_{[m]P})^2}{a^2 - b^2 x_{[m+1]P}} \right). \tag{5}
$$

Now, $y_{[m]P}$ can be computed by dividing both sides of the equality (5) by $2y_1$. This technique is known as y-coordinate recovery and it is widely used for the elliptic curve based digital signature algorithms. Also see [32] for a digital signature algorithm which does not require y-coordinate recovery. In this way, the x-only Montgomery ladder is readily extended to a scalar multiplication algorithm on $E(k)$ that inputs P and m and then outputs $[m]P$, see [23].

The formula (5) can be verified using a sequential execution of the previous and the following Magma [6] scripts. The following script is the continuation of the previous one and assumes $x_1 = \texttt{x1}$, $y_1 = \texttt{y1}$, $x_{[m]P} = \texttt{xm}$, $y_{[m]P} = \texttt{yk}$, and $x_{[m+1]P} = \texttt{xmplusone}$. The script composes $(\gamma^{-1}, \gamma^{-1}) \in k(M) \times k(M)$ with the addition morphism given in Algorithm 1, and then makes a final composition with γ.

```
SKK<x1,y1,xm,ym>:=AffineSpace(k,4); KK:=Scheme(SKK,[
    y1^2-(x1^3+(-a^2/b^2-b^2/a^2)*x1^2+x1),
    ym^2-(xm^3+(-a^2/b^2-b^2/a^2)*xm^2+xm)]);
SWW<u1,v1,u2,v2>:=AffineSpace(k,4); WW:=Scheme(SWW,[
    v1^2-(u1^3+a4*u1+a6), v2^2-(u2^3+a4*u2+a6)]);
seqKtoW:=DefiningPolynomials(KtoW);
KKtoWW:=map<KK->WW|[Evaluate(seqKtoW[1]/seqKtoW[3],[x1,y1,1]),
                    Evaluate(seqKtoW[2]/seqKtoW[3],[x1,y1,1]),
                    Evaluate(seqKtoW[1]/seqKtoW[3],[xm,ym,1]),
                    Evaluate(seqKtoW[2]/seqKtoW[3],[xm,ym,1])]>;
L:=(v2-v1)/(u2-u1); u3:=L^2-u1-u2; v3:=L*(u1-u3)-v1;
addW:=map<WW->W|[u3,v3,1]>; addK:=KKtoWW*addW*WtoK;
xmplusone:=DefiningPolynomials(addK)[1]/DefiningPolynomials(addK)[3];
0 eq RingOfFractions(CoordinateRing(KK))!(2*y1*ym-(
    (x1*xm+1)*(x1+xm)-(a^2/b^2)*(x1+xm)^2+
    (a^2/b^2-b^2/a^2)*(2*x1*xm+a^2*(x1-xm)^2/(a^2-b^2*xmplusone))
));
```

2   The Karatsuba-Friendly Prime p261

Fast integer arithmetic plays an important role in real-world applications of asymmetric cryptography. The performance of most popular cryptosystems such as RSA and ECC is centered around how fast we can multiply integers and reduce the product modulo some fixed integer. For arbitrary modulus one can use the long division algorithm which makes access to a built-in division instruction. However, using the division instruction usually leads to poor performance and non-constant running time. A faster choice is to use a general purpose modular arithmetic technique such as Barrett [1] or Montgomery [25] reduction.

ECC applications can further benefit from special prime modulus. These primes allows extremely fast reduction. The fastest primes that facilitate 128-bit conjectured security level in ECC implementations are listed in Table 1.

Table 1. List of fastest primes targeting 128-bit security level.

Name	Prime	Ref.
p2519	$2^{251} - 9$	[19]
p25519	$2^{255} - 19$	[2]
p2663	$2^{266} - 3$	[19]

Let f and g be integers written in radix 2^ℓ in the form $f_0 + 2^\ell f_1$ and $g_0 + 2^\ell g_1$ for some non-negative integer ℓ, respectively. The classic Karatsuba method for multiplying integers modulo a prime of the form $2^{2\ell} - t$ is given as

$$fg \equiv (A + tB) + 2^\ell \cdot (C - A - B) \quad (\text{mod } 2^{2\ell} - t)$$

where $A = f_0 g_0$, $B = f_1 g_1$, and $C = (f_0 + f_1)(g_0 + g_1)$. Such a method requires one multiplication by t and several linear operations. In comparison, the goldilock prime $p_{448} = 2^{448} - 2^{224} - 1$ has a structure which eliminates the multiplication by t and one linear operation. In particular, write f and g in the form $f_0 + 2^{224} f_1$ and $g_0 + 2^{224} g_1$, respectively. Hamburg [14] showed that

$$fg \equiv (A + B) + 2^{224} \cdot (C - A) \quad (\text{mod } p_{448}).$$

Building on this observation, one may question whether it is possible to do the same at the conjectured 128-bit security level. To achieve such a goal, one needs a prime of the form $2^{2\ell} - 2^\ell - t$ with $t = 1$ and 2ℓ near 256. However, no such prime exist for $216 < 2\ell < 322$. One can pick $t \neq 1$ as an alternative. For instance, $2\ell = 256$ and $t = 79$ gives a prime. But in such a situation, one needs to bear the cost of several multiplications by 79. We note that the popular prime $2^{255} - 19$ requires several multiplications by 19 in a similar way. To this end, we simply cannot find a Karatsuba-friendly prime with $t = 1$ in the aforementioned scenario.

We now explain our approach to the problem and present our solution. We let the prime to be of the form $r \cdot 2^{2\ell} - s \cdot 2^\ell - t$ for extremely small integers r, s and t. Now, the modular multiplication formulas read

$$fg \equiv (A + tB/r) + 2^\ell \cdot ((C - A - B) + sB/r) \quad (\text{mod } r \cdot 2^{2\ell} - s \cdot 2^\ell - t).$$

One obstacle in such a calculation is that division by r's are unlikely to be exact. To solve this problem we scale the congruence by r which gives

$$rfg \equiv (rA + tB) + 2^\ell \cdot (r(C - A - B) + sB) \quad (\text{mod } r \cdot 2^{2\ell} - s \cdot 2^\ell - t).$$

We arrived at a formula which produces rfg but not fg. This is of no problem for elliptic curve arithmetic since the representation of points in homogeneous projective coordinates allows non-zero scaling. For instance, a point $(X : Z)$ in $\mathbb{P}$ can also be represented by $(rX : rZ)$ with $r \neq 0$.

Now, we can search for primes satisfying this form. Since we target efficiency, it is reasonable to make the following additional assumptions: $r = s = 2$ and $t = 1$. The formula then simplifies to

$$2fg \equiv (2A + B) + 2^{\ell} \cdot (2C - 2A) \pmod{2 \cdot 2^{2\ell} - 2 \cdot 2^{\ell} - 1}. \tag{6}$$

At this stage, the question is whether there exist a prime of this form for 2ℓ close to 256. The answer is yes: $\ell = 130$ gives the Montgomery-friendly prime

$$\mathtt{p261} = 2^{261} - 2^{131} - 1.$$

The overhead of computing $2A$ and $2C$ are minor in comparison with the overhead of several multiplications by small constants. We emphasize that since $r = s$, we also eliminated an extra linear operation which is not possible for Karatsuba implementations of multiplication modulo primes of the form $2^{\alpha} - t$. In fact, even more optimizations are possible, which are not obvious at this level. See Sect. 3 for further details.

We investigated cryptographically secure elliptic curves over $GF(\mathtt{p261})$ in different elliptic curve forms through a rigid search. All of the proposed curves are twist-secure and have large CM discriminants. The numbers given in hexadecimal form are prime. The dash character is used to describe the non-trivial quadratic twists of the defined curve.

$$\mathcal{W}_{16417} \ : \ y^2 = x^3 - 3x + 16417 \quad \text{(Weierstrass)}$$
$$\#\mathcal{W}_{16417} = \mathtt{1FFFFFFFFFFFFFFFFFFFFFFFFFFFFFFFFF\backslash}$$
$$\mathtt{674A29D591C4954F6E0E4B49E39D45597}$$
$$\#\mathcal{W}'_{16417} = \mathtt{1FFFFFFFFFFFFFFFFFFFFFFFFFFFFFFFFF\backslash}$$
$$\mathtt{98B5D62A6E3B6AB091F1B4B61C62BAA69}$$

$$\mathcal{M}_{4318} \ : \ y^2 = x^3 + 4318x^2 + x \quad \text{(Montgomery)}$$
$$\#\mathcal{M}_{4318} = 4 \times \mathtt{7FFFFFFFFFFFFFFFFFFFFFFFFFFFFFFFF\backslash}$$
$$\mathtt{CD18A213CBB39E6C7CECB70A57CD1B49B}$$
$$\#\mathcal{M}'_{4318} = 4 \times \mathtt{7FFFFFFFFFFFFFFFFFFFFFFFFFFFFFFFF\backslash}$$
$$\mathtt{F2E75DEC344C6193831348F5A832E4B65}$$

$$\mathcal{K}_{281,271} : \; y^2 = x^3 + \left(-\frac{281}{271} - \frac{271}{281} \right) x^2 + x \quad \text{(Kummer)}$$

$$\#\mathcal{K}_{281,271} = 16 \times \texttt{1FFFFFFFFFFFFFFFFFFFFFFFFFFFFFFFFFF}\backslash$$
$$\texttt{8CB7C5196B18C220B76EA07799D19253}$$

$$\#\mathcal{K}'_{281,271} = 16 \times \texttt{1FFFFFFFFFFFFFFFFFFFFFFFFFFFFFFFFFF}\backslash$$
$$\texttt{73483AE694E73DDF48915F88662E6DAD}$$

$$(B^2 \colon A^2) = ((281 + 271) \colon (281 - 271)) = (276 \colon 5)$$

Some implementations use $A_{24} = (A - 2)/4$ instead of A. For the curve $\mathcal{M}_{4318}$, we have $A_{24} = (4318 - 2)/4 = 1079 = 13 \times 83$. We note that $\mathcal{M}_{4318}$ and $\mathcal{K}_{281,271}$ are not isomorphic over $\bar{k}$.

3 Implementation

There several different ways to carry out a modular multiplication. One classic approach is to compute the integer product fg with Karatsuba multiplication and then reduce the product modulo the prime. This approach is not able to benefit from the elimination of the linear operation explained in Sect. 2. Therefore, we closely follow the outline in therein.

10-limb representation. We provide implementation details in this part targeting $32 \times 32 \to 64$ bit multipliers and 64 bit adders without carry handling. The typical hardware platforms that suit this configuration are AVX, AVX2 and AVX-512. We set $k = 2^{26}$. We start by writing $f = f_0 + k^5 f_1$ where f_0 and f_1 are further specified in the form $f_0 = f_{00} + k f_{01} + k^2 f_{02} + k^3 f_{03} + k^4 f_{04}$ and $f_1 = f_{10} + k f_{11} + k^2 f_{12} + k^3 f_{13} + k^4 f_{14}$. Therefore, a field element is represented with 10 limbs. We note here that f_{14} accommodates the single bit that would reside in f_{15} in a standard radix 2^{26} representation.

Modular multiplication. We want to compute $2fg \bmod p$ for 10-limb integers f and g, see Sect. 2. First, we carry out the three integer multiplications $A = f_0 g_0$, $B = f_1 g_1$, $C = (f_0 + f_1)(g_0 + g_1)$. We use schoolbook multiplication algorithm where both A and B take $5 \times 5 = 25$ multiplications and 16 additions, and C takes $5 \times 5 = 25$ multiplications and $5 + 5 + 16 = 26$ additions. At this stage, each of A, B, and C are composed of 9 limbs where each limb can fit into 64 bits. We access these limbs with subscripts in the obvious way. E.g. A_0 is the least significant limb of A. Now, reducing $(2A + B) + 2^{130} \cdot (2C - 2A)$ modulo p261, the following the congruence is obtained:

$$
\begin{aligned}
2fg \equiv (\ & 2A_0 + B_0 + C_5 && - A_5 &&)\,k^0\ + \\
(\ & 2A_1 + B_1 + C_6 && - A_6 &&)\,k^1\ + \\
(\ & 2A_2 + B_2 + C_7 && - A_7 &&)\,k^2\ + \\
(\ & 2A_3 + B_3 + C_8 && - A_8 &&)\,k^3\ + \\
(\ & 2A_4 + B_4 && &&)\,k^4\ + \\
(\ & 2A_5 + B_5 + 2C_0 - 2A_0 + 2C_5 - 2A_5 &&)\,k^5\ + \\
(\ & 2A_6 + B_6 + 2C_1 - 2A_1 + 2C_6 - 2A_6 &&)\,k^6\ + \\
(\ & 2A_7 + B_7 + 2C_2 - 2A_2 + 2C_7 - 2A_7 &&)\,k^7\ + \\
(\ & 2A_8 + B_8 + 2C_3 - 2A_3 + 2C_8 - 2A_8 &&)\,k^8\ + \\
(\ & \qquad\quad + 2C_4 - 2A_4 + &&)\,k^9 \quad (\mathrm{mod}\ \mathrm{p261}).
\end{aligned}
$$

The congruence reflects a redundant reduction modulo p261. In addition to the linear simplification provided in (6), it is readily observed that several more operations can be removed. In particular, we delete the terms $2A_5$, $2A_6$, $2A_7$, $2A_8$, $-2A_5$, $-2A_6$, $-2A_7$, and $-2A_8$. The simplified formulas read as follows.

$$
\begin{aligned}
2fg \equiv (\ & B_0 + C_5 - A_5 + 2\,(&& A_0) &&)\,k^0\ + \\
(\ & B_1 + C_6 - A_6 + 2\,(&& A_1) &&)\,k^1\ + \\
(\ & B_2 + C_7 - A_7 + 2\,(&& A_2) &&)\,k^2\ + \\
(\ & B_3 + C_8 - A_8 + 2\,(&& A_3) &&)\,k^3\ + \\
(\ & B_4 \qquad\qquad\ + 2\,(&& A_4) &&)\,k^4\ + \\
(\ & B_5 \qquad\qquad\ + 2\,(&& C_5 + C_0 - A_0) &&)\,k^5\ + \\
(\ & B_6 \qquad\qquad\ + 2\,(&& C_6 + C_1 - A_1) &&)\,k^6\ + \\
(\ & B_7 \qquad\qquad\ + 2\,(&& C_7 + C_2 - A_2) &&)\,k^7\ + \\
(\ & B_8 \qquad\qquad\ + 2\,(&& C_8 + C_3 - A_3) &&)\,k^8\ + \\
(\ & \qquad\qquad\qquad + 2\,(&& C_4 - A_4) &&)\,k^9 \quad (\mathrm{mod}\ \mathrm{p261}).
\end{aligned}
$$

We note that all of the multiplications by 2 can be moved to the computation phase of A and C, which saves even more additions if $2f_0$, $2f_1$, $2f_2$, $2f_3$, $2f_4$, $2(f_0 + g_0)$, $2(f_1 + g_1)$, $2(f_2 + g_2)$, $2(f_3 + g_3)$, and $2(f_4 + g_4)$ are precomputed. Then, modular multiplication with a constant can be performed even faster.

The remaining single digit operations take only 27 additions and 9 subtractions. To this end, we use $3 \times 25 = 75$ multiplications and $16+16+26+27+9 = 94$ additions (or subtractions). In comparison, Chou [9] reported 109 multiplications and 95 additions for modular multiplication in $GF(2^{255} - 19)$. So, we do one less addition and save $109 - 75 = 34$ multiplications for p261; a prime having 6 more bits than p25519. Table 3 provides more detailed comparison of modular multiplication for different primes (Table 2 and 4).

Finally, we do the adjustments between the limbs in order to make them 26 bits, where we do not have any multiplications by small contants.

Modular Squaring. In a specialized squaring routine both A and B takes 15 multiplications, 6 additions, and 4 multiplications by 2. C takes 15 multiplications, 11 additions, and 4 multiplications by 2. These provide some saving in comparison with the modular multiplication routine. Furthermore, one can delay some of the multiplications by 2 until reduction which save even more time. More precisely, our implementation uses 45 multiplications, 52 additions, 13 subtractions,

Table 2. Comparison of modular multiplication of different primes without carries.

	p2519	p25519	p2663	p261
Multiplication (vpmuludq)	89	109	109	75
Addition (vpaddq)	80	95	90	85
Subtraction (vpsubq)	0	0	0	9
Data movement (vmovdqa)	11	20	27	18
Cycles (Skylake)	67.10	78.76	82.20	63.25

Table 3. Comparison of modular squaring of different primes without carries.

	p2519	p25519	p2663	p261
Multiplication (vpmuludq)	45	60	55	45
Shift left (vpsllq)	18	0	18	0
Addition (vpaddq)	55	53	62	54
Subtraction (vpsubq)	0	0	0	11
Data movement (vmovdqa)	3	10	12	12
Cycles (Skylake)	44.82	43.24	53.64	41.67

and 10 data movement intructions in total. We note that our implementation produces $2f^2$ rather than f^2, see Sect. 2.

4-way parallel Montgomery ladder. Our DH instances use the curves $\mathcal{M}_{4318}$ and $\mathcal{K}_{276,5}$. The implementation with $\mathcal{M}_{4318}$ is constructed with the 4-way ladder algorithm from [15], which makes no assumption on the underlying field, base points, and curve constants. An alternative algorithm is given in [27], which works fast if the squaring step can be efficiently distributed to SIMD channels. It is not clear how to perform such a distribution with p261 which requires frequently horizontal data transfers. The implementation with $\mathcal{K}_{276,5}$ is constructed with the 4-way ladder algorithm from [19].

Doing the Carries. Since the arithmetic of p261 does not involve multiplications with small constants, the limbs are allowed to accommodate some more bits before entering the modular multiplication (or squaring) routine. These extra bits comes from linear operations such as the Hadamard transform. We always delay doing the carries which occur only inside multiplication and squaring routines. This is a side benefit of using the prime p261. The costs regarding doing the carries is depicted in Table 3.

4   Results and Conclusion

There are several works in the literature which use these primes in order to provide speed recording instances of cryptographic primitives such as Diffie-

Hellmann Key Exchange. These implementations fix cryptographically interesting elliptic curves. A list of selected curves are provided in Table 5.

Table 4. Comparison of doing the carries.

	p2519	p25519	p2663	p261
Shift left (`vpsllq`)	2	2	0	0
Shift left (`vpsrlq`)	11	12	11	11
Addition (`vpaddq`)	12	14	13	13
Subtraction (`vpand`)	11	12	11	11
Cycles (Skylake)	17.48	16.14	24.75	16.94

Table 5. List of selected elliptic curves and DH Key Exchange cycle counts on Skylake 6500U processor.

Elliptic curve	Prime	Security	Cycles	Impl.Ref.
$\mathcal{K}_{683,18}$ [28]	p2663	132	105328	[28]
$\mathcal{M}_{486662}$ [2]	p25519	126	95437	[27]
$\mathcal{K}_{838,831}$ [28]	p25519	126.5	91151	[28]
$\mathcal{M}_{4698}$ [29]	p2519	124.5	87807	[29]
$\mathcal{K}_{276,5}$ (this work)	p261	128.5	85738	this work
$\mathcal{K}_{81,20}$ [19]	p2519	124.5	83424	[28]

Our $\mathcal{K}_{276,5}$ implementation does not set a new speed record but gets very competitive while providing the higher conjectured security then $\mathcal{K}_{81,20}$. This shows that the proposed prime p261 has potential to be used in applications of fast elliptic curve cryptography. We leave the problem of finding fast primes with $\ell > 130$ open.

Acknowledgements. Some parts of this work were completed when the first author was a student in Yasar University Graduate School and the second author was with Yasar University. We thank Craig Costello and Joseph Tonien for proofreading and corrections.

Appendix

The following Magma script verifies the multiplication formulas modulo p261.

```
k:=2^26; p261:=2^261-2^131-1;
_<f00,f01,f02,f03,f04,f10,f11,f12,f13,f14,\
  g00,g01,g02,g03,g04,g10,g11,g12,g13,g14>:=\
  PolynomialRing(GF(p261),20);
f0:=f00+f01*k+f02*k^2+f03*k^3+f04*k^4;
f1:=f10+f11*k+f12*k^2+f13*k^3+f14*k^4;
g0:=g00+g01*k+g02*k^2+g03*k^3+g04*k^4;
g1:=g10+g11*k+g12*k^2+g13*k^3+g14*k^4;
f:=f0+k^5*f1; g:=g0+k^5*g1;


//######## Multiplication starts ########//
f20:=f00+f10;  g20:=g00+g10;
f21:=f01+f11;  g21:=g01+g11;
f22:=f02+f12;  g22:=g02+g12;
f23:=f03+f13;  g23:=g03+g13;
f24:=f04+f14;  g24:=g04+g14;
A0:=f00*g00;
A1:=f00*g01+f01*g00;
A2:=f00*g02+f01*g01+f02*g00;
A3:=f00*g03+f01*g02+f02*g01+f03*g00;
A4:=f00*g04+f01*g03+f02*g02+f03*g01+f04*g00;
A5:=       f01*g04+f02*g03+f03*g02+f04*g01;
A6:=              f02*g04+f03*g03+f04*g02;
A7:=                     f03*g04+f04*g03;
A8:=                            f04*g04;
B0:=f10*g10;
B1:=f10*g11+f11*g10;
B2:=f10*g12+f11*g11+f12*g10;
B3:=f10*g13+f11*g12+f12*g11+f13*g10;
B4:=f10*g14+f11*g13+f12*g12+f13*g11+f14*g10;
B5:=       f11*g14+f12*g13+f13*g12+f14*g11;
B6:=              f12*g14+f13*g13+f14*g12;
B7:=                     f13*g14+f14*g13;
B8:=                            f14*g14;
C0:=f20*g20;
C1:=f20*g21+f21*g20;
C2:=f20*g22+f21*g21+f22*g20;
C3:=f20*g23+f21*g22+f22*g21+f23*g20;
C4:=f20*g24+f21*g23+f22*g22+f23*g21+f24*g20;
C5:=       f21*g24+f22*g23+f23*g22+f24*g21;
C6:=              f22*g24+f23*g23+f24*g22;
C7:=                     f23*g24+f24*g23;
C8:=                            f24*g24;
Z0:=B0+2*A0+C5-A5;   Z1:=B1+2*A1+C6-A6;
Z2:=B2+2*A2+C7-A7;   Z3:=B3+2*A3+C8-A8;
Z4:=B4+2*A4;         Z5:=B5+2*(C5+C0-A0);
Z6:=B6+2*(C6+C1-A1); Z7:=B7+2*(C7+C2-A2);
Z8:=B8+2*(C8+C3-A3); Z9:=   2*(  C4-A4);
//######## Multiplication ends ########//


2*f*g eq (Z0*k^0+Z1*k^1+Z2*k^2+Z3*k^3+Z4*k^4+
          Z5*k^5+Z6*k^6+Z7*k^7+Z8*k^8+Z9*k^9);
```

References

1. Barrett, P.: Implementing the Rivest Shamir and Adleman public key encryption algorithm on a standard digital signal processor. In: Andrew,M., Odlyzko (ed.) Advances in Cryptology — CRYPTO' 86, pp. 311–323. Berlin, Heidelberg, 1987. Springer Berlin Heidelberg (1987)
2. Bernstein, D.J.: Curve25519: new diffie-hellman speed records. In: Yung, M., Dodis, Y., Kiayias, A., Malkin, T. (eds.) PKC 2006. LNCS, vol. 3958, pp. 207–228. Springer, Heidelberg (2006). https://doi.org/10.1007/11745853_14

3. Bernstein, D.J., Chuengsatiansup, C., Kohel, D., Lange, T.: Twisted hessian curves. In: Lauter, K., Rodríguez-Henríquez, F. (eds.) LATINCRYPT 2015. LNCS, vol. 9230, pp. 269–294. Springer, Cham (2015). https://doi.org/10.1007/978-3-319-22174-8_15

4. Bernstein, D.J., Lange, T.: Faster addition and doubling on elliptic curves. In: Kurosawa, K. (ed.) ASIACRYPT 2007. LNCS, vol. 4833, pp. 29–50. Springer, Heidelberg (2007). https://doi.org/10.1007/978-3-540-76900-2_3

5. Boneh, D., Franklin, M.: Identity-based encryption from the weil pairing. In: Kilian, J. (ed.) CRYPTO 2001. LNCS, vol. 2139, pp. 213–229. Springer, Heidelberg (2001). https://doi.org/10.1007/3-540-44647-8_13

6. Bosma, W., Cannon, J., Playoust, C.: The Magma algebra system. I. the user language. J. Symbolic Comput. **24**(3-4), 235–265 (1997). Computational algebra and number theory (London, 1993)

7. Bosma, W., Lenstra, H.W.: Complete systems of two addition laws for elliptic curves. J. Number Theory **53**(2), 229–240 (1995)

8. Brier, É., Joye, M.: Weierstraß elliptic curves and side-channel attacks. In: Naccache, D., Paillier, P., (eds.) Public Key Cryptography, pp. 335–345, Berlin, Heidelberg, 2002. Springer Berlin Heidelberg (2002)

9. Chou, T.: Sandy2x: new Curve25519 speed records. In: Selected Areas in Cryptography - SAC 2015, pp. 145–160, Berlin, Heidelberg, 2015. Springer-Verlag (2015)

10. Feng, R., Nie, M., Wu, H.: Twisted Jacobi intersections curves. Theor. Comput. Sci. **494**, 24–35 (2013). Theory and Applications of Models of Computation (TAMC 2010)

11. Gaudry, P., Lubicz, D.: The arithmetic of characteristic 2 Kummer surfaces and of elliptic Kummer lines. Finite Fields Appl. **15**(2), 246–260 (2009)

12. Goldwasser, S., Kilian, J.: Almost all primes can be quickly certified. In: STOC'86, Proceedings of the 18th Annual ACM Symposium on the Theory of Computing (Berkeley, CA, 1986), pp. 316–329 (1986)

13. Günther, C.G.: An identity-based key-exchange protocol. In: Quisquater, J.J., Vandewalle, J., (eds.) Advances in Cryptology — EUROCRYPT '89, pp. 29–37, Berlin, Heidelberg, 1990. Springer Berlin Heidelberg (1990)

14. Hamburg, M.: Ed448-Goldilocks, a new elliptic curve. Cryptology ePrint Archive, Paper 2015/625, 2015. https://eprint.iacr.org/2015/625

15. Hisil, H., Egrice, B., Yassi, M.: Fast 4 way vectorized ladder for the complete set of Montgomery curves. Int. J. Inf. Secur. Sci. **11**(2), 12–24 (2022)

16. Hisil, H., Renes, J.: On Kummer lines with full rational 2-torsion and their usage in cryptography. ACM Trans. Math. Softw. **45**(4), 1–17 (2019)

17. Hisil, H., Wong, K.K.H., Carter, G., Dawson, E.: Jacobi quartic curves revisited. In: Boyd, C., Nieto, J.G., (eds.) Information Security and Privacy, pp.452–468, Berlin, Heidelberg, 2009. Springer Berlin Heidelberg (2009)

18. Jao, D., De Feo, L.: Towards quantum-resistant cryptosystems from supersingular elliptic curve isogenies. In: Yang, B.Y., (ed.) Post-Quantum Cryptography, pp. 19–34, Berlin, Heidelberg, 2011. Springer Berlin Heidelberg (2011)

19. Karati, S., Sarkar, P.: Kummer for genus one over prime order fields. In: Takagi, T., Peyrin, T. (eds.) ASIACRYPT 2017. LNCS, vol. 10625, pp. 3–32. Springer, Cham (2017). https://doi.org/10.1007/978-3-319-70697-9_1

20. Koblitz, N.: Elliptic curve cryptosystems. Math. Comput. **48**(177), 203–209 (1987)

21. Lange, H., Ruppert, W.: Complete systems of addition laws on abelian varieties. Invent. Math. **79**, 603–610 (1985)

22. Lenstra, H.W.: Factoring integers with elliptic curves. Ann. Math. **126**(3), 649–673 (1987)

23. López, J., Dahab, R.: Fast multiplication on elliptic curves over GF(2m) without precomputation. In: Çetin K. Koç and Christof Paar, (eds.) Cryptographic Hardware and Embedded Systems, pages 316–327, Berlin, Heidelberg, 1999. Springer Berlin Heidelberg (1999)

24. Miller, V.S.: Use of elliptic curves in cryptography. In: Williams, H.C. (ed.) CRYPTO 1985. LNCS, vol. 218, pp. 417–426. Springer, Heidelberg (1986). https://doi.org/10.1007/3-540-39799-X_31

25. Montgomery, P.L.: Modular multiplication without trial division. Math. Comput. **44**(170), 519–521 (1985)

26. Montgomery, P.L.: Speeding the Pollard and elliptic curve methods of factorization. Math. Comput. **48**(177), 243–264 (1987)

27. Nath, K., Sarkar, P.: Efficient 4-way vectorizations of the Montgomery ladder. IEEE Trans. Comput. **71**(3), 712–723 (2022)

28. Nath, K., Sarkar, P.: Kummer versus Montgomery face-off over prime order fields. ACM Trans. Math. Softw. **48**(2), 1–28 (2022)

29. Nath, K., Sarkar, P.: Security and efficiency trade-offs for elliptic curve Diffie-Hellman at the 128-bit and 224-bit security levels. J. Cryptogr. Eng. **12**, 107–121 (2022)

30. Okeya, K., Sakurai, K.: Efficient elliptic curve cryptosystems from a scalar multiplication algorithm with recovery of the y-coordinate on a montgomery-form elliptic curve. In: Koç, Ç.K., Naccache, D., Paar, C. (eds.) CHES 2001. LNCS, vol. 2162, pp. 126–141. Springer, Heidelberg (2001). https://doi.org/10.1007/3-540-44709-1_12

31. Renes, J., Costello, C., Batina, L.: Complete addition formulas for prime order elliptic curves. In: Fischlin, M., Coron, J.-S. (eds.) EUROCRYPT 2016. LNCS, vol. 9665, pp. 403–428. Springer, Heidelberg (2016). https://doi.org/10.1007/978-3-662-49890-3_16

32. Renes, J., Smith, B.: qDSA: small and secure digital signatures with curve-based Diffie–Hellman key pairs. In: Takagi, T., Peyrin, T., (eds.) Advances in Cryptology — ASIACRYPT 2017, pp. 273–302, Cham, 2017. Springer International Publishing (2017)

33. Shamir, A.: Identity-based cryptosystems and signature schemes. In: Blakley, G.R., Chaum, D., (eds.) Advances in Cryptology, pp. 47–53, Berlin, Heidelberg, 1985. Springer Berlin Heidelberg (1985)

34. Silverman, J.H.: The Arithmetic of Elliptic Curves, volume 106 of Graduate Texts in Mathematics. Springer-Verlag, 1st ed. 1986. Corr. 3rd printing (1994)

Safe curves for elliptic-curve cryptography

Daniel J. Bernstein[1,2] and Tanja Lange[3,2]

[1] University of Illinois at Chicago, USA
[2] Academia Sinica, Taiwan
djb@cr.yp.to
[3] Eindhoven University of Technology, Netherlands
tanja@hyperelliptic.org

Abstract. This paper surveys interactions between choices of elliptic curves and the security of elliptic-curve cryptography. Attacks considered include not just discrete-logarithm computations but also attacks exploiting common implementation pitfalls.

1   Introduction

In the original 1976 Diffie–Hellman (DH) key-exchange system [91, Section 3], user 1 has secret key X_1 and public key $Y_1 = g^{X_1}$; user 2 has secret key X_2 and public key $Y_2 = g^{X_2}$; and so on for any number of users. Here g is a "fixed primitive element of $GF(q)$", i.e., a generator of the multiplicative group $\mathbb{F}_q^*$, where q is a fixed prime number. To communicate with user i, user j computes a shared secret $g^{X_i X_j}$ as $Y_i^{X_j}$, and uses this shared secret as a key for symmetric-key cryptography to encrypt and authenticate messages. User i computes the same shared secret as $Y_j^{X_i}$.

The DH system is broken if an attacker can solve the "discrete-logarithm problem" for the group $\mathbb{F}_q^*$, the problem of computing X_i from g^{X_i}. The 1976 paper commented that "for certain carefully chosen values of q" this problem "requires on the order of $q^{1/2}$ operations, using the best known algorithm".

Author list in alphabetical order; see https://www.ams.org/profession/leaders/culture/CultureStatement04.pdf. This work was supported in part by the U.S. National Science Foundation under grant 1018836, the Deutsche Forschungsgemeinschaft (DFG, German Research Foundation) under Germany's Excellence Strategy–EXC 2092 CASA–390781972 "Cyber Security in the Age of Large-Scale Adversaries", the Academia Sinica Grand Challenge Seed Project AS-GCS-113-M07, the European Commision through the Horizon Europe program under project number 101135475 (TALER), and the Dutch Research Council (NWO) under grants 613.009.144 and 639.073.005. "Any opinions, findings, and conclusions or recommendations expressed in this material are those of the author(s) and do not necessarily reflect the views of the National Science Foundation" (or other funding agencies). Permanent ID of this document: 47f17793322fcaf3ef67f982e2c3ae86b34c17ce. Date: 2024.08.09.

© The Author(s), under exclusive license to Springer Nature Switzerland AG 2025
C. Boyd et al. (Eds.): EdDawsonFestschrift2024, LNCS 15600, pp. 124–191, 2025.
https://doi.org/10.1007/978-3-031-83490-5_7

The discrete-logarithm algorithms cited in that paper are "generic" algorithms that work for any group. They use about $\ell_1^{1/2} + \ell_2^{1/2} + \cdots$ operations if the order of the generator factors into primes $\ell_1, \ell_2, \ldots$ (not necessarily distinct). A careful choice of q for the DH system then takes, e.g., $q - 1 = 2\ell$ for a prime ℓ, so that the attacks take about $\ell^{1/2} \approx 0.7q^{1/2}$ operations; i.e., the DH security level against these attacks is about $(1/2) \log_2 q$ bits, where security level means logarithm base 2 of attack cost.

However, further analysis showed that a non-generic method called "index calculus"—which had been introduced in 1922 by Kraitchik [154, page 120], and which had been used at a much larger scale by Western and J. Miller [226]—had much better scalability in solving discrete-logarithm problems, reducing the security level to $(\log_2 q)^{1/2+o(1)}$ bits asymptotically. Index calculus applies more generally to discrete logarithms in $\mathbb{F}_q^*$ for arbitrary prime powers q, not just primes, and applies to integer factorization (see, e.g., Kraitchik's 1926 book [155, Chapitre XIV]), in all cases reducing the security level to $(\log_2 q)^{1/2+o(1)}$ bits.

There have been many further developments of index calculus since then. The security level dropped in the early 1980s to $(\log_2 q)^{1/3+o(1)}$ when q is a power of 2, and then a decade later to $(\log_2 q)^{1/3+o(1)}$ when q is a prime, and then two decades after that to $(\log_2 q)^{o(1)}$ when q is a power of 2; see generally [121]. Each of these exponent changes was preceded and followed by many speedups that had less effect on the asymptotics but that pushed many specific sizes of q across the line from "unbroken" to "broken".

1.1   Elliptic-curve cryptography (ECC)

The central idea of ECC is to *stop index calculus*, specifically by replacing the groups $\mathbb{F}_q^*$ in the DH system with elliptic-curve groups $E(\mathbb{F}_q)$. This idea was introduced in a 1986 paper by V. Miller [174] and, independently, a 1987 paper by Koblitz [152]. Miller gave arguments that index calculus "is not likely to work on elliptic curves". Koblitz wrote that "the analog of the discrete logarithm problem on elliptic curves is likely to be harder than the classical discrete logarithm problem, especially over $\mathrm{GF}(2^n)$".

The bird's-eye view is that this has been remarkably successful. Most cryptographic applications today rely on ECC, although there are still some uses of RSA. Computations in $E(\mathbb{F}_q)$ take more effort than computations in $\mathbb{F}_q^*$, but this is outweighed by the fact that for $E(\mathbb{F}_q)$ we can take q just large enough to resist generic discrete-logarithm algorithms, while for $\mathbb{F}_q^*$ we need much larger q to resist index calculus. More importantly, $E(\mathbb{F}_q)$ has maintained its security level much better than $\mathbb{F}_q^*$ has, and thus inspires more confidence than $\mathbb{F}_q^*$ does.

A closer look shows, however, that there have been many successful attacks against specific elliptic-curve cryptosystems—including some curves that had been specifically proposed for speed reasons. For example, "pairings" were shown in the mid-1990s (see Section 5.1) to reduce discrete logarithms in $E(\mathbb{F}_q)$ to discrete logarithms in $\mathbb{F}_q^*$ if $\#E(\mathbb{F}_q) = q - 1$; papers a few years later (see also Section 5.1) showed how to reduce discrete logarithms in $E(\mathbb{F}_q)$ to very easy discrete logarithms in $\mathbb{F}_q$ (not $\mathbb{F}_q^*$) if $\#E(\mathbb{F}_q) = q$; and further classes of "weak curves" are known when q is not a prime (see Section 2.1), where "weak" means that discrete logarithms involve noticeably fewer than $q^{1/2}$ operations.

A wave of standards then appeared specifying how to choose curves for ECC: ANSI X9.62 in 1999 [8], IEEE P1363 in 2000 [134], SEC 2 in 2000 [203], NIST FIPS 186-2 in 2000 [220], and ANSI X9.63 in 2001 [9]. Later elliptic-curve standards include Brainpool in 2005 [66], NSA Suite B in 2005 [184], and ANSSI FRP256V1 in 2011 [86]. These standards generally leave a wide berth around all known classes of weak curves; the goal is to make sure that the elliptic-curve discrete-logarithm problem (ECDLP) is very difficult.

1.2   ECC security risks

There are three important caveats regarding these ECC standards. First, it seems increasingly likely that future attackers will have quantum computers, breaking all of these cryptosystems. Second, it is conceivable that there are further classes of weak curves. Third, there are many attacks that break real-world ECC without solving ECDLP.

This third problem is not a future problem; it is not a problem that relies on the *possibility* of better ECDLP attacks; it is a real failure mode that we have seen again and again. None of the standards mentioned above do a good job of ensuring ECC security. See Appendix A for a chronology of ECC vulnerabilities.

We posted a "SafeCurves" web site [43] in 2013 aimed at improving the situation:

- The web site highlights the "core problem", namely that "**if you implement the standard curves, chances are you're doing it wrong**: Your implementation produces incorrect results for some rare curve points. Your implementation leaks secret data when the input isn't a curve point. Your implementation leaks secret data through branch timing. Your implementation leaks secret data through cache timing."
- The web site explains that these problems "are exploitable by real attackers, taking advantage of the gaps between ECDLP and real-world ECC: ECDLP is non-interactive. Real-world ECC handles attacker-controlled input. ECDLP reveals only nP. Real-world ECC also reveals timing (and, in some situations, much more side-channel information). ECDLP always computes nP correctly. Real-world ECC has failure cases. Secure implementations of the standard curves are theoretically possible but very hard."
- The web site explains that better curve choices help: "Most of these attacks would have been ruled out by better choices of curves that allow *simple* implementations to be *secure* implementations. This is the primary motivation for SafeCurves. **The SafeCurves criteria are designed to ensure ECC security, not just ECDLP security.**"

Note the word "most" here: better curve choices make ECC implementation failures less likely and are the focus of SafeCurves, but one needs to take further steps to eliminate the remaining failures. The web site notes, for example, that some attacks "would have been ruled out by better choices at higher levels of ECC protocols", such as the way that randomness is used in signature systems.

Ten years of further experience with ECC security failures have confirmed the importance of the SafeCurves criteria, in much the same way that decades of improvements in index calculus have confirmed the importance of switching from $\mathbb{F}_q^*$ to $E(\mathbb{F}_q)$. The point is not that everything is broken on one side of the line—it is certainly not true that *all* $\mathbb{F}_q^*$ have been broken, or that *all* implementations of curves failing the SafeCurves criteria have been broken—but rather that the switch reduces security risks.

1.3   This paper

The intention of this paper is to be "the SafeCurves paper": we present and justify the SafeCurves criteria, giving additional explanation and updated examples of why the criteria are important.

The fact that different curve choices have different effects on implementation simplicity is not something obvious: it relies on many years of research into elliptic-curve computations. The paper explains the relevant features of these computations, for example explaining why state-of-the-art ECC software uses formulas introduced in 1987 by Montgomery [**177**] in some situations and uses formulas introduced in 2008 by Hisil, Wong, Carter, and Dawson [**130**] in other situations.

The paper is organized into two parts. The first part is motivated by ECDLP attacks: Sections 2, 3, 4, 5, 6, and 7 cover, respectively, the field of definition, the curve equation, the order of the base point, the embedding degree, the CM field discriminant, and rigidity.

We emphasize that the SafeCurves criteria reject curves that are known to have faster ECDLP attacks, *and* proactively reject many further curves just in case there are further ECDLP attacks beyond what has been discovered. This is common practice in ECC standards, as noted above, but these sections point out some differences in the details.

The second part is motivated by ECC attacks *beyond* ECDLP attacks: specifically, Sections 8, 9, 10, and 11 cover requirements on "ladders", "twists", "completeness", and "indistinguishability". This is the central contribution of SafeCurves.

The general theme of this part is that there are tensions between the security, simplicity, and speed of ECC software—and these tensions are larger for some curves than for others. This matters because implementors are typically writing the simplest code that they can that passes some tests, and then modifying it for speed if there are speed complaints (or fears of speed complaints). Implementors can sometimes be convinced to take extra steps for security, especially if there are tools enforcing those steps; but needing more of those steps means more chances of disaster.

We do not repeat the tables of SafeCurves ratings here; the tables are easier to use on the web site [**43**]. However, for concreteness, we list three representative

name	curve equation over $\mathbb{F}_p$	prime p	source
NIST P-256	$y^2 = x^3 - 3x + b$; "large" b	$2^{256} - 2^{224} + 2^{192} + 2^{96} - 1$	[220]
brainpoolP256t1	$y^2 = x^3 - 3x + b$; "large" b	"dense"	[66]
Curve25519	$y^2 = x^3 + 486662x^2 + x$	$2^{255} - 19$	[23]

Table 1.3.1. Three examples of curves that have been proposed for cryptographic use. The "dense" p and "large" b values are listed in Sections 2 and 3 respectively.

examples of curves in Table 1.3.1. SafeCurves classifies one of these examples, Curve25519, as safe, meaning that the curve meets all of the SafeCurves criteria.

1.4 Context

We do not claim credit for the general idea of investigating the security consequences of implementation pitfalls. This is one of the main topics of the security literature. Regarding ECC in particular, this paper cites many examples of vulnerabilities in ECC implementations.

However, the processes used to select cryptosystems often assume perfect implementations. For example, NSA wrote the following in 1992 (see [7]) regarding the new NSA/NIST DSA proposal (and regarding the existing Data Encryption Standard, which remained a standard until 2005):

> We are unaware of any weaknesses in the DSS or in the DES when properly implemented and used for the purposes for which they both are designed.

Similarly, regarding the NIST curves, NIST wrote the following in 2019 [183]:

> NIST is not aware of any vulnerabilities to attacks on these curves when they are implemented correctly and used as described in NIST standards and guidelines.

Regarding better curves, [183] wrote that "their designers claim that they offer better performance and are easier to implement in a secure manner"; [183] did not cite any of the literature *demonstrating* the performance benefits and ease of secure implementation of these curves, and did not mention the likelihood and consequences of insecure implementation of the NIST curves.

There have been some recommendations to adjust cryptosystem-selection processes to predict and avoid implementation pitfalls. For example, one of Rivest's comments [204] in 1992 regarding DSA was as follows: "The poor user is given enough rope with which to hang himself—something a standard should not do." What we are asking in this paper is how curve choices influence the chance of implementations being secure.

This paper incorporates curve-selection material from documents we have previously posted, including [42], [43], [44], and [46]. Some of those documents look beyond curve choices at how other ECC design choices affect the speed, simplicity, and security of implementations.

2   Fields

To specify an elliptic curve to use in ECC, one specifies a prime number p and then an elliptic-curve equation "over" the finite field $\mathbb{F}_p$, i.e., an elliptic-curve equation with coefficients in $\mathbb{F}_p$.

For example, the NIST P-224 curve is defined over $\mathbb{F}_p$ where $p = 2^{224} - 2^{96} + 1$; the NIST P-256 curve is defined over $\mathbb{F}_p$ where $p = 2^{256} - 2^{224} + 2^{192} + 2^{96} - 1$; Curve25519 is defined over $\mathbb{F}_p$ where $p = 2^{255} - 19$; and brainpoolP256t1 is defined over $\mathbb{F}_p$ where

$$p = 76884956397045344220809746629001649093037950200943055203735601445031516197751.$$

See Table 1.3.1 and Section 3 for the elliptic-curve equations, and see the SafeCurves web site for further examples.

There are other types of elliptic curves. In particular, there are many ECC papers that consider elliptic curves over non-prime finite fields. However, the SafeCurves criteria require prime fields.

ECC standards from the turn of the century typically allowed binary curves. For example, NIST's FIPS 186-2 digital-signature standard specified 15 curves, of which 10 were defined over binary fields. However, the latest version of that standard, FIPS 186-5 from 2023, says that "Elliptic curves defined over binary curves ... are now deprecated". The Brainpool standard and NSA's Suite B standards had already required prime fields.

2.1   Is ECDLP broken for non-prime fields?

The security story for ECDLP over non-prime fields (e.g., binary extension fields $\mathbb{F}_q$ with $q = 2^n$) is more complicated and less stable than the security story for ECDLP over prime fields, as illustrated by [104], [116], [114], [89], and [195].

These attacks construct various non-prime fields $\mathbb{F}_q$ and elliptic curves over $\mathbb{F}_q$ for which attacks exploiting proper subfields of $\mathbb{F}_q$ break ECDLP noticeably faster than generic attacks do. There are some choices of q for which all curves are weak in this sense, and there are even some choices of q for which all curves are broken in time subexponential in $\log q$. On the other hand, there are still many ways to choose non-prime fields and curves that avoid these attacks.

We reiterate that security requirements go beyond avoiding known attacks. Requiring prime fields is *not* making the incorrect claim that non-prime fields are categorically broken; it is instead simplifying attack analysis by excluding the subfield structure used in various attacks. This removes cases where the known attacks apply, *and* proactively removes further cases that share the same structure.

One of the authors of this paper commented in 2006, in the paper [23] introducing Curve25519, that prime fields "have the virtue of minimizing the number of security concerns for elliptic-curve cryptography". There is general agreement that prime fields are the safe, conservative choice for ECC.

2.2 Are "special" primes dangerous?

Index calculus for $\mathbb{F}_p^*$ relies on the fact that integers often factor into small primes. The chance of this happening depends on how large the integers are. Optimized index calculus for $\mathbb{F}_p^*$ using the "number-field sieve" writes p as a low-degree polynomial, and performance depends on the size of the coefficients in this polynomial: quantitatively, security levels are reduced by about 20% when the polynomial has small coefficients.

However, the point of ECC has always been to avoid index calculus in the first place. All of the SafeCurves requirements can be met by "special" primes.

Most ECC standards require "special" primes for efficiency reasons. For example, NIST justifies its prime shape by saying that "modular multiplication can be carried out more efficiently than in general". However, Brainpool prohibits "special" primes for patent reasons [66, Section 3.1]:

> The prime p must not be of a special form in order to avoid patented fast arithmetic on the base field.

The context here is that U.S. patent 5159632 had been filed in September 1991 on elliptic-curve cryptography over $\mathbb{F}_p$ "where p is one of a class of numbers such that mod p arithmetic is performed in a processor using only shift and add operations", a common way to reduce modulo primes such as $2^{224} - 2^{96} + 1$. However, a paper by Bender and Castagnoli published in June 1990 [20] had already reported an implementation of ECDH using, e.g., the prime $2^{127} + 24933$, "which is convenient in computer arithmetic". We are not aware of any reports of enforcement attempts for the patent. The patent expired in 2011.

2.3 Are "random" primes dangerous?

Brainpool's choice of "random" primes p makes arithmetic in $\mathbb{F}_p$ roughly twice as slow. We do not know whether there are examples where this slowdown has motivated protocols using Brainpool to select, e.g., the brainpoolP192t1 curve instead of the brainpoolP256t1 curve; such cases would warrant adding a requirement to SafeCurves to prohibit "random" primes p. The question here is about protocol choices rather than internal implementation choices; if a protocol requires brainpoolP256t1 then interoperability will force each implementation to use brainpoolP256t1.

2.4 Are primes required to be 3 mod 4?

All of the SafeCurves requirements can be met by primes p with $p \equiv 1 \pmod 4$, and by primes p with $p \equiv 3 \pmod 4$.

Brainpool is more restrictive here: it requires $p \equiv 3 \pmod 4$. Brainpool does not claim that this has a security justification but instead claims that it "allows efficient point compression"; see [66, Section 3.1]. This boils down to the statement that computing square roots in $\mathbb{F}_p$ is efficient when $p \equiv 3 \pmod 4$, since one can compute a square root of s by computing $r = s^{(p+1)/4}$ and then checking whether $r^2 = s$. But computing square roots in $\mathbb{F}_p$ has practically identical efficiency when, e.g., $p \equiv 5 \pmod 8$, as in the case of Curve25519: compute $r = s^{(p+3)/8}$, check whether $r^2 = \pm s$, and multiply r by a precomputed $\sqrt{-1} \in \mathbb{F}_p$ if $r^2 = -s$.

We comment—looking ahead to, e.g., Section 9's coverage of invalid-curve attacks—that requiring extra steps can be a security risk if implementations that omit the extra steps *seem* to work while failing in situations that an attacker can trigger. This concern does not apply to the square-root procedure for $p \equiv 5 \pmod 8$: omitting the $\sqrt{-1}$ step for the case $r^2 = -s$ would not pass basic interoperability tests. Also, the difference in performance between the two square-root methods in the previous paragraph is unnoticeable, so the downgrading-security-levels concern from Section 2.3 does not apply.

3 Equations

There are several different ways to express elliptic curves over $\mathbb{F}_p$:

- The **short Weierstrass equation** $y^2 = x^3 + ax + b$, where $4a^3 + 27b^2$ is nonzero in $\mathbb{F}_p$, is an elliptic curve over $\mathbb{F}_p$. Every elliptic curve over $\mathbb{F}_p$ can be converted to a short Weierstrass equation if $p > 3$.
- The **Montgomery equation** $By^2 = x^3 + Ax^2 + x$, where $B(A^2 - 4)$ is nonzero in $\mathbb{F}_p$, is an elliptic curve over $\mathbb{F}_p$. Substituting $x = Bu - A/3$ and $y = Bv$ produces the short Weierstrass equation $v^2 = u^3 + au + b$ where $a = (3 - A^2)/(3B^2)$ and $b = (2A^3 - 9A)/(27B^3)$.
- The **Edwards equation** $x^2 + y^2 = 1 + dx^2y^2$, where $d(1 - d)$ is nonzero in $\mathbb{F}_p$, is an elliptic curve over $\mathbb{F}_p$. Substituting $x = u/v$ and $y = (u-1)/(u+1)$ produces the Montgomery equation $Bv^2 = u^3 + Au^2 + u$ where $A = 2(1 + d)/(1 - d)$ and $B = 4/(1 - d)$.

A 1987 paper by Montgomery [177] introduced Montgomery curves. A 2007 paper by Edwards [95] introduced Edwards curves in the case that d is a 4th power. For reasons explained in Section 10, SafeCurves requires Edwards curves to be **complete**, i.e., for d to not be a square; we introduced complete Edwards curves in a 2007 paper [36].

There are other possibilities, such as Hessian curves, which share some interesting properties with Edwards curves (see, e.g., [130]). As far as we know, there are no efforts to deploy specific Hessian curves in ECC. For simplicity, we focus on the three curve shapes specified above.

The **rational points** of a short Weierstrass curve are the pairs (x, y) of elements of $\mathbb{F}_p$ satisfying the equation, together with one extra "point at infinity". The **rational points** of a Montgomery curve are defined the same way. The **rational points** of a complete Edwards curve are the pairs (x, y) of elements of $\mathbb{F}_p$ satisfying the equation; there is no extra "point at infinity". In each of these cases, the set of rational points is written $E(\mathbb{F}_p)$, where E is the curve. There is a standard definition of a group structure on $E(\mathbb{F}_p)$; the neutral element is the point at infinity for a short Weierstrass curve or a Montgomery curve, or $(0, 1)$ for an Edwards curve.

As a concrete example, Curve25519 is the Montgomery curve $y^2 = x^3 + 486662x^2 + x$ over $\mathbb{F}_p$ with (as mentioned in Section 2) $p = 2^{255} - 19$. Here $B = 1$ and $A = 486662$, so $B(A^2 - 4) \neq 0$ in $\mathbb{F}_p$. As another example, NIST P-224 is the short Weierstrass curve $y^2 = x^3 + ax + b$ over $\mathbb{F}_p$ with $p = 2^{224} - 2^{96} + 1$, $a = -3$, and

$$b = 18958286285566608000408668544493926$$
$$41550468096867932107578723467256;$$

one can check that $4a^3 + 27b^2 \neq 0$ in $\mathbb{F}_p$. NIST P-256 and brainpoolP256t1 also have the form $y^2 = x^3 - 3x + b$, where

$$b = 41058363725152142129326129780047268409114$$
$$441015993725554835256314039467401291$$

for NIST P-256 and

$$b = 46214326585032579593829631435610129746736$$
$$367449296220983687490401182983727876$$

for brainpoolP256t1.

3.1 Are short Weierstrass equations required to have $a = -3$?

The first serious effort to optimize formulas for elliptic-curve group operations was in a 1986 paper [82, Section 4] from D. Chudnovsky and G. Chudnovsky. The paper considered what are now typically called short Weierstrass curves, Jacobi quartics, Jacobi intersections, and Hessian curves. In the case of short Weierstrass curves, the paper considered affine coordinates (x, y), but recommended instead using what are now typically called Jacobian coordinates (X, Y, Z) with $x = X/Z^2$ and $y = Y/Z^3$.

Note that the group operation on an elliptic curve is normally written as addition rather than multiplication. This is also the reason for "nP" in the quotes in Section 1, meaning the sum of n copies of P on the curve.

Discussions of costs frequently refer to the number of multiplications. It is important to be clear about whether these are multiplications in the field or multiplications of scalars n by curve points P. As in the literature, we use $\mathbf{M}$ to refer to the cost of multiplication in the field.

For Jacobian coordinates, [82] found doubling formulas taking $9\mathbf{M}$ plus 1 multiplication by a. Obviously choosing $a = 1$ removes the multiplication by a, but the paper said that it is "even smarter" to choose $a = -3$, where alternative formulas take just $8\mathbf{M}$. The paper also found general addition formulas taking $16\mathbf{M}$. The paper also considered an extension (X, Y, Z, Z^2, Z^3) of Jacobian coordinates, and projective coordinates (X, Y, Z) with $x = X/Z$ and $y = Y/Z$, in both cases reducing general addition from $16\mathbf{M}$ to $14\mathbf{M}$, but at the expense of doubling using $9\mathbf{M}$ for (X, Y, Z, Z^2, Z^3) or $10\mathbf{M}$ for (X, Y, Z).

IEEE P1363 suggests Jacobian coordinates, writing that "Other kinds of projective coordinates exist, but the ones given here provide the fastest arithmetic on elliptic curves. (See [CC87].)" P1363 also presents the $a = -3$ speedup from [82]. Similarly, the NIST curves use $y^2 = x^3 - 3x + b$ "for reasons of efficiency", and Brainpool uses $y^2 = x^3 - 3x + b$ for its "arithmetical advantages". Efficiency is also the rationale stated for various other choices in these standards: for example, NIST takes the "cofactor" (see Sections 7 and 9) to be "as small as possible" for "efficiency reasons". Recall also from Section 2.4 that Brainpool takes $p \equiv 3 \pmod 4$ for "efficient point compression".

If there are cases where the slowdown from using short Weierstrass equations *without* $a = -3$ has triggered a switch to lower security levels, then a requirement for short Weierstrass equations to use $a = -3$ can be justified on security grounds. See the analogous discussion in Section 2.3 of the (larger) speedup from avoiding "random" primes. Note also that one cannot object to an $a = -3$ requirement as potentially allowing an ECDLP attack: such an attack would imply an ECDLP attack against generic a, as explained in [**71**, Section 6].

4   The rho method

Along with specifying a curve, one specifies a base point G of prime order ℓ on that curve. The basic ECDH protocol is then as follows: user i has a secret key s_i, which is an integer; user i has a corresponding public key $s_i G$, which is a point on the elliptic curve; users i and j then compute a shared secret $s_i s_j G$, which is a point on the elliptic curve.

Note that, in the original 1976 DH protocol reviewed in Section 1, the base $g \in \mathbb{F}_q^*$ had order $q - 1$, which is never prime if $q > 3$ is a prime number (although the order can be prime if q is a power of 2). For a closer analogy to the previous paragraph, one can replace g in DH with g^2, which has prime order ℓ in the case $q - 1 = 2\ell$.

The size of ℓ puts an important limit on the security level. A standard attack [**197**], called the rho method, breaks ECDLP using, on average, approximately $0.886\sqrt{\ell}$ curve additions. For example, $0.886\sqrt{\ell}$ is approximately $2^{111.8}$ for NIST P-224, approximately $2^{125.8}$ for Curve25519, and approximately $2^{127.8}$ for NIST P-256.

4.1   Can rho finish sooner?

The $0.886\sqrt{\ell}$ cost for the rho method is an average over random choices made by the attacker: the method sometimes finishes more slowly and sometimes finishes more quickly. The success probability of the method after m additions is only about m^2/ℓ for small m. Common recommendations are to choose ℓ so that m^2/ℓ is negligible for any feasible value of m.

In 2013, we established a concrete lower limit for ℓ in SafeCurves as follows: "For example, if ℓ is around 2^{200}, then the success probability is around $1/2^{20}$ after 2^{90} additions. Performing 2^{90} additions in a year with state-of-the-art chip technology (as of 2013) would require hundreds of gigawatts of power. SafeCurves requires ℓ to be at least 2^{200}." We emphasized that SafeCurves does *not* recommend against larger values of ℓ:

> There are several reasons to use larger ℓ: chip technology can be expected to advance; $1/2^{20}$ is not an acceptable risk level for some users; very few ECC applications will notice the cost of increasing ℓ to, e.g., 2^{250}.

As an illustration of how chip technology has advanced after our estimates of what was possible with 2013 technology, consider the ANTMINER S21 [57], a Bitcoin-mining device released at the end of 2023 that uses 3500 watts and carries out 200 terahashes per second, nearly 2^{36} hashes per joule. Each hash uses about 2^{18} bit operations, while Appendix B indicates that a curve addition inside the rho method for, e.g., Curve25519 costs about 2^{20} bit operations, so using similar chip technology should carry out nearly 2^{34} curve additions per joule. Carrying out 2^{90} curve additions thus costs around 2^{56} joules; 2^{56} joules in a year is around 2 gigawatts.

To account for current chip efficiency and expected near-future improvements in chip efficiency, we are updating the SafeCurves lower limit on ℓ from 2^{200} to 2^{220}. We again emphasize that this is not a recommendation against larger values of ℓ: further improvements in chip technology would be unsurprising.

4.2   Can rho take advantage of multiple targets?

Yes. There is a square-root effect for multiple targets: breaking 1000000 keys with the rho method costs only about 1000 times as much as breaking a single key, not 1000000 times as much. See [156], [131], [162], and [40].

One can find standards as late as 2001 saying that "the computation of a single elliptic curve discrete logarithm has the effect of revealing a single user's private key. The same effort must be repeated in order to determine another user's private key". The second sentence is incorrect: the effort is reduced for each subsequent key.

For comparison, with secret-key ciphers there is a much worse effect for multiple targets. Breaking a single AES key costs about 2^{128} computations; breaking 1000000 AES keys costs, in total, about 2^{128} computations.

4.3   Does rho find some key more quickly when there are multiple targets?

No. The probability of finding *any* keys within m additions is still only about m^2/ℓ. The first key found will still cost approximately $0.886\sqrt{\ell}$ additions on average.

For comparison, if there are 1000000 AES keys to break, then some key will be found after only $2^{128}/1000000$ computations.

4.4   What is this 0.886? What exactly are the additions?

The 0.886 is actually $\sqrt{\pi/4}$. The additions are "batched affine" short-Weierstrass elliptic-curve additions, each consisting of 5 multiplications mod p, 1 squaring mod p, and an asymptotically negligible amount of extra work. (Short Weierstrass curves are the fastest known curve shapes for batched affine additions. This does not mean that other curves are harder to attack: the attacker converts other curves and the points on them to short Weierstrass form.) The algorithm can be efficiently parallelized and vectorized [187].

4.5   How stable is the security story for rho?

A 1971 paper by Shanks [217] introduced generic square-root DLP attacks. For curves that meet the SafeCurves requirements, the number of additions used in [217] is within a factor 2 of the number of additions used by state-of-the-art ECDLP attacks.

To be more precise, the Shanks method uses $1.5\sqrt{\ell}$ group operations on average. The low-memory rho method from Pollard [197] uses $\sqrt{\pi/2}\sqrt{\ell}$ group operations on average. This formula was used in, e.g., a draft of X9.62 in 1997 and in the Brainpool standard in 2005. There have been three main themes of research since 1971:

- Optimizing the number of additions. The largest change was a $\sqrt{2}$ "negation" speedup, replacing $\sqrt{\pi/2} \approx 1.253$ with $\sqrt{\pi/4} \approx 0.886$. See Wiener [228], Escott [96], and Duursma–Gaudry–Morain [94]; for further analysis see Bos–Kleinjung–Lenstra [60] and our paper [50] with Schwabe.
- Showing that there are no bottlenecks other than the arithmetic required for the additions: in particular, no serious memory use, no serialization, no serious communication, and no serious branching. Pollard [197] introduced the rho method, showing that square-root DLP attacks do not need much memory. Van Oorschot and Wiener [187] (drafts published as early as 1994) showed that a variant of the rho method is parallelizable with negligible communication costs, and [50] showed that a negating variant of the rho method is vectorizable.
- Optimizing the arithmetic inside the additions. See Appendix B.

5   Transfers

A "transfer" converts ECDLP into a "linear algebraic group" DLP. There are several types of transfers (see Section 5.1 for references) for an elliptic-curve group of prime order ℓ over a prime field $\mathbb{F}_p$:

- Additive transfer: applicable when $\ell = p$. The target group is the additive group $\mathbb{F}_p$, where DLP is very easy to solve.

- Degree-1 multiplicative transfer: applicable when ℓ divides $p - 1$. The target group is the multiplicative group $\mathbb{F}_p^*$, where DLP is solved in subexponential time by index calculus. The standard estimates are that current index-calculus methods break DLP in $\mathbb{F}_p^*$ at cost below 2^{128} for p up to roughly 2^{3000}.
- Degree-2 multiplicative transfer: applicable when ℓ divides $p^2 - 1$. The target group is the multiplicative group $\mathbb{F}_{p^2}^*$, where DLP is solved in subexponential time by index calculus. The standard estimates are that current index-calculus methods break DLP in $\mathbb{F}_{p^2}^*$ at cost below 2^{128} for p up to roughly 2^{1500}.
- Degree-3 multiplicative transfer: applicable when ℓ divides $p^3 - 1$. The target group is the multiplicative group $\mathbb{F}_{p^3}^*$, where DLP is solved in subexponential time by index calculus. The standard estimates are that current index-calculus methods break DLP in $\mathbb{F}_{p^3}^*$ at cost below 2^{128} for p up to roughly 2^{1000}.
- Et cetera.

The minimum possible multiplicative-transfer degree for a particular elliptic-curve group is called the **embedding degree** of that group. Standards vary in the requirements they place upon the embedding degree:

- SEC1 [203] requires the embedding degree to be at least 20.
- X9.62 [8] requires the embedding degree to be at least 20.
- P1363 [134] puts variable requirements upon the embedding degree, depending on the size of p, but never requires it to be more than 30.
- Brainpool [66] requires the embedding degree to be at least $(\ell - 1)/100$.

The SEC/X9.62/P1363 approach is risky: there is a long history of improvements to index calculus, and the point of ECC has always been to avoid index calculus. The Brainpool approach is clearly overkill, but is also non-controversial, since it rules out only a small fraction of curves [17].

SafeCurves takes the overkill approach. Pairing-based cryptography requires the risky approach, but pairing-based cryptography is outside the scope of SafeCurves.

5.1 How stable is the security story for transfers?

All of these transfers have been known since the 1990s. Multiplicative transfers were introduced by Menezes–Okamoto–Vanstone [172], Frey–Rück [105], and Semaev [214], and are often called the "MOV attack". Additive transfers were introduced by Semaev [215], Satoh–Araki [209], and Smart [218], and are often called the "Smart-ASS attack".

6 CM field discriminants

The number of rational points $\#E(\mathbb{F}_p)$ on an elliptic curve E over $\mathbb{F}_p$ is $p + 1 - t$ where t is the **trace** of E. Hasse's theorem states that t is between $-2\sqrt{p}$ and $2\sqrt{p}$. The prime order ℓ of the base point from Section 4 is a divisor of $p + 1 - t$.

If s^2 is the largest square dividing $t^2 - 4p$ then $(t^2 - 4p)/s^2$ is a squarefree negative integer. Define D as $(t^2 - 4p)/s^2$ if $(t^2 - 4p)/s^2 \equiv 1 \pmod 4$, otherwise as $4(t^2 - 4p)/s^2$. SafeCurves requires the absolute value of this **complex-multiplication field discriminant** D to be larger than 2^{100}. We are updating this to 2^{110} to keep pace with Section 4.1.

As in Section 5 (and unlike Section 4), this requirement is satisfied by the vast majority of elliptic curves. Looking beyond the scope of SafeCurves, we note the reasons that the literature sometimes intentionally chooses curves with small D: these curves make $\#E(\mathbb{F}_p)$ easier to compute (but $\#E(\mathbb{F}_p)$ does not take long to compute in any case), give a speedup in computing nP [**112**] at the expense of more complicated computation, and play a critical role in pairing-based cryptography.

6.1 How do I verify the trace?

Verifying that the base point has order ℓ guarantees that the curve cardinality $p+1-t$ is a multiple of ℓ. Typically ℓ is above $4\sqrt{p}$, so there is only one multiple of ℓ between $p + 1 - 2\sqrt{p}$ and $p + 1 + 2\sqrt{p}$; this multiple must be $p + 1 - t$.

In more detail, if all six of the following checks pass, then base point P has prime order ℓ and the curve trace is t: check that (1) ℓ is prime; (2) $\ell^2 > 16p$; (3) ℓ divides $p + 1 - t$; (4) $t^2 < 4p$; (5) P is not the neutral element; and (6) ℓP is the neutral element.

Proof: The order of P is a divisor of ℓ by condition 6, but ℓ is prime by condition 1, so the order of P is 1 or ℓ, but the order of P is larger than 1 by condition 5, so the order of P is exactly the prime ℓ as claimed. The order of P also divides $\#E(\mathbb{F}_p)$, since the order of each element divides the cardinality of the group. Write $t' = p+1-\#E(\mathbb{F}_p)$; then ℓ divides $p+1-t'$. Now $-2\sqrt{p} \le t' \le 2\sqrt{p}$ by Hasse's theorem, while $-2\sqrt{p} < t < 2\sqrt{p}$ by condition 4, so $|t - t'| < 4\sqrt{p}$. Also $4\sqrt{p} < \ell$ by condition 2, so $|t - t'| < \ell$. But ℓ divides $p+1-t$ by condition 3, so ℓ divides $t - t'$. This forces $t - t' = 0$; i.e., the curve trace t' is t as claimed.

6.2 Is ECDLP broken for curves with small $|D|$?

Slightly. Specifically, starting from the rho method (see Section 4), one can save time for some curves where $|D|$ is very small, using fast "endomorphisms" derived from D [**111**].

This is not a complete break. The limits of these speedups are reasonably well understood, and the literature does not indicate any mechanism that could allow further speedups for small $|D|$, except when pairings allow the transfers covered in Section 5. It is conceivable that there are much better attacks against the occasional curves with small $|D|$, but, in the opposite direction, it is conceivable that there are much better attacks against the usual curves with large $|D|$. What is clear is that the security story is more complicated for small $|D|$; SafeCurves therefore requires large $|D|$.

Brainpool contains a related requirement: the **class number**, a quantity related to D, is required to be larger than 1000000. The generalized Riemann hypothesis (a standard conjecture in number theory, backed by extensive evidence) implies that the class number is not far from the square root of $|D|$; it is thus reasonably clear that the Brainpool requirement is much weaker than the SafeCurves lower limit on $|D|$. With some computation one can compute exact class numbers, and with less computation one can verify the Brainpool class-number condition, but this has not been incorporated into SafeCurves.

7 Rigidity

There are documented instances (see, e.g., [219], [49], [194], and [26, Section 3.6]), and many more suspected instances, of standards being manipulated by attackers. This raises the question of how users of standard curves can be assured that the curves were not generated to be weak.

The SafeCurves criteria simplify the ECC security story by requiring prime fields (see Section 2). This still leaves various security dangers such as transfers (see Section 5) and invalid-curve attacks (see Section 9 below), but the SafeCurves tables check for these dangers in a publicly verifiable way. There is still a potential lack of assurance in the following corner case:

- public ECC cryptanalysis might have missed an attack that applies to a small fraction of curves,
- an attacker might have figured out this attack, and
- the attacker might have manipulated the choices of standard curves to be vulnerable to this secret attack.

Most ECC standards include mechanisms that supposedly block the third step in this scenario. However, further analysis has pointed out flaws in these mechanisms. This section highlights three examples of algorithms that—*if* they are given a small class of weak curves as input—manipulate curve choices to land in that class, despite claimed barriers to this manipulation.

7.1 Manipulation algorithm 1: seed search

The possibility of attackers manipulating standard curve choices was raised in the late 1990s, when NSA volunteered to "contribute" elliptic curves to the committee producing ANSI X9.62 [8]. NSA did in fact end up producing various elliptic curves later standardized by ANSI X9.62, SEC 2 [203], and NIST FIPS 186-2 [220]; these curves, the "NIST curves", were subsequently deployed in many applications.

(As an explanation for NSA's involvement, Koblitz and Menezes wrote the following [153]: "In 1997, counting the number of points on a random elliptic curve was still a formidable challenge." However, a 1998 implementation paper [141] reported counting points on 3569 curves with $p = 2^{240} + 115$, with early aborts, in a total of 52 hours on a 300MHz Pentium II, under a minute per curve, finding 16 examples of prime-order curves.)

In response to NSA's contributions, ANSI X9.62 developed "a method for selecting an elliptic curve *verifiably* at random", and a procedure to "verify that a given elliptic curve was indeed generated at random". ANSI X9.62 even claims that this procedure "serves as proof (under the assumption that SHA-1 cannot be inverted) that the parameters were indeed generated at random". However, this procedure does *not* verify randomness; it verifies only that the curve coefficients were produced as hash output. The claimed "proof" is nonexistent.

Concretely, NIST P-256 is a curve of the form $y^2 = x^3 - 3x + H(s)$, where s is a large public "seed" and H is a hash function. In 1999, shortly after the NIST curves were announced, Scott [212] pointed out that the curves were not, in fact, verifiably random:

> Now if the idea is to increase our confidence that these curves are therefore completely randomly selected from the vast number of possible elliptic curves and hence likely to be secure, I think this process fails. The underlying assumption is that the vast majority of curves are "good". Consider now the possibility that one in a million of all curves have an exploitable structure that "they" know about, but we don't.. Then "they" simply generate a million random seeds until they find one that generates one of "their" curves. Then they get us to use them. And remember the standard paranoia assumptions apply - "they" have computing power way beyond what we can muster. So maybe that could be 1 billion.

Scott recommended generating curve coefficients from digits of π as an alternative, and concluded his posting as follows: "So, sigh, why didn't they do it that way? Do they want to be distrusted?"

In 2000, SEC 2 version 1.0 copied the curves that NSA had produced for NIST, copied the claim that the curves were "chosen verifiably at random", and specifically claimed that the curves were chosen "by repeatedly selecting a random seed and counting the number of points on the corresponding curve until appropriate parameters were found". This claim might be correct, but is certainly not verifiable.

7.2   Manipulation algorithm 2: curve-generator search

In 2005, Brainpool identified the lack of explanation of the NSA/NIST curve seeds as a "major issue" [66, page 2]. Instead of claiming to generate seeds at random, Brainpool specified a deterministic procedure to generate seeds "in a systematic and comprehensive way", reminiscent of Scott's suggestion to use digits of π.

In a May 2013 talk [42], we again raised the possibility of NSA having searched through a billion curves. The main focus of the talk—and of the SafeCurves web site [43], which we announced in October 2013—was instead implementation issues, but we did include a "rigidity" criterion in SafeCurves. This criterion prohibits the NIST curves as "manipulatable": the process "has a large unexplained input, giving the curve generator a large space of curves to choose from". The criterion allows the Brainpool curves because the curve generators do not have "many bits of control", but we also pointed out that the Brainpool seed-generation mechanism was only partially explained:

> Why SHA-1 instead of, e.g., RIPEMD-160 or SHA-256? Why use 160 bits of hash input independently of the curve size? Why pi and e instead of, e.g., sqrt(2) and sqrt(3)? Why handle separate key sizes by more digits of pi and e instead of hash derivation? Why counter mode instead of, e.g., OFB? Why use overlapping counters for A and B (producing the repeated 26DC5C6CE94A4B44F330B5D9)? Why not derive separate seeds for A and B?

Together with Chou, Chuengsatiansup, Hülsing, Lambooij, Niederhagen, and van Vredendaal, we then refined the SafeCurves analysis, developing models for criteria applied to accept curves and quantifying the number of curves accepted by each model. Our paper [29] showed how to generate more than a billion different Brainpool-like curves, each claiming to be "verifiably pseudorandom". (We also computed more than a million such curves.) In other words, the Brainpool approach—despite obviously being more constrained than the NIST approach—would still have supported malicious generation of a curve having a one-in-a-billion weakness, perhaps indicating that the SafeCurves rigidity criterion should be strengthened to disallow this approach. We also showed how to generate hundreds of thousands of curves meeting a newer criterion of being "verifiably deterministic", and how to generate hundreds of Curve25519-like curves, each being the fastest curve meeting specified security criteria.

7.3 The NIST curves, revisited

NSA's Jerry Solinas—who had supplied the curves standardized by ANSI, NIST, etc.—sent email after the first version of [29] went online. Given public interest in these issues, we have decided to disclose the email exchange; see Appendix C. Solinas claimed that NSA had "built all the seeds via hashing (SHA-1, I think) from the ASCII representation of a humorous message ... I believe there was a counter rather than multiple hashing, but I don't know details. The message was along the lines of 'Give Bob and Jerry a raise' or 'Bob and Jerry rule' or something like that".

Note that this claim is incompatible with the claims of verifiable randomness reviewed in Section 7.1, such as the claim that the curves were generated "by repeatedly selecting a random seed and counting the number of points on the corresponding curve until appropriate parameters were found". The reader understands "random" to mean uniformly and independently at random, not a meaningful message accompanied by a counter.

We tried hashing many inputs along the lines sketched above, varying details much as in Section 7.2, hoping to find the original seed. After a while, we gave up and moved the computers to more productive projects. We have heard about more recent efforts to reconstruct the seed, apparently none succeeding yet.

Solinas claimed that "we could prove our innocence by disclosing the details, if only we could remember them". But success in recovering the seed would not provide any evidence of innocence. There are far more than a billion choices of plausible, efficiently enumeratable messages.[4] A malicious search hashing many seeds to target a one-in-a-billion weakness does not care whether the seeds were generated randomly or generated as meaningful messages.

7.4 Manipulation algorithm 3: isogenies

Koblitz and Menezes claimed in 2015 [**153**, 21 October 2015 eprint version, Section 3.1] that, since there are $p^{1+o(1)}$ isomorphism classes of elliptic curves over $\mathbb{F}_p$, an attacker knowing a class of weak curves and searching (say) $p^{1/4+o(1)}$ seeds would be able to find a curve in the class only if the class has size at least $p^{3/4+o(1)}$, a "huge class of weak curves".

We pointed out in 2017 that this argument is incorrect, even for the extreme case of "back door" weaknesses. Our curve-manipulation algorithm works as follows (see also [**67**] for portions of this structure):

- Write down $p^{1/4+o(1)}$ back-door keys. Map each key to a curve, and count the number of points on each curve. (We assume that the number of points on a backdoored curve looks random. One out of every $p^{o(1)}$ curves will have prime order.)
- Write down $p^{1/4+o(1)}$ seeds. Map each seed to a curve, and count the number of points on each curve.
- There is a good chance of a collision in the number of points, since this number is in an interval of length only $4p^{1/2}$ by Hasse's theorem.
- Given a back-door key and a seed producing the same number of points, find an efficient isogeny between the two curves as follows: compute $p^{1/4+o(1)}$ curves efficiently isogenous to the first curve; compute $p^{1/4+o(1)}$ curves efficiently isogenous to the second curve; find a collision.

This algorithm takes $p^{1/4+o(1)}$ operations to find a curve in a class of size only $p^{1/4+o(1)}$, far smaller than the $p^{3/4+o(1)}$ claimed in [**153**]. The memory consumption in the algorithm can easily be eliminated if the pool of back-door

---

[4] Consider, e.g., a simple request for money: "Bob" can instead be written "Bob Reiter" or "Robert Reiter" or "Robert Reiter Jr." or "Robert Reiter, Jr." or "Robert W. Reiter" or "Robert W. Reiter Jr." or "Robert W. Reiter, Jr."; "Dr." can be inserted in front of the name; if there were 20 people in the office with different names then there were 1330 choices of 2 or 3 names in alphabetical order; the request can end with an exclamation mark, a period, or no punctuation; the request can be all uppercase, all lowercase, or normal; a counter can be before or after the sentence; the counter can be separated by a space, a slash, a colon, or nothing; the counter can be zero-padded to 6 digits, or unpadded; the counter can be decimal, 0o octal, 0x hex, or 0X hex; the request can start with "please" or "we must" or nothing; the request can end with "today" or "right now" or "this year" or nothing; the request can be for a "raise" or a "bonus"; this can be "big" or "large" or "giant" or "massive" or "enormous"; etc.

keys is large enough (as it has to be for "nobody but us" back doors) and if the pool of seeds is large enough (as it is for the NIST curves).

Koblitz and Menezes responded that they estimate at least 2^{86} bit operations for this procedure for $p \approx 2^{256}$, "which almost certainly was beyond the NSA's capacity in 1997".

To put 2^{86} bit operations in perspective, observe that Bitcoin currently carries out 2^{87} bit operations every second. (See [58], which indicates that Bitcoin has reached 600 million terahashes per second; and recall that each hash uses about 2^{18} bit operations.) The question is whether this volume of computation would have taken, e.g., a year for NSA in 1997.

Appendix D uses information about Intel's mass-produced chips in 1997 to estimate the volume of chips that would have carried out 2^{86} bit operations in a year, and concludes that this would have been only about 10% of NSA's budget at the time, according to public information regarding that budget.

Of course, if records show that NSA was responding to an unpredictable curve-generation challenge in only M months, then an attack would have had to complete within M months. On the other hand, presumably more attention to the attack details would reduce the number of bit operations.

7.5   Attack discovery

The real question in [153] is whether it is plausible that NSA in 1997 knew curve weaknesses that are not known to the public today. Regarding a class of, e.g., 2^{209} weak curves, [153] says that it is "highly unlikely that such a large family of weak elliptic curves would have escaped detection by the cryptographic research community from 1997 to the present".

We do not see why the size of a weak-key class is relevant to the question of whether the weakness is detected by the public. The currently known classes of curves for which ECDLP has been broken range from the tiny class of curves subject to additive transfers (see Section 5) to the frequent curves for which the group order factors into small primes. Weak curves are detected by study of potential avenues of attack, not by Geiger counters.

If there are many smart people in public actively searching for better ECDLP attacks then the passage of time would suggest that no such attacks exist. However, public cryptanalysts with relevant knowledge are generally busy working on other topics, such as isogeny-based cryptography; so one would expect an elliptic-curve attack to appear only if it happens to be a spinoff of those other topics, as in [109].

7.6   Isn't it safest to choose cryptographic parameters at random?

Cryptographic *keys* lose security when they do not have enough randomness. There is a common confusion between public *parameters* and public *keys*, creating a common myth that public *parameters* lose security unless they are as random as possible.

The literature contains many counterexamples to this myth. For example, there are known attacks [**90**] that significantly reduce the security level of random genus-3 curves, but the attacks do not apply to specially structured genus-3 curves, namely *hyperelliptic* curves. As another example, ECC takes only unusual curves whose group orders have very large prime divisors, because uniform random curves are much less secure than these unusual curves. See [**151**, Section 11] for more subtle examples.

One should not conclude that uniform random parameters are necessarily bad: there are also examples where adding randomness to parameters is good. To see whether randomness is good or bad for the parameters of any particular system, one needs to study the details of attacks against that system.

All curves that meet the SafeCurves criteria are protected against all published attacks, use the most conservative bounds to stay far away from those attacks, and eliminate structure that has raised concerns about potential attacks. The criteria are computer-verified, with full details presented on our web page [**43**] to support third-party verification. It is conceivable that some of these curves are vulnerable to an attack that is not publicly known, but there is no basis for guessing whether any particular curve will be more or less vulnerable to attack than a random curve.

ECC users can reasonably choose their own random curves to protect against multiple-target rho attacks; see Section 4.2. However, giving a random curve to each user also has several obvious costs, whereas moving to a larger shared curve has lower costs and makes the same attacks even more expensive. This is why essentially all ECC applications use shared curves.

7.7   What about rigid choices of subgroups?

For each curve in the SafeCurves tables, the order ℓ of the specified subgroup of the group of rational points is prime and larger than $\sqrt{p} + 1$. A curve cannot have two different subgroups meeting this requirement.

7.8   What about rigid choices of base points?

For each curve in the SafeCurves tables, the specified base point is a generator of the specified subgroup. The SafeCurves criteria do not place restrictions on the choice of this base point. If there is a "weak" base point W allowing easy computations of discrete logarithms, then ECDLP is weak for every base point: an attacker can compute $\log_P Q$ as the ratio of $\log_W Q$ and $\log_W P$ modulo ℓ. Typical ECC protocols, such as signatures, are designed to be secure for all choices of base point.

There are some protocols where base-point rigidity is important. For example, a "random" ECDLP challenge, computing the discrete logarithm of Q base P, could have a back door for the challenge creator. Certicom's ECDLP challenges use rigid generators P and Q of the subgroup to prevent Certicom from choosing the discrete logarithm in advance. As another example, the CurveBall attack in 2020 [**173**] broke signature verification in Microsoft Windows CryptoAPI, allowing attackers to freely sign malicious executables under Microsoft's key, by exploiting the fact that CryptoAPI allowed certificates to provide their own base points.

For some curves, the specified base point is chosen rigidly. The usual choice is the generator with smallest possible x-coordinate for short Weierstrass curves or Montgomery curves, or smallest possible y-coordinate for Edwards curves. The reason for x vs. y here is that $y(-P) = y(P)$ for Edwards, allowing y as a ladder coordinate (see Section 8), while $x(-P) = x(P)$ for the others, allowing x as a ladder coordinate.

8 Ladders

This section focuses on the most important computation in ECC: namely, single-scalar variable-base-point multiplication. This means computing nP, given an integer n and a curve point P. This is what happens in each shared-secret computation in ECDH, when user i computes $s_i(s_jG)$ using their secret s_i and user j's public key s_jG before starting to communicate with j.

Given the emphasis on efficiency in the turn-of-the-century ECC standards (see the quotes in Section 3.1), it is puzzling that those standards chose to use short Weierstrass curves. This choice did not provide the fastest arithmetic known on elliptic curves; it was already outperformed by other options in [82] and [177], the fastest being the "Montgomery ladder" introduced in [177]. The Montgomery ladder is also a much *simpler* way to carry out ECDH computations, and naturally avoids various classes of security problems that we have seen repeatedly appearing in ECDH software.

This section begins by reviewing scalar-multiplication algorithms for short Weierstrass curves and for Montgomery curves, and then uses timing attacks to introduce the idea of different curve shapes having different chances of producing security problems. Sections 9 and 10 explain more ways that short Weierstrass curves produce security problems avoided by better choices of curves.

8.1 Scalar multiplication on short Weierstrass curves

As an example of how the literature suggests computing nP on a short Weierstrass curve, we quote the algorithm presented in the P1363 standard [134, Annex A.10.3, "Elliptic Scalar Multiplication"]:

1. If $n = 0$, then output O and stop.
2. If $n < 0$, then set $Q \leftarrow (-P)$ and $k \leftarrow (-n)$; else set $Q \leftarrow P$ and $k \leftarrow n$.
3. Let $h_l h_{l-1} \ldots h_1 h_0$ be the binary representation of $3k$, where the most significant bit h_l is 1.
4. Let $k_l k_{l-1} \ldots k_1 k_0$ be the binary representation of k.
5. Set $S \leftarrow Q$.
6. For i from $l - 1$ downto 1 do

Set $S \leftarrow 2S$.
If $h_i = 1$ and $k_i = 0$, then compute $S \leftarrow S + Q$ via A.10.1 or
A.10.2.
If $h_i = 0$ and $k_i = 1$, then compute $S \leftarrow S - Q$ via A.10.1 or
A.10.2.

7. Output S.

We focus on the case $n > 0$, where the first two steps of the algorithm can
be omitted. The algorithm builds an "addition-subtraction chain" for n using
approximately $\log_2 n$ doublings and $(\log_2 n)/3$ further group operations, each of
those group operations being an addition or a subtraction.

The standard also cites sources presenting addition-subtraction chains that are
more complicated but more efficient, replacing $(\log_2 n)/3$ with about $(\log_2 n)/5$
for typical sizes of n. These chains are organized as a preliminary computation
of a table containing, e.g., $3P, 5P, \ldots, 15P$, and then a series of doublings with
occasional additions or subtractions interspersed. The costs shown below assume
that these faster chains are used.

The implementor then needs to plug in formulas for curve doubling ("$2S$"),
addition ("$S+Q$"), and subtraction ("$S-Q$"), where Q is one of the precomputed
small multiples of P from the table. For short Weierstrass curves with $a = -3$
in Jacobian coordinates using the 1986 Chudnovsky–Chudnovsky formulas from
[82], each doubling costs 8M, and each addition or subtraction costs 16M, for a
total of about $8\mathbf{M} + 16\mathbf{M}/5 = 11.2\mathbf{M}$ per bit of n. There is also an inversion at
the end of the computation to replace Jacobian coordinates (X, Y, Z) with affine
coordinates $(x, y) = (X/Z^2, Y/Z^3)$ for communication.

A simple inversion method costs slightly over 1M per bit of p, which typically
means slightly over 1M per bit of n. More sophisticated inversion methods (see,
e.g., [53]) cost less. Sometimes inversions can be batched, reducing the cost very
close to 0M per bit. Using mixed coordinates from [83], which switches between
coordinate systems within a scalar multiplication, reduces the costs per additon
to 14M, for a cost per bit of $8\mathbf{M} + 14\mathbf{M}/5 = 10.8\mathbf{M}$ or, at the expense of an
extra inversion in $\mathbb{F}_q$, of $8\mathbf{M} + 11\mathbf{M}/5 = 10.2\mathbf{M}$. See generally [38] and [37] for
different coordinate systems and combinations.

8.2   Scalar multiplication on Montgomery curves

For a Montgomery curve $By^2 = x^3 + Ax^2 + x$ in Montgomery coordinates using
the Montgomery ladder, computation of nP follows a much simpler pattern
of one doubling and one "differential addition" for each bit of n. Differential
addition means computing $P + Q$ given P, Q, and $P - Q$.

Each point has just two coordinates (X, Z) with $x = X/Z$; the y-coordinate
is not used. The doubling and differential addition together cost just 9M plus
a multiplication by $(A + 2)/4$. Montgomery curves are normally chosen with
$(A+2)/4$ being small, so the overall cost is just 9M per bit of n, plus an inversion
at the end of the computation to convert (X, Z) to $x = X/Z$ for communication.

```
def montgomery(x1,n):
  A = 486662
  x2,z2,x3,z3 = 1,0,x1,1
  for i in reversed(range(255)):
    ni = bit(n,i)
    x2,x3 = cswap(x2,x3,ni)
    z2,z3 = cswap(z2,z3,ni)
    x3,z3 = 4*(x2*x3-z2*z3)**2,4*x1*(x2*z3-z2*x3)**2
    x2,z2 = (x2**2-z2**2)**2,4*x2*z2*(x2**2+A*x2*z2+z2**2)
    x3,z3 = x3%p,z3%p
    x2,z2 = x2%p,z2%p
    x2,x3 = cswap(x2,x3,ni)
    z2,z3 = cswap(z2,z3,ni)
  return (x2*pow(z2,p-2,p))%p
```

Fig. 8.2.1. Python code for the Montgomery ladder for Curve25519. The **bit** function extracts the coefficient of 2^i in n. The **cswap** function is a conditional swap, returning its first two inputs in the same order or reversed order depending on whether the third input is 0 or 1. Warning: integer arithmetic in Python takes variable time.

This is faster than any of the scalar-multiplication methods summarized in Section 8.1; in particular, it is about 1.5 times as fast as the method quoted from P1363. A more detailed cost analysis would consider, e.g., the costs of additions and subtractions in $\mathbb{F}_p$, the speedups from squarings in $\mathbb{F}_p$ being faster than general multiplications in $\mathbb{F}_p$, and the costs of communicating (x, y) for short Weierstrass curves vs. just x for Montgomery curves.

The 2006 paper [**23**] introducing X25519 (ECDH using Curve25519 with a Montgomery ladder)[5] presented X25519 software for various platforms more than twice as fast as previous results for NIST P-256 ECDH, and attributed the speedup partly to the curve choice. Subsequent work has consistently shown X25519 outperforming NIST P-256 ECDH; see Appendix E for examples of current speeds. The speedup is not entirely from the Montgomery ladder—for example, it is also affected by reductions mod $2^{255} - 19$ being easier than reductions mod $2^{256} - 2^{224} + 2^{192} + 2^{96} - 1$—but the speed of the Montgomery ladder certainly plays an important role.

What is even more remarkable than the speed of the Montgomery ladder is its simplicity. Figure 8.2.1, copied from the Python test suite in the lib25519 [**51**] software library for Curve25519, displays the Montgomery ladder in the case $A = 486662$ with a 255-bit n—except that the polynomials in the middle such as $x_2x_3 - z_2z_3$ are written for maximum conciseness, skipping the optimized computations of those polynomials from [**177**, page 261, "costs drop"]. These concise formulas were found independently by Chudnovsky–Chudnovsky [**82**, formula (4.19)]; but credit is normally assigned to Montgomery, who found the

---

[5] [**23**] used "Curve25519" to refer to X25519 rather than to the curve. X25519 was a subsequent renaming to allow separate names for the curve and the protocol.

concise formulas, the optimizations, and a simple statement of the curve shape. (As an example of these optimizations, the reader is invited to consider the two quantities $(x_2 - z_2)(x_3 + z_3) \pm (x_2 + z_2)(x_3 - z_3)$.)

Figure 8.2.1 has similar length to the much slower scalar-multiplication method quoted at the beginning of Section 8.1—but Figure 8.2.1 includes all of the necessary elliptic-curve computations! Furthermore, as we will see, the approach in Section 8.1 naturally leads to various security problems avoided by the Montgomery ladder.

8.3 Timing attacks

Care is required in computing the `cswap` operations in Figure 8.2.1. The obvious way to conditionally swap x_2 and x_3 if $n_i = 1$ is to write code such as

```
if ni == 1: x2,x3 = x3,x2
```

but this will take more time if $n_i = 1$. One then expects sufficiently detailed measurements of the total time of the computation to detect the number of i for which $n_i = 1$. More subtly, interactions with the timings of other programs (see, e.g., [10]) can leak each n_i. A typical way to proactively eliminate these timing leaks is to replace each secret-dependent branch with arithmetic:

```
x2,x3 = x2+ni*(x3-x2),x3-ni*(x3-x2)
```

Further work is then required to ensure that each lower-level operation, such as field addition, takes time independent of the inputs.

There are much larger timing leaks in the P1363 scalar-multiplication algorithm quoted in Section 8.1. For example, the case $(h_i, k_i) = (1, 0)$ triggers an entire curve-addition operation $S \leftarrow S + Q$, a much larger operation than swapping x_2 with x_3. Larger leaks tend to be exploitable in more situations—the timing information can be detected through more noise—and tend to be more annoying to fix. Regarding fixes in this case, one way to replace branches with arithmetic for both $S \leftarrow S + Q$ and $S \leftarrow S - Q$ is to

- conditionally select between Q and $-Q$,
- add the resulting $\pm Q$ to S, and
- conditionally select between S and $S \pm Q$;

also, as before, one needs to make sure that the conditional operations and lower-level arithmetic operations take constant time. Protection here takes more work than in the Montgomery ladder, with more steps that can go wrong. Furthermore, the resulting algorithm takes one curve addition and one doubling for a total of 24**M** per bit, making it more likely that implementors will switch to the more complicated chains mentioned in Section 8.1, using tables to reduce the number of additions. Those tables, in turn, open up further attacks that exploit timing variations in table lookups; see, e.g., the 2009 paper [**74**] from Brumley and Hakala demonstrating recovery of elliptic-curve keys from OpenSSL.

We are not saying that implementations *always* get this wrong. It is possible to write software for addition-subtraction chains, even chains at the aforementioned $(\log_2 n)/5$ level of performance, while avoiding secret-dependent conditional branches and secret-dependent table indices. What we are saying is that implementations are *more likely* to have security failures for short Weierstrass curves than for Montgomery curves: the natural pursuit of simplicity—and, in many cases, speed—pushes implementations farther away from security for short Weierstrass curves than for Montgomery curves. See Sections 9 and 10 for further examples of this tension.

8.4   The SafeCurves ladder criterion

The "ladder" criterion in SafeCurves is defined as follows:

> SafeCurves requires curves to support simple, fast, constant-time single-coordinate single-scalar multiplication, avoiding conflicts between simplicity, efficiency, and security. This is not a requirement specifically to use Montgomery curves: there are other types of curves that support simple, fast, constant-time ladders. "Fast" means that implementations of scalar multiplication for the same curve cannot be much faster, and "simple" means that reasonably fast implementations of scalar multiplication for the same curve cannot be much more concise. At this time there are no examples close enough to the edge to warrant quantification of "much".

In this criterion, "single-coordinate" refers to scalar multiplication taking just one coordinate as input and producing just one coordinate as output. "Ladder" refers to the structure used in Figure 8.2.1, with a doubling and differential addition of two points for each bit of n.

Beware that there are some papers erroneously referring to arbitrary ladders as "Montgomery ladders". The general ladder structure is much older than the Montgomery ladder. See, e.g., the discussion of the Lucas ladder in our paper [**45**, Section 4.2.1]; Montgomery's work started with the Lucas ladder.

8.5   Variable-length ladders

Figure 8.2.1 is an example of a constant-length ladder: it initializes the starting variables x2,z2,x3,z3 so that the algorithm correctly computes nP for any integer n with $0 \le n < 2^{255}$, always taking exactly 255 iterations.

One can find literature presenting ladders where the number of iterations is instead a variable i, namely the smallest integer $i \ge 0$ such that $n < 2^i$. This does not provide a noticeable speedup or code simplification, but implementors might end up using it simply because it appears in the literature, and then timing information leaks i. This was used in a 2011 timing attack [**75**] to extract secret keys remotely from OpenSSL's implementation of binary-field ECC.

We repeat Section 1's comment about the word "most": better curve choices make ECC implementation failures less likely and are the focus of SafeCurves, but one needs to take further steps to eliminate the remaining failures. In particular, to prevent problems in case implementors use fixed-length ladders, X25519 uses "a fixed position for the leading 1 in the secret key", as mentioned in the Curve25519 paper [23] in 2006.

8.6 Isomorphism (and birational equivalence)

As noted in Section 3, a simple change of variables converts a Montgomery curve into a short Weierstrass curve. This means that ECDH implementations for a Montgomery curve *can* use the approach from Section 8.1 rather than the much nicer Montgomery ladder. A library that already has software for the NIST curves might be tempted to handle a Montgomery curve this way. We do not claim that using Montgomery curves guarantees that all implementations are secure.

More interestingly, it is sometimes possible to invert this change of variables, converting a short Weierstrass curve $y^2 = x^3 + ax + b$ into a Montgomery curve as follows. Find r satisfying $r^3 + ar + b = 0$. Find s satisfying $s^2 = 3r^2 + a$. Define $u = (x - r)/s$, $B = 1/s^3$, and $A = 3r/s$. Then $By^2 = u^3 + Au^2 + u$. One can perform x-coordinate scalar multiplication on $y^2 = x^3 + ax + b$ by converting x to u, performing u-coordinate scalar multiplication on $By^2 = u^3 + Au^2 + u$ with the Montgomery ladder, and converting back.

The reason this does not always work is that, for the majority of curves, the field $\mathbb{F}_p$ does not contain suitable elements r and s. One can work around this by replacing $\mathbb{F}_p$ with an extension field, but this requires more complicated field operations inside scalar multiplication.

To be more precise, out of all isomorphism classes of elliptic curves over $\mathbb{F}_p$, the fraction that can be written as Montgomery curves is about $5/12$ if $p \equiv 1$ (mod 4), and about $3/8$ if $p \equiv 3$ (mod 4); see, e.g., [27]. A Montgomery curve E always has $\#E(\mathbb{F}_p) \equiv 0$ (mod 4), so curves E over $\mathbb{F}_p$ for which $\#E(\mathbb{F}_p)$ is a prime number, or 2 times an odd prime number, can never be converted to Montgomery curves over $\mathbb{F}_p$.

8.7 More ladders

Instead of trying to convert a short Weierstrass curve to a Montgomery curve, one can build a ladder directly on a short Weierstrass curve.

Every curve has a ladder. In the first ECC paper in 1986 [174, page 425, fourth paragraph], Miller commented that "only the x-coordinate needs to be transmitted" for ECDH on short Weierstrass curves $y^2 = x^3 + ax + b$, since "the x-coordinate of a multiple depends only on the x-coordinate of the original point"; one can convert the formulas given in [174] (attributed there to earlier sources) into a constant-time ladder.

We emphasize that merely having a ladder is not sufficient to meet the SafeCurves ladder criterion. The ladder has to also be "fast", meaning that "implementations of scalar multiplication for the same curve cannot be much faster", and "simple", meaning that "reasonably fast implementations of scalar multiplication for the same curve cannot be much more concise". This criterion is not simply asking whether a ladder *exists*; it is asking whether natural implementation incentives will lead to the ladder being *used*, as in the case of the Montgomery ladder.

In 2002, Brier and Joye [70] reported 19M per bit for a constant-time x-coordinate ladder applicable to every short Weierstrass curve $y^2 = x^3 + ax + b$. Scalar multiplication for the same curves as in Section 8.1 is much faster than the Brier–Joye ladder, so this ladder does not qualify as "fast". We commented on the SafeCurves web site that this ladder is an example of a "conflict between efficiency and security".

There has been more work on ladders since then. The latest news is a 2020 paper from Hamburg [124] reporting 11M per bit for an x-coordinate ladder. For comparison, recall that the best speed from Section 8.1 was 10.2M per bit. The performance gap turns out to be larger when one accounts for squarings being faster than general multiplications in $\mathbb{F}_p$, but one might still ask whether the word "much" now needs be quantified in the definition of "fast". Independently of that question, there is a different reason that we do not expect much use of this ladder: namely, this ladder appears to be covered by Hamburg's U.S. patent application 17/916,979. The patent application was assigned to Cryptography Research, a subsidiary of Rambus, and was filed before [124] was published.

9 Twist security

Imagine a careful implementation of NIST P-256 ECDH. The implementation multiplies the user's long-term secret key n by an incoming public key (x, y), using the scalar-multiplication methods from Section 8.1. The implementor is aware of timing attacks (see Section 8.3), and manages to eliminate all timing variations from the software. Also, let's be trendy here: the implementation is using computer-checked proofs that the arithmetic in $\mathbb{F}_p$ is always correct. The software isn't competitive in speed with X25519, but let's assume it's fast enough for the application. Everything is good at this point, right?

Unfortunately not. The implementation never checked that the incoming point (x, y) is on the curve. This has no effect on the normal operation of the protocol—but it exposes the software to an "invalid-curve attack" [54] where an attacker quickly extracts n by sending a few fake points (x, y). See Section 9.2.

We have seen again and again that implementations are vulnerable to invalid-curve attacks. For example:

- Vulnerability announcement CVE-2019-9155 [97] said that the OpenPGP.js software "allows an attacker who is able provide forged messages and gain feedback about whether decryption of these messages succeeded to conduct an invalid curve attack in order to gain the victim's ECDH private key".
- Vulnerability announcement CVE-2021-3798 [201] said that the "openCryptoki Soft token does not check if an EC key is valid when an EC key is created via `C_CreateObject`, nor when `C_DeriveKey` is used

with ECDH public data. This may allow a malicious user to extract the private key by performing an invalid curve attack".

- Vulnerability announcement CVE-2023-46324 [**175**] said that the free5GC udm software "allows an Invalid Curve Attack because it may compute a shared secret via an uncompressed public key that has not been validated. An attacker can send arbitrary SUCIs to the UDM, which tries to decrypt them via both its private key and the attacker's public key". SUCIs are 5G's "Subscription Concealed Identifiers". See [**107**] for more information.

Rather than blaming an apparently neverending series of implementors for not following security advice, the SafeCurves criteria have always proactively addressed this attack by moving to better curves:

- First, choose curves meeting the SafeCurves ladder criterion covered in Section 8, so that the incentives explained in that section encourage protocols to send just x rather than (x, y).
- Second, choose curves to be "twist-secure". This section covers the SafeCurves twist-security criteria, after explaining the motivating attacks.

The effectiveness of this approach is illustrated by a direct comparison in the 5G example cited above. According to [**107**, page 10], 5G requires implementations to support both Curve25519 and P-256 as options for SUCIs. As one would expect from the considerations in Section 8, the protocol is designed to send just x for Curve25519 but (x, y) for P-256. The attack from [**107**] worked against the P-256 option and failed against the X25519 option in the same software.

9.1 Small-subgroup attacks

Before reviewing invalid-curve attacks, we review **small-subgroup attacks** on ECDH. Small-subgroup attacks for multiplicative groups were introduced in a 1997 paper [**165**] by Lim and Lee.

As usual, we assume that E is an elliptic curve over $\mathbb{F}_p$, and that $G \in E(\mathbb{F}_p)$ is an ECDH base point of large prime order ℓ. This forces $\#E(\mathbb{F}_p) = h\ell$ for some positive integer h, called the "cofactor". We focus on the case that h is small, as in typical curve choices: e.g., $h = 8$ for Curve25519, and $h = 1$ for NIST P-256.

A small-subgroup attack proceeds as follows. Instead of sending a legitimate curve point eG to Bob, Eve sends Bob a point $Q \in E(\mathbb{F}_p)$ of small order, pretending that Q is her public key. Bob computes nQ as usual, where n is Bob's secret key; computes a hash of nQ as a shared secret key for, e.g., AES-GCM; and uses AES-GCM to encrypt and authenticate data. Because Q has small order, there are not many possibilities for nQ; Eve can simply enumerate the possibilities and check which possibility successfully verifies the data. This attack reveals n modulo the order of Q.

The only possible orders of curve points Q are

- divisors of h and
- ℓ times divisors of h.

In the second case, Q has order at least ℓ, giving too many possibilities for nQ to enumerate, so the attack does not work. Eve's best strategy—assuming the curve is cyclic, which typical curve choices are—is then to take a curve point Q of order h, so that the attack reveals n modulo h.

At this point we distinguish three scenarios. The first scenario is that Bob chose n as a uniform random integer modulo $h\ell$. Then, after this attack, there are still ℓ equally likely possibilities for n.

The second scenario is that Bob chose n as hs, where s is a uniform random integer modulo ℓ. Then the attack reveals nothing, and there are still ℓ equally likely possibilities for n. In both of these scenarios, Eve's best strategy is to continue with the rho method (see Section 4) in the group generated by G, a group of prime order ℓ.

The third scenario is that Bob instead chose n as a uniform random integer modulo ℓ. In this scenario, there is a slight loss of security: the attack reduces n to just ℓ/h possibilities, allowing a "kangaroo" computation [197], roughly $\sqrt{h}$ times faster than the rho method.

An implementor can stop a small-subgroup attack by rejecting any Q for which $hQ = 0$, either by carrying out a short computation or by checking against a precomputed list. But this creates a conflict between simplicity and security. An implementation that does not include this check is simpler and more likely to be produced, and will pass typical functionality tests.

A curve designer can protect against this type of attack by choosing curves with $h = 1$. A protocol designer can protect against this type of attack for any curve by specifying $n = hs$. Even without any defenses, the impact is limited to $\sqrt{h}$ for ECDH.

9.2 Invalid-curve attacks

Much more serious is an **invalid-curve** attack. In this case Eve sends Bob a point Q of small order *on another curve*.

For example, instead of sending Bob a point (x, y) satisfying a standard short Weierstrass equation $y^2 = x^3 + ax + b$, Eve sends a point (x, y) satisfying another short Weierstrass equation $y^2 = x^3 + ax + c$ where c is different from b. The standard formulas for scalar multiplication on short Weierstrass curves do not involve the constant coefficient b, so they automatically also work for $y^2 = x^3 + ax + c$. Bob will successfully compute $n(x, y)$ without realizing that anything is amiss.

The advantage of an invalid-curve attack, compared to a small-subgroup attack, is that Eve has many more points Q to choose from. Eve can run the attack using a point Q_2 of order 2 on one curve, a point Q_3 of order 3 on another curve, a point Q_5 of order 5 on another curve, etc., revealing n modulo 2, modulo 3, modulo 5, etc. Soon Eve has enough information to interpolate Bob's entire public key n using an explicit form of the Chinese remainder theorem.

Quantitatively, for fixed non-zero a, the short Weierstrass curves $y^2 = x^3 + ax + b$ cover roughly 25% or roughly 50% of all isomorphism classes of elliptic curves, depending on p. These curves have roughly $4\sqrt{p}$ different orders, and a huge number of points Q of small order.

Invalid-curve attacks were introduced in a 2000 paper [54] by Biehl, Meyer, and Müller. See also [55] for a variant breaking a Bluetooth security mechanism in which keys are used only once and x-coordinates are authenticated; the attack replaces (x, y) with $(x, 0)$.

Standards typically say that an implementation that receives a point (x, y) from another party *must* check whether (x, y) is on the curve. This takes very little computation time compared to scalar multiplication, and if it is done then it stops an invalid-curve attack. However, this again creates a conflict between simplicity and security. The CVEs show that this is still a frequent problem, more than 20 years after the attack was introduced.

9.3   Point compression

A protocol designer might try to help protect against invalid-curve attacks by specifying point compression. The idea is that an implementation that receives a compressed point, such as x and just one bit of y, will naturally detect invalid inputs when it reconstructs the missing coordinate. On the other hand, if an implementation was not checking the curve equation, then one has to ask what will happen if the implementation does not check squareness as part of a square-root computation to recover y; this question needs analysis. See Section 11.5.

Despite the obvious size advantage and potential security advantage of sending compressed points, it is common for protocols built on short Weierstrass curves to send uncompressed (x, y). We point out three factors that appear to have contributed to this.

The first factor is U.S. patent 6141420, which was filed in 1994 and expired in 2014. Claim 29 of the patent is on communicating a curve point by communicating one coordinate and having the recipient recover the other coordinate. Claim 30 of the patent is more specifically on also sending "identifying information of said other coordinate"—e.g., one bit of y.

Bodo Möller pointed out that point compression had already appeared in a 1992 paper [127, page 171] on ECDH, more than a year before the patent was filed. The patent also shared a coauthor with the paper. We doubt that the patent would have survived litigation. But the patent holder, Certicom, sent many letters regarding its patents, including the point-compression patent; see, e.g., [78]. In 2007, Certicom took Sony to court regarding other patents. It is understandable that protocol designers were hesitant to consider point compression.

(Certicom also filed, in 1997, a patent application on point validation, checking whether points are on curves. Certicom received U.S. patent 7215773 in 2007. That patent has also expired.)

A second factor weighing against point compression is the cost of recovering y, essentially the aforementioned square-root computation in $\mathbb{F}_p$. This involves some extra code and adds roughly 10% to the cost of scalar multiplication.

A third factor is the installed base. Once there are enough protocols and libraries using uncompressed points (x, y) on short Weierstrass curves, there is an incentive for new protocols to do what is most easily handled by the existing libraries, and for new libraries to focus on what is needed by the existing protocols. To be clear, we are not saying that something new can never be deployed; for example, [169] says that the "vast majority" of TLS connections are now using X25519. See also [72] and [73].

9.4   Twist attacks against ladders

Curves meeting the SafeCurves ladder criterion (see Section 8.4) naturally end up with protocols sending just single coordinates as ECDH public keys. This drastically limits the power of invalid-curve attacks.

Consider, for example, a Montgomery curve $By^2 = x^3 + Ax^2 + x$ over $\mathbb{F}_p$. Any input x that is not on the curve is guaranteed to be on the "twisted" curve $(B/u)y^2 = x^3 + Ax^2 + x$, where u is a non-square in $\mathbb{F}_p$. Specifically:

- If $(x^3 + Ax^2 + x)/B$ is a nonzero square in $\mathbb{F}_p$ then x represents two points $(x, \pm\sqrt{(x^3 + Ax^2 + x)/B})$ on the original curve.
- If $(x^3 + Ax^2 + x)/B$ is a non-square in $\mathbb{F}_p$ then x represents two points $(x, \pm\sqrt{(x^3 + Ax^2 + x)u/B})$ on the twisted curve.
- If $(x^3 + Ax^2 + x)/B$ is zero then x represents one point $(x, 0)$ on each curve.

The Montgomery ladder formulas for $By^2 = x^3 + Ax^2 + x$ also compute scalar multiplication for the twisted curve $(B/u)y^2 = x^3 + Ax^2 + x$, so the attacker can use points of small order on either of these curves, but the single input coordinate does not provide any other attack options. An invalid-curve attack using the twisted curve is called a "twist attack".

The general picture is that single-coordinate ladders work for curves isomorphic to the original curve and for one other isomorphism class of curves, namely all the **nontrivial quadratic twists** of the original curve. If the original curve has $p + 1 - t$ points then any nontrivial quadratic twist has $p + 1 + t$ points. Often a nontrivial quadratic twist is called "the twist".

An ECC implementor can stop an invalid-curve attack against ladders by checking whether the input coordinate x belongs to a point Q on the correct curve equation; this requires determining whether $x^3 + Ax^2 + x$ is a square. This computation is doable but noticeable in the overall computation of nQ; this also creates yet another conflict between simplicity and security.

A curve designer can protect against this attack by choosing better curves, namely twist-secure curves, meaning that the twist also has a small cofactor. This renders the checks unnecessary. See Section 9.5 for a quantitative analysis.

Twist-secure curves for DH were proposed in a 2001 talk [21] and posting [22] by one of the authors of this paper. See also the Curve25519 paper [23] and 2008 Fouque–Lercier–Réal–Valette [102].

9.5 Security against twist attacks

SafeCurves requires single-coordinate ladder ECDH to remain secure even if

- Bob chooses n only up to ℓ;
- Bob does not multiply n by the cofactor h for the original curve;
- Bob does not multiply n by the cofactor h' for the twist; and
- Bob does not bother to check whether incoming points are on the original curve.

Specifically, SafeCurves quantitatively evaluates **combined attacks** that use small-subgroup attacks as described above together with invalid-curve attacks using the twist. SafeCurves requires the security level against these attacks to be at least the square root of the lower limit on ℓ in the SafeCurves rho criterion. That lower limit was 2^{200} when we posted the SafeCurves web pages, so SafeCurves required at least 2^{100} security against these attacks, but note that we are now updating this limit; see Section 4.

If both cofactors are very small then the security level of this combined attack is close to the standard rho security level: for example, the combined attack costs $2^{120.3}$ for NIST P-256, and $2^{124.3}$ for Curve25519. In other cases the security level of this combined attack can be far below the standard rho security level: for example, the combined attack costs just $2^{58.4}$ for NIST P-224, and just $2^{44.5}$ for brainpoolP256t1.

Here are two examples showing how to optimize combined attacks:

1. Assume that the original curve has order $h\ell$ and that the twist has order $h'\ell'$ where ℓ and ℓ' are primes around 2^{200}, h and h' are around 2^{50}, and h and h' are coprime. Assume that Bob chooses n as a number less than ℓ. The attacker computes n modulo h in at most 2^{50} operations (trying all h possible values of nQ against some AES-GCM encrypted text); computes n modulo h' in at most 2^{50} operations; obtains n modulo hh' using CRT; and does a kangaroo attack against the $\ell/(hh')$ possibilities of n in time 2^{50}, for a total of $2^{51.6}$ operations. If h or h' factor further, the first two searches can be sped up at the expense of more interaction with Bob; however, this does not reduce the overall running time.

2. Assume instead that ℓ' is around 2^{94}; that ℓ is around 2^{200}; that h' is a product of primes q, r, and s around 2^{8}, 2^{18}, and 2^{90}; that h is around 2^{10}; and again that h and h' are coprime. Assume again that Bob chooses n as a number less than ℓ. In this situation the best attack is as follows: compute n modulo h in about 2^{10} operations; compute n modulo q and r in about 2^{18} operations; obtain n modulo hqr using CRT; apply a kangaroo attack to the remaining $\ell/(hqr)$ possibilities for n. Here hqr is around 2^{36}, so the kangaroo attack takes only about 2^{82} operations. Note that the attacker did not use a point of order s here, since searching all the multiples of the point would have taken 2^{90} operations; the combined attack balances the cost of the brute-force searches with the cost of a kangaroo attack on the remaining DLP in the main subgroup. Note also that a standard ECDLP problem for

the group of order ℓ' would have been much easier to solve, using only 2^{47} operations, but would have required Bob to expose a twisted curve point nQ to the attacker, rather than using a hash of nQ to encrypt data.

9.6 ECDLP security for the twist

SafeCurves also imposes all of its ECDLP security requirements upon the twist, specifically upon a subgroup of order ℓ', where ℓ' is the largest prime factor of $p + 1 + t$:

- ℓ' is required to reach the same lower limit as in Section 4.1, to protect against rho attacks. The rho security of this group is labeled **twist rho** in the SafeCurves tables.
- ℓ' is required to be different from p; i.e., the number of points on the original curve must not be $p + 2$. This requirement avoids additive transfers (see Section 5) for the twist.
- The embedding degree for ℓ' is required to be at least $(\ell' - 1)/100$. This requirement avoids multiplicative transfers (see Section 5) for the twist.

The field discriminant for the twist (see Section 6) is the same as the field discriminant for the original curve, so the twist does not need to be checked separately.

Some of the ECDLP security requirements for the twist are overkill for DH on the original curve: DH does not actually reveal nQ to Eve, so there is no obvious way for Eve to apply (e.g.) an additive transfer. There are, however, other ECC protocols that make full use of both the original curve and its twist, and twist security is important for these protocols. See, e.g., [148], [147], and [64].

10 Completeness

One of the pitfalls of using $E(\mathbb{F}_q)$ instead of $\mathbb{F}_q^*$ is that formulas for the group operations in $E(\mathbb{F}_q)$ do not always work correctly. See Section 10.1 for examples.

When implementations use sometimes-malfunctioning formulas, attackers can trigger the failure cases inside typical ECC protocols (by sending malicious inputs, as in Section 9), and in some cases can learn secret information by analyzing the responses. See, e.g., the 2002 "exceptional procedure attack" [142] by Izu and Takagi.

One fix is to mathematically characterize the failure cases and have implementations switch to correct formulas for those cases when those inputs appear. Such switches produce timing variations, which are sometimes exploitable as in Section 8.3; eliminating those timing variations takes further work. Even when the overheads here do not create a problematic slowdown, there is certainly more code. In short, these failure cases are another source of tension between simplicity and security.

One virtue of Montgomery curves is that the Montgomery ladder for ECDH (see Section 8.2) turns out to have no failure cases. To be more precise, given

$X_0(P)$ as input, the Montgomery ladder always produces $X_0(nP)$ as output; here X_0 is a modified x-coordinate, where $X_0(P)$ means 0 if P is the point at infinity and $X_0(P)$ means the x-coordinate of P otherwise. This was proven in [**23**, Appendix B] for Montgomery curves $y^2 = x^3 + Ax^2 + x$ with a unique point of order 2, i.e., with $A^2 - 4$ not a square, and in our 2017 paper [**45**, Theorem 4.5] for general Montgomery curves.

But what about protocols beyond ECDH? As an important example, what about elliptic-curve signatures? Elliptic-curve signature verification involves double-scalar multiplication, mapping m, n, P, Q to $mP + nQ$. The literature has various ways to adapt ladders to this situation (see, e.g., [**45**, Section 4.7]), but so far these adaptations do not have the impressive combination of speed, simplicity, and security provided by the original Montgomery ladder.

Another type of scalar multiplication for which the Montgomery ladder is not the speed leader is single-scalar *fixed-base-point* scalar multiplication. This means, for a fixed base point P, computing nP given n. Fixed base points appear in the key-generation step in ECDH and signatures, and in signature generation. For fixed base points one can precompute many more multiples than the $3P, 5P, \ldots, 15P$ mentioned in Section 8.1, with the result that nP can be computed very efficiently by summing up a secret selection of these precomputed points (for details see, e.g., [**31**]). This is faster than the Montgomery ladder. For all curve shapes, implementors pursuing speed for fixed-base-point scalar multiplication had an incentive to fall back to incomplete addition formulas.

This section explains how the underlying problem was resolved, starting with the advent of Edwards curves in 2007—which, fortunately, turn out to be compatible with Montgomery curves such as Curve25519. Before looking at the details, we point out one way to see how successful this has been.

ECDSA [**8**] is a standard signature system using short Weierstrass curves. EdDSA [**31**] is a now-standard signature system using Edwards curves. There is a long history of timing attacks against implementations of ECDSA, such as the following:

- The 2019 "TPM-FAIL" paper [**176**] recovered ECDSA secret keys from Trusted Platform Modules that had been manufactured by STM and Intel. Both TPMs were certified under FIPS 140-2. The STM TPM was also Common Criteria certified at EAL4+.
- The 2019 "Minerva" paper [**144**] recovered ECDSA keys from a FIPS-certified CC-certified Athena IDProtect smart card, pointed out seven other certified devices using the same ECDSA implementation, and reported timings indicating that a similar attack would work against ECDSA implementations in 4 out of 13 software libraries.
- In December 2023, Mozilla [**178**] announced that, in the Firefox browser, "multiple NSS NIST curves were susceptible to a side-channel attack known as 'Minerva.'"

The case of Minerva allows a direct comparison of how well ECDSA and EdDSA held up against these attacks. Out of the 13 software libraries covered in [**144**], 9 already supported EdDSA. In particular, out of the 4 software libraries where the timings in [144] indicated that ECDSA would be exploitable (libgcrypt, MatrixSSL, JDK, and Crypto++), all except JDK already supported EdDSA. None of the 9 EdDSA implementations were vulnerable.

The analysis in [25] shows that, in 8 of 9 cases, the underlying EdDSA code was designed to be constant-time—something that is easier to achieve for EdDSA than for ECDSA. This is connected to the choice of curves: Edwards curves make constant-time software easier than short Weierstrass curves do, for reasons explained below. The other case, libgcrypt, had variable-time EdDSA code but was rescued by a curve-independent feature of EdDSA, illustrating Section 1's comment about the word "most".

10.1   Incompleteness

We now consider again the P1363 algorithm from Section 8.1, computing nP given an integer n and a point P on a short Weierstrass curve. In applications where a further slowdown is acceptable, an implementor might eliminate the subtractions and use a simpler inner loop that looks like this:

- $Q \leftarrow Q + Q$.
- $Q \leftarrow Q + P$ if the current bit of n is set.

The simplest way to implement $+$ is to copy a readily available addition formula, such as one of the formulas cited in Section 8.1. The implementor then finds that this does not work: the scalar-multiplication formulas consistently fail random tests. The problem is that the so-called "addition formula" does not always work: in particular, it fails for the doublings $Q + Q$.

Because this implementation fails random tests, it will be fixed. The simplest fix has an inner loop that looks like this, with a "doubling formula" plugged in for $2Q$:

- $Q \leftarrow 2Q$.
- $Q \leftarrow Q + P$ if the current bit of n is set.

This passes random tests. Unfortunately, it still fails if Q happens to match P. This will *not* be caught by random tests.

A different fix is to modify "$+$" to check for its inputs being equal. But this produces a slower and more complicated implementation—and still does not catch all the failure cases. For example, the standard Weierstrass addition formula fails if Q happens to match $-P$. This is something else that will not be caught by random tests.

A typical presentation of the complete group operation on a short Weierstrass curve involves separate formulas for six different cases. This number of cases is not optimal: a 1995 theorem from Bosma and Lenstra [63, Theorem 1] states that "The smallest cardinality of a complete system of addition laws on E equals two". One might think that this means that any *single* addition formula must have failure cases; but, as we will see in a moment, the facts are more subtle than that.

10.2   Edwards curves

The original Edwards paper [**95**] stated that "The normal form $x^2 + y^2 = a^2 + a^2x^2y^2$ for elliptic curves simplifies formulas in the theory of elliptic curves and functions" and presented a remarkably simple addition formula for this curve shape. The constant a is required to be nonzero and to have $a^4 \neq 1$.

Replacing x and y with ax and ay respectively, and dividing by a^2, gives the curve shape $x^2 + y^2 = 1 + a^4x^2y^2$. In [**36**], we suggested generalizing this to $x^2 + y^2 = 1 + dx^2y^2$ for any $d \notin \{0, 1\}$, and showed that this includes a curve birationally equivalent over $\mathbb{F}_p$ to Curve25519. In this level of generality, the Edwards addition formula says that

$$(x_1, y_1) + (x_2, y_2) = \left(\frac{x_1y_2 + y_1x_2}{1 + dx_1x_2y_1y_2}, \frac{y_1y_2 - x_1x_2}{1 - dx_1x_2y_1y_2} \right).$$

We showed that addition in projective coordinates takes only 11**M** plus a multiplication by d, and that doubling takes only 7**M**. We also showed that, for Edwards curves where d is *not* a square, the Edwards addition formula is complete—it adds every pair of points correctly.

Why does this completeness not contradict the Bosma–Lenstra theorem? A superficial answer is that the theorem is stated only for Weierstrass curves; but one can see that the same concept applies to any shape of elliptic curve. The real answer is that the Bosma–Lenstra definition of incompleteness does not force failure cases for $E(\mathbb{F}_p)$; it forces failure cases for $E(K)$ for some field K *containing* $\mathbb{F}_p$. This is consistent with our completeness theorem—it simply means that d must be a square in K. Those failures do not affect computations in the group $E(\mathbb{F}_p)$ when d is not a square in $\mathbb{F}_p$.

Followup work found even better speeds for arithmetic on Edwards curves, and, more generally, for "twisted Edwards curves" $ax^2 + y^2 = 1 + dx^2y^2$, which were introduced in [**27**]. Any Montgomery curve is birationally equivalent to a twisted Edwards curve and vice versa. The speed records for addition are just 8**M** plus a multiplication by d, using complete formulas introduced by Hisil, Wong, Carter, and Dawson in a 2008 paper [**130**, Section 3.1] for the case $a = -1$ (which is compatible with, e.g., Curve25519). These formulas rely on "extended coordinates" introduced in the same paper; doublings take 8**M** in those coordinates, but skipping the extra coordinate when it is not needed produces doublings in 7**M** and additions in 8**M**, as explained in [**130**, Section 4.3].

The same paper [**130**] also showed that for addition one could achieve 8**M** *without* a multiplication by d, with the caveat of those formulas not being complete. There is a tension here between speed and security, but fortunately a very small tension for curves chosen to have small d.

In 2011, together with Duif, Schwabe, and Yang, we introduced the EdDSA signature system [**31**] (see also the extended version in [**32**]), and specifically Ed25519, which is EdDSA using Curve25519. As mentioned above, EdDSA relies on Edwards curves. The speed, simplicity, and completeness of Edwards addition contribute directly to the speed, simplicity, and security of Ed25519 software.

10.3   Completeness for more curves

Back in 2008, in joint work with Farashahi [**47**], we introduced "binary Edwards curves" as a new curve shape and designed complete addition formulas for it. In 2009, in joint work with Kohel [**35**] (see also [**30**]), we introduced a complete addition formula for "twisted Hessian curves". Finally, also in 2009, we introduced a complete addition formula that can safely be conjectured to cover all elliptic curves over non-binary finite fields; see [**24**]. We checked that all of the non-binary NIST curves were covered; see [**24**, page 23] for the case of NIST P-256. Arene, Kohel, and Ritzenthaler showed in 2012 [**14**, Theorem 4.3] that every elliptic curve over a large finite field has a complete addition formula in Weierstrass form.

Saying that a curve has a complete addition formula does not imply that sensible implementors will want to use the formula. Sometimes a complete addition formula is simple and fast, as the Edwards addition formula illustrates; but sometimes a complete addition formula is slower and more complicated than constant-time software that correctly merges two or more incomplete formulas.

In 2013, the SafeCurves web pages reviewed the basic completeness results for the Montgomery ladder and the Edwards addition formula, and continued as follows:

> Subsequent research has introduced other complete scalar-multiplication formulas. However, many of these formulas are considerably slower and more complicated than standard incomplete scalar-multiplication formulas, creating major conflicts between simplicity, efficiency, and security.
>
> SafeCurves requires curves to support simple, fast, *complete*, constant-time single-coordinate single-scalar multiplication. This includes the SafeCurves ladder requirement but goes further by requiring completeness. SafeCurves also requires curves to support simple, fast, *complete*, constant-time multi-scalar multiplication.

See Section 8 for the definitions of "simple" and "fast".

This SafeCurves criterion is satisfied by, e.g., Curve25519: the Montgomery ladder provides simple, fast, complete, constant-time single-coordinate single-scalar multiplication, and standard multi-scalar-multiplication techniques on top of the Edwards addition formula provide simple, fast, complete, constant-time multi-scalar multiplication. Note that "simple" and "fast" are relative to single-scalar multiplication in the first case and relative to multi-scalar multiplication in the second case; fast multi-scalar multiplication on top of the Edwards addition formula is certainly not as simple as the Montgomery ladder.

There has been further work on completeness for other curve shapes. In 2015, Renes, Costello, and Batina [**202**] showed that one of the Bosma–Lenstra formulas takes just 12**M** for short Weierstrass curves E in projective coordinates; this particular formula is complete for $E(\mathbb{F}_p)$ if $\#E(\mathbb{F}_p)$ is odd. However, the complete doubling formulas in [**202**] for the same coordinate system take 11**M**. This approach to complete scalar multiplication is much slower than incomplete scalar multiplication on the same curves (see [**211**] for quantification), never mind questions of simplicity; so it does not meet this SafeCurves criterion.

There is a statement in [**202**] that the formulas in that paper are "comparably efficient". That statement appears to be a comparison to earlier *complete* formulas for the same curves. What matters for this SafeCurves criterion is instead the comparison to the simplest, fastest scalar-multiplication algorithms for the same curves *without regard to security*. This is also what matters for predicting security risks.

Vulnerability announcement CVE-2023-24532 [**120**] illustrates how powerful the implementation incentives are. There was a valiant effort to deploy the formulas from [**202**] as part of the "crypto/elliptic" library for the Go programming language—but the library ended up using faster P-256 software instead. The vulnerability announcement indicates that the faster software has a bug stemming from its use of incomplete formulas: "The ScalarMult and ScalarBaseMult methods of the P256 Curve may return an incorrect result if called with some specific unreduced scalars (a scalar larger than the order of the curve)." It is not clear whether the library has applications where the bug is exploitable. What is clear is that larger tensions between simplicity, efficiency, and security make it more likely that security will be lost.

11   Strings as group elements

Beyond the core ECC tasks of ECDH as in X25519 and signatures as in Ed25519, there is a vast literature on further cryptographic protocols using elliptic curves. Complications arise in many of these protocols because of the interface gap between

- bit strings—the standard interchange format for data stored inside computers—and
- elliptic-curve points—the central objects appearing in ECC.

This section introduces the central issue, and then explains a simple workaround known for *some* curves.

11.1   The gap between strings and curve points

In symmetric cryptography, stream encryption of a message m produces ciphertext $c = m \oplus s$. Here s is the output of, e.g., AES-CTR applied to a "nonce" (a number used once; e.g., number i for the ith message) and a secret key; and $\oplus$ is the exclusive-or operation on bit strings.

For comparison, consider the ElGamal encryption system using the multiplicative group $\mathbb{F}_p^*$. Alice's secret key is a, and Alice's public key is g^a for a fixed generator $g \in \mathbb{F}_p^*$. To send a message m, Bob generates n randomly for this message, and sends the pair (g^n, mg^{an}). Alice divides mg^{an} by g^{an} to reconstruct m.

In this ElGamal example, m is implicitly an element of $\mathbb{F}_p^*$, whereas one expects a message to instead be a bit string. This distinction might not seem worth commenting on:

- There is a standard representation of elements of $\mathbb{F}_p^*$ as strings of $\lceil \log_2 p \rceil$ bits, namely the usual little-endian encodings of the integers $1, 2, \ldots, p-1$.
- If m is a message consisting of, say, $\lfloor \log_2(p-1) \rfloor$ bits then one can zero-pad m to $\lceil \log_2 p \rceil$ bits, replace the all-zero string with the encoding of $p-1$, and observe that the result is the representation of some element of $\mathbb{F}_p^*$.

In short, there is an efficient bijection between strings of $\lfloor \log_2(p-1) \rfloor$ bits and a large subset of the group elements. This provides a clean interface for protocols viewing strings as group elements.

The semantic gap here becomes more of a problem in the elliptic-curve version of the ElGamal system. Alice's public key is then aG for a fixed base point $G \in E(\mathbb{F}_p)$, and Bob encrypts $m \in E(\mathbb{F}_p)$ as the pair $(nG, m + naG)$. How does one view bit strings as elements of $E(\mathbb{F}_p)$?

There are again standard representations of elements of $E(\mathbb{F}_p)$ as strings. Consider, for example, a compressed representation of elements of $E(\mathbb{F}_p)$ as in Section 9.3 when E is a short Weierstrass curve: a point (x, y) is represented as x and one bit of y (and the point at infinity is represented as some otherwise unused string; this exists by Hasse's theorem when p is large), taking $\lceil \log_2 p \rceil + 1$ bits. The problem is that one cannot reliably obtain strings in this representation by zero-padding slightly shorter messages: $x(E(\mathbb{F}_p))$ covers only about half of the elements of $\mathbb{F}_p$, and not simply an interval as in the $\mathbb{F}_p^*$ case. So this representation does not seem useful for a protocol that needs to reliably encode bit strings as curve points.

11.2   Protocols using strings as group elements

One can dismiss the ElGamal example from Section 11.1 by saying that its basic purpose, namely encryption, is better achieved by combining DH with a symmetric cipher, as proposed in the original DH paper. When Section 9.1 mentioned producing, e.g., an AES-GCM key by hashing an ECDH shared secret, it was implicitly representing the ECDH shared secret as a bit string for input to the hash function. This relies on mapping elliptic-curve points *to* bit strings; it does not need a bijection. Similarly, EdDSA does not need a bijection.

However, more advanced protocols frequently encounter the problem of viewing strings as group elements. Here is an illustrative example, namely password-authenticated key exchange (PAKE).

The goal of PAKE is to upgrade a not-very-high-entropy password shared by Alice and Bob into a high-entropy shared secret. In the simplest PAKE protocol, Alice generates an integer m and uses (a hash of) the password as a key for a block cipher to encrypt the block mG; Bob generates an integer n and similarly encrypts nG; Alice and Bob each compute (a hash of) mnG. For each subsequent communication session, Alice and Bob repeat this process with fresh integers m

and n. (One might wonder why Alice and Bob do not reuse secrets across sessions, or share a higher-entropy secret in the first place; the typical answer is that Alice and Bob are humans with limited memory and want their devices to forget all secrets as quickly as possible.)

An attacker starting with a correct guess of the password before the protocol trivially breaks security of this protocol by forging messages, but this has probability only $1/W$ of success per session if there are W equally likely passwords, so on average it takes about $W/2$ sessions before success.

A much more efficient "partition attack", introduced by Patel [191] in 1997 for multiplicative groups and adapted to elliptic-curve groups in 2001 by Boyd, Montague, and Nguyen [64, Section 5.1], is as follows: try decrypting the encrypted mG and nG using various guesses for the password, and reject any guess for which the results are not group elements. The critical observation here is that most block-length strings are not encodings of group elements. Consequently, these trials rapidly reject most passwords by observing a single session, and confidently identify the correct password after a logarithmic number of sessions—at which point an active attack breaks security with probability 1. Even if point mG is represented by its x-coordinate $x(mG)$, only about half of all strings give valid x-coordinates, still permitting a partition attack to succeed in about $\log_2 W$ steps.

For multiplicative groups $\mathbb{F}_p^*$, it is easy to block partition attacks by equating block-length strings with group elements as in Section 11.1 and taking g to generate $\mathbb{F}_p^*$ (rather than to have prime order). This does not equate strings with *all* group elements—if g^m does not correspond to a string then Alice has to try again; same for Bob—but all block-length strings are covered by the elements g^m that correspond to strings. For p of the form $p = 2^t - s$ for very small s it is also safe to take t-bit strings, which mean no retries, as the chance that any candidate decryption ever lands in the forbidden interval $[p, 2^t - 1]$ is negligible.

For elliptic-curve groups $E(\mathbb{F}_p)$, a more complicated protocol "secure against partition attacks" was proposed in [64, Section 5.2]. Alice encrypts either $x(mG)$ or $x(m'G')$, chosen randomly for each session, where G generates $E(\mathbb{F}_p)$ and G' generates the twist. The idea here is that these x-coordinates cover $\mathbb{F}_p$, and thus cover all strings (after retries as in the previous paragraph). Bob sends back unencrypted points $x(nG)$ and $x(n'G')$, and then Alice and Bob use either $x(mnG)$ or $x(m'n'G')$, depending on whether Alice had chosen $x(mG)$ or $x(m'G')$ in the first place.

The literature has many more examples of complications stemming from the interface gap between strings and elements of $E(\mathbb{F}_p)$; see, e.g., the references in our 2013 paper [34] with Hamburg and Krasnova. As an illustration of these complications being a security risk, [34] pointed out the following active attack against the protocol from [64]: the attacker replaces $x(n'G')$ with random data, and, if the protocol continues successfully, concludes that Alice was using $x(mG)$ in the first place. A partition attack then eliminates half of the passwords, and repeating for a logarithmic number of sessions breaks the protocol.

11.3 Strings as curve points: a dangerous approach

A simple-sounding, and presumably correct, method to view bit strings as curve points is as follows. Take bit strings that are, say, 10 bits shorter than compressed point representations. Given a bit string m, consider the 1024 possible point representations starting with m, and take the lexicographically smallest that represents a point. This fails if none of the 1024 strings represents a point; presumably such failures do not occur for, e.g., 256-bit primes p.

One issue with this (presumed) bijection is that stopping after the first point representation that works—as part of mapping a bit string to a point, or as part of deciding whether a point corresponds to a string—leaks information through timing. Constant-time software instead has to try all 1024 possibilities. Another issue is that the bijection does not cover a large fraction of curve points. Protocols trying group elements until they find elements represented by strings, as in some of the protocols considered in Section 11.2, might have to try thousands of times.

In 2019, Vanhoef and Ronen [221] announced Dragonblood, breaking every analyzed implementation of the WPA3 Dragonfly handshake. Most implementations were vulnerable to invalid-curve attacks as in Section 9.2, but there were exceptions, such as hostapd, which [221] instead broke with a timing attack. Dragonfly used a lexicographic computation of a point from a bit string, and the timing attack targeted this computation.

Another implementation covered in [221], namely FreeRADIUS, stopped the lexicographic map after just 10 possibilities. This was not a problem for functionality: >99.9% of handshakes would succeed, and users would not notice failure cases if handshakes were retried automatically. Security was a different story: the failure cases were efficiently exploitable, as shown in [221, Section 7]. FreeRADIUS was also vulnerable to invalid-curve attacks.

11.4 Strings as curve points: a better approach

A 2006 paper by Shallue and van de Woestijne [216] introduced a formula mapping $\mathbb{F}_p$ to a reasonably large fraction of $E(\mathbb{F}_p)$. There are many followup papers refining this "hash-to-curve" idea; see, e.g., the references in [34, Section 1.4]. For protocols that simply want to map bit strings to points, such as Dragonfly, these formulas are much nicer for implementations than the lexicographic approach described in Section 11.3. However, "hash-to-curve" formulas are typically not bijections, so they do not address the foundational interface gap highlighted in Section 11.1 and exploited in Section 11.2.

Efficient bijections are known for *some* elliptic curves. For example, for $p \equiv 2$ (mod 3), the function $y \mapsto ((y^2 - b)^{1/3}, y)$ is an efficient bijection between $\mathbb{F}_p$ and $\{(x, y) : (x, y) \in E(\mathbb{F}_p)\}$, where E is the curve $y^2 = x^3 + b$. This curve has, however, more basic security problems. Miller commented in 1986 [174, page 425] that another curve having $p + 1$ points is convenient for calculations but that "it may be prudent to avoid curves with complex multiplication because the extra structure of these curves might somehow be used to give a better algorithm". This avoidance is the topic of Section 6, and these curves with $p + 1$

points were then discovered to be weak, specifically because of multiplicative transfers; see Section 5.

More interestingly, efficient bijections are known for essentially all curves E for which $\#E(\mathbb{F}_p) \equiv 0 \pmod 2$, via the "Elligator 2" construction from [34]. For many of the curves, [103] had already introduced a slightly more complex injective map to the curve, which [34] showed how to invert; see also [88] for further techniques and references. For each of these curves E, the fraction of $E(\mathbb{F}_p)$ covered by strings is between about $1/4$ and about $1/2$, so retries as in Section 11.2 are not very expensive. Of course, it would be even better to have an efficient bijection covering all of $E(\mathbb{F}_p)$.

The issues addressed by these bijections are not as central to ECC as the issues from Sections 8, 9, and 10. However, looking at the broader ECC literature shows frequent error-prone contortions to work around the interface gap between strings and points, as illustrated by the PAKE example in Section 11.2 and many more examples cited in [34]. We therefore include an "indistinguishability" criterion in SafeCurves, asking for an efficient constant-time bijection between all b-bit strings and a large fraction of curve points. We allow an undetectable fraction of b-bit strings to be skipped, although one can tweak the known constructions of bijections to avoid this at the expense of replacing b with $b-1$.

11.5 Encodings enforcing group membership

An efficient bijection between the set of b-bit strings and (many) curve points has another interesting property: if a protocol requires a curve point to be communicated as a b-bit string, then decoding always produces a point on the correct curve, automatically avoiding invalid-curve attacks.

This does not mean that a protocol as simple as ECDH should use these encodings: ECDH software is simpler if one uses x-coordinates with the Montgomery ladder, as in Figure 8.2.1, and chooses a twist-secure curve. However, looking at a much wider range of ECC protocols shows that security analyses typically assume that incoming points are in $E(\mathbb{F}_p)$. Rather than trusting each implementation to check this, one can have each protocol use a general-purpose encoding that forces inputs to be in $E(\mathbb{F}_p)$.

Two complications appear at this level of generality. First, one cannot expect all protocols to be willing and able to handle the possibility of a point not being representable as a string. Second, security analyses sometimes assume that incoming points are specifically in the order-ℓ group generated by $G \in E(\mathbb{F}_p)$. This group matches $E(\mathbb{F}_p)$ if $E(\mathbb{F}_p) = \ell$, but the known efficient bijections require larger cofactors.

As an illustration of the second complication, the Monero blockchain announced in 2017 [166] that it had patched a vulnerability allowing each coin to be spent 8 times. Monero used Curve25519, which has cofactor 8, so there are 8 points $T \in E(\mathbb{F}_p)$ such that $8T$ is the neutral element; Monero's security analysis was expecting a point P to be in the order-ℓ group, but the software was accepting $P + T$ as a separate expenditure for each of the 8 points T. Note that switching to cofactor 1 exacerbates the core problem here: it leads to invalid-curve attacks even against basic ECDH, as illustrated by the recent attacks cited in Section 9.

These considerations have triggered interest in ways to encode elements of the order-ℓ group as b-bit strings, with decoders rejecting all other b-bit strings. What would be best is a bijection, so that nothing needs to be rejected. In the absence of a bijection, some possibilities are the following:

- When $E(\mathbb{F}_p)$ is, e.g., a group of order ℓ in short Weierstrass form, one can encode a curve point as (x, y) (with some handling of the point at infinity, although some protocols will want to reject this point). The decoder is then required to check whether (x, y) is on the curve. To limit the damage just in case the check is omitted, it seems safer to replace y with one bit of y as noted in Section 9.3, using a square-root computation to recover y. However, the strength of this protection is unclear: the literature does not show what will happen if an invalid x is sent and the resulting y is not tested against the putative y^2.
- To handle general curves, one could similarly send (x, y) or a compressed version of (x, y), and add an explicit test whether (x, y) has order ℓ, which seems to be a useful protection in any case. For typical Edwards curves, there are alternative representations of the order-ℓ group that advertise efficient encoding and decoding; see, e.g., [**123**]. With any of these encodings, one has to ask what will happen if the decoder's tests are omitted.

Without a thorough analysis of failure cases, there seems to be no alternative to making sure that the decoding (and encoding) software works correctly, but at least this software can be shared across many protocols asking for an order-ℓ group. Within *correct* implementations of order-ℓ groups, the most efficient groups known rely on Edwards curves, and on the formulas from [**130**].

References

[1]   — (no editor), *1997 IEEE symposium on security and privacy, May 4–7, 1997, Oakland, CA, USA*, IEEE Computer Society, 1997. ISBN 0-8186-7828-3. URL: https://ieeexplore.ieee.org/xpl/conhome/4693/proceeding. See [191].

[2]   — (no editor), *27th IEEE symposium on computer arithmetic, ARITH 2020, Portland, OR, USA, June 7–10, 2020*, IEEE, 2020. ISBN 978-1-7281-7120-3. URL: https://ieeexplore.ieee.org/xpl/conhome/9146973/proceeding. See [56].

[3]   — (no editor), *2020 IEEE symposium on security and privacy, SP 2020, San Francisco, CA, USA, May 18–21, 2020*, IEEE, 2020. URL: https://ieeexplore.ieee.org/xpl/conhome/9144328/proceeding. See [221].

[4]   — (no editor), *30th IEEE annual international symposium on field-programmable custom computing machines, FCCM 2022, New York City, NY, USA, May 15–18, 2022*, IEEE, 2022. ISBN 978-1-6654-8332-2. DOI: 10.1109/FCCM53951.2022. See [230].

[5]   — (no editor), *IEEE European symposium on security and privacy, EuroS&P 2023—workshops, Delft, Netherlands, July 3–7, 2023*, IEEE, 2023. ISBN 979-8-3503-2720-5. DOI: 10.1109/EuroSPW59978.2023. See [169].

[6]   "Bushing", Hector Martin "marcan" Cantero, Segher Boessenkool, Sven Peter, *PS3 epic fail* (2010). URL: `https://events.ccc.de/congress/2010/Fahrplan/attachments/1780_27c3_console_hacking_2010.pdf`. Citations in this document: §A.

[7]   Joe Abernathy, *The following is the written response to my request for an interview with the NSA* (1992). URL: `https://archive.epic.org/crypto/dss/nsa_abernathy_letter.html`. Citations in this document: §1.4.

[8]   Accredited Standards Committee X9, *ANSI x9.62-1999: Public key cryptography for the financial services industry: the elliptic curve digital signature algorithm (ECDSA)* (1999). Citations in this document: §1.1, §5, §7.1, §10.

[9]   Accredited Standards Committee X9, *ANSI X9.63-2001: Public key cryptography for the financial services industry: key agreement and key transport using elliptic curve cryptography* (2001). URL: `https://web.archive.org/web/20010724160111/https://grouper.ieee.org/groups/1363/Research/Other.html`. Citations in this document: §1.1.

[10]   Onur Aciiçmez, Billy Bob Brumley, Philipp Grabher, *New results on instruction cache attacks*, in CHES 2010 [**168**] (2010), 110–124. URL: `https://iacr.org/archive/ches2010/62250105/62250105.pdf`. Citations in this document: §8.3.

[11]   Alejandro Cabrera Aldaya, Billy Bob Brumley, *When one vulnerable primitive turns viral: novel single-trace attacks on ECDSA and RSA*, IACR Trans. Cryptogr. Hardw. Embed. Syst. **2020** (2020), 196–221. URL: `https://eprint.iacr.org/2020/055`. DOI: `10.13154/tches.v2020.i2.196-221`. Citations in this document: §A.

[12]   Thomas Allan, Billy Bob Brumley, Katrina Falkner, Joop van de Pol, Yuval Yarom, *Amplifying side channels through performance degradation*, in ACSAC 2016 [**210**] (2016), 422–435. URL: `https://eprint.iacr.org/2015/1141`. Citations in this document: §A.

[13]   Diego F. Aranha, Felipe Rodrigues Novaes, Akira Takahashi, Mehdi Tibouchi, Yuval Yarom, *LadderLeak: breaking ECDSA with less than one bit of nonce leakage*, in CCS 2020 [**164**] (2020), 225–242. URL: `https://eprint.iacr.org/2020/615`. DOI: `10.1145/3372297.3417268`. Citations in this document: §A.

[14]   Christophe Arene, David R. Kohel, Christophe Ritzenthaler, *Complete addition laws on abelian varieties*, LMS J. Comput. Math. **15** (2012), 308–316. DOI: `10.1112/s1461157012001027`. Citations in this document: §10.3.

[15]   Vijay Atluri, Claudia Díaz (editors), *Computer security—ESORICS 2011—16th European symposium on research in computer security, Leuven, Belgium, September 12–14, 2011, proceedings*, Lecture Notes in Computer Science, 6879, Springer, 2011. ISBN 978-3-642-23821-5. See [75].

[16]   Daniel V. Bailey, Brian Baldwin, Lejla Batina, Daniel J. Bernstein, Peter Birkner, Joppe W. Bos, Gauthier van Damme, Giacomo de Meulenaer, Junfeng Fan, Tim Güneysu, Frank Gurkaynak, Thorsten Kleinjung, Tanja Lange, Nele Mentens, Christof Paar, Francesco Regazzoni, Peter Schwabe, Leif Uhsadel, *Breaking ECC2K-130* (2009). URL: `https://eprint.iacr.org/2009/466`. Citations in this document: §B.

[17]   R. Balasubramanian, Neal Koblitz, *The improbability that an elliptic curve has subexponential discrete log problem under the Menezes–Okamoto–Vanstone algorithm*, J. Cryptol. **11** (1998), 141–145. Citations in this document: §5.

[18]   James Bamford, *The NSA is building the country's biggest spy center (watch what you say)* (2012). URL: `https://www.wired.com/2012/03/ff-nsadatacenter/`. Citations in this document: §D.3.

[19] Mihir Bellare (editor), *Advances in cryptology—CRYPTO 2000, 20th annual international cryptology conference, Santa Barbara, California, USA, August 20–24, 2000, proceedings*, Lecture Notes in Computer Science, 1880, Springer, 2000. ISBN 3-540-67907-3. See [54].

[20] Andreas Bender, Guy Castagnoli, *On the implementation of elliptic curve cryptosystems*, in [**68**] (1990), 186–192. MR 91d:11154. Citations in this document: §2.2.

[21] Daniel J. Bernstein, *A software implementation of NIST P-224* (29 Oct 2001). URL: `https://cr.yp.to/talks.html#2001.10.29`. Citations in this document: §9.4.

[22] Daniel J. Bernstein, *Re: Current consensus on ECC* (1 Nov 2001). URL: `https://groups.google.com/g/sci.crypt/c/mu_paShEU3w/m/m491pYxHbtAJ`. Citations in this document: §9.4.

[23] Daniel J. Bernstein, *Curve25519: new Diffie-Hellman speed records*, in PKC 2006 [**231**] (2006), 207–228. URL: `https://cr.yp.to/papers.html#curve25519`. Citations in this document: §1.3, §2.1, §8.2, §8.2, §8.5, §9.4, §10, §B, §E.2.

[24] Daniel J. Bernstein, *Complete addition laws for all elliptic curves over finite fields* (2009). URL: `https://cr.yp.to/talks.html#2009.07.17`. Citations in this document: §10.3, §10.3.

[25] Daniel J. Bernstein, *Why EdDSA held up better than ECDSA against Minerva* (2019). URL: `https://blog.cr.yp.to/20191024-eddsa.html`. Citations in this document: §10.

[26] Daniel J. Bernstein, *Cryptographic competitions*, Journal of Cryptology **37** (2024), article 7. URL: `https://cr.yp.to/papers.html#competitions`. Citations in this document: §7.

[27] Daniel J. Bernstein, Peter Birkner, Marc Joye, Tanja Lange, Christiane Peters, *Twisted Edwards curves*, in Africacrypt 2008 [**223**] (2008), 389–405. Citations in this document: §8.6, §10.2.

[28] Daniel J. Bernstein, Tung Chou, *CryptAttackTester: formalizing attack analyses*, in Crypto 2024, to appear (2023). URL: `https://eprint.iacr.org/2023/940`. Citations in this document: §B.1.

[29] Daniel J. Bernstein, Tung Chou, Chitchanok Chuengsatiansup, Andreas Hülsing, Eran Lambooij, Tanja Lange, Ruben Niederhagen, Christine van Vredendaal, *How to manipulate curve standards: A white paper for the black hat*, in [**79**] (2015), 109–139. URL: `https://bada55.cr.yp.to`. Citations in this document: §7.2, §7.3.

[30] Daniel J. Bernstein, Chitchanok Chuengsatiansup, David Kohel, Tanja Lange, *Twisted Hessian curves*, in Latincrypt 2015 [**161**] (2015), 269–294. URL: `https://eprint.iacr.org/2015/781`. DOI: `10.1007/978-3-319-22174-8_15`. Citations in this document: §10.3.

[31] Daniel J. Bernstein, Niels Duif, Tanja Lange, Peter Schwabe, Bo-Yin Yang, *High-speed high-security signatures*, in CHES 2011 [**199**] (2011), 124–142; see also newer version [**31**]. Citations in this document: §10, §10, §10.2.

[32] Daniel J. Bernstein, Niels Duif, Tanja Lange, Peter Schwabe, Bo-Yin Yang, *High-speed high-security signatures*, Journal of Cryptographic Engineering **2** (2012), 77–89; see also older version [**31**]. URL: `https://eprint.iacr.org/2011/368`. Citations in this document: §10.2, §E.2.

[33] Daniel J. Bernstein, Susanne Engels, Tanja Lange, Ruben Niederhagen, Christof Paar, Peter Schwabe, Ralf Zimmermann, *Faster elliptic-curve discrete logarithms on FPGAs* (2016). URL: `https://eprint.iacr.org/2016/382`. Citations in this document: §B.3.

[34] Daniel J. Bernstein, Mike Hamburg, Anna Krasnova, Tanja Lange, *Elligator: elliptic-curve points indistinguishable from uniform random strings*, in CCS 2013 [**207**] (2013), 967–980. URL: `https://eprint.iacr.org/2013/325`. Citations in this document: §11.2, §11.2, §11.4, §11.4, §11.4, §11.4.

[35] Daniel J. Bernstein, David Kohel, Tanja Lange, *Projective coordinates for twisted Hessian curves* (2009). URL: `https://hyperelliptic.org/EFD/g1p/auto-twistedhessian-projective.html`. Citations in this document: §10.3.

[36] Daniel J. Bernstein, Tanja Lange, *Faster addition and doubling on elliptic curves*, in Asiacrypt 2007 [**157**] (2007), 29–50. URL: `https://eprint.iacr.org/2007/286`. Citations in this document: §3, §10.2.

[37] Daniel J. Bernstein, Tanja Lange, *Explicit-Formulas Database* (2007), first posted in 2007, also updated afterwards. URL: `https://hyperelliptic.org/EFD/`. Citations in this document: §8.1.

[38] Daniel J. Bernstein, Tanja Lange, *Analysis and optimization of elliptic-curve single-scalar multiplication*, Contemporary Mathematics **46** (2008), 1–20. URL: `https://eprint.iacr.org/2007/455`. Citations in this document: §8.1.

[39] Daniel J. Bernstein, Tanja Lange, *Type-II optimal polynomial bases*, in WAIFI 2010 [**128**] (2010), 41–61. URL: `https://eprint.iacr.org/2010/069`. Citations in this document: §B.

[40] Daniel J. Bernstein, Tanja Lange, *Computing small discrete logarithms faster*, in INDOCRYPT 2012 [**110**] (2012), 317–338. URL: `https://eprint.iacr.org/2012/458`. Citations in this document: §4.2.

[41] Daniel J. Bernstein, Tanja Lange, *Two grumpy giants and a baby*, in ANTS 2012 [**132**] (2013), 87–111. URL: `https://eprint.iacr.org/2012/294`. Citations in this document: §B.1.

[42] Daniel J. Bernstein, Tanja Lange, *Security dangers of the NIST curves* (31 May 2013). URL: `https://cr.yp.to/talks.html#2013.05.31`. Citations in this document: §1.4, §7.2.

[43] Daniel J. Bernstein, Tanja Lange, *SafeCurves: choosing safe curves for elliptic-curve cryptography* (2013). URL: `https://safecurves.cr.yp.to`. Citations in this document: §1.2, §1.3, §1.4, §7.2, §7.6, §D.1.

[44] Daniel J. Bernstein, Tanja Lange, *Failures in NIST's ECC standards* (2016). URL: `https://cr.yp.to/papers.html#nistecc`. Citations in this document: §1.4.

[45] Daniel J. Bernstein, Tanja Lange, *Montgomery curves and the Montgomery ladder*, in [**61**] (2017), 82–115. Citations in this document: §8.4, §10, §10.

[46] Daniel J. Bernstein, Tanja Lange, *Failures in NIST's ECC standards, part 2* (2020). URL: `https://csrc.nist.gov/files/pubs/sp/800/186/final/docs/sp800-186-draft-comments-received.pdf`. Citations in this document: §1.4.

[47] Daniel J. Bernstein, Tanja Lange, Reza Rezaeian Farashahi, *Binary Edwards curves*, in CHES 2008 [**190**] (2008), 244–265. URL: `https://cr.yp.to/papers.html#edwards2`. Citations in this document: §10.3.

[48] Daniel J. Bernstein, Tanja Lange, Chloe Martindale, Lorenz Panny, *Quantum circuits for the CSIDH: optimizing quantum evaluation of isogenies*, in Eurocrypt 2019 [**140**] (2019), 409–441. URL: `https://cr.yp.to/papers.html#qisog`. DOI: `10.1007/978-3-030-17656-3_15`. Citations in this document: §B, §B, §B.3, §D.1.

[49] Daniel J. Bernstein, Tanja Lange, Ruben Niederhagen, *Dual EC: A standardized back door*, in [**206**] (2016), 256–281. URL: `https://www.projectbullrun.org/dual-ec/index.html`. Citations in this document: §7, §A.

[50] Daniel J. Bernstein, Tanja Lange, Peter Schwabe, *On the correct use of the negation map in the Pollard rho method*, in PKC 2011 [**77**] (2011), 128–146. URL: `https://eprint.iacr.org/2011/003`. Citations in this document: §4.5, §4.5.

[51] Daniel J. Bernstein, Kaushik Nath, *lib25519* (2024). URL: `https://lib25519.cr.yp.to`. Citations in this document: §8.2, §E.1.

[52] Daniel J. Bernstein, Peter Schwabe, *NEON crypto*, in CHES 2012 [**200**] (2012), 320–339. URL: `https://cr.yp.to/papers.html#neoncrypto`. Citations in this document: §E.2.

[53] Daniel J. Bernstein, Bo-Yin Yang, *Fast constant-time gcd computation and modular inversion*, IACR Trans. Cryptogr. Hardw. Embed. Syst. **2019** (2019), 340–398. URL: `https://tches.iacr.org/index.php/TCHES/article/view/8298`. Citations in this document: §8.1.

[54] Ingrid Biehl, Bernd Meyer, Volker Müller, *Differential fault attacks on elliptic curve cryptosystems*, in Crypto 2000 [**19**] (2000), 131–146. URL: `https://www.iacr.org/archive/crypto2000/18800131/18800131.pdf`. Citations in this document: §9, §9.2, §A, §A.

[55] Eli Biham, Lior Neumann, *Breaking the Bluetooth pairing—the fixed coordinate invalid curve attack*, in SAC 2019 [**192**] (2019), 250–273. DOI: `10.1007/978-3-030-38471-5_11`. Citations in this document: §9.2, §A.

[56] Mojtaba Bisheh-Niasar, Rami El Khatib, Reza Azarderakhsh, Mehran Mozaffari Kermani, *Fast, small, and area-time efficient architectures for key-exchange on Curve25519*, in ARITH 2020 [**2**] (2020), 72–79. DOI: `10.1109/ARITH48897.2020.00019`. Citations in this document: §E.2.

[57] BITMAIN, *Bitcoin Miner S21* (2023). URL: `https://shop.bitmain.com/product/detail?pid=00020240311180613891frupBW6406B2`. Citations in this document: §4.1.

[58] Blockchain.com, *Total Hash Rate (TH/s)* (2024), accessed 15 June 2024. URL: `https://www.blockchain.com/explorer/charts/hash-rate`. Citations in this document: §7.4.

[59] Joppe W. Bos, J. Alex Halderman, Nadia Heninger, Jonathan Moore, Michael Naehrig, Eric Wustrow, *Elliptic curve cryptography in practice*, in FC 2014 [**81**] (2014), 157–175. URL: `https://eprint.iacr.org/2013/734`. Citations in this document: §A.

[60] Joppe W. Bos, Thorsten Kleinjung, Arjen K. Lenstra, *On the use of the negation map in the Pollard rho method*, in ANTS 2010 [**125**] (2010), 66–82. URL: `https://www.joppebos.com/files/negation.pdf`. Citations in this document: §4.5.

[61] Joppe W. Bos, Arjen K. Lenstra (editors), *Topics in computational number theory inspired by Peter L. Montgomery*, Cambridge University Press, 2017. ISBN 978-1107109353. See [45].

[62] Joppe W. Bos, Martijn Stam (editors), *Computational cryptography: algorithmic aspects of cryptology*, Cambridge University Press, 2021. DOI: `https://doi.org/10.1017/9781108854207`. See [121].

[63] Wieb Bosma, Hendrik W. Lenstra, Jr., *Complete systems of two addition laws for elliptic curves*, Journal of Number Theory **53** (1995), 229–240. MR 96f:11079. URL: `https://www.math.ru.nl/~bosma/pubs/JNT1995.pdf`. Citations in this document: §10.1.

[64] Colin Boyd, Paul Montague, Khanh Quoc Nguyen, *Elliptic curve based password authenticated key exchange protocols*, in [**222**] (2001), 487–501. Citations in this document: §9.6, §11.2, §11.2, §11.2.

[65] Colin Boyd, Leonie Simpson (editors), *Information security and privacy—18th Australasian conference, ACISP 2013, Brisbane, Australia, July 1–3, 2013, proceedings*, Lecture Notes in Computer Science, 7959, Springer, 2013. ISBN 978-3-642-39058-6. DOI: `10.1007/978-3-642-39059-3`. See [103].

[66] ECC Brainpool, *ECC Brainpool standard curves and curve generation* (2005). URL: `https://web.archive.org/web/20070814070853/http://www.ecc-brainpool.org/download/Domain-parameters.pdf`. Citations in this document: §1.1, §1.3, §2.2, §2.4, §5, §7.2.

[67] Luis Brandao, Rene Peralta, *Deniable and not self-harming trapdoors*, Talk at Rump session of Crypto 2014 (2014). URL: `https://crypto.2014.rump.cr.yp.to/7bad0b876b1c65ff7d0727be9afcbcf8.pdf`. Citations in this document: §7.4.

[68] Gilles Brassard (editor), *Advances in cryptology—CRYPTO '89*, Lecture Notes in Computer Science, 435, Springer, Berlin, 1990. ISBN 0–387–97317–6. MR 91b:94002. See [20].

[69] Luca Breveglieri, Shay Gueron, Israel Koren, David Naccache, Jean-Pierre Seifert (editors), *Fifth international workshop on fault diagnosis and tolerance in cryptography, 2008, FDTC 2008, Washington, DC, USA, 10 August 2008*, IEEE Computer Society, 2008. ISBN 978-0-7695-3314-8. URL: `https://ieeexplore.ieee.org/xpl/conhome/4599542/proceeding`. See [102].

[70] Eric Brier, Marc Joye, *Weierstraß elliptic curves and side-channel attacks*, in PKC 2002 [**179**] (2002), 335–345. URL: `https://marcjoye.github.io/papers/BJ02espa.pdf`. Citations in this document: §8.7.

[71] Eric Brier, Marc Joye, *Fast point multiplication on elliptic curves through isogenies*, in AAECC 2003 [**101**] (2003), 43–50. URL: `https://marcjoye.github.io/papers/BJ03isog.pdf`. DOI: `10.1007/3-540-44828-4_6`. Citations in this document: §3.1.

[72] Nicolai Brown, *Things that use Curve25519* (2024). URL: `https://ianix.com/pub/curve25519-deployment.html`. Citations in this document: §9.3.

[73] Nicolai Brown, *Things that use Ed25519* (2024). URL: `https://ianix.com/pub/ed25519-deployment.html`. Citations in this document: §9.3.

[74] Billy Bob Brumley, Risto M. Hakala, *Cache-timing template attacks*, in Asiacrypt 2009 [**170**] (2009), 667–684. URL: `https://www.iacr.org/archive/asiacrypt2009/59120664/59120664.pdf`. DOI: `10.1007/978-3-642-10366-7_39`. Citations in this document: §8.3, §A.

[75] Billy Bob Brumley, Nicola Tuveri, *Remote timing attacks are still practical*, in ESORICS 2011 [**15**] (2011), 355–371. URL: `https://eprint.iacr.org/2011/232`. Citations in this document: §8.5, §A.

[76] Srdjan Capkun, Franziska Roesner (editors), *29th USENIX security symposium, USENIX Security 2020, August 12–14, 2020*, USENIX Association, 2020. ISBN 978-1-939133-17-5. URL: `https://www.usenix.org/conference/usenixsecurity20`. See [176].

[77] Dario Catalano, Nelly Fazio, Rosario Gennaro, Antonio Nicolosi (editors), *Public key cryptography—PKC 2011—14th international conference on practice and theory in public key cryptography, Taormina, Italy, March 6–9, 2011, proceedings*, Lecture Notes in Computer Science, 6571, Springer, 2011. ISBN 978-3-642-19378-1. See [50].

[78] Certicom, *Letter to IEEE* (2002). URL: `https://www.ieee802.org/15/pub/Patent_Letters/15.3/certicom%2015.3.pdf`. Citations in this document: §9.3.

[79] Liqun Chen, Shin'ichiro Matsuo (editors), *Security standardisation research—second international conference, SSR 2015, Tokyo, Japan, December*

15–16, 2015, proceedings, Lecture Notes in Computer Science, 9497, Springer, 2015. ISBN 978-3-319-27151-4. See [29].

[80] Tung Chou, *Sandy2x: New Curve25519 speed records*, in SAC 2015 [**93**] (2015), 145–160. URL: https://eprint.iacr.org/2015/943. DOI: 10.1007/978-3-319-31301-6_8. Citations in this document: §E.2.

[81] Nicolas Christin, Reihaneh Safavi-Naini (editors), *Financial cryptography and data decurity: 18th international conference, FC 2014, Christ Church, Barbados, March 3–7, 2014*, Lecture Notes in Computer Science, 8437, Springer, 2014. See [59].

[82] David V. Chudnovsky, Gregory V. Chudnovsky, *Sequences of numbers generated by addition in formal groups and new primality and factorization tests*, Advances in Applied Mathematics **7** (1986), 385–434. MR 88h:11094. Citations in this document: §3.1, §3.1, §3.1, §8, §8.1, §8.2.

[83] Henri Cohen, Atsuko Miyaji, Takatoshi Ono, *Efficient elliptic curve exponentiation using mixed coordinates*, in Asiacrypt 1998 [**186**] (1998), 51–65. URL: https://dspace02.jaist.ac.jp/dspace/bitstream/10119/4458/1/73-53.pdf. Citations in this document: §8.1.

[84] Neil Costigan, Peter Schwabe, *Fast elliptic-curve cryptography on the Cell Broadband Engine*, in Africacrypt 2009 [**198**] (2009), 368–385. URL: https://cryptojedi.org/users/peter/#celldh. Citations in this document: §E.2.

[85] Brooke Crothers, *Intel has bug-repair program* (1997). URL: https://www.cnet.com/tech/tech-industry/intel-has-bug-repair-program/. Citations in this document: §D.2.

[86] Agence nationale de la sécurité des systèmes d'information, *Publication d'un paramétrage de courbe elliptique visant des applications de passeport électronique et de l'administration électronique française* (Nov 2011). URL: https://www.ssi.gouv.fr/fr/anssi/publications/publications-scientifiques/autres-publications/publication-d-un-parametrage-de-courbe-elliptique-visant-des-applications-de.html. Citations in this document: §1.1.

[87] Yvo Desmedt (editor), *Public Key Cryptography—PKC 2003, 6th international workshop on theory and practice in public key cryptography, Miami, FL, USA, January 6–8, 2003, proceedings*, Lecture Notes in Computer Science, 2567, Springer, 2002. ISBN 3-540-00324-X. See [142].

[88] Nafissatou Diarra, Djiby Sow, Ahmed Youssef Ould Cheikh Khlil, *On indifferentiable deterministic hashing into elliptic curves*, European Journal of Pure and Applied Mathematics **10** (2017), 363–391. URL: https://ejpam.com/index.php/ejpam/article/view/2623. Citations in this document: §11.4.

[89] Claus Diem, *On the discrete logarithm problem in elliptic curves*, Compositio Mathematica **147** (2011), 75–-104. DOI: 10.1112/S0010437X10005075. Citations in this document: §2.1, §A.

[90] Claus Diem, Emmanuel Thomé, *Index calculus in class groups of non-hyperelliptic curves of genus three*, J. Cryptol. **21** (2008), 593–611. URL: https://members.loria.fr/EThome/files/non-he-genus3.pdf. Citations in this document: §7.6.

[91] Whitfield Diffie, Martin Hellman, *New directions in cryptography*, IEEE Transactions on Information Theory **22** (1976), 644–654. ISSN 0018-9448. MR 55:10141. URL: https://ee.stanford.edu/~hellman/publications/24.pdf. Citations in this document: §1.

[92] Michael Düll, Björn Haase, Gesine Hinterwälder, Michael Hutter, Christof Paar, Ana Helena Sánchez, Peter Schwabe, *High-speed Curve25519 on 8-bit, 16-bit, and 32-bit microcontrollers*, Designs, Codes and Cryptography **77** (2015), 493–514. URL: `https://link.springer.com/article/10.1007/s10623-015-0087-1/fulltext.html`. Citations in this document: §E.2.

[93] Orr Dunkelman, Liam Keliher (editors), *Selected areas in cryptography—SAC 2015—22nd international conference, Sackville, NB, Canada, August 12–14, 2015, revised selected papers*, Lecture Notes in Computer Science, 9566, Springer, 2016. ISBN 978-3-319-31300-9. DOI: `10.1007/978-3-319-31301-6`. See [80].

[94] Iwan M. Duursma, Pierrick Gaudry, François Morain, *Speeding up the discrete log computation on curves with automorphisms*, in Asiacrypt 1999 [**158**] (1999), 103–121. URL: `https://inria.hal.science/inria-00511639/PDF/automorphisms.pdf`. Citations in this document: §4.5.

[95] Harold M. Edwards, *A normal form for elliptic curves*, Bulletin of the American Mathematical Society **44** (2007), 393–422. URL: `https://www.ams.org/bull/2007-44-03/S0273-0979-07-01153-6/home.html`. Citations in this document: §3, §10.2.

[96] Adrian Escott, *Implementing a parallel Pollard rho attack on ECC* (1998). URL: `https://cacr.uwaterloo.ca/conferences/1998/ecc98/escott.ps`. Citations in this document: §4.5.

[97] Wolfgang Ettlinger, *Multiple vulnerabilities in Openpgp.js* (2019). URL: `https://sec-consult.com/vulnerability-lab/advisory/multiple-vulnerabilities-in-openpgp-js/`. Citations in this document: §9, §A.

[98] Federation of American Scientists, *Intelligence agency budgets: Commission recommends no release but releases them anyway* (1996). URL: `https://irp.fas.org/commission/budget.htm`. Citations in this document: §D.3.

[99] Marc Fischlin, Jean-Sébastien Coron (editors), *Advances in cryptology—EUROCRYPT 2016—35th annual international conference on the theory and applications of cryptographic techniques, Vienna, Austria, May 8–12, 2016, proceedings, part I*, Lecture Notes in Computer Science, 9665, Springer, 2016. ISBN 978-3-662-49889-7. DOI: `10.1007/978-3-662-49890-3`. See [202].

[100] Agner Fog, *Instruction tables: Lists of instruction latencies, throughputs and micro-operation breakdowns for Intel, AMD and VIA CPUs* (2024). URL: `https://agner.org/optimize/`. Citations in this document: §D.1.

[101] Marc P. C. Fossorier, Tom Høholdt, Alain Poli (editors), *Applied algebra, algebraic algorithms and error-correcting codes, 15th international symposium, aaecc-15, toulouse, France, May 12–16, 2003, proceedings*, 2643, Springer, 2003. ISBN 3-540-40111-3. DOI: `10.1007/3-540-44828-4`. See [71].

[102] Pierre-Alain Fouque, Reynald Lercier, Denis Réal, Frédéric Valette, *Fault attack on elliptic curve Montgomery ladder implementation*, in FDTC 2008 [**69**] (2008), 92–98. URL: `https://www.di.ens.fr/~fouque/pub/fdtc08.pdf`. DOI: `10.1109/FDTC.2008.15`. Citations in this document: §9.4.

[103] Pierre-Alain Fouque, Antoine Joux, Mehdi Tibouchi, *Injective encodings to elliptic curves*, in ACISP 2013 [**65**] (2013), 203–218. DOI: `10.1007/978-3-642-39059-3_14`. Citations in this document: §11.4.

[104] Gerhard Frey, *How to disguise an elliptic curve (Weil descent)* (1998). URL: `https://cacr.uwaterloo.ca/conferences/1998/ecc98/slides.html`. Citations in this document: §2.1, §A.

[105] Gerhard Frey, Hans-Georg Rück, *A remark concerning m-divisibility and the discrete logarithm problem in the divisor class group of curves*, Math. Comp. **62** (1994), 865–874. URL: `https://www.ams.org/journals/mcom/1994-62-206/S0025-5718-1994-1218343-6/`. Citations in this document: §5.1, §A.

[106] Hayato Fujii, Diego F. Aranha, *Curve25519 for the Cortex-M4 and beyond*, in LatinCrypt 2017 [**159**] (2017), 109–127. DOI: `10.1007/978-3-030-25283-0_6`. Citations in this document: §E.2.

[107] Tobias Funke, David Rupprecht, *Invalid curve attack on the 5G SUCI privacy feature* (2023). URL: `https://www.gsma.com/solutions-and-impact/technologies/security/wp-content/uploads/2023/10/0073-invalid_curve.pdf`. Citations in this document: §9, §9, §9, §A.

[108] Tim Güneysu, Helena Handschuh (editors), *Cryptographic hardware and embedded systems—CHES 2015—17th international workshop, Saint-Malo, France, September 13–16, 2015, proceedings*, Lecture Notes in Computer Science, 9293, Springer, 2015. ISBN 978-3-662-48323-7. See [133].

[109] Steven Galbraith, *Climbing and descending tall volcanos* (2024), ANTS 2024. URL: `https://eprint.iacr.org/2024/924`. Citations in this document: §7.5.

[110] Steven D. Galbraith, Mridul Nandi (editors), *Progress in cryptology—INDOCRYPT 2012, 13th international conference on cryptology in India, Kolkata, India, December 9–12, 2012, proceedings*, Lecture Notes in Computer Science, 7668, Springer, 2012. ISBN 978-3-642-34930-0. See [40].

[111] Robert P. Gallant, Robert J. Lambert, Scott A. Vanstone, *Improving the parallelized Pollard lambda search on anomalous binary curves*, Math. Comput. **69** (2000), 1699–1705. URL: `https://www.ams.org/journals/mcom/2000-69-232/S0025-5718-99-01119-9/`. Citations in this document: §6.2, §A.

[112] Robert P. Gallant, Robert J. Lambert, Scott A. Vanstone, *Faster point multiplication on elliptic curves with efficient endomorphisms*, in Crypto 2001 [**150**] (2001), 190–200. URL: `https://iacr.org/archive/crypto2001/21390189.pdf`. Citations in this document: §6.

[113] Qingguan Gao, Kaisheng Sun, Jiankuo Dong, Fangyu Zheng, Jingqiang Lin, Yongjun Ren, Zhe Liu, *V-Curve25519: efficient implementation of Curve25519 on RISC-V architecture*, in Inscrypt 2023 [**117**] (2023), 130–149. DOI: `10.1007/978-981-97-0945-8_8`. Citations in this document: §E.2.

[114] Pierrick Gaudry, *Index calculus for abelian varieties of small dimension and the elliptic curve discrete logarithm problem*, J. Symb. Comput. **44** (2009), 1690–1702. URL: `https://inria.hal.science/inria-00337631`. Citations in this document: §2.1, §A.

[115] Pierrick Gaudry, Emmanuel Thomé, *The mp$\mathbb{F}_q$ library and implementing curve-based key exchanges* (2007). URL: `https://inria.hal.science/inria-00168429`. Citations in this document: §E.2.

[116] Pierrick Gaudry, Florian Hess, Nigel P. Smart, *Constructive and destructive facets of Weil descent on elliptic curves*, Journal of Cryptology **15(1)** (2002), 19–46. URL: `https://inria.hal.science/inria-00512763`. Citations in this document: §2.1, §A.

[117] Chunpeng Ge, Moti Yung (editors), *Information security and cryptology—19th international conference, Inscrypt 2023, Hangzhou, China, December 9–10, 2023, revised selected papers, part II*, Lecture Notes in Computer Science, 14527, Springer, 2024. ISBN 978-981-97-0944-1. DOI: `10.1007/978-981-97-0945-8`. See [113].

[118] Rosario Gennaro, Matthew Robshaw (editors), *Advances in cryptology—CRYPTO 2015—35th annual cryptology conference, Santa Barbara, CA, USA, August 16–20, 2015, proceedings, part I*, Lecture Notes in Computer Science, 9215, Springer, 2015. ISBN 978-3-662-47988-9. DOI: 10.1007/978-3-662-47989-6. See [123].

[119] Diana Goehringer, Marco Domenico Santambrogio, João M. P. Cardoso, Koen Bertels (editors), *Reconfigurable computing: architectures, tools, and applications—10th international symposium, ARC 2014, Vilamoura, Portugal, April 14–16, 2014, proceedings* (2014). ISBN 978-3-319-05959-4. See [208].

[120] Go Project, *CVE-2023-24532: Incorrect calculation on P256 curves in crypto/internal/nistec* (2023). URL: https://www.cve.org/CVERecord?id=CVE-2023-24532. Citations in this document: §10.3, §A.

[121] Robert Granger, Antoine Joux, *Computing discrete logarithms*, in [**62**] (2021), 106–139. URL: https://eprint.iacr.org/2021/1140. Citations in this document: §1.

[122] Tom R. Halfhill, *Intel ups the ante*, BYTE Magazine **FEB** (1996), 156–156. URL: https://web.archive.org/web/19981206022744/http://byte.com/art/9602/sec14/art2.htm. Citations in this document: §D.2.

[123] Mike Hamburg, *Decaf: eliminating cofactors through point compression*, in Crypto 2015 [**118**] (2015), 705–723. URL: https://eprint.iacr.org/2015/673. DOI: 10.1007/978-3-662-47989-6_34. Citations in this document: §11.5.

[124] Mike Hamburg, *Faster Montgomery and double-add ladders for short Weierstrass curves*, IACR Trans. Cryptogr. Hardw. Embed. Syst. **2020** (2020), 189–208. URL: https://tches.iacr.org/index.php/TCHES/article/view/8681. Citations in this document: §8.7, §8.7.

[125] Guillaume Hanrot, François Morain, Emmanuel Thomé (editors), *Algorithmic number theory, 9th international symposium, ANTS-IX, Nancy, France, July 19–23, 2010, proceedings*, Lecture Notes in Computer Science, 6197, Springer, 2010. ISBN 978-3-642-14517-9. See [60].

[126] Feng Hao, Sushmita Ruj, Sourav Sen Gupta (editors), *Progress in cryptology—INDOCRYPT 2019—20th international conference on cryptology in India, Hyderabad, India, December 15–18, 2019, proceedings*, Lecture Notes in Computer Science, 11898, Springer, 2019. ISBN 978-3-030-35422-0. DOI: 10.1007/978-3-030-35423-7. See [211].

[127] Greg Harper, Alfred Menezes, Scott A. Vanstone, *Public-key cryptosystems with very small key length*, in Eurocrypt 1992 [**205**] (1992), 163–173. DOI: 10.1007/3-540-47555-9_14. Citations in this document: §9.3.

[128] M. Anwar Hasan, Tor Helleseth (editors), *Arithmetic of finite fields, third international workshop, WAIFI 2010, Istanbul, Turkey, June 27–30, 2010, proceedings*, Springer, 2010. ISBN 978-3-642-13796-9. See [39].

[129] Florian Hess, Sebastian Pauli, Michael E. Pohst (editors), *Algorithmic number theory, 7th international symposium, ANTS-VII, Berlin, Germany, July 23–28, 2006, proceedings*, Lecture Notes in Computer Science, 4076, Springer, 2006. ISBN 3-540-36075-1. DOI: 10.1007/11792086. See [216].

[130] Huseyin Hisil, Kenneth Koon-Ho Wong, Gary Carter, Ed Dawson, *Twisted Edwards curves revisited*, in Asiacrypt 2008 [**196**] (2008). URL: https://eprint.iacr.org/2008/522. Citations in this document: §1.3, §3, §10.2, §10.2, §10.2, §11.5.

[131] Yvonne Hitchcock, Paul Montague, Gary Carter, Ed Dawson, *The efficiency of solving multiple discrete logarithm problems and the implications for the*

security of fixed elliptic curves, Int. J. Inf. Sec. **3** (2004), 86–98. Citations in this document: §4.2.

[132] Everett W. Howe, Kiran S. Kedlaya (editors), *ANTS X: proceedings of the tenth algorithmic number theory symposium, San Diego 2012*, Mathematical Sciences Publishers, 2013. ISBN 978-1-935107-01-9. See [41].

[133] Michael Hutter, Jürgen Schilling, Peter Schwabe, Wolfgang Wieser, *NaCl's* crypto_box *in hardware*, in CHES 2015 [108] (2015), 81–101. URL: https://cryptojedi.org/papers/#naclhw. Citations in this document: §E.2.

[134] Institute of Electrical and Electronics Engineers, *IEEE Std 1363-2000: IEEE standard specifications for public key cryptography* (2000). URL: https://perso.telecom-paristech.fr/guilley/recherche/cryptoprocesseurs/ieee/00891000.pdf. Citations in this document: §1.1, §5, §8.1.

[135] Intel, *Pentium Processor Family Developer's Manual, volume 3: Architecture and Programming Manual* (1995). URL: https://stuff.mit.edu/afs/sipb/contrib/doc/specs/ic/cpu/x86/pentium/vol3.pdf. Citations in this document: §D.1, §D.1, §D.1.

[136] Intel, *Intel delivers the next level of computing with the new Pentium II processor* (1997). URL: https://www.intel.com/pressroom/archive/releases/1997/DP050797.HTM. Citations in this document: §D.1, §D.2, §D.2.

[137] Intel, *Form 10-K* (1998). URL: https://www.intc.com/filings-reports/annual-reports/content/0000050863-98-000031/0000050863-98-000031.pdf. Citations in this document: §D.1, §D.2.

[138] Intel, *Pentium II processor at 233 MHz, 266 MHz, 300 MHz, and 333 MHz* (1998). URL: https://web.archive.org/web/20240413014621/https://datasheets.chipdb.org/Intel/x86/Pentium%20II/24333503.PDF. Citations in this document: §D.1.

[139] Intel, *Intel Architecture Optimization Reference Manual* (1999). URL: https://download.intel.com/design/PentiumII/manuals/24512701.pdf. Citations in this document: §D.1.

[140] Yuval Ishai, Vincent Rijmen (editors), *Advances in cryptology—EUROCRYPT 2019—38th annual international conference on the theory and applications of cryptographic techniques, Darmstadt, Germany, May 19–23, 2019, proceedings, part II*, Lecture Notes in Computer Science, 11477, Springer, 2019. ISBN 978-3-030-17655-6. DOI: 10.1007/978-3-030-17656-3. See [48].

[141] Tetsuya Izu, Jun Kogure, Masayuki Noro, Kazuhiro Yokoyama, *Efficient implementation of Schoof's algorithm*, in Asiacrypt 1998 [186] (1998), 66–79. DOI: 10.1007/3-540-49649-1_7. Citations in this document: §7.1.

[142] Tetsuya Izu, Tsuyoshi Takagi, *Exceptional procedure attack on elliptic curve cryptosystems*, in PKC 2003 [87] (2002), 224–239. URL: https://www.iacr.org/archive/pkc2003/25670224/25670224.pdf. Citations in this document: §10, §A.

[143] Tibor Jager, Jörg Schwenk, Juraj Somorovsky, *Practical invalid curve attacks on TLS-ECDH*, in ESORICS 2015 [193] (2015), 407–425. URL: https://www.nds.rub.de/research/publications/ESORICS15/. DOI: 10.1007/978-3-319-24174-6_21. Citations in this document: §A.

[144] Jan Jancar, Vladimir Sedlacek, Petr Svenda, Marek Sýs, *Minerva: the curse of ECDSA nonces: systematic analysis of lattice attacks on noisy leakage of bit-length of ECDSA nonces*, IACR Trans. Cryptogr. Hardw. Embed. Syst. **2020** (2020), 281–308. DOI: 10.13154/tches.v2020.i4.281-308. Citations in this document: §10, §10, §10, §A.

[145] Thomas R. Johnson, *American cryptology during the cold war, 1945–1989, Book III: retrenchment and reform, 1972–1980*, 2013, distributed inside NSA in 1998, partially declassified in 2013. URL: `https://archive.org/details/cold_war_iii-nsa`. Citations in this document: §D.3.

[146] Thomas R. Johnson, *American cryptology during the cold war, 1945–1989, Book IV: cryptologic rebirth, 1981–1989*, 2013, distributed inside NSA in 1999, partially declassified in 2013. URL: `https://archive.org/details/cold_war_iv-nsa`. Citations in this document: §D.3.

[147] Burton S. Kaliski Jr, *Elliptic curves and cryptography: A pseudorandom bit generator and other tools*, Ph.D. thesis, MIT, 1988. URL: `https://dspace.mit.edu/handle/1721.1/14709`. Citations in this document: §9.6.

[148] Burton S. Kaliski Jr., *A pseudo-random bit generator based on elliptic logarithms*, in Crypto 1986 [185] (1986), 84–103. DOI: `10.1007/3-540-47721-7_7`. Citations in this document: §9.6.

[149] Burton S. Kaliski Jr. (editor), *Advances in cryptology—CRYPTO '97, 17th annual international cryptology conference, Santa Barbara, California, USA, August 17–21, 1997, proceedings*, Lecture Notes in Computer Science, 1294, Springer, 1997. ISBN 3-540-63384-7. See [165].

[150] Joe Kilian (editor), *Advances in cryptology—CRYPTO 2001, 21st annual international cryptology conference, Santa Barbara, California, USA, August 19–23, 2001, proceedings*, Lecture Notes in Computer Science, 2139, Springer, 2001. ISBN 3-540-42456-3. See [112].

[151] Ann Hibner Koblitz, Neal Koblitz, Alfred Menezes, *Elliptic curve cryptography: The serpentine course of a paradigm shift*, Journal of Number Theory **131** (2011), 781–814. URL: `https://eprint.iacr.org/2008/390`. Citations in this document: §7.6.

[152] Neal Koblitz, *Elliptic curve cryptosystems*, Mathematics of Computation **48** (1987), 203–209. ISSN 0025-5718. MR 88b:94017. URL: `https://www.ams.org/journals/mcom/1987-48-177/S0025-5718-1987-0866109-5/`. Citations in this document: §1.1.

[153] Neal Koblitz, Alfred Menezes, *A riddle wrapped in an enigma*, IEEE Security & Privacy **14** (2016), 34–42. URL: `https://eprint.iacr.org/2015/1018`. DOI: `10.1109/MSP.2016.120`. Citations in this document: §7.1, §7.4, §7.4, §7.5, §7.5, §D.

[154] Maurice Kraitchik, *Théorie des nombres I*, Gauthier-Villars, 1922. URL: `https://archive.org/details/thoriedesnombres01krai`. Citations in this document: §1.

[155] Maurice Kraitchik, *Théorie des nombres II*, Gauthier-Villars, 1926. URL: `https://archive.org/details/thoriedesnombres02krai`. Citations in this document: §1.

[156] Fabian Kuhn, Rene Struik, *Random walks revisited: extensions of Pollard's rho algorithm for computing multiple discrete logarithms*, in [224] (2001), 212–229. URL: `https://www.distcomp.ethz.ch/publications.html`. Citations in this document: §4.2.

[157] Kaoru Kurosawa (editor), *Advances in cryptology—ASIACRYPT 2007, 13th international conference on the theory and application of cryptology and information security, Kuching, Malaysia, December 2–6, 2007, proceedings*, Lecture Notes in Computer Science, 4833, Springer, 2007. ISBN 978-3-540-76899-9. See [36].

[158] Kwok-Yan Lam, Eiji Okamoto, Chaoping Xing (editors), *Advances in cryptology—ASIACRYPT '99, international conference on the theory and applications of cryptology and information security, Singapore, November 14–18, 1999, proceedings*, Lecture Notes in Computer Science, 1716, Springer, 1999. ISBN 3-540-66666-4. See [94].

[159] Tanja Lange, Orr Dunkelman (editors), *Progress in cryptology—LATINCRYPT 2017—5th international conference on cryptology and information security in Latin America, Havana, Cuba, September 20–22, 2017, revised selected papers*, Lecture Notes in Computer Science, 11368, Springer, 2019. ISBN 978-3-030-25282-3. DOI: 10.1007/978-3-030-25283-0. See [106].

[160] Adam Langley, Andrew Moon, *Implementations of a fast elliptic-curve Digital Signature Algorithm* (2013). URL: https://github.com/floodyberry/ed25519-donna. Citations in this document: §E.2.

[161] Kristin E. Lauter, Francisco Rodríguez-Henríquez (editors), *Progress in cryptology—LATINCRYPT 2015—4th international conference on cryptology and information security in Latin America, Guadalajara, Mexico, August 23–26, 2015, proceedings*, Lecture Notes in Computer Science, 9230, Springer, 2015. ISBN 978-3-319-22173-1. DOI: 10.1007/978-3-319-22174-8. See [30].

[162] Hyung Tae Lee, Jung Hee Cheon, Jin Hong, *Accelerating ID-based encryption based on trapdoor DL using pre-computation* (2011). URL: https://eprint.iacr.org/2011/187. Citations in this document: §4.2.

[163] Donald J. Lewis (editor), *1969 Number Theory Institute*, Proceedings of Symposia in Pure Mathematics, 20, American Mathematical Society, Providence, Rhode Island, 1971. ISBN 0–8218–1420–6. MR 47:3286. See [217].

[164] Jay Ligatti, Xinming Ou, Jonathan Katz, Giovanni Vigna (editors), *CCS '20: 2020 ACM SIGSAC conference on computer and communications security, virtual event, USA, November 9–13, 2020*, ACM, 2020. ISBN 978-1-4503-7089-9. DOI: 10.1145/3372297. See [13].

[165] Chae Hoon Lim, Pil Joong Lee, *A key recovery attack on discrete log-based schemes using a prime order subgroup*, in Crypto 1997 [**149**] (1997), 249–263. DOI: 10.1007/BFb0052240. Citations in this document: §9.1.

[166] Luigi1111, Riccardo Spagni, *Disclosure of a major bug in CryptoNote based currencies* (2017). URL: https://www.getmonero.org/2017/05/17/disclosure-of-a-major-bug-in-cryptonote-based-currencies.html. Citations in this document: §11.5.

[167] Eric M. Mahé, Jean-Marie Chauvet, *Fast GPGPU-based elliptic curve scalar multiplication* (2014). URL: https://eprint.iacr.org/2014/198. Citations in this document: §E.2.

[168] Stefan Mangard, François-Xavier Standaert (editors), *Cryptographic Hardware and Embedded Systems, CHES 2010, 12th international workshop, Santa Barbara, CA, USA, August 17–20, 2010, proceedings*, Lecture Notes in Computer Science, 6225, Springer, 2010. ISBN 978-3-642-15030-2. See [10].

[169] Dimitri Mankowski, Thom Wiggers, Veelasha Moonsamy, *TLS → post-quantum TLS: inspecting the TLS landscape for PQC adoption on Android*, in EuroSPW [**5**] (2023), 526–538. DOI: 10.1109/EuroSPW59978.2023.00065. Citations in this document: §9.3.

[170] Mitsuru Matsui (editor), *Advances in cryptology—ASIACRYPT 2009, 15th international conference on the theory and application of cryptology and information security, Tokyo, Japan, December 6–10, 2009, proceedings*, Lecture Notes in Computer Science, 5912, Springer, 2009. ISBN 978-3-642-10365-0. DOI: 10.1007/978-3-642-10366-7. See [74].

[171] Mohamad Ali Mehrabi, Christophe Doche, *Low-cost, low-power FPGA implementation of ED25519 and CURVE25519 point multiplication*, Inf. **10** (2019), 285. DOI: 10.3390/info10090285. Citations in this document: §E.2.

[172] Alfred J. Menezes, Tsuaki Okamoto, Scott A. Vanstone, *Reducing elliptic curve logarithms to a finite field*, IEEE Transactions on Information Theory **39** (1993), 1639–1646. DOI: 10.1145/103418.103434. Citations in this document: §5.1, §A.

[173] Microsoft, *Windows CryptoAPI spoofing vulnerability* (2020). URL: https://msrc.microsoft.com/update-guide/en-US/advisory/CVE-2020-0601. Citations in this document: §7.8, §A.

[174] Victor S. Miller, *Use of elliptic curves in cryptography*, in Crypto 1985 [**229**] (1986), 417–426. MR 88b:68040. DOI: 10.1007/3-540-39799-X_31. Citations in this document: §1.1, §8.7, §8.7, §11.4.

[175] MITRE, *CVE-2023-46324* (2023). URL: https://www.cve.org/CVERecord?id=CVE-2023-46324. Citations in this document: §9.

[176] Daniel Moghimi, Berk Sunar, Thomas Eisenbarth, Nadia Heninger, *TPM-FAIL: TPM meets timing and lattice attacks*, in USENIX Security 2020 [**76**] (2020), 2057–2073. URL: https://www.usenix.org/conference/usenixsecurity20/presentation/moghimi-tpm. Citations in this document: §10, §A.

[177] Peter L. Montgomery, *Speeding the Pollard and elliptic curve methods of factorization*, Mathematics of Computation **48** (1987), 243–264. ISSN 0025-5718. MR 88e:11130. URL: https://www.ams.org/journals/mcom/1987-48-177/S0025-5718-1987-0866113-7/. Citations in this document: §1.3, §3, §8, §8, §8.2.

[178] Mozilla Foundation, *Security Advisory 2023-56* (2023). URL: https://www.mozilla.org/en-US/security/advisories/mfsa2023-56/. Citations in this document: §10, §A.

[179] David Naccache, Pascal Paillier (editors), *Public Key Cryptography, 5th international workshop on practice and theory in public key cryptosystems, PKC 2002, Paris, France, February 12–14, 2002, proceedings*, Lecture Notes in Computer Science, 2274, Springer, 2002. ISBN 3-540-43168-3. See [70].

[180] Kaushik Nath, Palash Sarkar, *Efficient arithmetic in (pseudo-)Mersenne prime order fields*, Adv. Math. Commun. **16** (2022), 303–348. DOI: 10.3934/amc.2020113. Citations in this document: §E.2.

[181] Kaushik Nath, Palash Sarkar, *Security and efficiency trade-offs for elliptic curve Diffie-Hellman at the 128-bit and 224-bit security levels*, J. Cryptogr. Eng. **12** (2022), 107–121. DOI: 10.1007/s13389-021-00261-y. Citations in this document: §E.2.

[182] Kaushik Nath, Palash Sarkar, *Efficient 4-way vectorizations of the Montgomery ladder*, IEEE Trans. Computers **71** (2022), 712–723. DOI: 10.1109/TC.2021.3060505. Citations in this document: §E.2.

[183] National Institute of Standards and Technology, *Request for Comments on FIPS 186-5 and SP 800-186*, Federal Register **84** (2019), 58373–58375. URL: https://www.federalregister.gov/documents/2019/10/31/2019-23742/request-for-comments-on-fips-186-5-and-sp-800-186. Citations in this document: §1.4, §1.4, §1.4.

[184] National Security Agency, *Fact Sheet NSA Suite B Cryptography* (2005). URL: https://web.archive.org/web/20051125141648/https://www.nsa.gov/ia/industry/crypto_suite_b.cfm. Citations in this document: §1.1.

[185] Andrew M. Odlyzko (editor), *Advances in cryptology—CRYPTO '86, Santa Barbara, California, USA, 1986, proceedings*, Lecture Notes in Computer Science, 263, Springer, 1987. See [148].

180   Daniel J. Bernstein and Tanja Lange

[186] Kazuo Ohta, Dingyi Pei (editors), *Advances in cryptology—ASIACRYPT '98, International conference on the theory and applications of cryptology and information security, Beijing, China, October 18–22, 1998, proceedings*, Lecture Notes in Computer Science, 1514, Springer, 1998. ISBN 3-540-65109-8. DOI: 10.1007/3-540-49649-1. See [83], [141].

[187] Paul C. van Oorschot, Michael Wiener, *Parallel collision search with cryptanalytic applications*, Journal of Cryptology **12** (1999), 1–28. ISSN 0933-2790. DOI: 10.1007/PL00003816. Citations in this document: §4.4, §4.5.

[188] OpenSSL Project, *Bignum squaring may produce incorrect results (CVE-2014-3570)* (2015). URL: https://www.openssl.org/news/secadv/20150108.txt. Citations in this document: §A, §A.

[189] OpenSSL Project, *OpenSSL 3.2.2* (2024). URL: https://www.openssl.org/source/. Citations in this document: §E.1.

[190] Elisabeth Oswald, Pankaj Rohatgi (editors), *Cryptographic hardware and embedded systems—CHES 2008, 10th International Workshop, Washington, D.C., USA, August 10–13, 2008, Proceedings*, Lecture Notes in Computer Science, 5154, Springer, 2008. ISBN 978-3-540-85052-6. See [47].

[191] Sarvar Patel, *Number theoretic attacks on secure password schemes*, in S&P 1997 [1] (1997), 236–247. DOI: 10.1109/SECPRI.1997.601340. Citations in this document: §11.2.

[192] Kenneth G. Paterson, Douglas Stebila (editors), *Selected areas in cryptography—SAC 2019—26th international conference, Waterloo, ON, Canada, August 12–16, 2019, revised selected papers*, Lecture Notes in Computer Science, 11959, Springer, 2020. ISBN 978-3-030-38470-8. DOI: 10.1007/978-3-030-38471-5. See [55].

[193] Günther Pernul, Peter Y. A. Ryan, Edgar R. Weippl (editors), *Computer security—ESORICS 2015—20th European symposium on research in computer security, Vienna, Austria, September 21–25, 2015, proceedings, part I*, Lecture Notes in Computer Science, 9326, Springer, 2015. ISBN 978-3-319-24173-9. DOI: 10.1007/978-3-319-24174-6. See [143].

[194] Léo Perrin, *Partitions in the S-box of Streebog and Kuznyechik*, IACR Trans. Symmetric Cryptol. **2019** (2019), 302–329. URL: https://who.paris.inria.fr/Leo.Perrin/pi.html. Citations in this document: §7.

[195] Christophe Petit, Jean-Jacques Quisquater, *On polynomial systems arising from a Weil descent*, in Asiacrypt 2012 [**225**] (2012), 451–466. URL: https://www.iacr.org/archive/asiacrypt2012/76580446/76580446.pdf. Citations in this document: §2.1, §A.

[196] Josef Pieprzyk (editor), *Advances in cryptology — ASIACRYPT 2008, 14th international conference on the theory and application of cryptology and information security, Melbourne, Australia, December 7–11, 2008*, Lecture Notes in Computer Science, 5350, 2008. ISBN 978-3-540-89254-0. See [130].

[197] John M. Pollard, *Monte Carlo methods for index computation mod p*, Mathematics of Computation **32** (1978), 918–924. URL: https://www.ams.org/journals/mcom/1978-32-143/S0025-5718-1978-0491431-9/. Citations in this document: §4, §4.5, §4.5, §9.1.

[198] Bart Preneel (editor), *Progress in cryptology—AFRICACRYPT 2009, second international conference on cryptology in Africa, Gammarth, Tunisia, June 21–25, 2009, proceedings*, Lecture Notes in Computer Science, 5580, Springer, 2009. See [84].

[199] Bart Preneel, Tsuyoshi Takagi (editors), *Cryptographic Hardware and Embedded Systems—CHES 2011—13th international workshop, Nara, Japan, September 28–October 1, 2011, proceedings*, Lecture Notes in Computer Science, 6917, Springer, 2011. ISBN 978-3-642-23950-2. See [31].

[200] Emmanuel Prouff, Patrick Schaumont (editors), *Cryptographic hardware and embedded systems—CHES 2012—14th international workshop, Leuven, Belgium, September 9–12, 2012, proceedings*, Lecture Notes in Computer Science, 7428, Springer, 2012. ISBN 978-3-642-33026-1. See [52].

[201] Red Hat, *CVE-2021-3798* (2022). URL: https://www.cve.org/CVERecord?id=CVE-2021-3798. Citations in this document: §9, §A, §A.

[202] Joost Renes, Craig Costello, Lejla Batina, *Complete addition formulas for prime order elliptic curves*, in Eurocrypt 2016 [**99**] (2016), 403–428. URL: https://eprint.iacr.org/2015/1060. DOI: 10.1007/978-3-662-49890-3_16. Citations in this document: §10.3, §10.3, §10.3, §10.3.

[203] Certicom Research, *SEC 2: recommended elliptic curve domain parameters, version 1.0* (2000). URL: https://www.secg.org/SEC2-Ver-1.0.pdf. Citations in this document: §1.1, §5, §7.1.

[204] Ronald L. Rivest, Martin E. Hellman, John C. Anderson, John W. Lyons, *Responses to NIST's proposal*, Communications of the ACM **35** (1992), 41–54. URL: https://people.csail.mit.edu/rivest/pubs/RHAL92.pdf. Citations in this document: §1.4.

[205] Rainer A. Rueppel (editor), *Advances in cryptology—EUROCRYPT '92, workshop on the theory and application of of cryptographic techniques, Balatonfüred, Hungary, May 24–28, 1992, proceedings*, Lecture Notes in Computer Science, 658, Springer, 1993. ISBN 3-540-56413-6. DOI: 10.1007/3-540-47555-9. See [127].

[206] Peter Y. A. Ryan, David Naccache, Jean-Jacques Quisquater (editors), *The New Codebreakers—Essays dedicated to David Kahn on the occasion of his 85th birthday*, Lecture Notes in Computer Science, 9100, Springer, 2016. ISBN 978-3-662-49300-7. See [49].

[207] Ahmad-Reza Sadeghi, Virgil D. Gligor, Moti Yung (editors), *2013 ACM SIGSAC conference on computer and communications security, CCS'13, Berlin, Germany, November 4–8, 2013*, ACM, 2013. ISBN 978-1-4503-2477-9. See [34].

[208] Pascal Sasdrich, Tim Güneysu, *Efficient elliptic-curve cryptography using Curve25519 on reconfigurable devices*, in ARC 2014 [**119**] (2014), 25–36. URL: https://citeseerx.ist.psu.edu/document?repid=rep1&type=pdf&doi=ddbd39a27e4db00813a4c5d2da0e19d6fb50bbcb. Citations in this document: §E.2.

[209] Takakzu Satoh, Kiyomichi Araki, *Fermat quotients and the polynomial time discrete log algorithm for anomalous elliptic curves*, Commentarii Mathematici Universitatis Sancti Pauli **47** (1998), 81–92. URL: https://rikkyo.repo.nii.ac.jp/records/9910. Citations in this document: §5.1, §A.

[210] Stephen Schwab, William K. Robertson, Davide Balzarotti (editors), *Proceedings of the 32nd annual conference on computer security applications, ACSAC 2016, Los Angeles, CA, USA, December 5–9, 2016*, ACM, 2016. ISBN 978-1-4503-4771-6. DOI: 10.1145/2991079. See [12].

[211] Peter Schwabe, Amber Sprenkels, *The complete cost of cofactor h = 1*, in INDOCRYPT 2019 [**126**] (2019), 375–397. URL: https://eprint.iacr.org/2019/1166. DOI: 10.1007/978-3-030-35423-7_19. Citations in this document: §10.3.

[212] Michael Scott, *Re: NIST annouces set of Elliptic Curves.* (1999). URL: `https://groups.google.com/g/sci.crypt/c/mFMukSsORmI/m/FpbHDQ6hM_MJ`. Citations in this document: §7.1.

[213] Igor A. Semaev, *On computing logarithms on elliptic curves*, Diskretnaya Matematika **8** (1996), 65–71, in Russian; see also newer version [**214**]. DOI: `10.4213/dm516`.

[214] Igor A. Semaev, *On computing logarithms on elliptic curves*, Discrete Mathematics and Applications **6** (1996), 69–76; see also older version [**213**]. DOI: `10.1515/dma.1996.6.1.69`. Citations in this document: §5.1, §A.

[215] Igor A. Semaev, *Evaluation of discrete logarithms in a group of p-torsion points of an elliptic curve in characteristic p*, Mathematics of Computation **67** (1998), 353–356. URL: `https://www.ams.org/journals/mcom/1998-67-221/S0025-5718-98-00887-4/`. Citations in this document: §5.1, §A.

[216] Andrew Shallue, Christiaan E. van de Woestijne, *Construction of rational points on elliptic curves over finite fields*, in ANTS 2006 [**129**] (2006), 510–524. DOI: `10.1007/11792086_36`. Citations in this document: §11.4.

[217] Daniel Shanks, *Class number, a theory of factorization, and genera*, in [**163**] (1971), 415–440. MR 47:4932. Citations in this document: §4.5, §4.5.

[218] Nigel P. Smart, *The discrete logarithm problem on elliptic curves of trace one*, Journal of Cryptology **12(3)** (1999), 193–196. DOI: `10.1007/s001459900052`. Citations in this document: §5.1, §A.

[219] David L. Sobel, *New NIST/NSA Revelations* (1993). URL: `https://web.archive.org/web/20200229145033/https://catless.ncl.ac.uk/Risks/14/59#subj7`. Citations in this document: §7.

[220] National Institute for Standards and Technology, *Digital signature standard*, Federal Information Processing Standards Publication **186-2** (2000). URL: `https://csrc.nist.gov/publications/fips/archive/fips186-2/fips186-2.pdf`. Citations in this document: §1.1, §1.3, §7.1.

[221] Mathy Vanhoef, Eyal Ronen, *Dragonblood: analyzing the Dragonfly handshake of WPA3 and EAP-pwd*, in S&P 2020 [**3**] (2020), 517–533. URL: `https://eprint.iacr.org/2019/383`. DOI: `10.1109/SP40000.2020.00031`. Citations in this document: §11.3, §11.3, §11.3, §11.3, §A.

[222] Vijay Varadharajan, Yi Mu (editors), *Information security and privacy, 6th Australasian conference, ACISP 2001, Sydney, Australia, July 11–13, 2001, proceedings*, Lecture Notes in Computer Science, 2119, Springer, 2001. ISBN 3-540-42300-1. See [64].

[223] Serge Vaudenay (editor), *Progress in Cryptology—AFRICACRYPT 2008, First international conference on cryptology in Africa, Casablanca, Morocco, June 11–14, 2008, proceedings*, Lecture Notes in Computer Science, 5023, Springer, 2008. ISBN 978-3-540-68159-5. See [27].

[224] Serge Vaudenay, Amr M. Youssef (editors), *Selected Areas in Cryptography: 8th annual international workshop, SAC 2001, Toronto, Ontario, Canada, August 16–17, 2001, revised papers*, Lecture Notes in Computer Science, 2259, Springer, 2001. ISBN 3-540-43066-0. MR 2004k:94066. See [156].

[225] Xiaoyun Wang, Kazue Sako (editors), *Advances in cryptology—ASIACRYPT 2012—18th international conference on the theory and application of cryptology and information security, Beijing, China, December 2–6, 2012, proceedings*, Lecture Notes in Computer Science, 7658, Springer, 2012. ISBN 978-3-642-34960-7. See [195].

[226] A.E. Western, Jeffery Charles Percy Miller, *Tables of indices and primitive roots* (1968). URL: `https://books.google.com/books?id=amw5wwEACAAJ`. Citations in this document: §1.

[227] Zack Whittaker, *New leaked documents detail secret U.S. intelligence 'black budget' figures* (2013). URL: `https://www.zdnet.com/article/new-leaked-documents-detail-secret-u-s-intelligence-black-budget-figures/`. Citations in this document: §D.3.

[228] Michael J. Wiener, Robert J. Zuccherato, *Faster attacks on elliptic curve cryptosystems* (1998). URL: `https://grouper.ieee.org/groups/1363/Research/contributions/attackEC.ps`. Citations in this document: §4.5, §A.

[229] Hugh C. Williams (editor), *Advances in cryptology: CRYPTO '85*, Lecture Notes in Computer Science, 218, Springer, Berlin, 1986. ISBN 3–540–16463–4. See [174].

[230] Guiming Wu, Qianwen He, Jiali Jiang, Zhenxiang Zhang, Xin Long, Yuan Zhao, Yinchao Zou, *A high-performance hardware architecture for ECC point multiplication over Curve25519*, in FCCM 2022 [4] (2022), 1–9. DOI: `10.1109/FCCM53951.2022.9786192`. Citations in this document: §E.2.

[231] Moti Yung, Yevgeniy Dodis, Aggelos Kiayias, Tal Malkin (editors), *Public Key Cryptography—PKC 2006—9th international conference on theory and practice in public-key cryptography, New York, NY, USA, April 24–26, 2006, proceedings*, Lecture Notes in Computer Science, 3958, Springer, 2006. ISBN 978-3-540-33851-2. See [23].

A   Chronology of ECC vulnerabilities

This appendix reviews the timeline of ECC vulnerabilities. In this appendix, "demo" means that an attack has been demonstrated; "vulnerability" means that analysis indicates that an attack should work; "potential vulnerability" means that the attacker has extra power but further analysis is required to determine whether there is a vulnerability; "speedup" means that attacks are faster but not necessarily feasible.

This appendix focuses on the core ECC tasks, namely ECDH and signatures; this excludes, e.g., Dual EC (see [49]) and many breaks of advanced protocols built using ECC. For side-channel attacks, this appendix focuses on timing attacks and excludes power attacks, electromagnetic attacks, etc.

The timeline is organized by publication date. Two types of publications are included: publications pointing out new attack strategies (e.g., [54] pointing out invalid-curve vulnerabilities), and publications pointing out vulnerabilities in specific implementations (e.g., [201] pointing out an invalid-curve vulnerability in openCryptoki). The timeline is as follows:

- 1993 [172], independently 1994 [105], independently 1996 [214]: multiplicative transfers against curves with $p - 1$ points, $p + 1$ points, etc.
- 1998 [215], independently 1998 [209], independently 1999 [218]: additive transfers against curves with p points.
- 1998 [104]: sketch of speedup against some curves over non-prime fields.
- 1998 [228]: negation speedup.

- 2000 [111]: speedup using other fast endomorphisms for some curves.
- 2000 [54]: invalid-curve vulnerabilities in general.
- 2002 [116]: speedup against some curves over non-prime fields.
- 2002 [142]: exceptional-procedure vulnerabilities in general.
- 2009 [114]: speedup against some curves over non-prime fields.
- 2009 [74]: cache-timing demo against OpenSSL (0.9.8k and under).
- 2010 [6]: repeated-nonce demo extracting the Sony PlayStation 3 ECDSA signing key.
- 2011 [89]: speedup against some curves over non-prime fields.
- 2011 [75]: timing demo extracting NIST B-163 ECDSA secret keys from OpenSSL.
- 2012 [195]: speedup against some curves over non-prime fields.
- 2013 [59]: repeated-nonce demo extracting some Bitcoin ECDSA secret keys.
- 2015 [188]: potential invalid-curve vulnerability in OpenSSL because of an arithmetic bug inside a point-on-curve test. The arithmetic bug applies to occasional inputs, and [188] says the "exact impact is difficult to determine".
- 2015 [12]: timing demo extracting secp256k1 ECDSA secret keys from OpenSSL.
- 2015 [143]: invalid-curve demo extracting TLS ECDH secret keys from 2 out of 8 analyzed libraries: "Oracle's default Java TLS implementation (JSSE with a SunEC provider) and TLS servers using the Bouncy Castle library)".
- 2019 [97]: invalid-curve vulnerability in OpenPGP.js.
- 2019 [144]: "Minerva" timing demo extracting ECDSA secret keys from a FIPS-certified CC-certified Athena IDProtect smart card. Same vulnerability in seven other certified devices, and in 4 out of 13 software libraries.
- 2019 [176]: "TPM-FAIL" timing demo extracting ECDSA secret keys from two certified TPMs.
- 2019 [55]: invalid-curve demo against Bluetooth pairing.
- 2019 [221]: "Dragonblood" demo against the WPA3 Dragonfly handshake, including invalid-curve attacks and timing attacks.
- 2020 [173]: "CurveBall" parameter-substitution vulnerability in ECDSA in Windows 10.
- 2020 [11]: timing demo extracting ECDSA secret keys from mbedTLS.
- 2020 [13]: "LadderLeak" timing demo extracting ECDSA secret keys from OpenSSL in some scenarios.
- 2022 [201]: invalid-curve vulnerability in the openCryptoki soft token.
- 2023 [120]: potential exceptional-procedure vulnerability for NIST P-256 in the crypto/elliptic library for Go.
- 2023 [107]: invalid-curve vulnerability for 5G Subscription Concealed Identifiers in the free5GC udm software.
- 2023 [178]: timing vulnerability for NIST curves in the NSS cryptographic library in the Firefox browser.

B   Bit operations for elliptic-curve discrete logarithms

This appendix reviews the number of bit operations used in state-of-the-art ECDLP attacks for curves meeting the SafeCurves criteria. Note that faster attacks are known against various curves not meeting the SafeCurves criteria.

This appendix takes Curve25519 as a concrete example, with $p = 2^{255} - 19$ and $\ell \approx 2^{252}$. It was stated in [23] that every attack known at that time was "more expensive than performing a brute-force search on a typical 128-bit secret-key cipher"; this is also true for every attack known today.

Structurally, this appendix counts the number of iterations in an attack (Appendix B.1), counts the number of multiplications in each iteration (Appendix B.2), and takes optimized bit-operation counts from [48] for each multiplication (Appendix B.3). The reader is cautioned that this analysis omits two small effects in opposite directions: first, there is overhead in each iteration beyond multiplications; second, the operation counts from [48] can still be improved. See Appendix B.3 for further details. It would be interesting to analyze the exact number of bit operations for an optimized iteration, accounting for these improvements and for all overheads. See our paper [39] (and, for more background, [16]) for a detailed analysis of bit-operation counts for ECC2K-130, a binary-field ECDL challenge.

B.1   Iterations

As mentioned in Section 4, a standard negating rho attack takes about $\sqrt{\pi \ell / 4}$ iterations on average: e.g., $2^{125.8}$ iterations for Curve25519.

We showed in [41] that the constant $\sqrt{\pi / 4} \approx 0.886$ is not optimal in cost models that allow free memory access. Perhaps an improvement is possible even when one counts the bit operations involved in memory access. In the generic-group model augmented with free negation, the constant cannot be better than $2/3 \approx 0.667$; e.g., $2^{125.4}$ iterations for Curve25519.

For comparison, brute-force search on a 128-bit secret-key cipher takes about 2^{127} iterations on average, but the iterations are typically much less expensive in the cipher case. For example, [28] shows that a complete AES-128 attack iteration uses under $2^{14.9}$ bit operations, whereas Appendices B.2 and B.3 below indicate that the main operations in a Curve25519 attack iteration are close to 2^{20} bit operations. Presumably the costs of routing data will also be larger for a Curve25519 attack iteration than for an AES-128 attack iteration, but this appendix focuses on bit operations. See also Sections 4.2 and 4.3 regarding multi-target attacks.

B.2   Multiplications per iteration

The main work in an iteration inside the standard negating rho attack is an addition on a short Weierstrass curve in affine coordinates. Addition in affine coordinates involves a division, but the division is batched across many parallel attack iterations, reducing the effective cost of each division to 4**M** and the total cost of each iteration to 6**M**.

The details are as follows. On the curve $y^2 = x^3 + ax + b$, the sum of two points (x_1, y_1) and (x_2, y_2) is (x_3, y_3) where $\lambda = (y_2 - y_1)/(x_2 - x_1)$, $x_3 = \lambda^2 - x_1 - x_2$, and $y_3 = (x_1 - x_3)\lambda - y_1$. Failure cases in these formulas (see Section 10) are not relevant to the attack.

The inversion of $x_2 - x_1$ costs 3M as part of a large batch. There is then 1M to multiply by $y_2 - y_1$, 1M to square λ, and 1M to multiply by $x_1 - x_3$.

B.3   Bit operations per multiplication

Asymptotically, each multiplication in $\mathbb{F}_p$ uses $(\log p)^{1+o(1)}$ bit operations. For concrete numbers, we focus on the case of Curve25519.

An unrolled circuit for 255-bit integer multiplication, including Karatsuba's method and many lower-layer speedups, uses 173954 bit operations, according to the software from [48]. A 255-bit squaring circuit uses 103000 bit operations, according to the same software. Five multiplications and a squaring with these circuits use $972770 \approx 2^{19.89}$ bit operations.

As noted above, this analysis omits some known improvements. Karatsuba's method saves time when inputs are reused across multiplications; batched divisions reuse some inputs. Also, [33, footnote 5] points out that iteration details can be set up to guarantee that some trailing bits of $x_2 - x_1$ are zero, saving time in multiplications. As a possible further improvement, more advanced multiplication methods such as Toom's method asymptotically outperform Karatsuba's method, and perhaps already save operations for 255-bit inputs.

In the opposite direction, these are just the multiplication costs. There are also some costs for subtractions, reductions mod $2^{255} - 19$, "distinguished point" management, etc.

C   An email exchange

```
Subject: Greetings from evil Jerry
From: "Jerome A. Solinas" <jasolin@tycho.ncsc.mil>
Date: Wed, 23 Jul 2014 13:49:32 -0400
To: djb@cr.yp.to


Dr. Dan,

   Enjoyed your new paper.  Now I can cross "become an evil Internet meme"
off my bucket list.

   I will be at PQC Waterloo, so I'll see you and Tanja there if you're
going.


Regards,

-- Jerry


Subject: Re: Greetings from evil Jerry
From: "D. J. Bernstein" <djb@cr.yp.to>
```

Date: 6 Sep 2014 08:54:43 -0000
To: "Jerome A. Solinas" <jasolin@tycho.ncsc.mil>

Hi Jerry,

Unfortunately we won't be able to make it to PQCrypto. Maybe we'll see
you at the NIST events in the Spring.

Out of curiosity, where _did_ you get the seeds for NIST P-256 etc.?

---Dan

Subject: Re: Greetings from evil Jerry
From: "Jerome A. Solinas" <jasolin@tycho.ncsc.mil>
Date: Tue, 16 Sep 2014 14:53:14 -0400
To: "D. J. Bernstein" <djb@cr.yp.to>

On 09/06/2014 04:54 AM, D. J. Bernstein wrote:
> Hi Jerry,
>
> Unfortunately we won't be able to make it to PQCrypto. Maybe we'll see
> you at the NIST events in the Spring.
>
> Out of curiosity, where _did_ you get the seeds for NIST P-256 etc.?
>
> ---Dan

Interesting question. We built all the seeds via hashing (SHA-1, I think)
from the ASCII representation of a humorous message. Unfortunately, we can
remember neither the (exact) message nor the details of how we hashed.   Too
bad, since we could prove our innocence by disclosing the details, if only
we could remember them.

-- j

Subject: Re: Greetings from evil Jerry
From: "D. J. Bernstein" <djb@cr.yp.to>
Date: 14 Jun 2015 03:15:54 -0000
To: "Jerome A. Solinas" <jasolin@tycho.ncsc.mil>

Jerome A. Solinas writes, back in September:
> We built all the seeds via hashing (SHA-1, I think) from the ASCII
> representation of a humorous message. Unfortunately, we can remember
> neither the (exact) message nor the details of how we hashed.

Do you have some examples of similar messages? Kevin already mentioned
that it was something along the lines of "Jerry will get a raise", but
the next question is where you would have put a counter (or could it

have been repeated hashing?) to try multiple seeds. I'd be happy to
throw some cluster time at this.

---Dan

Subject: Re: Greetings from evil Jerry
From: "Jerome A. Solinas" <jasolin@tycho.ncsc.mil>
Date: Wed, 17 Jun 2015 10:27:34 -0400
To: "D. J. Bernstein" <djb@cr.yp.to>

On 06/13/2015 11:15 PM, D. J. Bernstein wrote:
> Jerome A. Solinas writes, back in September:
> > We built all the seeds via hashing (SHA-1, I think) from the ASCII
> > representation of a humorous message. Unfortunately, we can remember
> > neither the (exact) message nor the details of how we hashed.
> Do you have some examples of similar messages? Kevin already mentioned
> that it was something along the lines of "Jerry will get a raise", but
> the next question is where you would have put a counter (or could it
> have been repeated hashing?) to try multiple seeds. I'd be happy to
> throw some cluster time at this.
>
> ---Dan

I believe there was a counter rather than multiple hashing, but I don't know
details. The message was along the lines of "Give Bob and Jerry a raise" or
"Bob and Jerry rule" or something like that. It was Bob Reiter who actually
wrote the code, and he doesn't remember the details either. Nor were we
able to find archives from so long ago. If they exist, they are no doubt
sitting on a hard drive near the Ark of the Covenant.

I know this isn't much to go on. We really didn't think it would ever
matter.

-- Jerry

D   Chips available to attackers

This appendix investigates the claim from [153, 2018 eprint version] that "2^{86}
bit operations ... almost certainly was beyond the NSA's capacity in 1997".

D.1   An example of CPU efficiency

Consider the 266 MHz Intel Pentium II. This CPU was released in May 1997,
according to [136] and [137, pages 2–3]. The CPU carried out "one FMUL per
two clock cycles", according to [100, page 83] (see also [139, page 2-30]); i.e.,
the CPU carried out 133 million FMUL instructions per second.

Each FMUL instruction multiplies two inputs in "FPU registers" (see, e.g., [135, page 25-117]), each of which is a floating-point number in "extended format" (see, e.g., [135, page 6-25]), meaning an 80-bit floating-point number with a 64-bit mantissa (see, e.g., [135, page 6-23]). The software from [48] reports 17402 bit operations for 64-bit integer multiplication. The CPU was also carrying out many further bit operations for instruction decoding, out-of-order execution, etc. We estimate at least 2^{15} bit operations in total per FMUL, and thus at least 2^{42} bit operations per second for the CPU.

Intel's data sheet for the processor [138, page 22] indicated that the CPU core would draw at most 12.7 A at 2.8 V, plus at most 1.44 A at 3.3 V for L2 cache; i.e., at most 40 watts. We estimate 2^6 watts to account for supporting circuitry, power-supply inefficiency, etc., and conclude that this CPU was carrying out at least 2^{36} bit operations per joule.

For comparison, the current Bitcoin-mining equipment cited in Section 4.1 carries out 2^{54} bit operations per joule. This indicates about 1.5 years per doubling of energy efficiency of a bit operation. Interpolating would suggest 2^{47} bit operations per joule in 2013, in line with our estimate [43] at the time.

D.2 Scaling to many chips

Given the above estimate of at least 2^{36} bit operations per joule with 1997 chip technology, 2^{86} bit operations would have consumed at most 2^{50} joules. Spreading 2^{50} joules over a year means 2^5 megawatts. At 2^6 watts per chip, 2^5 megawatts means half a million chips, equivalent to a few hundred million dollars at Intel's original $775 sales price (see [136]) for the 266 MHz Pentium II.

For comparison, a 1997 news report [85] said that Intel "is shipping close to 100 million chips a year". Intel's annual report in early 1998 [137, pages 3 and 26] said that "sales of Pentium Pro and Pentium II microprocessors became an increasing portion of the Company's revenues and gross margin in 1996 and a significant portion in 1997", and that Intel's net revenues in 1997 were $25 billion. Intel was already manufacturing earlier "CPUs in volume on a 0.35-micron process" in 1995, according to [122]; the 266 MHz Pentium II was also manufactured at 350nm, according to [136]. There is no reason to think that producing half a million 350nm CPUs for an attack would have run into any manufacturing limits.

D.3 NSA resources

The Federation of American Scientists used public data to conclude in 1996 [98] that the "NSA budget is around $3.6 billion", including "roughly 20,000 direct-hire NSA staff". Even if personnel expenses for an average staff member were as high as $100000, NSA would have had $1.6 billion in 1996 to spend on equipment.

Declassification requests by journalists led to partial declassification in 2013 of internal NSA history books from 1998 and 1999. These books confirm the 20,000 number; see, e.g., [145, page 23]. These books also say [146, page 291]

that NSA spent $199 million in 1984 on a single contract to buy 21,000 IBM PC
XTs so as to put a PC on each desk; that NSA spent $150 million in 1985 on a
single network-hardware contract; and that "computer power was the essential
ingredient in cryptanalysis".

Spending a few hundred million dollars in 1996 on chips to carry out
attacks would have been enough to carry out 2^{86} bit operations in 1997 (see
Appendices D.1 and D.2), even if there were no contributions from chips bought
in previous years, and would have been only 10% of NSA's budget. There is
no evident reason that NSA would not have spent even more than this on such
chips, say 30% of its budget, in which case an attack consuming 2^{86} bit operations
would have been only one of multiple large-scale attacks that NSA could have
afforded to carry out at the same time.

For comparison, news reports in 2013 such as [**227**] indicated that NSA's
yearly budget was around $10 billion, with half spent on "management, facilities,
and support". A news report in 2012 regarding just one of NSA's computer
centers, the Bluffdale center [**18**], indicated that the center cost $2 billion, that
construction had begun in 2011, and that the center "should be up and running
in September 2013", so that center by itself accounted for close to 10% of NSA's
budget for those years.

E Speed

X25519 has been consistently observed to outperform NIST P-256 ECDH,
as noted in Section 8.2; similarly, Ed25519 has been consistently observed
to outperform NIST P-256 ECDSA. As quantification, this appendix reports
measurements of recent software on a spectrum of different CPU cores.

E.1 Data collection

We picked machines with a spread of 10 CPUs introduced over the past decade.
Table E.1.1 provides detailed information about the CPU in each machine.

On each machine, we compiled OpenSSL 3.2.2 (released in June 2024 [**189**])
and used OpenSSL's speed utility to measure NIST P-256. This utility reports
ECDH time, ECDSA signing time, and ECDSA verification time. Key-generation
time is not reported (ECDH time means only shared-secret computation),
but key generation and signing have the same primary bottleneck, namely
single-scalar fixed-base-point multiplication.

The speed utility runs experiments on a single CPU core. The numbers in
Appendix E.2 are operation counts per second on one core. It is reasonable to
expect that a CPU with, e.g., 4 cores can carry out operations 4 times more
quickly. This expectation would be invalid with overclocking mechanisms such
as "Turbo Boost", since overclocking is much more effective when only one core
is active; we disabled those mechanisms.

For X25519 and Ed25519, we measured the performance of lib25519 [**51**] on
the same CPUs. To maximize comparability, we performed these measurements

machine	CPU	cores	MHz	microarchitecture	year
alder	Intel Core i3-12100	4	3300	Golden Cove	2022
cezanne	AMD Ryzen 5 PRO 5650G	6	3900	Zen 3	2021
jasper3	Intel Celeron N5105	4	2000	Tremont	2021
panther	Intel Core i7-1165G7	4	2800	Tiger Lake	2020
rome1	AMD EPYC 7742	64	2245	Zen 2	2019
pi4b	Broadcom BCM2711	4	1500	Cortex-A72	2019
gemini	Intel Celeron N4020	2	1100	Goldmont Plus	2019
pi3aplus	Broadcom BCM2837B0	4	1400	Cortex-A53	2018
rumba7	AMD Ryzen 7 1700	8	3000	Zen	2017
nucnuc	Intel Pentium N3700	4	1600	Airmont	2015
samba	Intel Xeon E3-1220 v5	4	3000	Skylake	2015

Table E.1.1. CPUs used for the measurements in Table E.2.1. "Year" is the year that the CPU was introduced. The machine named `rome1` has two identical CPUs; "cores" is the number of cores per CPU.

machine	P-256 DH	X25519 DH	P-256 Ed25519 sign	sign	P-256 Ed25519 verify	verify
alder	18700	48075	47009	118851	14450	35893
cezanne	23184	53152	53564	132900	17918	34131
jasper3	6047	9252	15613	23476	4662	7111
panther	15526	43282	36826	91401	11855	25868
rome1	12920	24068	29073	73521	9809	17326
pi4b	3810	10947	8636	13642	2893	3639
gemini	2837	4455	7227	11427	2192	3450
rumba7	14595	25527	32723	76847	10811	18921
nucnuc	2341	3692	5772	9083	1811	2891
samba	17698	35981	38669	88640	13170	28468

Table E.2.1. Speed of readily available software for NIST P-256 and Curve25519 on various CPU cores. See Table E.1.1 for descriptions of the CPUs. Each number is for operations carried out per second on a single CPU core, with overclocking disabled.

with OpenSSL's `speed` utility, using a "provider" that plugs lib25519 into OpenSSL.

E.2 Results

Table E.2.1 reports the speed of each operation on each machine. For previous reports of Curve25519 speeds in various environments, often with in-depth analyses of the speeds, see [23], [115], [84], [32], [52], [160], [167], [208], [80], [92], [133], [106], [171], [56], [180], [181], [182], [230], and [113].

Asymptotic Complexity and Performance Comparison of FALCON and SOLMAE using their C Implementation

Kwangjo Kim[1(✉)] and YeonJun Kim[2]

[1] International Research Institute for Cyber Security(IRCS)/KAIST, Daejeon, Korea
kkj@kaist.ac.kr
[2] LGUPLUS, Yongsan, Korea
cherryk@lguplus.co.kr

Abstract. In 2023, NIST selected FALCON as one of the quantum–resistant digital signatures, which uses the hash-and-sign paradigm in the style of Gentry–Peikert–Vaikuntanathan framework and instantiated over NTRU lattices. SOLMAE, as a variant of FALCON, was submitted to KpqC competition by taking all the pros of FALCON and MITAKA and reducing their cons as much as possible.

In this paper, we analyze the asymptotic computational complexity of FALCON and SOLMAE that take $\Theta(n \log n)$ in their KeyGen, Sign and Verif procedures simultaneously and verify their performance by ANSI C language implementation. Our experiment shows that SOLMAE achieves the same high security and short key and signature sizes as FALCON, but it has faster Sign procedure than FALCON, while taking a bit longer time in KeyGen procedure. However, the Sign and Verif procedures of SOLMAE-512 is about 10 times faster than those of ECDSA P256r1 currently used in TSL or SSL.

Keywords: Lattice-based cryptography · Hash-and-sign paradigm · NTRU trapdoors · Discrete Gaussian sampling · C language implementation

1 Introduction

Shor [19] proposed an efficient randomized algorithm on a hypothetical quantum computer in 1999 to integer factorization and discrete logarithm problems in a polynomial time. Building for the powerful computing environment at that time was beyond imagination. Currently the threat of attacking the current (or classical) secure system by using the quantum computer is expected to be right at our fingertips due to the aggressive road map by IBM quantum computing [8].

We are very concerned about so-called *Harvest Now, Decrypt Later* attack [20] which is a surveillance strategy that relies on the acquisition and long-term storage of currently unreadable encrypted data awaiting possible breakthroughs in decryption technology that would render it readable in the future.

© The Author(s), under exclusive license to Springer Nature Switzerland AG 2025
C. Boyd et al. (Eds.): Ed Dawson Festschrift 2024, LNCS 15600, pp. 192–213, 2025.
https://doi.org/10.1007/978-3-031-83490-5_8

Due to the substantial amount of research on quantum computers, large-scale quantum computers if built, can break many public-key cryptosystems based on the number–theoretic hard problems in use. In 2016, NIST [16] has initiated Post Quantum Cryptography (PQC) project to solicit, evaluate, and standardize one or more quantum-resistant cryptographic algorithms for Key Encapsulation Mechanism (KEM) and Digital Signature (DS) worldwide. After several rounds, NIST has finally selected CRYSTALS-Kyber [18] for KEM and CRYSTALS-Dilithium [13], FALCON [2], and SPHINCS+ [7] for DS in 2022.

Influenced by this NIST PQC project, Korean cryptographic society led by KpqC task force [12] has called for soliciting Korean PQC candidates by the end of Oct. in 2022. By the due of submission, 7 candidates KEM and 8 candidates DS for KpqC competition were submitted and their details are available at https://kpqc.or.kr/.

SOLMAE which stands for an acronym of quantum–Secure algOrithm for Long–term Message Authentication and Encryption was submitted to KpqC Competition as one of DS candidate algorithms which is a lattice-based signature scheme inspired by several pioneering works based on the hash-then-sign signature paradigm proposed by Gentry, Peikert and Vaikuntanathan [4]. SOLMAE is inspired from FALCON's design. Some of the new theoretical foundations were laid out in the presentation of MITAKA [1] while keeping the security level of FALCON with 5 NIST levels of security I to V. At a high level, SOLMAE removes the inherent technicality of the sampling procedure, and most of its induced complexity from an implementation standpoint, for *free*, that is with no loss of efficiency. This theoretical simplicity translates into faster operations while preserving signatures and verification key sizes, on top of allowing for additional features absent from FALCON, such as enjoying cheaper masking and being parallelizable.

The companion work of this paper was published at Proc. of ICSICS2023 [10] to discuss the performance comparison using their Python implementation of both algorithms which cannot represent their exact performance evaluation in real-time applications. On the other hand, this paper discusses the real performance comparison between 2 algorithms by their ANSI C implementations which is more valuable to the practitioners and gives easy to grasp their execution times. To the best of our knowledge, there is no open literature to compare FALCON and SOLMAE directly from the point of their asymptotic complexity and performance. In this paper, after giving a brief description from the specification of FALCON and SOLMAE, we discuss their asymptotic computational complexity of `KeyGen`, `Sign` and `Verif` procedures from the theoretical point of view and suggest our performance evaluation including performance comparison of SOLMAE-512 and ECDSA P256r1.

The organization of this paper is as follows: In Sect. 2, we define our notations and definition used in this paper. In Sects. 3 and 4, we describe how FALCON and SOLMAE work summarized from their specifications, respectively. In Sect. 5, we discuss the asymptotic computational complexity of FALCON and SOLMAE. Section 6 suggests our performance analysis of FALCON and SOLMAE in total and commonly-used computations in their C language reference implementation and gives an exact comparison the performance of SOLMAE-512 and ECDSA P256r1 at the same level of security. Finally, we will give concluding remarks and challenging issues.

2   Notations and Definition

To keep the consistency to understand FALCON and SOLMAE correctly, we will use the following notations and definitions used their specification throughout this paper.

Matrices, Vectors, and Scalars

Matrices will usually be in bold uppercase (e.g. $\mathbf{B}$), vectors in bold lowercase (e.g. $\mathbf{v}$), and scalars - which include polynomials - in italic (e.g. s). We use the row convention for vectors. The transpose of a matrix $\mathbf{B}$ may be noted $\mathbf{B}^t$. It is to be noted that for a polynomial f, we do *not* use f' to denote its derivative in this document.

Quotient Rings

Let $\mathbb{Z}$ and $\mathbb{N}$ denote a set of integers and a set of all numbers starting from 1, respectively. $\mathbb{Q}$ and $\mathbb{R}$ denote a set of rational numbers and a set of real numbers,respectively. For $q \in \mathbb{N}^\times$, we denote by $\mathbb{Z}_q$ the quotient ring $\mathbb{Z}/q\mathbb{Z}$. In FALCON and SOLMAE, an integer modulus $q = 12,289$ is prime, so $\mathbb{Z}_q$ is also a finite field. We denote by $\mathbb{Z}_q^\times$ the group of invertible elements of $\mathbb{Z}_q$, and by φ Euler's totient function: $\varphi(q) = |\mathbb{Z}_q^\times| = q - 1 = 3 \cdot 2^{12}$ since q is prime. The rings $\mathbb{Q}[x]/(\phi)$, $\mathbb{Z}[x]/(\phi)$, and $\mathbb{R}[x]/(\phi)$ where ϕ is a monic minimal polynomial will be interchangeably written as $\mathcal{Q}$, $\mathcal{Z}$, and $K_\mathbb{R}$, respectively for the sake of our convenience.

DFT Representation

For $d = 2^n$, we use $\phi(x) = x^d + 1$. It is a monic polynomial of $\mathbb{Z}[x]$, irreducible in $\mathbb{Q}[x]$ and with distinct roots over $\mathbb{C}$. Then $\zeta_j = exp(i(2j-1)\pi/d)$ for $j = 1, 2, \cdots d$ are roots of $\phi(x)$. For $f = \Sigma f_i x^i \in K_\mathbb{R}$, we define the coefficient representation as $\mathbf{f} = (f_0, f_1, \cdots f_{d-1})$ and Discrete Fourier Transform (DFT) representation $\varphi(f) = (\varphi_1(f), \cdots, \varphi_d(f))$.

Number Fields

Let $a = \sum_{i=0}^{d-1} a_i x^i$ and $b = \sum_{i=0}^{d-1} b_i x^i$ be arbitrary elements of the number field $\mathcal{Q} = \mathbb{Q}[x]/(\phi)$. We note a^* and call (Hermitian) adjoint of a the unique element of $\mathcal{Q}$ such that for any root ζ of ϕ, $a^*(\zeta) = \overline{a(\zeta)}$, where $\overline{\cdot}$ is the usual complex conjugation over $\mathbb{C}$. For $\phi = x^d + 1$, the Hermitian adjoint a^* can be expressed simply:

$$a^* = a_0 - \sum_{i=1}^{d-1} a_i x^{d-i} \tag{1}$$

We extend this definition to vectors and matrices: the adjoint $\mathbf{B}^*$ of a matrix $\mathbf{B} \in \mathcal{Q}^{n \times m}$ (resp. a vector $\mathbf{v}$) is the component-wise adjoint of the transpose of $\mathbf{B}$ (resp. $\mathbf{v}$):

$$\mathbf{B} = \begin{bmatrix} a & b \\ c & d \end{bmatrix} \quad \Leftrightarrow \quad \mathbf{B}^* = \begin{bmatrix} a^* & c^* \\ b^* & d^* \end{bmatrix} \tag{2}$$

Inner Product

The inner product $\langle \cdot, \cdot \rangle$ over $\mathcal{Q}$ and its associated norm $\| \cdot \|$ are defined as:

$$\langle a, b \rangle = \frac{1}{\deg(\phi)} \sum_{0 < i \le d} \varphi_i(a) \cdot \overline{\varphi_i(b)} \tag{3}$$

$$\|a\| = \sqrt{\langle a, a \rangle} \tag{4}$$

These definitions can be extended to vectors: for $u = (u_i)$ and $v = (v_i)$ in $\mathcal{Q}^m$, $\langle u, v \rangle = \sum_i \langle u_i, v_i \rangle$. For our choice of ϕ, the inner product coincides with the usual coefficient-wise inner product:

$$\langle a, b \rangle = \sum_{0 \le i < d} a_i b_i; \tag{5}$$

From an algorithmic point of view, computing the inner product or the norm is most easily done using Eq.(3) if polynomials are in FFT representation, and using Eq.(5) if they are in coefficient representation. By substituting $b = a$ in Eqs. (3) and (5), we get

$$\|\varphi(a)\| = \sqrt{d} \cdot \|a\|. \tag{6}$$

where $\| \cdot \|$ is Euclidean norm. Since we know that

$$\|\varphi(a)\| = \sqrt{2} \cdot \|(Re(\varphi_1(a)), Im(\varphi_1(a)), \cdots Re(\varphi_{d/2}(a)), Im(\varphi_{d/2}(a)))\|, \tag{7}$$

we get

$$\|(Re(\varphi_1(a)), Im(\varphi_1(a)), \cdots Re(\varphi_{d/2}(a)), Im(\varphi_{d/2}(a)))\| = \sqrt{\frac{d}{2}} \cdot \|a\|. \tag{8}$$

If $a \in K_{\mathbb{R}}$ follows the d-dimensional standard normal distribution, it is known that

$$(Re(\varphi_1(a)), Im(\varphi_1(a)), \cdots Re(\varphi_{d/2}(a)), Im(\varphi_{d/2}(a))) \text{ follows } \mathcal{N}_{d/2}, \tag{9}$$

where $\mathcal{N}_{d/2}$ denotes continuous Gaussian distribution with zero mean and $\frac{d}{2} \cdot I_d(i.e., \text{Identity matrix})$ variance.

Ring Lattices

For the rings $\mathcal{Q} = \mathbb{Q}[x]/(\phi)$ and $\mathcal{Z} = \mathbb{Z}[x]/(\phi)$, positive integers $m \geq n$, and a full-rank matrix $\mathbf{B} \in \mathcal{Q}^{n \times m}$, we denote by $\Lambda(\mathbf{B})$ and call lattice generated by $\mathbf{B}$, the set $\mathcal{Z}^n \cdot \mathbf{B} = \{z\mathbf{B} \mid z \in \mathcal{Z}^n\}$. By extension, a set Λ is a lattice if there exists a matrix $\mathbf{B}$ such that $\Lambda = \Lambda(\mathbf{B})$. We may say that $\Lambda \subseteq \mathcal{Z}^m$ is a q-ary lattice if $q\mathcal{Z}^m \subseteq \Lambda$.

NTRU Lattices

Let q be an integer, and $f \in \mathbb{Z}[x]/(x^d + 1)$ such that f is invertible modulo q (equivalently, $\det[f]$ is coprime to q). Let $h = g/f \bmod q$ and consider the NTRU module associated to h:

$$\mathcal{M}_{\mathrm{NTRU}} = \{(u, v) \in K_{\mathbb{R}}^2 : hu - v = 0 \bmod q\},$$

and its lattice version

$$\mathcal{L}_{\mathrm{NTRU}} = \{(\mathbf{u}, \mathbf{v}) \in \mathbb{Z}^{2d} : [h]\mathbf{u} - \mathbf{v} = 0 \bmod q\}.$$

This lattice has volume q^d. Over $K_{\mathbb{R}}$, it is generated by (f, g) and any (F, G) such that $fG - gF = q$. For such a pair $(f, g), (F, G)$, this means that $\mathcal{L}_{\mathrm{NTRU}}$ has a basis of the form

$$\mathbf{B}_{f,g} = \begin{bmatrix} [f] & [F] \\ [g] & [G] \end{bmatrix}.$$

One checks that $([h], -\mathrm{Id}_d) \cdot \mathbf{B}_{f,g} = 0 \bmod q$, so the verification key is h. The NTRU-search problem is : given $h = g/f \bmod q$, find any $(f' = x^i f, g' = x^i g)$. In its decision variant, one must distinguish $h = g/f \bmod q$ from a uniformly random $h \in R_q := \mathbb{Z}[x]/(q, x^d + 1) = (\mathbb{Z}/q\mathbb{Z})[x]/(x^d + 1)$. These problems are assumed to be intractable for large d.

Discrete Gaussians

For $\sigma, \mu \in \mathbb{R}$ with $\sigma > 0$, we define the Gaussian function $\rho_{\sigma,\mu}$ as $\rho_{\sigma,\mu}(x) = \exp(-|x - \mu|^2/2\sigma^2)$, and the discrete Gaussian distribution $D_{\mathbb{Z},\sigma,\mu}$ over the integers as:

$$D_{\mathbb{Z},\sigma,\mu}(x) = \frac{\rho_{\sigma,\mu}(x)}{\sum_{z \in \mathbb{Z}} \rho_{\sigma,\mu}(z)} \tag{10}$$

The parameter μ may be omitted when it is equal to zero.

Gram-Schmidt Orthogonalization

Any matrix $\mathbf{B} \in \mathcal{Q}^{n \times m}$ can be decomposed as follows:

$$\mathbf{B} = \mathbf{L} \times \tilde{\mathbf{B}} \tag{11}$$

where $\mathbf{L}$ is lower triangular with 1's on the diagonal, and the rows $\tilde{b}_i$'s of $\tilde{\mathbf{B}}$ verify $\langle \tilde{b}_i, \tilde{b}_j \rangle = 0$ for $i \neq j$. When $\mathbf{B}$ is full-rank, this decomposition is unique, and it is called the Gram-Schmidt orthogonalization (or GSO). We also call the Gram-Schmidt norm of $\mathbf{B}$ the following value:

$$\|\mathbf{B}\|_{GS} = \max_{\mathbf{b}_i \in \tilde{\mathbf{B}}} \|\tilde{\mathbf{b}}_i\| \tag{12}$$

The LDL* Decomposition

The LDL* decomposition writes any full-rank Gram matrix as a product LDL*, where $\mathbf{L} \in \mathcal{Q}^{n \times n}$ is lower triangular with 1's on the diagonal, and $\mathbf{D} \in \mathcal{Q}^{n \times n}$ is diagonal. The LDL* decomposition and the GSO are closely related as for a basis $\mathbf{B}$, there exists a unique GSO $\mathbf{B} = \mathbf{L} \cdot \tilde{\mathbf{B}}$, and for a full-rank Gram matrix $\mathbf{G}$, there exists a unique LDL* decomposition $\mathbf{G} = \mathbf{LDL}^*$. If $\mathbf{G} = \mathbf{BB}^*$, then $\mathbf{G} = \mathbf{L} \cdot (\tilde{\mathbf{B}}\tilde{\mathbf{B}}^*) \cdot \mathbf{L}^*$ is a valid LDL* decomposition of $\mathbf{G}$. As both decompositions are unique, the matrices $\mathbf{L}$ in both cases are actually the same. In a nutshell:

$$[\mathbf{L} \cdot \tilde{\mathbf{B}} \text{ is the GSO of } \mathbf{B}] \Leftrightarrow [\mathbf{L} \cdot (\mathbf{B}\tilde{\mathbf{B}}^*) \cdot \mathbf{L}^* \text{ is the LDL*decomposition of } (\mathbf{BB}^*)].\tag{13}$$

The reason why we present both equivalent decompositions is that the GSO is a more familiar concept in lattice-based cryptography, whereas the use of LDL* decomposition is faster and therefore makes more sense from an algorithmic point of view.

3   FALCON Algorithm

Hoffstein, Pipher and Silverman [6] suggested a new public–key cryptosystem based on a polynomial ring in 1997 as an alternative to RSA and DH whose difficulties are based on number–theoretic hard problems such as integer factorization and discrete log problem, respectively. They founded the company so–called as NTRU[1] Cryptosystem with Lieman and initiated an open–source lattice-based cryptography consisting of two algorithms: NTRUENCRYPT used for encryption/decryption and NTRUSIGN used for digital signatures. Their security relies on the presumed difficulty of factoring certain polynomials in a truncated polynomial ring into a quotient of two polynomials having very small coefficients.

NTRUSIGN was designed based on the GGH signature scheme [5] which was proposed in 1995 based on solving the closest vector problem (CVP) in a lattice and asymptotically is more efficient than RSA in the computation time for encryption, decryption, signing, and verifying are all quadratic in the natural security parameter. The signer demonstrates knowledge of a good basis for the lattice by using it to solve CVP on a point representing the message; the

---

[1] Number Theorists 'R' Us, or Number Theory Research Unit, or N–th degree TRuncated polynomial Ring.

verifier uses a bad basis for the same lattice to verify that the signature under consideration is actually a lattice point and is sufficiently close to the message point.

On the other hand, Min *et al.* [14] suggested a weak property of malleability of NTRUSIGN using the annihilating polynomial from a given message and signature pair to generate a valid signature. Nguyen and Regev [15] had cryptanalyzed the original GGH signature scheme including NTRUSIGN in 2006 successfully extracting secret information from many known signatures characterized by multivariate optimization problems. Their experiments showed that 90,000 signatures are sufficient to recover the NTRUSIGN–251 secret key.

In a nutshell, FALCON follows a framework introduced in 2008 by Gentry, Peikert, and Vaikuntanathan [4] which we call the GPV framework for short over the NTRU lattices and uses a typically hash–and–sign paradigm. Their high–level idea is the following:

1. The public key is a long basis of a q–ary lattice.
2. The private key is (essentially) a short basis of the same lattice.
3. In the signing procedure, the signer:
   (a) generates a random value, *salt*;
   (b) computes a target $\mathbf{c} = H(M\|salt)$, where H is a hash function sending input to a random–looking point (on the grid);
   (c) uses his knowledge of a short basis to compute a lattice point $\mathbf{v}$ close to the target $\mathbf{c}$;
   (d) outputs $(salt, \mathbf{s})$, where $\mathbf{s} = \mathbf{c} - \mathbf{v}$.
4. The verifier accepts the signature $(salt, \mathbf{s})$ if and only if:
   (a) the vector $\mathbf{s}$ is short;
   (b) $H(M\|salt) - \mathbf{s}$ is a point on the lattice generated by his public key.

Only the signer should be able to *efficiently* compute v close enough to an arbitrary target. This is a decoding problem that can be solved when a basis of *short* vectors is known. On the other hand, anyone wanting to check the validity of a signature should be able to verify lattice membership. The KeyGen, Sign and Verif procedures for FALCON will be introduced briefly in the later Section by restating the original specification as in [2]. For details, the readers can refer to [2].

3.1   Key Generation of FALCON

For the class of NTRU lattices, a trapdoor pair is $(h, \mathbf{B}_{f,g})$ where $h = f^{-1}g$, $\mathbf{B}_{f,g}$ is a trapdoor basis over $\mathcal{L}_{\mathrm{NTRU}}$ and Pornin & Prest [17] showed that a completion (F, G) can be computed in $O(d \log d)$ time from short polynomials $f, g \in \mathcal{Z}$. In practice, their implementation is as efficient as can be for this technical procedure: it is called NtruSolve in FALCON. Their algorithm only depends on the underlying ring and has now a stable version for $\mathbb{Z}[x]/(x^d + 1)$, where $d = 2^n$.

Figure 1 illustrates the flowchart of the key generation procedure for FALCON. Algorithm 1 describes the pseudo–code for key generation of FALCON.

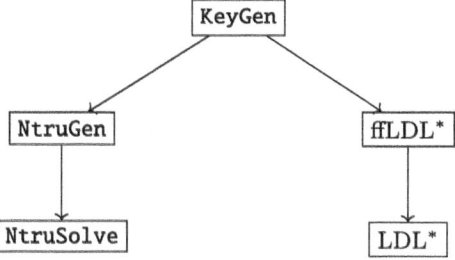

Fig. 1. Flowchart of KeyGen for FALCON

Algorithm 1: KeyGen of FALCON

Input: A monic polynomial $\phi \in \mathbb{Z}[x]$, a modulus q
Output: A secret key sk, a public key pk

  1: $f, g, F, G \leftarrow$ NtruGen ;   /* Solving the NTRU equation */

  2: $\mathbf{B} \leftarrow \begin{bmatrix} g & -f \\ G & -F \end{bmatrix}$;

  3: $\hat{\mathbf{B}} \leftarrow$ FFT($\mathbf{B}$) ;   /* Compute FFT for each $\{g, -f, G, -F\}$ */

  4: $\mathbf{G} \leftarrow \hat{\mathbf{B}} \times \hat{\mathbf{B}}^*$;

  5: $\mathrm{T} \leftarrow$ ffLDL*($\mathbf{G}$);   /* Compute the LDL* tree */

  6: for each leaf of T do

  7:     $leaf.value \leftarrow \sigma/\sqrt{leaf.value}$;   /* Normalization step */

  8: sk $\leftarrow (\hat{\mathbf{B}}, \mathrm{T})$;

  9: $h \leftarrow gf^{-1} \mathrm{mod} q$;

10: pk $\leftarrow h$;

11: **return** sk, pk;

3.2 Signing of FALCON

At a high level, the signing procedure in FALCON is at first to compute a hashed value $c \in \mathbb{Z}_q[x]/(\phi)$ from the message, M and a salt r, then using the secret key, f, g, F, G to generate two short values (s_1, s_2) such that $s_1 + s_2 h = c \bmod q$. An interesting feature is that only the *first half* of the signature (s_1, s_2) needs to be sent along the message, as long as h is available to the verifier. This comes from the identity $hs_1 = s_2 \bmod q$ defining these lattices, as we will see in the Verif algorithm description.

The core of FALCON signing is to use ffSampling (Algorithm 11 in [2]) which applies a randomizing rounding according to Gaussian distribution on the coefficient of $t = (t_0, t_1) \in (\mathbb{Q}[x]/(\phi))^2$ stored in the FALCON Tree, $\mathbf{T}$ at the KeyGen procedure of FALCON.

This fast Fourier sampling algorithm can be seen as a recursive version of Klein's well–known trapdoor sampler, but *cannot be computed in parallel* also known as the GPV sampler. Klein's sampler uses a matrix $\mathbf{L}$ and the norm of Gram–Schmidt vectors as a trapdoor while FALCON are using a tree of non-trivial elements in such matrices. Note that Fouque *et al.* [3] suggested Gram-Schmidt norm leakage in FALCON by timing side channels in the implementation of the one-dimensional Gaussian samplers.

FALCON cannot output two different signatures for a message. This well-known concern of the GPV framework can be addressed in several ways, for example, making a stateful scheme or by hash randomization. FALCON chose the latter solution for efficiency purposes. In practice, Sign adds a random "salt"

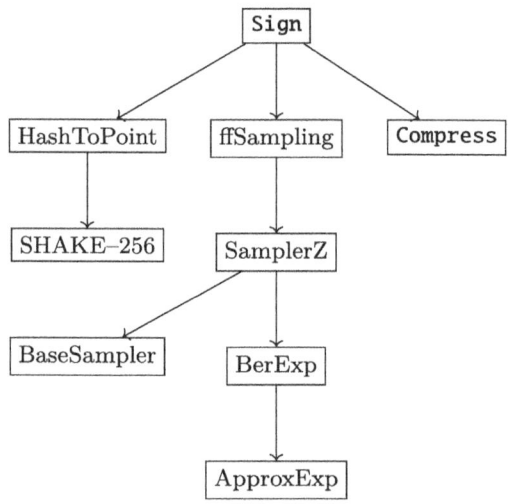

Fig. 2. Flowchart of Sign for FALCON.

Algorithm 2: Sign of FALCON

Input: A message $M \in \{0,1\}^*$, secret key sk, a bound γ.
Output: A pair $(r, \text{Compress}(s_1))$ with $r \in \{0,1\}^{320}$ and $\|(s_1, s_2)\| \leq \gamma$.

1: $r \leftarrow \mathcal{U}(\{0,1\}^{320})$;
2: $c \leftarrow \text{HashToPoint}(r\|M, q, n)$;
3: $t \leftarrow (-\frac{1}{q}\text{FFT}(c) \odot \text{FFT}(F), \frac{1}{q}\text{FFT}(c) \odot \text{FFT}(f))$; /* $t = (\text{FFT}(c), \text{FFT}(0)) \cdot \hat{\mathbf{B}}^{-1}$ */
4: do
5:      do
6:          $z \leftarrow \text{ffSampling}_n(t, T)$;
7:          $s = (t - z)\hat{\mathbf{B}}$;   /* At this point, s follows Gaussian distribution. */
8:      while $\|s\|^2 > \gamma$
9:      $(s_1, s_2) \leftarrow \text{FFT}^{-1}(s)$;
10:     $s \leftarrow \text{Compress}(s_2, 8 \cdot \text{sbytelen} - 328)$;   /* Remove 1 byte for the header, and 40 bytes for r */
11: while$(s = \bot)$
12: **return** (r, s);

$r \in \{0,1\}^k$, where k is large enough that an unfortunate collision of messages is unlikely to happen, that is, it hashes $(r||M)$ instead of M. A signature is then $\mathtt{sig} = (r, \mathtt{Compress}(\mathbf{s}_1))$.

Figure 2 and Algorithm 2 sketches the signing procedure for FALCON and shows its pseudo-code for FALCON, respectively.

3.3 Verification of FALCON

The last step of the scheme is thankfully simpler to describe. Upon receiving a signature $(r, \mathbf{s})$ and message M, the verifier decompresses $\mathbf{s}$ to a polynomial $\mathbf{s}_1$ and $\mathbf{c} = (0, \mathtt{H}(r||M))$, then wants to recover the full signature vector $\mathbf{v} = (\mathbf{s}_1, \mathbf{s}_2)$. If $\mathbf{v}$ is a valid signature, the verification identity is $(h, -1) \cdot (\mathbf{c} - \mathbf{v}) = -\mathtt{H}(r||M) - h\mathbf{s}_1 + \mathbf{s}_2 \bmod q = 0$, or equivalently the verifier can compute

$$\mathbf{s}_2 = \mathtt{H}(r||M) + h\mathbf{s}_1 \bmod q.$$

This is computed in the ring R_q, and can be done very efficiently for a good choice of modulus q using the Number Theoretic Transform (NTT). FALCON currently follow the standard choice of $q = 12,289$, as the multiplication in NTT format amounts to d integer multiplications in $\mathbb{Z}/q\mathbb{Z}$. The last step is to check that $\|(\mathbf{s}_1, \mathbf{s}_2)\|^2 \leq \gamma^2$: the signature is only accepted in this case. The rejection bound γ comes from the expected length of vectors outputted by $\mathtt{Sample}$ described as Algorithm 4 in [11].

Since they are morally Gaussian, they concentrate around their standard deviation; a "slack" parameter $\tau = 1.042$ is tuned to ensure that 90% of the vectors generated by $\mathtt{Sample}$ will get through the loop:

$$\gamma = \tau \cdot \sigma_{\mathtt{sig}} \cdot \sqrt{2d}.$$

Algorithm 3 shows the pseudo–code of verification procedure of FALCON.

Algorithm 3: $\mathtt{Verif}$ of FALCON

Input: A signature $(r, \mathbf{s})$ on M, a public key $\mathtt{pk} = h$, a bound γ.
Output: Accept or Reject.

1: $\mathbf{s}_1 \leftarrow \mathtt{Decompress}(\mathbf{s})$;
2: $\mathbf{c} \leftarrow \mathtt{H}(r||M)$;
3: $\mathbf{s}_2 \leftarrow \mathbf{c} + h\mathbf{s}_1 \bmod q$;
4: **if** $\|(\mathbf{s}_1, \mathbf{s}_2)\|^2 > \gamma^2$ **then**
$\natural$: **return** Reject.
    end
6: **return** Accept.

---

4 SOLMAE Algorithm

While its predecessor FALCON could be summed-up as *an efficient instantiation of the GPV framework*, SOLMAE takes it one step further. The main ingredients in SOLMAE are:

- **Hybrid sampler** is a faster, simpler, parallelizable, and maskable Gaussian sampler to generate signatures;
- **Optimally tuned key generation algorithm**, enhancing the security of the used hybrid sampler to that of FALCON's level[2];
- **Dedicated compression techniques** to reduce bandwidth consumption even further, at no cost on the security according to our analyses.

The KeyGen, Sign and Verif procedures for SOLMAE will be introduced briefly in the later Section by restating the original specification in [11]. For details, the readers can refer to [11].

4.1 Key Generation of SOLMAE

An important concern here is that not all pairs $(f, g), (F, G)$ gives good trapdoor pairs for Sample described as **Algorithm** 4 in [11]. Schemes such as FALCON and MITAKA solve this technicality essentially by sieving among all possible bases to find the ones that reach an acceptable quality for the Sample procedure. This technique is costly, and many tricks were used to achieve an acceptable KeyGen. *This sieving routine was bypassed by redesigning completely how good quality bases can be found.* This improves the running time of KeyGen and also increases the security offered by Sample. In any case, note that NtruSolve's running time largely dominates the overall time for KeyGen: this is not avoidable as the basis completion algorithm requires working with quite large integers and relatively high-precision floating-point arithmetic.

At the end of the procedure, the secret key contains not only the secret basis but also the necessary data for Sign and Sample. This additional information can be represented by elements in $K_{\mathbb{R}}$ and is computed during or at the end of NtruSolve. All-in-all, KeyGen outputs:

$$\mathbf{sk} = (\mathbf{b}_1 = (f, g), \mathbf{b}_2 = (F, G), \widetilde{\mathbf{b}}_2 = (\widetilde{F}, \widetilde{G}), \Sigma_1, \Sigma_2, \beta_1, \beta_2),$$

$$\mathbf{pk} = (h, q, \sigma_{\mathsf{sig}}, \eta),$$

where we recall that $h = g/f \bmod q$. These parameters and a table of their practical values are described more thoroughly in [11].

Informally, they correspond to the following:

- $(f, g), (F, G)$ is a good basis of the lattice $\mathcal{L}_{\mathrm{NTRU}}$ associated to h, with quality $\mathcal{Q}(f, g) = \alpha$, and $\widetilde{\mathbf{b}}_2$ is the Gram-Schmidt orthogonalization of (F, G) with respect to (f, g);
- $\sigma_{\mathsf{sig}}, \eta$ are respectively the standard deviation for signature vectors, and a tight upper bound on the "smoothing parameter of $\mathbb{Z}^d$";
- $\Sigma_1, \Sigma_2 \in K_{\mathbb{R}}$ represent covariance matrices for two intermediate Gaussian samplings in Sample;
- the vectors $\beta_1, \beta_2 \in K_{\mathbb{R}}^2$ represent the orthogonal projections from $K_{\mathbb{R}}^2$ onto $K_{\mathbb{R}} \cdot \mathbf{b}_1$ and $K_{\mathbb{R}} \cdot \widetilde{\mathbf{b}}_2$ respectively. In other words, they act as "getCoordinates" for vectors in $K_{\mathbb{R}}^2$. They are used by Sample and are precomputed for efficiency.

---

[2] This corresponds to NIST-I and NIST-V requirements.

Algorithm 4 computes the necessary data for signature sampling, then outputs the key pair. Note that NtruSolve could also compute the sampling data and the public key, but for clarity, the pseudo-code gives these tasks to KeyGen of SOLMAE. Figure 3 sketches the key generation procedure of SOLMAE

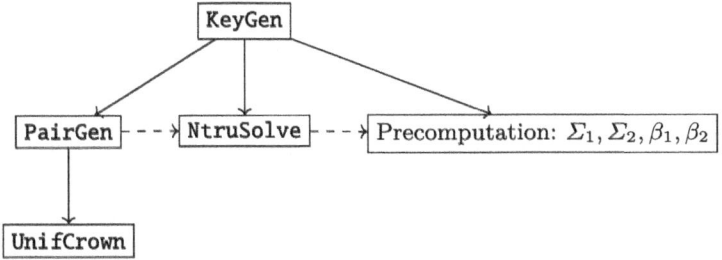

Fig. 3. Flowchart of KeyGen of SOLMAE.

Algorithm 4: KeyGen of SOLMAE

Input: A modulus q, a target quality parameter $1 < \alpha$, parameters $\sigma_{\texttt{sig}}, \eta > 0$

Output: A basis $((f, g), (F, G)) \in R^2$ of an NTRU lattice $\mathcal{L}_{\text{NTRU}}$ with $\mathcal{Q}(f, g) = \alpha$;

1: **repeat**

| $\mathbf{b}_1 := (f, g) \leftarrow \texttt{PairGen}(q, \alpha, R_-, R_+)\}$

  until f *is invertible modulo* q;

    ;   /* Secret basis computation between R_- and R_+ */

2: $\mathbf{b}_2 := (F, G) \leftarrow \texttt{NtruSolve}(q, f, g)$:

3: $h \leftarrow g/f \bmod q$;   /* Public key data computation */

4: $\gamma \leftarrow 1.1 \cdot \sigma_{\texttt{sig}} \cdot \sqrt{2d}$;   /* tolerance for signature length */

5: $\beta_1 \leftarrow \frac{1}{\langle \mathbf{b}_1, \mathbf{b}_1 \rangle_K} \cdot \mathbf{b}_1$;   /* Sampling data computation, in Fourier domain */

6: $\Sigma_1 \leftarrow \sqrt{\frac{\sigma_{\texttt{sig}}^2}{\langle \mathbf{b}_1, \mathbf{b}_1 \rangle_K} - \eta^2}$;

7: $\widetilde{\mathbf{b}}_2 := (\widetilde{F}, \widetilde{G}) \leftarrow \mathbf{b}_2 - \langle \beta_1, \mathbf{b}_2 \rangle \cdot \mathbf{b}_1$;

8: $\beta_2 \leftarrow \frac{1}{\langle \widetilde{\mathbf{b}}_2, \widetilde{\mathbf{b}}_2 \rangle_K} \cdot \widetilde{\mathbf{b}}_2$;

9: $\Sigma_2 \leftarrow \sqrt{\frac{\sigma_{\texttt{sig}}^2}{\langle \widetilde{\mathbf{b}}_2, \widetilde{\mathbf{b}}_2 \rangle_K} - \eta^2}$;

10: $\texttt{sk} \leftarrow (\mathbf{b}_1, \mathbf{b}_2, \widetilde{\mathbf{b}}_2, \Sigma_1, \Sigma_2, \beta_1, \beta_2)$;

11: $\texttt{pk} \leftarrow (q, h, \sigma_{\texttt{sig}}, \eta, \gamma)$;

12: **return** sk, pk;

The function of two subroutines `PairGen` and `NtruSolve` are described below:

1. The `PairGen` algorithm generates d complex numbers $(x_j e^{i\theta_j})_{j \leq d/2}$, $(y_j e^{i\theta_j})_{j \leq d/2}$ to act as the FFT representations of two *real* polynomial $f^{\mathbb{R}}, g^{\mathbb{R}}$ in $K_{\mathbb{R}}$. The magnitude of these complex numbers is sampled in a planar annulus whose small and big radii are set to match a target $\mathcal{Q}(f, g)$ with `UnifCrown` [11]. It then finds close elements $f, g \in \mathcal{Z}$ by round-off, unless maybe the rounding error was too large. When the procedure ends, it outputs a pair (f, g) such that $\mathcal{Q}(f, g) = \alpha$, where α depends on the security level.

2. `NtruSolve` is exactly Pornin & Prest's algorithm and implementation [17]. It takes as input $(f, g) \in \mathcal{Z}^2$ and a modulus q, and outputs $(F, G) \in \mathcal{Z}^2$ such that $(f, g), (F, G)$ is a basis of $\mathcal{L}_{\text{NTRU}}$ associated to $h = g/f \bmod q$. It does so by solving the Bézout-like equation $fG - gF = q$ in $\mathcal{Z}$ using recursively the tower of subfields for optimal efficiency.

4.2   Signing of SOLMAE

Recall that NTRU lattices live in $\mathbb{R}^{2d}$. Their structure also helps to simplify the preimage computation. Indeed, the signer only needs to compute $\mathbf{m} = \mathrm{H}(M) \in \mathbb{R}^d$, as then $\mathbf{c} = (0, \mathbf{m})$ is a valid preimage: the corresponding polynomials satisfy $(h, 1) \cdot \mathbf{c} = \mathbf{m}$.

As the same with `Sign` procedure of FALCON, an interesting feature is that only the *first half* of the signature $(\mathbf{s_1}, \mathbf{s_2}) \in \mathcal{L}_{\text{NTRU}}$ needs to be sent along the message, as long as h is available to the verifier. This comes from the identity $h\mathbf{s_1} = \mathbf{s_2} \bmod q$ defining these lattices, as we will see in the `Verif` algorithm description.[3]

Because of their nature as Gaussian integer vectors, signatures can be encoded to reduce the size of their bit-representation. The standard deviation of `Sample` is large enough so that the $\lfloor \log \sqrt{q} \rfloor$ least significant bits of one coordinate are essentially random.

In practice, `Sign` adds a random "salt" $r \in \{0, 1\}^k$, where k is large enough that an unfortunate collision of messages is unlikely to happen, that is, it hashes $(r||M)$ instead of M—our analysis in this regard is identical to FALCON. A signature is then $\mathtt{sig} = (r, \mathtt{Compress}(\mathbf{s_1}))$. SOLMAE cannot output two different signatures for a message like FALCON which was mentioned in Sect. 3.2.

Figure 4 sketches the signing procedure of SOLMAE and Algorithm 5 shows its pseudo–code.

---

[3] The same identity can also be used to check the validity of signatures only with a hash of the public key h, requiring this time send both $\mathbf{s_1}$ and $\mathbf{s_2}$, but we will not consider this setting here.

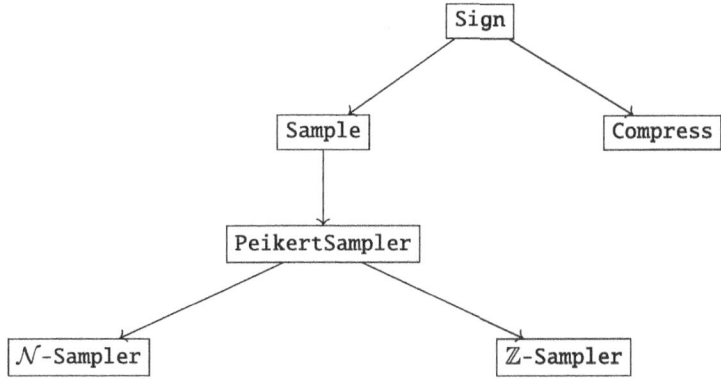

Fig. 4. Flowchart of Sign of SOLMAE.

Algorithm 5: Sign of SOLMAE

Input: A message $M \in \{0,1\}^*$, a tuple
   $\mathrm{sk} = ((f, g), (F, G), (\widetilde{F}, \widetilde{G}), \sigma_{\mathrm{sig}}, \Sigma_1, \Sigma_2, \eta)$, a rejection parameter
   $\gamma > 0$.
Output: A pair $(r, \mathrm{Compress}(\mathbf{s}_1))$ with $r \in \{0,1\}^{320}$ and $\|(\mathbf{s}_1, \mathbf{s}_2)\| \leq \gamma$.
   1: $r \leftarrow \mathcal{U}(\{0,1\}^{320})$;
   2: $\mathbf{c} \leftarrow (0, \mathrm{H}(r\|M))$;
   3: $\hat{\mathbf{c}} \leftarrow \mathrm{FFT}(\mathbf{c})$;
   4: **repeat**
   $\quad|\quad (\hat{s}_1, \hat{s}_2) \leftarrow \hat{\mathbf{c}} - \mathrm{Sample}(\hat{\mathbf{c}}, \mathrm{sk})$;   /* $(\mathbf{s}_1, \mathbf{s}_2) \leftarrow D_{\mathcal{L}_{\mathrm{NTRU}}, \mathbf{c}, \sigma_{\mathrm{sig}}}$ */
   $\quad\quad$ **until** $\|(\mathrm{FFT}^{-1}(\hat{s}_1), \mathrm{FFT}^{-1}(\hat{s}_2))\|^2 \leq \gamma^2$;
   5: $s_1 \leftarrow \mathrm{FFT}^{-1}(\hat{s}_1)$;
   6: $s \leftarrow \mathrm{Compress}(s_1)$;
   $\quad$ **return** (r, s);

4.3   Verification of SOLMAE

This is the same as the Verification of FALCON stated in Sect. 3.3.

5   Asymptotic Complexity of FALCON and SOLMAE

To the best of our allowable knowledge as of writing this paper, we first suggest the asymptotic computational complexity of FALCON and SOLMAE algorithms with their pseudo–codes described their specifications based on the following assumptions to make our computation work to be simple:

(i) Multiplication of large integers can be done by integer–type Karatsuba algorithm or Schönhage-Strassen algorithm. However, we assumed that multiplication of large integers can be done linearly in the given bitsize.

(ii) The multiplication and division of polynomials in $\mathbb{Z}[x]/(x^d+1)$ or $\mathbb{Q}[x]/(x^d+1)$ are assumed to compute the polynomial–type Karatsuba algorithm or operate pointwise in Fourier domain. It is known that the time complexity of the Karatsuba algorithm and FFT(or FFT^{-1}) are $\Theta(d^{3/2})$ and $\Theta(d\log(d))$, respectively. We assume that all polynomial operations are done in the Fourier domain, so polynomial multiplication and division in $\mathbb{Z}[x]/(x^d+1)$ or $\mathbb{Q}[x]/(x^d+1)$ takes $\Theta(d\log(d))$ time. Since every inverse element of $\mathbb{Z}_q$ is stored in the list and the division of polynomials in $\mathbb{Z}_q[x]/(x^d+1)$ can be done in the NTT domain, the division of polynomials in $\mathbb{Z}_q[x]/(x^d+1)$ also takes $\Theta(d\log d)$ by ignoring the complexity of computing the inverse.

(iii) Some number of rejection samplings may inevitably happen in FALCON and SOLMAE. If one–loop for rejection sampling takes t times and its probability of the acceptance is p, the expectation value of the total time is $\Sigma_{k=1}^{\infty} p(1-p)^{k-1} \cdot kt = \frac{t}{p} \approx t$ since the value $1/p$ does not influence our asymptotic analysis due to its fixed constant value. So, we may ignore the number of rejections occurred in the rejection sampling. In fact, our experiment reveals that more or less 5 times rejections have occurred.

(iv) Ignore some minor operations and trivial computations which do not affect the total asymptotic complexity so much.

5.1   Asymptotic Complexity of FALCON

Using the previous assumption stated in Sect. 5, Table 1 is the detailed analysis of the asymptotic complexity of KeyGen in FALCON from its algorithm whose total complexity to complete takes $\Theta(d\log d)$.

Table 1. Asymptotic complexity of KeyGen in FALCON

No.	Computation	Complexity	Location	Comment(d is degree)
1	NTRUGen(ϕ, q)	$\Theta(d\log d)$	Step 1 of Alg. 1	See below [†]
2	FFT(f)	$\Theta(d\log d)$	Step 3 of Alg. 1	
3	$\mathbf{B} \times \hat{\mathbf{B}}^*$	$\Theta(d\log d)$	Step 4 of Alg. 1	Polynomial multiplications
4	ffLDL$^*(\mathbf{G})$	$\Theta(d\log d)$	Step 5 of Alg. 1	See below [‡]
5	Normalization	$\Theta(d)$	Step 6–7 of Alg. 1	d leaf nodes in FALCON tree
6	$gf^{-1} \bmod q$	$\Theta(d\log d)$	Step 9 of Alg. 1	See the beginning of Sect. 5
Total Complexity of KeyGen : $\Theta(d\log d)$				

[†] In Algorithm 6: NTRUGen(), Step 2 and Step 5(or 6) take $\Theta(d)$ and $\Theta(d\log d)$, respectively. Since the recurrence relation of NtruSolve is $T(d) = T(d/2) + \Theta(d\log d)$, thus Step 8 in Algorithm 6 takes $\Theta(d\log d)$.
[‡] Algorithm 9: ffLDL$^*(\mathbf{G})$ in [2] recursively calls ffLDL$^*(\mathbf{G}_0)$ and ffLDL$^*(\mathbf{G}_1)$, and other processes such as LDL* and Splitfft both take $\Theta(d)$, so the recursive formula is $T(d) = 2T(d/2) + \Theta(d)$. From this, we can get $T(d) = \Theta(d\log d)$.

Tables 2 and 3 are the asymptotic complexity of Sign and Verif in FALCON, respectively whose total complexity to complete takes $\Theta(d\log d)$.

Algorithm 6: NTRUGen(ϕ, q)

Input: A monic polynomial $\phi \in \mathbb{Z}[x]$ of degree n, a modulus q
Output: Polynomials f, g, F, G

1: $\sigma \leftarrow 1.17\sqrt{q/2n}$;
2: **for** i *from* 0 *to* $n-1$ **do**
$\quad\big|\quad f_i \leftarrow D_{\mathbb{Z},\sigma_{\{f,g\}},0}$;
$\quad\big|\quad g_i \leftarrow D_{\mathbb{Z},\sigma_{\{f,g\}},0}$;
$\quad$**end**
3: $f \leftarrow \Sigma_i f_i x^i$;
4: $g \leftarrow \Sigma_i g_i x^i$;
5: **if** *NTT(f) contains 0 as a coefficient* **then**
$\quad\big|\quad$ restart
$\quad$**end**
6: $\gamma \leftarrow max\{\|(g, -f)\|, \|(\frac{qf*}{ff*+gg*}, \frac{qg*}{ff*+gg*})\|\}$;
7: **if** $\gamma > 1.17\sqrt{q}$ **then**
$\quad\big|\quad$ restart
$\quad$**end**
$\quad$;
8: $F, G \leftarrow$ NtruSolve$_{n,q}(f, g)$;
9: **if** $(F, G) = \perp$ **then**
$\quad\big|\quad$ restart
$\quad$**end**
$\quad$**return** f, g, F, G;

Table 2. Asymptotic complexity of `Sign` in FALCON

No.	Computation	Complexity	Location	Comment(d is degree)
1	HashToPoint($r \| M, q, n$)	$\Theta(d)$	Step 2 of Alg. 2	
2	FFT	$\Theta(d \log d)$	Step 3 of Alg. 2	
3	ffSampling$_n$(**t**, T)	$\Theta(d \log d)$	Step 6 of Alg. 2	See below †
4	(**t** − **z**)$\hat{\mathbf{B}}$	$\Theta(d \log d)$	Step 7 of Alg. 2	Polynomial multiplications
5	$\|\mathbf{s}\|^2$	$\Theta(d)$	Step 8 of Alg. 2	Calculating norm
6	invFFT	$\Theta(d \log d)$	Step 9 of Alg. 2	
7	Compress	$\Theta(d)$	Step 10 of Alg. 2	See below ‡
	Total Complexity of `Sign`:	$\Theta(d \log d)$		

† ffSampling$_d$ recursively calls ffSampling$_{d/2}$ two times, and other processes such as
splitfft and mergefft take $\Theta(d)$. So, the recursive formula is $T(d) = 2T(d/2) + \Theta(d)$.
If we solve this, we get $T(d) = \Theta(d \log d)$.
‡ The compression function converts d degree polynomial into string of length $slen(=$
666). $slen \approx d$, so it is irrelevant to say that the compression function takes $\Theta(d)$.

Table 3. Asymptotic complexity of `Verif` in FALCON

No.	Computation	Complexity	Location	Comment(d is degree)
1	HashToPoint($r \| m, q, n$)	$\Theta(d)$	Step 1 of Alg. 3	
2	Decompress(**s**, $8 \cdot$ sbytelen − 328)	$\Theta(d)$	Step 2 of Alg. 3	on par with Compress in Table 2
3	$c - s_2 h \bmod q$	$\Theta(d \log d)$	Step 5 of Alg. 3	Polynomial multiplication
4	$\|(s_1, s_2)\|^2$	$\Theta(d)$	Step 6 of Alg. 3	Calculating norm
	Total Complexity of `Verif`:	$\Theta(d \log d)$		

5.2 Asymptotic Complexity of SOLMAE

Based on the previous assumption stated in Sect. 5 as the same manner as we analyze the asymptotic complexity of FALCON, Table 4 is the asymptotic complexity of KeyGen in SOLMAE whose total complexity to complete takes $\Theta(d \log d)$.

Table 4. Asymptotic complexity of KeyGen in SOLMAE

No.	Computation	Complexity	Location	Comment(d is degree)
1	Pairgen	$\Theta(d \log d)$	Step 1 of Alg. 4	See below †
2	NtruSolve(q, f, g)	$\Theta(d \log d)$	Step 2 of Alg. 4	Explained in Table 1
3	$g/f \bmod q$	$\Theta(d \log d)$	Step 3 of Alg. 4	Polynomial operations
4	Key computations	$\Theta(d \log d)$	Step 4–9 of Alg. 4	Polynomial operations
Total Complexity of KeyGen: $\Theta(d \log d)$				

† In **Algorithm 7**:PairGen, Steps 1,3,and 5 all take $\Theta(d)$ time. Steps 2 and 4 take $\Theta(d \log d)$ time.

Algorithm 7: PairGen

Input: A modulus q, a target quality parameter $1 < \alpha$, two radii
　　　　parameters $0 < R_- < R_+$
Output: A pair (f, g) with $\mathcal{Q}(f,g) = \alpha$
1: **for** $i = 1$ *to* $d/2$ **do**
$\quad x_i, y_i \leftarrow$ UnifCrown(R_-, R_+) ;　　　/* see **Algorithm 9** in [11] */
$\quad \theta_x, \theta_y \leftarrow \mathcal{U}(0,1)$;
$\quad \varphi_{f,i} \leftarrow |x_i| \cdot e^{2i\pi\theta_x}$;
$\quad \varphi_{g,i} \leftarrow |y_i| \cdot e^{2i\pi\theta_y}$;
$\quad$ **end**

2: $(f^{\mathbb{R}}, g^{\mathbb{R}}) \leftarrow \big(\mathsf{FFT}^{-1}((\varphi_{f,i})_{i \leq d/2}), \mathsf{FFT}^{-1}((\varphi_{g,i})_{i \leq d/2})\big)$;
3: $(\mathbf{f}, \mathbf{g}) \leftarrow (\lfloor f_i^{\mathbb{R}} \rceil)_{i \leq d/2}, (\lfloor g_i^{\mathbb{R}} \rceil)_{i \leq d/2}$;
4: $(\varphi(f), \varphi(g)) \leftarrow (\mathsf{FFT}(\mathbf{f}), \mathsf{FFT}(\mathbf{g}))$;
5: **for** $i = 1$ *to* $d/2$ **do**
$\quad$ **if** $q/\alpha^2 > |\varphi_i(f)|^2 + |\varphi_i(g)|^2$ *or* $\alpha^2 q < |\varphi_i(f)|^2 + |\varphi_i(g)|^2$ **then**
$\quad\quad |$ restart;
$\quad$ **end**
$\quad$ **end**
$\quad$ **return** $(\mathbf{f}, \mathbf{g})$;

Table 5 is the asymptotic complexity of Sign in SOLMAE whose total complexity to complete takes $\Theta(d \log d)$.

The asymptotic complexity of verification in SOLMAE is omitted since the algorithm is identical to verification in FALCON. Our asymptotic analysis discussed here is the first step to estimate the execution time of FALCON and

Table 5. Asymptotic complexity of `Sign` in SOLMAE

No.	Computation	Complexity	Location	Comment(d is degree)
1	$\mathbf{H}(r\|M)$	$\Theta(d)$	Step 2 of Alg. 5	This is same as HashToPoint()
2	$\mathsf{FFT}(\mathbf{c})$	$\Theta(d\log d)$	Step 3 of Alg. 5	
3	$\mathsf{Sample}(\hat{c}, sk)$	$\Theta(d\log d)$	Step 4 of Alg. 5	See below †
4	$\mathsf{FFT}^{-1}(\hat{s_1})$	$\Theta(d\log d)$	Step 5 of Alg. 5	
5	$\mathsf{Compress}(s_1)$	$\Theta(d)$	Step 6 of Alg. 5	Explained in Table 2
Total Complexity of `Sign`: $\Theta(d\log d)$				

† In `Sample` (Algorithm 4 in [11],) there are some polynomial multiplications and additions which take $\Theta(d\log d)$ and calls PeikertSampler(**Algorithm** 5 in [11]) two times. In PeikerSampler, Step 1 takes $\Theta(d)$ (Generating normal vector with N–sampler takes $\Theta(d)$ and multiplying Σ takes $\Theta(d)$ since Σ is a diagonal matrix.). Steps 2, 3, and 5 take $\Theta(d\log d)$ since FFT computation is required. Step 4 takes $\Theta(d)$ simply since the loop iterates d times.

SOLMAE roughly. We can claim that `KeyGen`, `Sign`, `Verif` procedures take $\Theta(d\log d)$ together with FALCON and SOLMAE here. This analysis does imply that FALCON and SOLMAE show the same execution times regardless of its implemented platform.

6 Performance Analysis

As mentioned before, we verified asymptotic complexities of FALCON and SOL-MAE in `KeyGen`, `Sign` and `Verif` procedures and suggested that both take asymptotically similar $\Theta(d\log(d))$ complexity that is difficult to evaluate their exact performance. Using the reference implementations of FALCON and SOL-MAE which will be available over the github in C language under the same platform, we discuss the performance comparison between them and show the specific execution times here.

6.1 Description of Platform

Timings below have been collected on two cores of Intel Xeon CPU E5–2640 v3 2.60GHz 4.00GB RAM under Ubuntu–20.04 server using `CFLAGS = -Wall -Wextra -march=native -O3` compiling flag of gcc. All the tests were executed 10,000 times and the average value were taken for the sake of the good evaluation.

6.2 Performance of Our Reference Implementation

For this test, the input messages are chosen 1,024 byte randomly per 10,000 times with each count using different key pairs. FALCON performance numbers are also provided using the `speed` tool included in the official code archive

At first we checked and compared the performance of the FALCONwith different security level having 256 (no NIST level), 512 (NIST level I) and 1024 (NIST level V) in Fig. 5. The Sign procedure consumes more time than KeyGen and Verif procedures.

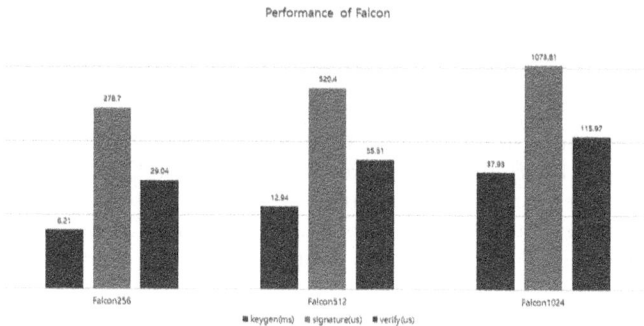

Fig. 5. Performance Comparison of FALCON-{256, 512, 1024}

The average clock cycle and time (μs) during KeyGen, Sign and Verif procedures using SOLMAE-512 and SOLMAE-1024 are shown in Table 6.

Table 6. Performance comparison of SOLMAE and FALCON

		SOLMAE-512	SOLMAE-1024	FALCON−512	FALCON−1024
KeyGen time	Mcycles	58.77	137.76	33.65	98.65
	time (ms)	22.6	52.97	12.94	37.93
pk size	Bytes	896	1,792	896	1,792
Sign time	Kcycles	758.3	1,512.9	1,353.15	2,792.22
	time (μs)	291.63	581.82	520.4	1,073.81
sgn size	Bytes	666	1,375	666	1,280
Verif time	Kcycles	121.3	289.48	144.31	301.52
	time (μs)	46.66	111.34	55.51	115.97

From these experiments, we found that SOLMAE without compression and decompression consistently outperforms FALCON in Sign and Verif procedures in equal dimension, while its KeyGen procedure is slightly slower due to its extra computation of additional data for the private key in advance. The time to execute compression and decompression can be ignored.

The average time in μs of internal common computations such as FFT, pointwise multiplication and Gaussian sampling, *etc.* which are commonly used for SOLMAE-{512 and 1024} also FALCON as well are shown in Table 7.

Table 7. Average time (μs) of common computations for SOLMAE-{512 and 1024}

	FFT	poly-add	pointwise-mult	FFT-mul-adj	poly-div-FFT	dis. Gauss	Gauss sampl.
SOLMAE-512	4.62	0.17	0.21	0.21	0.68	68.85	46.06
SOLMAE-1024	8.94	0.3	0.4	0.38	1.37	139.07	89.99

On the other hand, in Table 8 we made performance comparison of SOL-MAE-512 with Shake-128 and ECDSA P256r1 with SHA256 provided by Dream-security Engineer [9] using our publicly available SOLMAE-512 C language reference implementation under their computing platform. Compared with ECDSA, the keygen of SOLMAE-512 is slower than EDCSA P256r1 by online computation[4]. But the signing and verification of SOLMAE-512 is about 10 times faster than those of ECDSA P256r1 currently used in TSL or SSL which makes no speed degradation when we apply quantum-secure SOLMAE for PKI and various security applications.

Table 8. Comparison of SOLMAE and ECDSA

		SOLMAE	ECDSA
Specification		512	P256r1
Size(Bytes)	pk	1,792	65
	sgn	1,375	32
Time	KeyGen(ms)	30.21	2.53
	Sign(μs)	288.2	2,582.8
	Verif(μs)	55.6	7,744.7

7 Concluding Remarks

FALCON is claimed to have the advantage of providing short public keys and signatures as well as high–security levels; plagued by a contrived signing algorithm, not very fast for signing and hard to parallelize; very little flexibility in terms of parameter settings. However, SOLMAE has a simple, fast, parallelizable signing algorithm, with flexible parameters with its novel key generation algorithm.

In this paper, after giving a brief description of the specification of FALCON and SOLMAE, we found that their asymptotic computational complexity of KeyGen, Sign and Verif procedures take $\Theta(n \log n)$ simultaneously. Also, our computer experiments using their C language implementation exhibit empirically that KeyGen of SOLMAE takes a bit longer time than that of SOLMAE, but executes faster Sign procedure. Amazingly enough, the Sign and Verif

---

[4] Note that keygen of SOLMAE can be operated online/offline together in parallel.

procedures of SOLMAE-512 is about 10 times faster than those of ECDSA P256r1 currently used in TSL or SSL.

Further work such as elaborated analysis of computational complexity on FALCON and SOLMAE asymptotically is left to do next.

References

1. Espitau, T., et al.: Mitaka: a simpler, parallelizable, maskable variant of falcon. In: Advances in Cryptology, Proceedings of EUROCRYPTO 2022, Part III, pp. 222–253 (2022)
2. Fouque, P.A., et al.: Falcon: Fast-fourier lattice-based compact signatures over ntru, https://falcon-sign.info/
3. Fouque, P.A., Kirchner, P., Tibouchi, M., Wallet, A., Yu, Y.: Key recovery from gram-schmidt norm leakage in hash-and-sign signatures over ntru lattices. Cryptology ePrint Archive, Paper 2019/1180 (2019). https://eprint.iacr.org/2019/1180, https://eprint.iacr.org/2019/1180
4. Gentry, C., Peikert, C., Vaikuntanathan, V.: Trapdoors for hard lattices and new cryptographic constructions. In: Ladner, R.E., Dwork, C. (eds.) 40th ACM STOC, pp. 197–206. ACM Press (May 2008). https://doi.org/10.1145/1374376.1374407
5. Goldreich, O., Goldwasser, S., Halevi, S.: Public-key cryptosystems from lattice reduction problems. In: Advances in Cryptology, Proceedings of Crypto 1997, pp. 112–131 (1997)
6. Hoffstein, J., Pipher, J., Silverman, J.H.: NTRU: A ring-based public key cryptosystem. In: Buhler, J.P. (ed.) ANTS 1998. LNCS, vol. 1423, pp. 267–288. Springer, Heidelberg (1998). https://doi.org/10.1007/BFb0054868
7. Hulsing, A., et al.: Sphincs+. https://sphincs.org/
8. IBM: Expanding the ibm quantum roadmap to anticipate the future of quantum-centric supercomputing (2022). https://research.ibm.com/blog/ibm-quantum-roadmap-2025
9. Kim, H.: Personal correspondence (2023). will provide upon request
10. Kim, K.: Theoretical and empirical analysis of falcon and solmae using their python implementation. In: Information Security and Cryptology -ICISC2023. Lecture Notes in Computer Science, vol. 14562. Springer (2024)
11. Kim, K., et al.: Solmae : Algorithm specification. Updated SOLMAE, IRCS Blog (2023). https://ircs.re.kr/?p=1714
12. KpqC: Korean post-quantum crytography (2020). https://kpqc.or.kr/
13. Lyubashevsky, V., et al.: Crystal–dilithum. https://pq-crystals.org/dilithium/index.shtml
14. Min, S.J., Yamamoto, G., Kim, K.: Weak property of malleability in NTRUSign. In: Wang, H., Pieprzyk, J., Varadharajan, V. (eds.) ACISP 2004. LNCS, vol. 3108, pp. 379–390. Springer, Heidelberg (2004). https://doi.org/10.1007/978-3-540-27800-9_33
15. Nguyen, P.Q., Regev, O.: Learning a parallelepiped: cryptanalysis of ggh and ntru signatures. J. Cryptol. **22**(2), 139–160 (2009)
16. NIST: Post-quantum crytography (2016). https://csrc.nist.gov/projects/post-quantum-cryptography
17. Pornin, T., Prest, T.: More efficient algorithms for the NTRU key generation using the field norm. In: Lin, D., Sako, K. (eds.) PKC 2019. LNCS, vol. 11443, pp. 504–533. Springer, Cham (2019). https://doi.org/10.1007/978-3-030-17259-6_17

18. Schwabe, P., et al.: Crystal–kyber. https://pq-crystals.org/kyber/index.shtml
19. Shor, P.W.: Polynomial-time algorithms for prime factorization and discrete logarithms on a quantum computer. SIAM Rev. **41**(2), 303–332 (1999)
20. Wikipedia: Harvest now, decrypt later (2023). https://en.wikipedia.org/wiki/Harvest_now_decrypt_later

Falsifiability, Composability, and Comparability of Game-Based Security Models for Key Exchange Protocols

Chris Brzuska[1], Cas Cremers[2], Håkon Jacobsen[3], Douglas Stebila[4(✉)], and Bogdan Warinschi[5]

[1] Aalto University, Espoo, Finland
[2] CISPA Helmholtz Center for Information Security, Saarbrücken, Germany
[3] University of Oslo, Oslo, Norway
[4] University of Waterloo, Waterloo, Canada
dstebila@uwaterloo.ca
[5] University of Bristol and DFINITY, Bristol, UK

Abstract. A security proof for a key exchange protocol requires writing down a security definition. Authors typically have a clear idea of the level of security they aim to achieve, e.g., forward secrecy. Defining the model formally additionally requires making choices on games vs. simulation-based models, partnering, on having one or more Test queries and on adopting a style of avoiding trivial attacks: exclusion, penalizing or filtering. We elucidate the consequences, advantages and disadvantages of the different possible model choices.

Concretely, we show that a model with multiple Test queries composes tightly with symmetric-key protocols while models with a single Test query require a hybrid argument that loses a factor in the number of sessions. To illustrate the usefulness of models with multiple Test queries, we prove the Naxos protocol security in said model and obtain a tighter bound than adding a hybrid argument on top of a proof in a single Test query model.

Our composition *model* exposes partnering information to the adversary, circumventing a previous result by Brzuska, Fischlin, Warinschi, and Williams (CCS 2011) showing that the *protocol* needs to provide public partnering. Moreover, our baseline theorem of key exchange partnering shows that partnering by *key equality* provides a joint baseline for most known partnering mechanisms, countering previous criticism by Li and Schäge (CCS 2017) that security in models with existential quantification over session identifiers is non-falsifiable.

1 Introduction

Key exchange protocols are at the heart of most secure real world communication protocols: they establish a shared secret session key for further use, typically a symmetric-key based secure channel. Additionally they usually also provide a form of authentication, referred to as *authenticated key exchange* (AKE).

© The Author(s), under exclusive license to Springer Nature Switzerland AG 2025
C. Boyd et al. (Eds.): Ed Dawson Festschrift 2024, LNCS 15600, pp. 214–255, 2025.
https://doi.org/10.1007/978-3-031-83490-5_9

Given the ubiquity of AKE protocols, one might expect that they meet a well-understood and standard security notion. Unfortunately, this is not the case. Security models for AKE protocols are surprisingly diverse and complex, mainly owing to the diversity and complexity of AKE protocols themselves, but also because of the large number of different definitional choices one can make when modeling them. Specifically, in coming up with a good security model for AKE protocols one has to decide on the kind of *adversary capabilities* considered, what type of *security properties* the protocol ought to provide, as well as various other *functionality* related aspects of the protocol. We briefly expand upon these points below.

Adversary Capabilities. An AKE protocol consists of a polynomial number of parties, running a polynomial number of instances, or sessions, of the protocol concurrently. Following the seminal work of Dolev and Yao [33] and Bellare and Rogaway [10], the adversary is typically assumed to be in full control of the network, meaning that it can drop, re-order, delay, modify and re-route messages as it sees fit. In addition, it is also assumed that the adversary can learn various secret information from the parties. Here, the models differ significantly depending on the protocol being modeled. For example, the adversary can typically corrupt long-term keys of parties (statically or adaptively) and learn session keys of sessions of its choice. But many models go beyond this and grant the adversary additional capabilities, such as the ability to register long-term keys of its own choosing, reveal internal state, subvert random number generators, and so on.

Security Properties. The main desired security property of an AKE protocol is to provide secrecy of the established session keys. Technically, the keys should be indistinguishable from random keys, since this makes the keys suitable for applications that assume random keys. In addition to session key secrecy, an AKE protocol should also provide authentication to one (unilateral), or possibly both (mutual), ends of a protocol run. By authentication we mean that a protocol participant is assured that the established session key is only shared with its intended communication partner.

These security properties, however, cannot always hold. For example, if the adversary corrupts all secrets of a party, it can impersonate this party and break authentication as well as break key indistinguishability. Similarly, if the adversary learns the session key computed by one party, it can easily distinguish the partner's session key from random, since they computed the same key. Both of these attacks are examples of trivial, i.e., unavoidable, attacks. However, other attacks may or may not be avoidable, depending on the protocol. To delineate the trivial attacks from the non-trivial attacks, security models typically come with a *freshness predicate* that marks sessions as either fresh or non-fresh. With respect to key secrecy, the fresh sessions are those for whom the model expects security to hold, i.e., their session keys should be indistinguishable from random. Different models differ greatly in which sessions they consider fresh.

For example, the original Bellare-Rogaway model [10] considers sessions fresh only if their long-term keys are not corrupted. Their next model [11] introduced *forward secrecy*, where sessions remain fresh even when the long-term keys are corrupted—as long as the corruption happens *after* the session completed. Later, Bellare and Rogaway, together with Pointcheval, introduced a model where sessions would remain fresh even if their internal state is compromised [9]. Similar ideas are also present in the so-called (e)CK model [25,53].

In addition to choosing a freshness predicate for key secrecy, an AKE model typically also specifies in which setting we expect authentication guarantees. These conditions are similarly varied across different security models [65].

Protocol Functionality. Finally, examples of protocol functionality choices are the number of parties that can jointly establish a key; whether authentication is based on public keys, shared symmetric keys, or passwords; and whether parties know their intended peer's identity in advance or if it is learned during the execution of the protocol and whether keys are static or evolving.

Additional Model Choices. The aforementioned security model choices (i.e., adversary capabilities, security properties, and protocol functionality) have, in many different ways, all been incorporated into distinct, and often incomparable security models. See [17, Ch. 2] for an extensive introduction and further details on the impact of these three definitional choices on security models.

However, it turns out that there are *other*—less commonly discussed—technical choices that must be made in addition when defining an AKE security model. These choices might also make a model stronger or weaker in subtle, technical ways (more details below), but they may also impact other aspects of a security model, such as its ease-of-use or conceptual clarity. It is *these* additional choices we focus on this paper.

Contributions. In this paper we provide conceptual discussions, and formally substantiated insights, on the consequences of four different definitional choices for AKE security models. Specifically, we consider the following four aspects:

1. Game-based vs. simulation-based security: impact on composability.
2. Partnering definitions (i.e., how a model defines what the partner session is that is expected to compute the same key): impact on composability, falsifiability, comparability and agreement properties.
3. Single vs. multiple test queries: impact on the tightness of composition proofs.
4. Exclusion vs. penalizing vs. filtering of trivial attacks: impact on expressibility, comparability, strength and (subjective) clarity of the model.

We expand on these aspects in Sects. 1.1 to 1.4, and illustrate how existing models for key exchange instantiate them in Table 1. Having explored various consequences of these modeling choices, we then proceed to:

- develop a security model for key exchange protocols that deals consistently with each of the above four choices;

- prove a general composition theorem that shows how to compose a key exchange protocol with symmetric-key protocols, with weaker preconditions than previous results; and
- prove a lemma on key exchange partnering that partnering by *key equality* is a joint baseline for most models.

As a case study for some of our model choices, we prove the Naxos protocol secure with a tighter bound than in the original paper.

1.1 Game-Based vs. Simulation-Based Security

While it was originally thought that simulation-based security is inherently more composable than game-based security, the lines between the two notions have become blurred over the years. In the end, a security game can often be seen as an *instantiation* of a simulation-based definition. For example, for key exchange security, the simulation-based definition postulates the existence of a simulator which simulates a protocol run independently of the key, whereas the game-based security notion can be seen as using a standard protocol run (independently from the session key) as a simulation. Indeed, Canetti and Krawczyk [26] show that Bellare–Rogaway secure key exchange protocols imply (a variant of) UC-security and thus compose securely with other UC-protocols. Brzuska, Fischlin, Warinschi and Williams [22] later showed that Bellare–Rogaway secure key exchange protocols compose securely also with arbitrary symmetric-key-based games. Nowadays, there is a plethora of variants of game-based key exchange definitions with varying levels of strength, each of which would require its own composition theorem. In this paper, we show via a unified composition theorem that our security model composes securely with symmetric-key protocols; as our security model is parameterizable to capture different variants, this yields composability for all variants in our model.

1.2 Partnering Mechanisms

Partnering mechanisms are used in AKE security models to identify *related* sessions. Most AKE security models give the adversary the power to reveal session keys, but only of sessions *unrelated* to the target session that the adversary is supposed to attack (by trying to distinguishing its real session key from random). If we want any protocol to be secure with respect to a model, the adversary cannot be allowed to reveal the session key of the target session itself, since this is the real key by design. But there is another session that also ought to be off-limits: the one residing at the target session's communication peer in a normal protocol run, because by correctness, this session *should* compute the same key as the target session. To model this, we must be able to identify this partner session within the model. This is one of the main purposes of the partnering mechanism.[1]

We can divide security models into two main classes based on their partnering mechanism: ones using *universal* partnering, and ones using *existential* partnering. For models based on universal partnering there is a single fixed partnering mechanism used for all protocols within the model, and a protocol is considered secure in the model if it can be proven secure with respect to this single mechanism. On the other hand, for models based on existential partnering, there is not a single fixed partnering mechanism. Instead, a protocol is considered secure in the model only if there *exists* a partnering mechanism for which the protocol can be proven secure.

Universal Partnering. The most common form of universal partnering is *matching conversations*, where two sessions are partners if they have the same transcript of messages sent and received (except possibly the last message which may have been dropped by the adversary); this partnering mechanism originates from the first AKE security model by Bellare and Rogaway [10][2]; a small sample of important models that employ it include [13,15,30,32,45,49,54,57]. Other forms of universal partnering include key-partnering [42,48] and original-key-partnering [43,56].

Existential Partnering. In their second AKE paper, Bellare and Rogaway [11] introduced existential partnering via *partner functions*. In this model a protocol is secure if there exists some partnering function for which it can be proven secure. It is up to the prover to demonstrate such a partner function exists, either by construction or by proving that it must exist. Other papers working with partnering functions generically include [19,66]. Models using *session identifiers* (SIDs) [3,9,21–25,34,38,47,51,63] can also be seen as using existential partnering. Specifically, the SID can be viewed as a function that simply computes the SID string based on various inputs (including, e.g., a partial transcript, secret information, or externally provided information). Of course, matching conversations, and any of the other universal partnering mechanisms, are also suitable, and thus security models using partner functions can be seen as a generalization of security models using universal partnering.

Falsifiability. We refer to the process of showing that a protocol is insecure in a model as *falsifiability*: one falsifies the security of a protocol (with respect to a model, and the model should support this possibility). To show that a protocol

---

[1] The partnering mechanism is also sometimes used to define authentication, e.g., authentication is broken if there exists a session that accepted without a partner (provided the intended peer's authentication credential was uncompromised), or used to determine if the attacker was temporarily passive. For now, we focus on partnering for defining session key indistinguishability, and deal with authentication separately later.

[2] Note that the Bellare and Rogaway version also required strict temporal ordering of the individual messages sent and received, excluding e.g. pre-plays; this requirement was dropped by later works.

is insecure in a model with universal partnering, one can demonstrate an attack that breaks security with respect to the partnering mechanism specified by the model.

On the other hand, to show that a protocol is insecure in a model with existential partnering, one would have to demonstrate attacks that break security for all possible partnering functions, which could be substantially harder. How, then, should one interpret the absence of a proof of security with respect to a particular session identifier or partner function? Is it possible to demonstrate an attack against the same protocol in the same model with respect to a different session identifier? What constitutes a *good* session identifier? And how do we know whether a protocol is insecure or whether we merely failed to find a suitable session identifier?

Thus, models with universal partnering offer a more direct path to falsifiability. However, partnering using, e.g., matching conversations could be too strong a requirement, since adding an irrelevant bit to a secure protocol suddenly makes it insecure, defying our intuition. Indeed, Li and Schäge [56] showed a class of "no-match" attacks that demonstrated flaws in several existing security proofs in models based on matching conversations.

One alternative universal partnering mechanism is *key partnering* [42,48], where two sessions are considered partners if they have computed the same session key. Li and Schäge [56] however argue that *original-key partnering* should be used, where two sessions are considered partners if they would have computed the same session key in the presence of a passive adversary.

Key Partnering. We show that key partnering is a universal choice for AKE partnering mechanisms, together with a partnering oracle that is added to the model and allows the adversary to determine whether two sessions have the same key. From the perspective of writing proofs, key partnering is relatively easy to work with, especially compared to original-key partnering.

Importantly, we demonstrate in Sect. 3 that key partnering comes with strong falsifiability properties: we show that if an attack is shown against a protocol in a model where key partnering is used, then that attack would be present in the model with respect to *any* valid partnering mechanism. We prove this falsifiability result by establishing the contrapositive. Namely, we show what we call the *baseline theorem of partnering in key exchange*: for any fixed freshness condition, if a key exchange protocol provides key indistinguishability in the model using a partnering mechanism that satisfies certain soundness properties, then that protocol is also secure in the model using key partnering.

A consequence of our baseline theorem of key exchange partnering is that researchers retain the option of proving security using session identifiers or other partner functions, but can be assured of falsifiability by also proving that their partner function satisfies the soundness conditions required by the baseline theorem.

Composability. Our aforementioned composability result for key agreement protocols with symmetric-key protocols indeed relies on *key partnering*, sidestepping a seeming no-go result of Brzuska, Fischlin, Warinschi, and Williams [22], which states that composability requires the *protocol* to provide public partnering mechanism. We circumvent their impossibility result by giving the adversary an oracle to learn which two sessions are partnered. This only makes the model stronger and simplifies composition, as we will show in Sect. 4.2.

Comparability. The central benchmark around which to compare models is normally the capabilities granted to the attacker. For example, a model in which the adversary can learn both the parties' long-term keys *and* the sessions' internal randomness ought to be stronger than a model where it can only do the former. Of course, not all models are formally comparable. For instance, a model where only long-term keys can be revealed is not necessarily stronger nor weaker than a model where only internal randomness can be revealed. But even in the case where two models do provide the same attacker queries, they can still differ in strength due to how the access to these queries are controlled, i.e., they have different freshness conditions.

Cremers and Feltz [32, 37] formalized these observations, defining a security model to be precisely the collection of adversary capabilities (queries) and a freshness condition. They could then compare the relative strengths of a large number of models. However, it turns out that there are further factors that can additionally influence the comparability between models, and which were not covered by Cremers and Feltz [32]. The first is the choice of partnering mechanism. Indeed, Cremers [31] shows that the extended Canetti–Krawczyk (eCK) model [53] is in fact formally incomparable with the original CK model [24] – partially due to a mismatch in the partnering definitions.

Agreement Properties. The model we develop, besides key indistinguishability, also covers agreement and authentication properties. These properties provide guarantees of the following form: if two parties agree on a session key, then they also agree on various other variables determined during the protocol run. Examples of such variables include: party identities, communication roles, and negotiated ciphersuites. An easy way to achieve such a property in practice is by hashing the entire transcript into the key. In the case such a practice is adopted, the notions key partnering and matching conversations coincide under the assumption that the key derivation function is collision-resistant. Transcript hashing has been adopted in TLS 1.3 and is generally considered good practice. In addition, the parties might hash further agreement data into their key. In this case, agreement on the transcript alone does not imply agreement on further variables, while agreement on the key still implies their equality.

1.3   Single vs. Multiple Test Queries

From the perspective of *building* an AKE protocol, we want a security model that facilitates a tight reduction from the security of the AKE protocol to the security of its underlying primitives. Later works have started to develop tight reductions of this form [4, 5, 29, 43].

In addition, from the perspective of *using* an AKE protocol, we also want a security model that facilitates a tight reduction from the composition "AKE protocol + symmetric-key protocol" to the security of the underlying AKE protocol. It is this composition we focus on here. Unfortunately, traditional models tend to lose at least a factor in the number sessions, sometimes even a square. To see why, recall that key exchange models like the BR model [10] typically have a single TEST query. This means that in the composition proof we cannot replace the session keys all at once, but instead need to employ a hybrid argument where they are replaced one-by-one (as illustrated by the proof of the composition result in [22]). Indeed, this incurs a tightness loss [27,28] in the number of session keys replaced. If the AKE protocol itself had a non-tight proof with a linear loss in the number of sessions n, then we are now up to an $O(n^2)$ loss of tightness for the whole composition; in real-world protocols like TLS, the number of sessions could be on the order of billions, so an n^2 tightness loss would have a substantial impact on the selection of parameters.

It seems more useful if an AKE model supports tight composition with the symmetric-key protocol, and the natural response is to allow *multiple* TEST queries. But how should these TEST queries be answered? Should each query be answered independently as real-or-random (and the adversary wins if it can distinguish at least one query), or should all answers be either all-real or all-random?

Let's call the first approach n-FtG (for Find-then-Guess) and the second RoR (for Real-or-Random), where n is the number of TEST queries. Unfortunately, n-FtG is no better than 1-FtG for the purposes of composability: even if n-FtG has multiple TEST queries, during the composition proof they cannot be used to replace the session keys with random all at once, since each query is independently answered with either real or random.

In contrast, the RoR notion *does* allow all keys to be replaced all at once during the composition proof, resulting in no additional security loss for the combined construction (we will make this more precise in Sect. 5). The conclusion is that RoR is the most appropriate model to use for composing AKE protocols, justifying its use in our model in Sect. 2.

Note that switching from 1-FtG to RoR does not necessarily move the tightness problem elsewhere in the chain of results: perhaps surprisingly, our case study of NAXOS+ in Appendix A achieves the same advantage bounds in RoR as the original proof in the 1-FtG notion. In general, we suggest the use of multiple Test queries with the same secret bit to enable tightness of reductions.

1.4   Misbehaving Adversaries: Exclusion, Penalizing, and Filtering

A key exchange model needs to define which adversaries are considered valid. Specifically, the freshness condition defines the class of misbehaving adversaries as those that trivially win by violating the predicate. Naturally, we only want to measure the success probability of non-misbehaving adversaries. In the literature, there are essentially three ways to do this: (a) the *exclusion* approach [8], in which one only quantifies over the class of valid adversaries; (b) the *penalizing* approach [19], where, posteriori, misbehaving adversaries are penalized for their actions; and (c) the *filtering* approach [42, 64] where responses to misbehaving adversaries are silenced.

Model Strength and Comparability. We argue that security with respect to the *filtering* approach implies security with respect to the *exclusion* approach, while the implication in the other direction is false. The reason is that an adversary which is valid according to the exclusion approach is valid with respect to the filtering approach, but not vice versa. Additionally, the adversary might learn additional information via the filtering feedback which it receives from the model. By the principle of choosing the stronger model when in doubt, it seems useful to deploy the filtering approach. In addition, this means that one's security statement is at least as strong as those made by others, all other things being equal (which, admittedly, is rarely the case in key exchange models).

Expressibility. It turns out that the penalizing approach is somewhat incomparable to filtering. Namely, eCK-security inherently relies on the penalizing approach: The adversary is first permitted to Test a session, even though the game does not know yet whether this session is fresh or not. The adversary is then penalized in case it turns out the session does not become fresh. An analogous mechanism cannot be achieved via exclusion or filtering. If such after-the-fact-freshness properties are needed, one has to adapt a penalizing or exclusion approach. In all other cases, filtering seems to be the preferred option which is why we adopt it in our model family.

2   Security Model

In this section we specify a parameterized model that defines a family of key exchange models. Our models can capture a variety of relevant security properties within the same carefully constructed formalism that results in security definitions that are comparable (at least amongst each other), support falsifiability and tight composition results. To formalize this family, we employ a two-step approach. First, we abstract the main security goal into a *security predicate*, and give predicates representing common key exchange security goals, such as session-key indistinguishability (in Appendix B we also address authentication security goals). Second, we allow a *freshness condition* to refine the security goal to capture security against different attacker models such as forward secrecy, which also simplifies the comparison of models, in the spirit of works such as [16, 36].

Both the issue of partnering and how misbehaving adversaries (cf. Sect. 1.4) are handled, are in some sense technicalities. Unlike the attacker capabilities and freshness predicates, they do not correspond to our intuitive idea of model strength. Thus, an essential step in facilitating comparison between models is fixing as many of the components of the model as possible, with the only variable being the freshness condition encoding different attacker capabilities. But what to fix these to? In particular, which partnering mechanism should you choose, and how should you capture misbehaving adversaries?

Following our earlier observations, we fix the partnering mechanism to key partnering. Our baseline theorem of key exchange partnering implies that this choice does not sacrifice comparability, as long as the partnering mechanism satisfies the required conditions.

As for dealing with a misbehaving adversary, we suggest the filtering approach which makes rules of accepted behavior explicit in the game code (see Fig. 2, lines 307–311) and yields monotonic winning conditions. We showcase the filtering approach in our case study (Appendix A), where we encode game hops by successively modifying the game's filter function with each hop, until the adversary can, information-theoretically, not win anymore.

For maximal comparability, we recommend encoding the filtering rules as publicly checkable predicates, which makes exclusion-style and filtering-style definitions equivalent (see Sect. 6). The ISPARTNERED oracle we use in our general security experiment is an instance of such a public encoding: it allows publicly checking whether the adversary may reveal a session key or not.

Table 1. Various AKE security models in terms of our four characteristics

Model	Partnering Mechanism	Existential / Universal	Public Partnering	TEST's Hidden Bit	Parameterizable Freshness	Adversary Behaviour
BR family						
BR93/BWM [10,15]	matching conversations	U	●	1-FtG	○	penalize
BR95 [11]	partner function	E	●	1-FtG	○	exclude
BPR [9]	session identifiers + key partnering	E	○	1-FtG	○	penalize
AFP [3]	session identifiers	E	◖	RoR	○	filter
KSS [48]	key partnering	U	○	1-FtG	○	penalize
Tight (BHJKL) [4]	matching conversations	U	●	n-FtG	○	penalize
Tight (CCGJJ) [29]	matching conversations	U	●	RoR	○	exclude
CK family						
CK01 [24]	session identifiers	E	◖	1-FtG	○	exclude
CK$_{HMQV}$ [49]	transcript	U	●	1-FtG	○	exclude
eCK family						
eCK [53]	transcript	U	●	1-FtG	○	penalize
MU08 [57]	matching conversations	U	●	1-FtG	○	penalize
eCK-PFS, eCK^w [32]	transcript + origin sessions	U	●	1-FtG	●	exclude
"Darmstadt family"						
Composable BR [22]	public session identifiers	E	●	1-FtG	○	penalize
Less is more [21]	session identifiers	E	◖	1-FtG	○	penalize
State-separating proofs [18]	partner functions	E	via oracle	RoR	○	exclude
TLS 1.3 [34]	session + contributive identifiers	E	○	n-FtG	○	penalize
Others						
George-Rackoff [42]	key partnering	U	via oracle	1-FtG	○	filter
ASICS [16]	partner function	E	◖	1-FtG	●	exclude
Li–Schage [56]	original-key partnering	U	◖	1-FtG	○	—
This paper	**key partnering**	**U**	**via oracle**	**RoR**	**●**	**filter**

Legend: ● yes; ◖ not necessarily; ○ no;—not applicable

We begin with the abstract algorithms ("syntax") that we use as the interface to a key exchange model and correctness thereof. Next we describe the AKE security experiment, which is parameterized over a freshness condition and a security predicate. We can then define the security properties of key indistinguishability and key confinement. Properties related to authentication are given in Appendix B.

Notation. $y \leftarrow A(x)$ denotes running a deterministic algorithm A with input x, and storing the output in the variable y. Similarly, $y \leftarrow_\$ A(x)$ denotes running a probabilistic algorithm A with (implicit) uniform random coins. We often use superscript to indicate function parameters, e.g., $A^O(x)$ to denote an algorithm with access to oracle O. We write $A(x) \mapsto y$ when presenting the type of A: A takes arguments x and yields y, after which we describe A's domain (for x) and range (for y). We denote by $L = [x_1, \ldots, x_n]$ that L is a list of n elements, where $L[i]$ denotes its i-th element. We write $L \leftarrow x$ to denote appending the element x to the list L, or adding x to the set L. We write $L_1 \| L_2$ to denote the concatenation of two lists. We also write $L[x]$ to denote the entry for key x in the dictionary L. Party identities are elements of $\mathbb{N}$. The equality test $\equiv$ treats two values as equal only if they have previously been defined, i.e., $x \equiv y \Leftrightarrow (x = y) \wedge (x \text{ and } y \text{ are defined})$.

2.1   Syntax of Key Exchange

As noted above, for simplicity we focus on two-party key exchange algorithms authenticated using public keys.

Definition 1 (Key exchange protocol). *A* key exchange protocol *is a tuple of algorithms* $\Pi = (\text{KG}, \text{NEW}, \text{RUN})$*:*

- KG() $\mapsto$ (sk, pk)*: a probabilistic* long-term key generation algorithm *that outputs a private/public key pair* (sk, pk)*.
- NEW$(U, \text{sk}_U, \text{pk}_U, \text{role}, V, \text{PK}) \mapsto (\pi, m)$*: the probabilistic* protocol activation algorithm *takes as input the long-term key pair* $(\text{sk}_U, \text{pk}_U)$ *of party* U*, its role (*role*) in this protocol run, its intended peer* V *(or an empty value* $\star$*), and a dictionary* PK *of all parties' long-term public keys, indexed by party identity. It outputs a new instance state* π *(defined next) at party* U *and a (possibly empty) outgoing initial message* m*.
- RUN$(\pi, m) \mapsto (\pi', m')$*: the deterministic* protocol execution algorithm *takes as input an instance state* π *and an incoming message* m*, and outputs an updated state* π' *and (possibly empty) outgoing message* m'*.[3]

---

[3] RUN is deterministic; all per-instance randomization is incorporated in the instance variable π.rand generated during the NEW algorithm.

We allow each party U to run multiple instances ("sessions") of the protocol; all data related to a specific instance is recorded in an *instance state* π, which contains the following variables set by NEW:

- π.owner: the party to which the instance π belongs
- π.sk, π.pk: the long-term private/public key pair of party π.owner
- π.role: the role of this party in this run of the protocol, either init or resp
- π.peerID: the party identity of π's intended peer
- π.PK: the dictionary of public keys
- π.status: π's status: running, accepted, or rejected
- π.transcript: list of all messages sent and received by π in chronological[4] order
- π.rand: randomness used by π
- π.k: the session key derived by π. If no key has been derived yet, we use the symbol $\bot$; when we compare the session keys of two sessions, if both are $\bot$, we will not consider those session keys to be equal

A key exchange protocol is *correct* if, when messages are relayed faithfully between two honest sessions, both sessions accept, compute the same session key, and have each recorded the other as its peer. Note that we have two versions of the correctness definition, one for protocols that allow post-specified peers (i.e., the responder learns its intended peer's identity during the execution of the protocol), and one for protocols only allowing pre-specified peers (the responder must be initialized with its intended peer's identity at the beginning of the session).

Definition 2 (AKE correctness, post-specified peer model). *A k-message AKE protocol Π allowing post-specified peers is ε-correct if for all $U, V \in \mathbb{N}$, and all $u \in \{U, \star\}$, we have*

$$\Pr[\mathsf{Corr}_{\Pi, U, V, u}() \Rightarrow 1] \geq 1 - \varepsilon \ ,$$

where Corr *is the experiment defined in Fig. 1.*

AKE correctness for the pre-specified peer model is as Definition 2 except for requiring that the responder is initialized with $u = U$.

---

[4] We do not assume a global clock; this denotes the local order within U's session.

$\underline{\mathsf{Corr}_{\Pi, U, V, u}()}$

101 // Set up long-term key pairs
102 $(\mathsf{sk}_U, \mathsf{pk}_U) \twoheadleftarrow_\$ \Pi.\mathsf{KG}(), \mathsf{PK}[U] \leftarrow \mathsf{pk}_U$
103 $(\mathsf{sk}_V, \mathsf{pk}_V) \twoheadleftarrow_\$ \Pi.\mathsf{KG}(), \mathsf{PK}[V] \leftarrow \mathsf{pk}_V$
104 // Initialize initiator and responder sessions
105 $(\pi, m) \twoheadleftarrow_\$ \Pi.\mathrm{NEW}(U, \mathsf{sk}_U, \mathsf{pk}_U, \mathsf{init}, V, \mathsf{PK})$
106 $(\pi', \bot) \twoheadleftarrow_\$ \Pi.\mathrm{NEW}(V, \mathsf{sk}_V, \mathsf{pk}_V, \mathsf{resp}, u, \mathsf{PK})$
107 // Relay messages back and forth between initiator and responder,
108 // updating their respective states π and π'
109 **for** $i \leftarrow 1$ **to** $\lfloor k/2 \rfloor$:
110      $(\pi', m') \leftarrow \Pi.\mathrm{RUN}(\pi', m)$
111      $(\pi, m) \leftarrow \Pi.\mathrm{RUN}(\pi, m')$
112 **if** k **odd:**
113      $(\pi', \bot) \leftarrow \Pi.\mathrm{RUN}(\pi', m)$ // initiator sends the last message
114 // Check correctness condition
115 **return** $(\pi.\mathsf{status} = \mathsf{accepted}) \wedge (\pi'.\mathsf{status} = \mathsf{accepted}) \wedge$
116      $(\pi.\mathsf{k} = \pi'.\mathsf{k}) \wedge (\pi.\mathsf{peerID} = V) \wedge (\pi'.\mathsf{peerID} = U)$

Fig. 1. Correctness experiment for a k-message key exchange protocol Π between parties U and V, with responder's intended peer being u.

2.2 Security Experiment

In experiment $\mathbf{Exp}_{\Pi,n}^{\mathsf{SecPred},F}(\mathcal{A})$, shown in Fig. 2, we specify a common execution model that is parametrized by a security predicate $\mathsf{SecPred}$ which we later use to capture the different security properties a key exchange protocol might have. In addition, experiment $\mathbf{Exp}_{\Pi,n}^{\mathsf{SecPred},F}(\mathcal{A})$ is parametrized on the protocol Π, the number of parties n to run in the experiment, and freshness condition F.

The session-key indistinguishability property is built into the experiment via the TEST query; but other properties can be considered as well. For instance, later in this section we show the less-often-stated property of session key confinement (Confined), i.e., a session key should be shared among at most two sessions. In subsequent sections, we provide additional security predicates to prove our falsification theorem (the soundness and inverse soundness properties in Sect. 3) and predicates capturing authentication properties in Appendix B.

The freshness condition F models different attacker capabilities (such as forward secrecy); see Sect. 2.3.

Our approach of encoding each security goal explicitly in its own predicate is different from the modern approach of encoding all goals implicitly through the key indistinguishability property. Our approach yields a modular security model, in which different predicates can be used for protocols with different goals.

Experiment Overview. Lines 201–211 of Fig. 2 initialize the experiment, which includes: picking a random challenge bit b for the session key indistinguishability game; setting up lists to record session states ($\mathcal{S}$), the adversary's queries ($\mathcal{Q}$), and the sessions that have been tested ($\mathcal{T}$); and generating long-term key pairs

$\mathbf{Exp}_{\Pi,n}^{\mathsf{SecPred},F}(\mathcal{A})$

201 // Pick hidden challenge bit
202 $b \leftarrow\!\!\$ \{0,1\}$
203 // Initialize lists for experiment
204 $S \leftarrow []$ // List of session states
205 $Q \leftarrow []$ // List of queries
206 $T \leftarrow \emptyset$ // Set of tested sessions
207 cnt $\leftarrow 0$ // Session counter
208 // Generate all long-term key pairs
209 **for all** $U \in \{1, \ldots, n\}$:
210 $(\mathsf{sk}_U, \mathsf{pk}_U) \leftarrow\!\!\$ \Pi.\mathsf{KG}$
211 $\mathsf{PK}[U] \leftarrow \mathsf{pk}_U$
212 // Global experiment state
213 $\Phi \leftarrow \{b, S, Q, T, \mathsf{cnt}, \mathsf{PK}\}$
214 // Run the adversary
215 $b' \leftarrow\!\!\$ \mathcal{A}^{\mathcal{O}}(\mathsf{PK})$
216 // If key indistinguishability, check guess
217 **if** SecPred = KI:
218   **output** $(b = b')$
219 **else**
220   // Experiment ended so winning condition wasn't triggered
221   **output** 0

// All adversary queries are "filtered" through $\mathcal{O}$
$\mathcal{O}(\mathrm{QUERY}, x)$

301 // Save the current global experiment state
302 $\Phi' \leftarrow \Phi$
303 // Run the adversary's query
304 $y \leftarrow \mathrm{QUERY}(x)$
305 $Q \leftarrow\!\!\langle \mathrm{QUERY}, x, y \rangle$
306 // Check if all tested sessions would remain fresh
307 **if** $\forall i \in T . F(\Phi, i)$:
308   **return** y
309 **else**
310      $\Phi \leftarrow \Phi'$ // Revert effects of bad query
311   **return** $\diamond$ // Silence response

INIT(U, role, V)

401 cnt $\leftarrow$ cnt $+ 1$
402 $(S[\mathsf{cnt}], m) \leftarrow\!\!\$ \Pi.\mathsf{NEW}(U, \mathsf{sk}_U, \mathsf{pk}_U, \mathsf{role}, V, \mathsf{PK})$
403 **if** (SecPred $\neq$ KI) $\wedge \neg$SecPred(Φ, cnt):
404   terminate experiment with **output** 1
405 **return** (cnt, m)

SEND(i, m)

501 $(S[i], m') \leftarrow \Pi.\mathsf{RUN}(S[i], m)$
502 // Continuously evaluate whether adversary has won
503 **if** (SecPred $\neq$ KI) $\wedge \neg$SecPred(Φ, i):
504   terminate experiment with **output** 1
505 **return** $(S[i].\mathsf{status}, m')$

REVSK(i)

601 **return** $S[i].\mathsf{k}$

REVRAND(i)

701 **return** $S[i].\mathsf{rand}$

REVLTK(U)

801 **return** sk_U

TEST(i)

901 **if** $i \in T$:
902   **return** $\perp$
903 **if** $\exists j . S[i].\mathsf{k} = S[j].\mathsf{k} \wedge j \in T$:
904   **return** $\perp$
905 $T \leftarrow i$
906 $\mathsf{k}_0 \leftarrow S[i].\mathsf{k}$
907 $\mathsf{k}_1 \leftarrow\!\!\$ \mathcal{K}$
908 **return** k_b

ISPARTNERED(i, j)

1001 **return** $(S[i].\mathsf{k} \equiv S[j].\mathsf{k})$

Fig. 2. Generic key exchange security experiment for protocol Π with n parties against an adversary $\mathcal{A}$, for security property specified by predicate SecPred with freshness condition F.

for all users. The global experiment state consists of all of those values, and is represented as Φ. Line 215 runs the adversary, who is given all public keys as input, has access to a single oracle $\mathcal{O}$ through which all queries are made, and finally outputs a guess bit b'. For the session-key indistinguishability security property, the adversary's guess of the hidden challenge bit is checked on line 218. For the other security properties, the adversary's success in breaking the security property is checked throughout the experiment, specifically on line 503 of the SEND query.

For KI, which is a distinguishing property, we want to bound

$$\left| \Pr\left[\mathbf{Exp}_{\Pi,n}^{\mathsf{KI},F}(\mathcal{A}) \Rightarrow 1 \right] - \frac{1}{2} \right|.$$

For our remaining properties SecPred, which are win/lose, we want to bound $\Pr\left[\mathbf{Exp}_{\Pi,n}^{\mathsf{SecPred},F}(\mathcal{A}) \Rightarrow 1\right]$. For the latter, we will sometimes write $\Pr[\overline{\mathsf{SecPred}}]$, when F, Π, n, and $\mathcal{A}$ are clear from the context.

Oracle and Queries. Our model provides queries that model an adversary's ability to control all network communications, as well as compromise certain secrets.

The following two queries model normal protocol operation. The adversary uses the INIT query to direct a party U to start a new session with a given role and optional intended peer identifier. The adversary uses the SEND query to deliver a message to a session. Due to the genericity of our experiment, we decided that the INIT and SEND queries *continuously evaluate* the winning condition SecPred every time they are called, and the experiment terminates immediately once the condition is met. This avoids some problems that would develop if the winning condition is not *monotonic*, i.e., if it was possible for a session to enter the winning state, then leave the winning state by the end of the game. (Session-key indistinguishability is still evaluated at the end, since we must wait for the adversary's guess.)

The REVSK, REVRAND, and REVLTK queries model the adversary's ability to learn the session key or randomness, or a party's long-term key. Some AKE security models also allow the registration of malicious public keys (e.g., [16]), but we omit that from our model for simplicity.

The TEST query models the session key indistinguishability security property. As long as the adversary has not already tested this session or its partner (if any), we give the adversary either the real session key or a randomly chosen value. Note that the same hidden challenge bit b is used for every TEST query, so either all TEST queries return real keys, or all TEST queries return random values; Sect. 5 gives the rationale behind using real-or-random with a single bit across all TEST queries.

The ISPARTNERED query permits the adversary to check whether two sessions are partnered, i.e., have computed the same session key. This enables composability for protocols without public partnering; see Sect. 4.

However, the adversary is not allowed to query any of these oracles directly. Instead, all queries go through the oracle $\mathcal{O}$. This follows the "silencing" approach of Rogaway and Zhang [64], where the adversary only learns the output of a query if it does not cause tested sessions to become unfresh. E.g., if the adversary queries REVSK for a tested session, this would be a "trivial win" because it would allow the adversary to immediately determine the hidden challenge bit b. If $\mathcal{O}$ silences the query, a special silence symbol $\diamond$ is returned, and any changes to the game state are undone. Section 6 discusses alternatives: quantifying over adversaries that never violate freshness, or "penalizing" such adversaries by artificially recording a "loss".

2.3 Freshness

Our model is parameterized by a freshness condition F, which is used to capture security against different attacker capabilities, such as forward secrecy or the different permitted reveal patterns allowed in the CK [24] or eCK [53] models. Localizing the different attacker capabilities into a parameterized freshness condition follows the approach of Boyd, Cremers, Feltz, Paterson, Poettering, and Stebila [16] and permits comparing the relative strength of security models solely by comparing their freshness conditions. For more discussion, we refer the reader to Sect. 6.

A freshness condition F with input (Φ, i) checks whether a particular session $S[i]$ is fresh based on the global experiment state Φ, which includes all current session states, the list of all non-filtered queries, and the list of tested sessions.

For example, Fig. 3 shows a freshness condition (F^{eCK}) capturing the core attacker capabilities of the extended Canetti–Krawczyk (eCK) model [53]. In the eCK model, a session is considered fresh as long as all of the following are satisfied:

$F^{\mathsf{eCK}}(\Phi, i)$

```
1101  // The session's session key has not been revealed
1102  if ⟨RevSK, i, *⟩ ∈ Q:
1103      return false
1104  // At most one of the session's ephemeral randomness or
1105  // the owner's long-term key has been revealed
1106  if ⟨RevLTK, S[i].owner, *⟩ ∈ Q and ⟨RevRand, i, *⟩ ∈ Q:
1107      return false
1108
1109  // For all partner sessions
1110  for all j ≠ i . S[i].k ≡ S[j].k:
1111      // The partner's session key has not been revealed
1112      if ⟨RevSK, j, *⟩ ∈ Q:
1113          return false
1114      // At most one of the partner's ephemeral randomness or
1115      // the peer's long-term key has been revealed
1116      if ⟨RevLTK, S[j].owner, *⟩ ∈ Q and ⟨RevRand, j, *⟩ ∈ Q:
1117          return false
1118
1119  // If there is no partner session, the peer's long-term key
1120  // has not been revealed
1121  if ∄j ≠ i . S[i].k = S[j].k and ⟨RevLTK, S[i].peerID, *⟩ ∈ Q:
1122      return false
1123
1124  return true
```

Fig. 3. Freshness conditions capturing attacker capabilities similar to the eCK security model [53]. Recall that $\equiv$ treats two values as equal only if they have previously been defined, see notation in Sect. 2.

1. the session's session key has not been revealed;
2. both the session's ephemeral randomness and the session's owner's long-term secret key have not been revealed (but revealing one or the other is okay);
3. for all partner sessions that exist, we have that both:
   (a) the partner session's session key has not been revealed;
   (b) both the partner session's ephemeral randomness and the peer's long-term secret key have not been revealed (revealing one or the other is okay); and
4. if no partner sessions exist, the peer's long-term secret key has not been revealed.

Different freshness conditions can be used to capture different attacker capabilities, e.g., prohibiting any REVRAND query to capture the BR93/BWM model [10,15], or prohibiting revealing the peer's long-term key before acceptance to capture forward secrecy. Figure 4 shows example freshness conditions for attacker capabilities in the BR93/BWM model and the eCK-PFS model [32].[5]

$F^{\text{BWM}}(\Phi, i)$

```
1201  // The session's session key has not been revealed
1202  if ⟨REVSK, i, *⟩ ∈ Q:
1203      return false
1204  // For all partner sessions
1205  for all j ≠ i . S[i].k ≡ S[j].k:
1206      // The partner's session key has not been revealed
1207      if ⟨REVSK, j, *⟩ ∈ Q:
1208          return false
1209  // Neither party's long-term key was revealed
1210  if ⟨REVLTK, S[i].owner, *⟩ ∈ Q ∨ ⟨REVLTK, S[i].peerID, *⟩ ∈ Q:
1211      return false
1212  // No ephemeral randomness revealed anywhere
1213  if ⟨REVRAND, *, *⟩ ∈ Q:
1214      return false
1215
1216  return true
```

$F^{\text{eCK-PFS}}(\Phi, i)$

```
1301  //
1302  // same as Lines 1101 to 1117 of F^eCK
1315  //
1316  // If there is no partner session, the peer's long-term key has not been revealed before
      the session accepted
1317  if ∄j . S[i].k = S[j].k and ∃r < s .
1318      Q[r] = ⟨REVLTK, S[i].peerID, *⟩ and
1319      Q[s] = ⟨SEND, (i, *), (accepted, *)⟩:
1320          return false
1321
1322  return true
```

Fig. 4. Freshness conditions capturing attacker capabilities similar to the Blake-Wilson–Menezes model [15] (the public key analog of BR93 [10]) and the eCK model with forward secrecy ("eCK-PFS" in [32]).

---

[5] We do not claim that our models with the corresponding freshness conditions are *equivalent* to the original security models from the literature. For example, BR93 and BWM use matching conversations for partnering, rather than key partnering. Our intention is to represent the permitted query patterns that capture attacker capabilities at a high level.

In the remainder of this section, we define two core security properties in our model.

2.4   Session Key Indistinguishability

The first security property that we define using our experiment is session key indistinguishability. As already mentioned, this property is often considered the most central security goal for key exchange protocols. An adversary is deemed to have broken session key indistinguishability if it can distinguish real session keys from random; this is captured in the adversary's ability to guess the hidden challenge bit b. We model this in the security experiment by checking if the security predicate is equal to the distinguished symbol KI, which leads to several special cases in the experiment. This allows us to define key indistinguishability as follows:

Definition 3. *For a freshness condition F and number of parties $n \in \mathbb{N}$, a protocol Π provides ϵ-key-indistinguishability against an adversary $\mathcal{A}$ if*

$$\mathsf{Adv}_{\Pi,n}^{\mathsf{KI},F}(\mathcal{A}) := \left| \Pr\left[\mathbf{Exp}_{\Pi,n}^{\mathsf{KI},F}(\mathcal{A}) \Rightarrow 1 \right] - \frac{1}{2} \right| \leq \epsilon \ .$$

2.5   Session Key Confinement

Our second security property, *session key confinement*, models the common expectation of two-party key exchange that a particular session key ends up in at most two different sessions. We can capture this either implicitly through key-indistinguishability or explicitly as its own security goal.

In the implicit approach, the adversary is supposed to be able to capitalize on the event that more than two sessions share the same session key by distinguishing the challenge key. That is, once three sessions end up with the same key, they are by definition not considered partners anymore, so the adversary can reveal the session key of one of them and use it to break any of the other two.

While this is a valid encoding of session key confinement, we prefer to state security properties explicitly and thus reward the adversary directly if it manages to get more than two sessions to agree on the same key. Thus, we define session key confinement via the event:

$$\mathsf{Confined}(\varPhi, i) \colon \ \left| \{ j \mid \varPhi.\mathcal{S}[j].\mathsf{k} \equiv \varPhi.\mathcal{S}[i].\mathsf{k} \} \right| \leq 2. \tag{1}$$

Definition 4 (Session key confinement). *For a freshness condition F and number of parties $n \in \mathbb{N}$, a protocol Π provides ϵ-(session key) confinement against adversary $\mathcal{A}$ if*

$$\mathsf{Adv}_{\Pi,n}^{\mathsf{Confined},F}(\mathcal{A}) := \Pr\left[\mathbf{Exp}_{\Pi,n}^{\mathsf{Confined},F}(\mathcal{A}) \Rightarrow 1 \right] \leq \epsilon.$$

When using key-partnering, key-indistinguishability does *not* imply confinement. For example, consider the non-interactive key exchange protocols of Freire, Hofheinz, Kiltz, and Paterson [40], where there may be several sessions between the same pair of parties, each of which is established non-interactively using the same long-term keys and thus leads to the same session key every time. Such protocols provide session key indistinguishability under key partnering (since none of the sessions sharing the same session key can be revealed), but clearly violate confinement

Note that Eq. (1) does not require sessions to be fresh: the adversary may reveal *all* secrets in the experiment. This might seem to make confinement very difficult to achieve. However, for protocols that derive their session keys from a key derivation function (KDF), confinement can usually be proven either by the random oracle assumption, or in the standard model, by assuming collision resistance (satisfied by, e.g., HKDF [50]).

3   Falsifiability and Partnering

As noted in the introduction, key exchange security models using existential partnering [3,9,11,19,21–25,34,38,47,51,63,66] allow the prover to state a session identifier or partner function for which their protocol can be proven secure, rather than the model providing one. We call this a *partnering mechanism*: the security model explicitly defines a relation that decides whether two sessions should be considered partners or not.

Without further restrictions on this relation, it is possible to define unnatural and pathological mechanisms that allow intuitively insecure protocols to be proven secure, or mechanisms that make *all* protocols insecure.

For example, a partnering mechanism that partners *all* sessions artificially limits the adversary's powers, since it cannot reveal the session key of *any* session. As a result, protocols where the session key of different sessions are not independent of each other can be proven secure. More generally, allowing a partnering mechanism that partners everyone—even sessions with different session keys—is an example of *over-provisioning*, since it partners sessions that intuitively should have nothing to do with each other.

At the other end of the spectrum is a partnering mechanism which partners *no one*. This is an example of partner *under-provisioning* since it allows attacks in the model that do not correspond to any real-world attacks.

In this section we formalize soundness and "inverse soundness" that capture over- and under-provisioning respectively. We then show that a protocol that is secure with respect to a partnering mechanism that does not over- or under-provision is also secure with respect to key partnering; we call this the baseline theorem of key exchange partnering.

3.1   Partnering

Definition 5 (Partnering mechanism). *Let $\mathcal{I}$ be the space of all instance states. A* partnering mechanism *is a binary relation on $\mathcal{I}$.*

For example, key partnering is $P_{\text{key}}(\pi, \pi') = (\pi.\text{k} = \pi'.\text{k})$; matching conversations is

$$P_{\text{mc}}(\pi, \pi') = (\pi.\text{transcript} = \pi'.\text{transcript})$$
$$\lor\ (\exists m\ .\ \pi.\text{transcript} = \pi'.\text{transcript}\|[m]))$$
$$\lor\ (\exists m\ .\ \pi.\text{transcript}\|[m] = \pi'.\text{transcript}))$$

Our security experiment and freshness conditions in Sect. 2 are stated with key-partnering already built into the definitions. For the purposes of this section, we need to generalize them to an arbitrary partnering mechanism P, which is done simply by replacing all session key equality checks with the general partnering check.

In particular, we define $\mathbf{Exp}_{\Pi,n}^{\text{SecPred},F,P}$ by making the following modifications in Fig. 2:

- TEST line 903 becomes: "if $\exists j\ .\ P(\mathcal{S}[i], \mathcal{S}[j])$ and $j \in \mathcal{T}$:"
- IsPARTNERED line 1001 becomes: "return $P(\mathcal{S}[i], \mathcal{S}[j])$"

The freshness condition F is also allowed to depend on the partnering mechanism P. For example, in Fig. 3:

- F^{eCK} line 1110 becomes: "for all $j\ .\ P(\mathcal{S}[i], \mathcal{S}[j])$:"
- F^{eCK} line 1121 becomes: "if $\nexists j\ .\ P(\mathcal{S}[i], \mathcal{S}[j])$ and $\exists \ldots$"

Note that our partnering mechanism compares session states, so our security experiment uses indices i, j, etc. to index into the list of sessions $\mathcal{S}$ and then evaluates the partnering mechanism on session states $\mathcal{S}[i], \mathcal{S}[j]$.

We now turn to assessing whether a partnering mechanism over- or under-provisions session partners, which we will model by certain soundness properties.[6]

Beginning with the problem of over-provisioning, we demand that partners should derive the same session key. This is captured by the following event defined on security experiment $\mathbf{Exp}_{\Pi,n}^{\text{SecPred},F,P}$:

$$\mathsf{Sound}_P(\varPhi, i)\colon \forall \pi, \pi' \in \varPhi.\mathcal{S}\ .\ P(\pi, \pi') \implies \pi.\text{k} = \pi'.\text{k}.$$

ϵ-soundness is defined analogously to Definition 4.

To deal with the issue of under-provisioning, we demand that any two sessions that derive the same session key should also be partners. We call this *inverse soundness*, defined by the event:

$$\mathsf{InvSound}_P(\varPhi, i)\colon \forall \pi, \pi' \in \varPhi.\mathcal{S}\ .\ \pi.\text{k} \equiv \pi'.\text{k} \implies P(\pi, \pi').$$

ϵ-inverse-soundness is defined analogously to Definition 4.

---

[6] Here, "soundness" refers to a property of the partnering mechanism; we use the term "correctness" for the property that honest parties, in the absence of active adversarial interference, derive equal session keys.

Notice both soundness and inverse soundness are required to hold unconditionally with respect to session freshness: each must hold even when the adversary can obtain any secret value it wants.

Soundness is one of the conditions required of Match security [22]. Inverse soundness is seldom mentioned in key exchange models, but was described by Kudla and Paterson [52] as *strong partnering*. Together, these two properties allow us to prove in the next section our baseline theorem relating security under key partnering to security under arbitrary partnering mechanisms.

3.2   Baseline Theorem of Key Exchange Partnering

Theorem 1 (Baseline theorem of key exchange partnering). *Let Π be a key exchange protocol. For any security property SecPred, Π is secure under key-partnering if and only if it is secure under P-partnering, as long as the partnering mechanism P is sound and inverse-sound. More precisely, for all SecPred, Π, n, F, P, and $\mathcal{A}$,*

$$\left| \mathsf{Adv}^{\mathsf{SecPred},F,P_{\mathsf{key}}}_{\Pi,n}(\mathcal{A}) - \mathsf{Adv}^{\mathsf{SecPred},F,P}_{\Pi,n}(\mathcal{A}) \right| \leq \Pr[\overline{\mathsf{Sound}_P}] + \Pr[\overline{\mathsf{InvSound}_P}]. \quad (2)$$

Note that while the same F is used in the two experiments in (2), that F may call the partnering mechanism used in the respective experiment, so we would have "F-with-P_{key}" or "F-with-P". Also recall that we use $\Pr[\overline{\mathsf{Sound}_P}]$ and $\Pr[\overline{\mathsf{InvSound}_P}]$ as a short-hand for the advantage an adversary has in breaking soundness or inverse-soundness of Π with P. Interestingly, de Saint Guilhem, Fischlin and Warinschi [65, Theorem 5.1] prove that if Match security holds, then equal keys implies equal partners already so that the requirement of inverse soundness might seem superfluous. However, their implication only holds for *fresh* sessions and thus, the additional requirement of inverse soundness is needed in our theorem.

A direct consequence of Theorem 1 is the falsifiability of security models using session identifiers or general partnering functions. If an attack is shown against a security property of a key exchange protocol when using a sound and inverse-sound partnering mechanism, then that is indeed an attack against the protocol under key partnering or (by transitivity) under any other sound or inverse-sound partnering mechanism.

Proof. Consider the run of $\mathbf{Exp}^{\mathsf{SecPred},F,P}_{\Pi,n}(\mathcal{A})$ with the same random coins for the experiment and the adversary as in the run of $\mathbf{Exp}^{\mathsf{SecPred},F,P_{\mathsf{key}}}_{\Pi,n}(\mathcal{A})$, but using P instead of P_{key}. Let Same be the event that $P(\pi,\pi') = P_{\mathsf{key}}(\pi,\pi')$ at every evaluation of the partnering mechanism in the experiment and freshness conditions, as described earlier in Sect. 3.1; $\overline{\mathsf{Same}}$ is the complement of Same. Then the two runs behave identically as long as $\overline{\mathsf{Same}}$ does not occur, i.e.,

$$\left| \mathsf{Adv}^{\mathsf{SecPred},F,P_{\mathsf{key}}}_{\Pi,n}(\mathcal{A}) - \mathsf{Adv}^{\mathsf{SecPred},F,P}_{\Pi,n}(\mathcal{A}) \right| \leq \Pr[\overline{\mathsf{Same}}]. \quad (3)$$

If $\overline{\mathsf{Same}}$ occurs, and thus there is some point in time for which there is some pair of sessions π,π' for which $P(\pi,\pi') \neq P_{\mathsf{key}}(\pi,\pi')$, then either (a) $P(\pi,\pi')$

but $\pi.\mathsf{k} \neq \pi'.\mathsf{k}$ (which we will show violates soundness for P), or (b) $\pi.\mathsf{k} = \pi'.\mathsf{k}$ but $\neg P(\pi, \pi')$ (which will violate inverse-soundness for P).

There are three places within the experiment which can cause the event $\overline{\mathsf{Same}}$ to occur, namely the three places where we modified $\mathbf{Exp}_{\Pi,n}^{\mathsf{SecPred},F}$ to $\mathbf{Exp}_{\Pi,n}^{\mathsf{SecPred},F,P}$ at the start of Sect. 3.1:

- Line 903 of the $\mathrm{TEST}(i)$ query: If there is some j for which $P(\mathcal{S}[i], \mathcal{S}[j]) \neq P_{\mathsf{key}}(\mathcal{S}[i], \mathcal{S}[j])$, then this would also have been true at the most recent INIT or SEND query involving either $\mathcal{S}[i]$ or $\mathcal{S}[j]$. Note that we only have to consider INIT and SEND queries since they are the only queries that modify session variables, and we only have to consider the most recent such query involving one of those sessions since INIT or SEND queries to other sessions do not affect the partnering of $\mathcal{S}[i]$ or $\mathcal{S}[j]$.
- Line 1001 of the $\mathrm{ISPARTNERED}$ query: Similarly.
- Inside the call to F on line 307 of the $\mathcal{O}$ oracle: The freshness condition F may evaluate the partner predicate zero or more times, on two arbitrary sessions $\pi, \pi' \in \mathcal{S}$. Note that F uses the partnering mechanism of its experiment, therefore it is either F-with-P_{key} or F-with-P, depending on whether we are in $\mathbf{Exp}_{\Pi,n}^{\mathsf{SecPred},F,P_{\mathsf{key}}}(\mathcal{A})$ or $\mathbf{Exp}_{\Pi,n}^{\mathsf{SecPred},F,P}(\mathcal{A})$. If, at any of F's evaluations of the partnering mechanism, we have that $P(\pi, \pi') \neq P_{\mathsf{key}}(\pi, \pi')$, then it would also have been true at the most recent INIT or SEND query involving either π or π'.

Thus, if $\overline{\mathsf{Same}}$ occurs in $\mathbf{Exp}_{\Pi,n}^{\mathsf{SecPred},F,P}(\mathcal{A})$, then either the game $\mathbf{Exp}_{\Pi,n}^{\mathsf{Sound},F,P}(\mathcal{A})$ or the experiment $\mathbf{Exp}_{\Pi,n}^{\mathsf{InvSound},F,P}(\mathcal{A})$ (with the same random coins for the experiment and adversary) outputs 1. Hence

$$\Pr[\overline{\mathsf{Same}}] \leq \Pr[\overline{\mathsf{Sound}}_P] + \Pr[\overline{\mathsf{InvSound}}_P]..$$

Combining (3) with the above inequality yields the result.

Note that key partnering is clearly perfectly sound and inverse-sound.

At first glance, Theorem 1 might seem vacuous: security with P-partnering approximates security with key-partnering if P-partnering approximates k-partnering. However, there are variants of $\mathbf{Exp}_{\Pi,n}^{\mathsf{SecPred},F}$ for which proving the baseline theorem becomes unclear. For example, we initially tried to write $\mathbf{Exp}_{\Pi,n}^{\mathsf{SecPred},F}$ with all security predicates evaluated at the end of the main experiment on line 218, rather than continuously evaluating non-KI predicates in the SEND query as Fig. 2 shows. We were unable to prove the corresponding baseline theorem: soundness/inverse-soundness would only be guaranteed at the end of the experiment, but there might have been intermediate points where it was temporarily violated, which might result in different behavior between the experiment using key-partnering versus P-partnering.

Theorem 1 uses a generic security predicate: it holds for, e.g., session-key indistinguishability, confinement, and the authentication properties in Appendix B.

4   Composition Should Be Possible

Brzuska, Fischlin, Warinschi, and Williams [22] (BFWW) show that if a key exchange protocol is composable, then it is possible to (weakly) determine which sessions derive the same keys only based on the public *protocol* transcript. However, BFWW consider a model that does not expose a session matching oracle, and we argue now, that if the *model* itself exposes a session matching oracle, then the key exchange protocol can actually be composable without admitting a public session-matching algorithm based on transcripts only. That is, we show that the class of key exchange protocols that are securely composable is bigger than the class identified by BFWW. In this section, we first explain why a key exchange secure in security model with a session matching oracle is composable and then discuss a separating example of a key exchange protocol that is composable, intuitively and provably, but was excluded by BFWW due to the absence of a public session-matching algorithm.

4.1   Composability

In order to prove that a key exchange model provides composability with a symmetric-key primitive, one first needs a definition of security for the symmetric-key primitive and a definition of a composed game. Let's think of $k \leftarrow_\$ \{0,1\}^n$ as being a line of pseudo-code in the game defining the security of the symmetric primitive. The composed game will replace this line by using the session key of the key exchange game. Besides, the composed game will expose the same queries to the adversary as the game defining the security of the symmetric primitive and the key exchange game, except for TEST and REVEAL queries. The composed game uses bit $b = 0$ for the key exchange, and the adversary wins the composed game based on the winning condition of the symmetric primitive.

To reduce the composed security to the two underlying building blocks, one first reduces to the key exchange security to replace real session keys with random session keys. Then, one can reduce to the security of the symmetric-key protocol. Making this proof outline rigorous is less straightforward than one might think. A tricky part in the proof is that the symmetric primitive game needs to be multi-session and key exchange sessions that belong together must be mapped to the same instance of the symmetric primitive. Therefore, in the reduction to the key exchange, the reduction needs to know which two sessions are partnered. BFWW [22] thus argued that a protocol must have a public matching algorithm. This approach was also followed by [20] for composition of non-forward secure key exchange protocols and by Skrobot and Lancrenon [67] for password-based authenticated key exchange. Moreover, due to the session identifiers in Universal Composability, also Canetti and Krawczyk [26] assumed the protocol to have public partnering. In turn, Brzuska, Delignat-Levaud, Fournet, Kohbrok, and Kohlweiss [18] and George and Rackoff [42] provide the adversary with a session-matching oracle that tells the adversary which pairs of sessions are partnered.

In this paper, we argue for the advantages of the latter choice. Namely, it allows to establish secure composability of a larger class of protocols.

4.2   A Separating Example

Let Π be a key exchange protocol that is secure in an arbitrary key exchange model with mutual authentication and pre-specified peers. We now add public-keys for a re-randomizable encryption scheme to Π and encrypt all messages of the original Π protocol with re-randomizable encryption of the intended peer. (Here, we use mutual authentication and pre-specified peers). We obtain a new protocol Π'. In the previous subsection, we showed that protocols secure in a model with a partnering oracle are composable. In this section, we show that Π' is indeed secure in a model with a partnering oracle but Π' does not have a public partnering mechanism.

Π' *is secure in a model with a partnering oracle* Let $\mathcal{A}$ be an adversary against Π' in a model with a partnering oracle. We now build an adversary $\mathcal{B}$ against Π. $\mathcal{B}$ first draws all keys for the rerandomizable encryption scheme and whenever a party P_i with intended peer P_j sends a message m, then $\mathcal{B}$ encrypts m under the public key of P_j with the rerandomizable encryption scheme. In turn, when the adversary makes a $\text{SEND}(i, m)$ query to session i, and P is the owner of session i, then $\mathcal{B}$ first decrypts m using the secret key of P of the rerandomizable encryption scheme and forwards the decrypted message to the experiment. All other oracle queries are forwarded. The soundness of the simulation is a bit hard to argue in an arbitrary model, but the emulation of the SEND query is perfect, REVSK, ISPARTNERED, REVLTK (here, we need to add the secret key) also return the same answer, REVRAND (here, we need to add the randomness for the rerandomizable encryption scheme).

Π' *does not have public partnering* Consider an adversary $\mathcal{A}$ that creates two sessions for P_i and two sessions for P_j, flips a bit to see which one is matched to which and then re-randomizes messages. By security of rerandomizable encryption, from the public transcript, one cannot tell which session is matched with which session. If one wants these probabilities to be more dramatic, one can take many pairs of such sessions and gets a guessing probability of $\frac{1}{2}^c$, where c is the number of sessions: the guessing probability is upper bounded by $\frac{1}{2}^c$ or the probability of breaking the rerandomizable encryption scheme. If c is polynomial, the guessing probability is negligible.

4.3   A General Composition Theorem

We can bypass the aforementioned counterexample and impossibility result by Brzuska, Fischlin, Warinschi and Williams [22], as we added a partnering oracle to our model which tells the adversary whether two sessions are partnered or not. A similar observation was made by Brzuska, Delignat-Lavaud, Fournet, Kohbrok and Kohlweiss [18] who establish composability of a specific eCK variant. We can generalize their theorem to arbitrary key exchange protocols which can be formalized in our above model, regardless of their freshness predicate. To prove such a general composability theorem, we need to formalize the above mechanism that defines the composition of a key exchange protocol with a symmetric-key primitive. To be able to do this, we use the technique of [18] to slice code into several pieces of code. The first object we need is a keys array which will replace some of the code of the Test oracle.

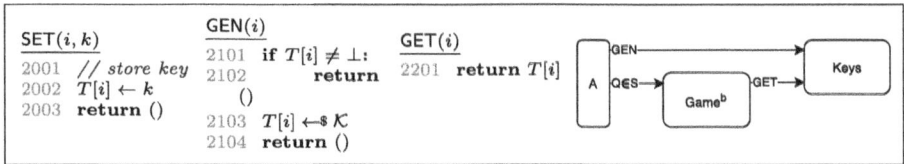

Fig. 5. Keys Array

Definition 6 (Keys Array). *A* Keys *array is a piece of pseudocode which exposes the oracles* SET, GEN *and* GET *which behave as specified in Fig. 5.*

Now, we first define a symmetric-key security game which relies on the Keys array and then modify our key exchange experiment to interact with the Keys array, too.

Definition 7 (Symmetric-Key Security Game). *Let* G^0 *and* G^1 *be stateful pieces of pseudocode that expose the same set* S *of oracles to the adversary and make queries to the* GET *oracle of a* Keys *array. Then, we define the game* $G^b \to$ Keys *as the game where an adversary can call oracles* $S \cup \{$GEN$\}$*, where* GEN *calls of the adversary are executed by* Keys. $G^b \to$ Keys *is depicted on the right side of Fig. 5. For an adversary* $\mathcal{A}$ *interacting with* $G^b \to$ Keys*, we define the advantage as*

$$\epsilon_{G \to \text{Keys}}(\mathcal{A}) := \left| \Pr[1 = \mathcal{A} \to G^0 \to \text{Keys}] - \Pr[1 = \mathcal{A} \to G^1 \to \text{Keys}] \right|$$

The key exchange experiment $\mathbf{Exp}_{\Pi,n}^{\mathsf{KI},F}(\mathcal{A})$ does not terminate early and it always terminates in line 215. Additionally, it does not rewind the adversary. We can thus *externalize* the adversary and write $\mathcal{A} \to \mathbf{Exp}_{\Pi,n}^{\mathsf{KI},F}$ as an adversary which interacts with the oracles of $\mathbf{Exp}_{\Pi,n}^{\mathsf{KI},F}$. Additionally, we can fix the bit b in $\mathbf{Exp}_{\Pi,n}^{\mathsf{KI},F,b}$ and change the Test query such that, instead of returning a key to the adversary, it writes the key into Keys via a SET(i, k) query if $b = 0$ and makes a GEN(i) query to Keys if $b = 1$. The adversary is now given access to the GET oracle of Keys.

Definition 8 (Composable Key Exchange Game). *Let* $\mathcal{A} \to \mathbf{Exp}_{\Pi,n}^{\mathsf{KI},F}$ *be an adversary that interacts with the oracles of* $\mathbf{Exp}_{\Pi,n}^{\mathsf{KI},F}$*, where we fix* b *in* $\mathbf{Exp}_{\Pi,n}^{\mathsf{KI},F,b}$*. Let the Test query write the key into* Keys *via a* SET(i, k) *query if* $b = 0$ *and make* a GEN(i) query to Keys if $b = 1$. The adversary is given access to the GET oracle of Keys. We define the adversary's external advantage as $\epsilon_{\mathbf{Exp}_{\Pi,n}^{\mathsf{KI},F} \to \mathsf{Keys}}(\mathcal{A}) :=$

$$\left| \Pr[1 = \mathcal{A} \to \mathbf{Exp}_{\Pi,n}^{\mathsf{KI},F,0} \to \mathsf{Keys}] - \Pr[1 = \mathcal{A} \to \mathbf{Exp}_{\Pi,n}^{\mathsf{KI},F,1} \to \mathsf{Keys}] \right|.$$

Note that $\epsilon_{\mathbf{Exp}_{\Pi,n}^{\mathsf{KI},F} \to \mathsf{Keys}}(\mathcal{A})$ is twice the standard advantage. We can now naturally define the composed game where $\mathbf{Exp}_{\Pi,n}^{\mathsf{KI},F,b}$ is connected to Keys via a SET query (if $b = 0$) or via a GEN query (if $b = 1$), $G^{b'}$ is connected to Keys via a GET query, and the adversary has access to the oracles of $\mathbf{Exp}_{\Pi,n}^{\mathsf{KI},F}$ and G (but not to any oracle of Keys). In line with [18], we denote the parallel composition of two games by a fraction notation.

Definition 9 (Composed Game). *Let* $\mathbf{Exp}_{\Pi,n}^{\mathsf{KI},F}(\mathcal{A})$ *be a key exchange game from our family, let* G^0 *and* G^1 *be a symmetric-key security game, then we define the advantage of* $\mathcal{A}$ *against their composition as* $\epsilon_{comp}(\mathcal{A}) :=$

$$\left| \Pr[1 = \mathcal{A} \to \frac{\mathbf{Exp}_{\Pi,n}^{\mathsf{KI},F,0}}{G^0} \to \mathsf{Keys}] - \Pr[1 = \mathcal{A} \to \frac{\mathbf{Exp}_{\Pi,n}^{\mathsf{KI},F,1}}{G^1} \to \mathsf{Keys}] \right|.$$

Theorem 2. *Let* $\mathbf{Exp}_{\Pi,n}^{\mathsf{KI},F}(\mathcal{A})$ *be a key exchange game from our family, let* G^0 *and* G^1 *be a symmetric-key security game, then*

$$\epsilon_{comp}(\mathcal{A}) \le \epsilon_{\mathbf{Exp}_{\Pi,n}^{\mathsf{KI},F} \to \mathsf{Keys}}(\mathcal{A} \to G^0) + \epsilon_{G \to \mathsf{Keys}}(\mathcal{A} \to \mathbf{Exp}_{\Pi,n}^{\mathsf{KI},F,1})$$

Proof. The proof is purely syntactical. In the first game hop, we move from $\frac{\mathbf{Exp}_{\Pi,n}^{\mathsf{KI},F,0}}{G^0} \to \mathsf{Keys}$ to $\frac{\mathbf{Exp}_{\Pi,n}^{\mathsf{KI},F,1}}{G^0} \to \mathsf{Keys}$ by making the code of G^0 part of the adversary, i.e., we consider $\mathcal{A} \to G^0$ together as an adversary against the key exchange. In the game-hop from $\frac{\mathbf{Exp}_{\Pi,n}^{\mathsf{KI},F,1}}{G^0} \to \mathsf{Keys}$ to $\frac{\mathbf{Exp}_{\Pi,n}^{\mathsf{KI},F,1}}{G^1} \to \mathsf{Keys}$, we do the converse, i.e., we make the code of $\mathbf{Exp}_{\Pi,n}^{\mathsf{KI},F,1}$ part of the adversary and consider $\mathcal{A} \to \mathbf{Exp}_{\Pi,n}^{\mathsf{KI},F,1}$ as an adversary against G^b. This concludes the proof.

5 Composition Should Be Tight

In the previous section we argued that for an AKE security notion to be useful it should be possible to compose it with other security notions. Here we go one step further and argue that composition should also be efficient. By efficient we mean in the sense of practice-oriented provable security [62]: a reduction from the composed protocol to the AKE should be *tight* [27,28]. More concretely, suppose you have a protocol $\Pi = \mathsf{KE}; \Sigma$ consisting of the composition of an AKE protocol KE and symmetric protocol Σ, i.e., where the keys used by Σ are generated by KE. Now assume KE is secure according to some composable AKE security notion AKE, Σ is secure according to some notion X, and the goal is to show that Π is secure according to some notion Y. Then we want the Y-security of Π to be tightly reducible to the AKE-security of KE and the X-security of Σ, informally stated:

$$\mathsf{Adv}^Y_{\mathsf{KE};\Sigma} \leq \mathsf{Adv}^{\mathsf{AKE}}_{\mathsf{KE}} + \mathsf{Adv}^X_\Sigma. \tag{4}$$

For example, Σ could be an authenticated encryption scheme, X could be the security notion of multi-user authenticated encryption (mu-AE) [46], and Y could be the security notion of authenticated and confidential channel establishment (ACCE) [45].

Intuitively, this should be possible since an AKE protocol is fundamentally a multi-user object, and so the security of KE should "line-up" with the multi-user security of Σ to provide security for their composition Π. In particular, we want the AKE security notion to support the following natural proof strategy: start by replacing the session keys of all fresh sessions with random keys (which can be done since KE is secure), then appeal to the X-security of Σ to argue that the composition $\Pi = \mathsf{KE};\Sigma$ now satisfies Y-security. This argument has been formalized by Brzuska, Fischlin, Warinschi, and Williams [22], showing that BR-secure AKE protocols can be composed with arbitrary symmetric-key protocols. Unfortunately, the reduction given in [22] is not quite of the form (4), but rather

$$\mathsf{Adv}^Y_{\mathsf{KE};\Sigma} \leq q \cdot \mathsf{Adv}^{\mathsf{AKE}}_{\mathsf{KE}} + \mathsf{Adv}^X_\Sigma, \tag{5}$$

where the factor $q = n_U^2 \cdot n_s$ depends on the number of users n_U and the number of sessions per user n_s. For systems with billions of users and sessions such as TLS, the factor q can become very substantial. As a result, if parameters are to be selected in a theoretically sound manner supported by reductions, they would have to be increased significantly, thereby hurting performance.

So where does the factor q in (5) come from? It comes from a hybrid argument in [22] where, one-by-one, the session keys of all fresh sessions are replaced with random keys. The hybrid argument is necessary since the AKE model in [22] only allows one TEST query. A 1-TEST model is thus not conducive to a tight composition result like (4). More conceptually, we see the 1-TEST model as failing to reflect the multi-user nature of key exchange.

n-FtG vs. RoR. Given that a 1-TEST model is inadequate for tight composition, the natural solution is to use an n-TEST model where the adversary can make multiple TEST queries. But there are two reasonable ways in which this can be done: the n-FtG (Find-then-Guess) model, where each session is equipped with its own independent secret bit b_i and each TEST query is answered real-or-random based on the corresponding session's secret bit; or the RoR (Real-or-Random) model, where all TEST queries are either all answered with real keys, or all are answered with random keys, based a *single* secret bit b.[7] Both the n-FtG model [4,34,38,43] and the RoR model [1–3] have seen use in the literature. So which one should you prefer? Answer: RoR.

The n-FtG model is no better than the 1-FtG model when it comes to tight composition, because in the reduction it does not allow replacement of all fresh

---

[7]   The FtG and RoR labels are inspired by the similarly-named IND-CPA security notions for symmetric encryption [7].

session keys with random keys in one big swoop due to the secret bits b_i being independent. On the other hand, the RoR model allows all fresh session keys to be replaced at once. Thus, the proof of (4) is simply a matter of "lining up" the keys from KE with the correct instances of the symmetric protocol Σ. In fact, Skrobot and Lancrenon [67] have carried out exactly this proof by adapting the composition framework of BFWW [22] to the RoR setting (albeit for password-based protocols).

Comparing the RoR and n-FtG models (see Fig. 6), one can show that RoR tightly implies n-FtG, while n-FtG only implies RoR with a tightness loss of n. Moreover, this loss is inherent. All of these claims can be proven by adapting the corresponding proofs in [3] to our model given in Sect. 2. Note that this is not just an exercise in moving definitions around so that a tightness gap is hidden elsewhere. For example, our proof in Appendix A of the security of the NAXOS++ protocol obtains the same tightness gap to the underlying hardness assumptions in the RoR model as the original proof of the NAXOS+ protocol did in the 1-FtG model [55], but due to the RoR-model there is no additional gap when composing the AKE protocol with a subsequent symmetric protocol.

Finally, we note a peculiarity of the n-FtG model. For security to be meaningfully defined in the 1-FtG and RoR models all test sessions must be fresh, otherwise the adversary could trivially win the game. However, in the n-FtG model—where the adversary's output (i, b') is a guess of the singular session i's secret bit—one could technically allow the compromise of all the *other* test sessions, since this wouldn't necessarily trivialize the game. But we do not recommend this variant of n-FtG. First of all, we find it conceptually wrong, since the whole purpose of the TEST query is to measure the adversary's ability to distinguish session keys of valid targets. If the adversary really wanted to learn the keys of the other test sessions it should have used the REVEAL query. Second, with this variant we can no longer prove the implication RoR $\implies$ n-FtG.

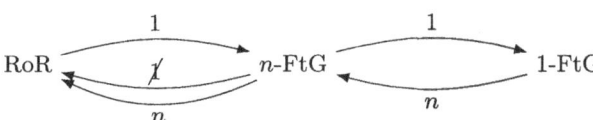

Fig. 6. Relationship between notions; $X \xrightarrow{L} Y$ indicates that notion X implies notion Y with security loss $O(L)$.

Tight AKE Constructions vs. Tight AKE Composition. This section has focused on the usefulness of the AKE security notion itself, i.e., how tightly can the security of a complex protocol be reduced to the security of the underlying AKE? In a sense, we have focused on the *user* of the AKE security notion.

In contrast, tightness considerations in the literature have mainly focused on the *construction* of the AKE protocol itself, i.e., how tightly can the security of the AKE protocol be reduced to the security of some underlying assumptions, such as Diffie-Hellman or RSA? Some examples of AKE protocols with tight, or nearly tight, reductions in this sense are [4,5,29,41,43,44,58–61].

Note that these two types of tightness considerations are complementary. For the security proof of the overall system to be maximally meaningful (in the sense of practice-oriented provable security [6,28,62]), both the construction and the composition need to be tight.

6   Comparability of Models

The main reason to compare key exchange security models is to compare the relative *strength* of a considered adversary, i.e., which capabilities are the adversary assumed to have in the model? However, existing models typically entangle the capabilities in slightly different ways, and hence there are no common capability parameters that could serve as a basis for comparison.

If one commits to only using a specific family of models parametrized solely by a freshness condition (such as the one in [16,32], or our $\mathbf{Exp}_{\Pi,n}^{\mathsf{SecPred},F}$ in Sect. 2), then the comparison boils down to comparing the freshness conditions. However, in practice, other aspects may also differ, such as the choice of partnering mechanism [31]. Nevertheless, our baseline theorem shows that the behavior of different partnering mechanisms is approximately the same, provided they satisfy the two natural soundness properties. Thus, here we focus instead on another source of incomparability, namely the treatment of adversarial misbehavior, which has not been considered by previous works. ·

For a given property, we aim to determine a protocol's security against adversaries that do not violate the freshness condition; what we will call *well-behaved* adversaries. Surprisingly, there is no consensus on how to ensure that only well-behaved adversaries are considered in the security definition, as illustrated by the following different approaches taken in the literature.

A) Exclusion-style. In this approach one simply quantify over the well-behaved adversaries only. The security experiment is typically formulated as follows (see, e.g., [16]):

1. The experiment begins, and the adversary can issue any permissible query.
2. At some point it issues a TEST query to a *fresh* session.
3. It continues issuing queries, *under the condition that the test session remains fresh.*
4. Finally, the adversary outputs a guess b'.

While the exclusion-style formulation is probably the one most commonly found in the literature, it has some conceptual drawbacks. Quoting Rogaway and Zhang [64]:

Exclusion-style definitions compel consideration of adversary classes. They disqualify adversaries that only rarely misbehave. They ignore whether or not an adversary can 'know' it has misbehaved. And they promote ambiguity, as the relevant restrictions are not expressed in game code.

We refer the reader to [64] for further details.

B) Penalty-style. Another approach is to quantify over *all* adversarial behaviors, but then penalize the misbehavior at the end of the experiment (e.g., by outputting a random bit on the adversary's behalf). The difference between the exclusion-style and the penalty-style definitions has previously been considered by Bellare, Hofheinz, and Kiltz [8] in the context of IND-CCA security for public-key encryption. Examples of models using the penalty-style are given in [9,19,35,55]. For a proof using a penalty-style definition, the relevant adversary restrictions will manifest themselves during the probability analysis where one needs to check that indeed, the reduction will not be penalized by the game it is playing and/or that it is penalized if and only if the original adversary would have been penalized in its game as well. These analyses can sometimes be quite subtle.

C) Filtering-Style. Finally, we have the approach we prefer, where queries that constitute adversarial misbehavior are not executed, and no response is returned to the adversary. This filtering-style definition is inspired by George and Rackoff [42] and the work of Rogaway and Zhang [64].[8] The advantage of a filtering-style definition is that it makes the accepted adversarial behaviour explicit in the game code, and it avoids the need for subtle freshness analyses at the end of the proof.

Relations Between Notions. The relationship between the three notions is subtle. First, security in a filter-style model implies security in an exclusion-style model, but not the other way around. The problem is that one cannot always publicly check whether a query is valid or not. However, if the validity can be publicly checked (i.e., if it does not depend on secret game state), then exclusion-style security implies filter-style security. This is similar to a result by Rogaway and Zhang [64].

For penalty-style security the situation is much more complicated. First, similar to the direction exclusion-style security $\rightarrow$ filter-style security, security in a penalty-style model only implies security in a filter-style model if one can publicly check validity. However, in the converse direction filter-style security fails to imply penalty-style security. To illustrate this, consider a penalty-style adversary $\mathcal{A}$ for which we aim to build a filter-style adversary $\mathcal{B}$ (against the same protocol) using the eCK-like freshness predicate F^{eCK} given in Fig. 3. Now suppose $\mathcal{A}$ behaves as follows: (1) it reveals all long-term keys; (2) it forwards messages passively between two sessions until one of them accepts; (3) it tests this session; (4) it delivers the test session's final message to the other one (so they become partners); (5) it stops and outputs a guess. The problem for $\mathcal{B}$ occurs in step (3): at this point the test-session is non-fresh according to F^{eCK}, so it won't get a response back if it forwards $\mathcal{A}$'s TEST query to its own filter-style game. However, it can't simply abort, because $\mathcal{A}$ is a valid penalty-style

---

[8] In the *silencing* definition of Rogaway and Zhang [64], the game state is updated and only the response is suppressed, whereas our formulation in Fig. 2 reverts the game state if the response is to be suppressed.

adversary due to step (4) (since the test-session eventually gets a partner, it is fresh by the time of step (5)).

The reason for this issue is that in a penalty-style model the "intermediate" freshness state of a session could be *non-monotonic*. I.e., even though a session is fresh when the experiment ends, it could have been considered unfresh at certain points during the experiment. In our view, this non-monotonic aspect of the penalty-style model is counter-intuitive and complicates reasoning. Also, it is not clear whether the obstacle to proving that filter-style security implies penalty-style security represents an actual security difference, or whether it is merely a proof technicality.

7   Discussion

For the cryptographer developing a protocol, we offer a family of key exchange models in Sect. 2, parameterized by a freshness condition tailored to capture the intended adversarial attack capabilities. A proof in one of our models ensures that no attack exists under a different reasonable partnering mechanism, and that efficient composition with a symmetric-key protocol is possible.

Our results are useful beyond the family of models: for those who prefer to use session identifiers rather than key partnering for your proof, our baseline theorem of key exchange partnering says this is fine, as long as soundness of the session identifiers is proven. For those who prefer to penalize adversaries that violate the freshness condition, rather than filtering the response from unfresh queries, the IsPartnered oracle provides the public checkability of partnering to show these equivalent.

Our results show that by some careful choices for key exchange models, one can relatively easily obtain sanity in interpreting and relating different key exchange security models, and assurance that protocols satisfying those models can be composed in reasonable ways.

Acknowledgements. We thank Konrad Kohbrok for discussions on the baseline theorem of key partnering at early stages of this work. We thank Eric Cornelissen for helpful comments on the presentation.

D.S. is supported in part by Natural Sciences and Engineering Research Council of Canada (NSERC) Discovery grant RGPIN-2022-03187. This work was supported by the Research Council of Finland.

A   Case Study: Analyzing NAXOS+ in Our Model

In this section we showcase the security model we defined in Sect. 2 by providing a proof of the NAXOS+ protocol [55]. In fact, we consider a slight variant of NAXOS+ we call NAXOS++, whose only difference is that it includes the full protocol transcript into the key derivation function.

Specifically, in NAXOS++, each party U has a long-term Diffie-Hellman key pair over a group $\mathbb{G}$ of prime order p, generated by a generator g, i.e.:

$$\mathrm{KG}() \mapsto (\mathsf{sk}, \mathsf{pk}) : a \leftarrow_\$ \{1, .., p\}, \mathsf{sk} \leftarrow a, \mathsf{pk} \leftarrow g^a$$

Each party draws an ephemeral random string esk and computes its ephemeral Diffie-Hellman exponent using the NAXOS trick, i.e.:

$$\text{NEW}(U, \text{sk}_U, \text{pk}_U, \text{role}, V, \text{PK}) \mapsto (\pi, m) :$$
$$\text{esk} \leftarrow_\$ \{1, .., p\},$$
$$\text{if role} = \text{init} : x \leftarrow H_1(\text{esk}, \text{sk}_U), \ X \leftarrow g^x, \ m \leftarrow X$$
$$\text{if role} = \text{resp} : y \leftarrow H_1(\text{esk}, \text{sk}_U), \ Y \leftarrow g^y, \ m \leftarrow \bot$$

The initiator and responder then both compute all possible combinations of Diffie-Hellman secrets and hash them together with their long-term public-keys and the ephemeral Diffie-Hellman public shares (including these public-shares is somewhat redundant, but it makes the key material uniqueness argument for NAXOS++ a little easier than the analogous argument about NAXOS+), i.e.:

$$\text{RUN}(\pi, m) \mapsto (\pi', m') : \quad // \ \pi.\text{owner} = U, \pi.\text{pid} = V$$
$$\textbf{if role} = \textbf{init} :$$
$$m' \leftarrow \bot, \ \textbf{parse } Y \leftarrow m$$
$$\text{keymat} \leftarrow (\text{pk}_U, \text{pk}_V, X, Y, \text{pk}_V^{\text{sk}_U}, Y^{\text{sk}_U}, \text{pk}_V^x, Y^x)$$
$$\textbf{if role} = \textbf{resp} :$$
$$m' \leftarrow Y, \ \textbf{parse } X \leftarrow m$$
$$\text{keymat} \leftarrow (\text{pk}_V, \text{pk}_U, X, Y, \text{pk}_V^{\text{sk}_U}, \text{pk}_V^y, X^{\text{sk}_U}, X^y)$$
$$k \leftarrow H_2(\text{keymat})$$

We now state our theorem for NAXOS++ $\Pi = (\text{KG}, \text{NEW}, \text{RUN})$ and observe that, although we prove security for an arbitrary number of TEST sessions, the bounds and the conceptual reduction arguments remain essentially the same as in Lee and Park [55], only the additive statistical terms Theorem 3 are slightly increased. Recall that we prove security in the tightly composable RoR model while Lee and Park [55] prove security in the 1-FtG model, cf. Figure 6.

Theorem 3. *For all adversaries $\mathcal{A}$, there are efficient, explicit constructions of adversaries $\mathcal{B}_1(\mathcal{A})$, $\mathcal{B}_2(\mathcal{A})$ and $\mathcal{B}_3(\mathcal{A})$ such that*

$$
\begin{aligned}
\text{Adv}_{\Pi,n}^{\text{KI},F^{\text{eCK}}}(\mathcal{A}) \leq{} & n \cdot \text{Adv}_{\mathbb{G},g}^{\text{dlog}}(\mathcal{B}_1(\mathcal{A})) \\
& + n_s^2 \cdot \text{Adv}_{\mathbb{G},g}^{\text{CDH}}(\mathcal{B}_2(\mathcal{A})) \\
& + nn_s \cdot \text{Adv}_{\mathbb{G},g}^{\text{CDH}}(\mathcal{B}_3(\mathcal{A})) \\
& + \frac{q_1^2 + q_2^2 + 2n_s^3 q_2 + 2n_s^2 q_1 q_2 + n_s^2 q_2^2}{2^\lambda} \\
& + \frac{n^2 + n_s^2 + 2nn_s q_2 + 2nn_s^2 q_1 q_2}{p}
\end{aligned}
\tag{6}
$$

where n denotes number of users, n_s is the (total) number of sessions, q_1 is the number of queries to random oracle H_1, q_2 is the number of queries to random *oracle H_2,* dlog *is the Discrete Logarithm problem, and* CDH *is the Computational Diffie-Hellman problem.*

Proof. The proof proceeds through a sequence of six game-hops that are summarized in Fig. 7. G_0 is equal to $\mathbf{Exp}_{\Pi,n}^{\mathsf{KI},F^{\mathsf{eCK}}}(\mathcal{A})$. The lines following G_ℓ are only executed in games G_m with $m \geq \ell$. Note that in our game-hops, we use our filtering mechanism to ensure that fewer and fewer bad events can occur. Essentially, this captures "identical-up-to-bad" reasoning [12], but without the complexity of conditional probabilities. Instead, we simply modify the game such that the undesirable behavior cannot occur anymore.

From game G_0 to G_1, we remove collisions on the long-term keys. From game G_1 to G_2, we remove random oracle collisions on the random oracles H_1 and H_2. From game G_2 to G_3, we remove collisions between the randomness that is drawn by each session. From game G_3 to G_4, we remove the case that there exists a party U with long-term secret sk such that the adversary $\mathcal{A}$ makes a random oracle query $H_1(*, \mathsf{sk}_U)$ before, or without, making a REVLTK(U) query. From game G_4 to G_5, we remove random oracle queries to H_2 with the key material of a Test session i that is not partnered. From game G_5 to G_6, we remove random oracle queries to H_2 with the key material of a Test session i that is partnered. In game G_6, the adversary cannot make random oracle queries to the random oracle H_2 with the key material of any Test session, and thus, the adversary's advantage in G_6 is the statistical distance between random keys and non-colliding keys (since several collisions have been removed).

We now bound the difference between each subsequent pair of games. In the following, let ϵ_i denote $\mathcal{A}$'s advantage in game G_i. For the first three game hops, simple collision arguments gives

$$|\epsilon_0 - \epsilon_1| \leq \frac{n^2}{p}, \ |\epsilon_1 - \epsilon_2| \leq \frac{q_1^2}{2^\lambda} + \frac{q_2^2}{2^\lambda} \text{ and } |\epsilon_2 - \epsilon_3| \leq \frac{n_s^2}{p} \ .$$

Bounding game G_3 and game G_4 is analogous to the reduction to the discrete logarithm problem (DLOG) given by Lee and Park [55]. They lose a factor n when *guessing* a random party whereas we simply perform a hybrid argument over the number of parties, yielding a stronger claim with the same security loss and the same reasoning. Only the constant additive term gets increased by the hybrid argument when compared with the guessing argument.

$$\epsilon_3 - \epsilon_4 \leq n \cdot \left(\mathsf{Adv}_{\mathbb{G},g}^{\mathsf{dlog}}(\mathcal{B}_1(\mathcal{A})) + \frac{2n_s q_2}{p} \right) \tag{7}$$

The two remaining game-hops involve reductions to the Computational Diffie-Hellman (CDH) assumption. Again, the proofs are analogous to reductions for the corresponding events in [55]. For the step from G_4 to G_5, Lee and Park [55] guess a pair of random sessions where they embed the challenge Diffie-Hellman share. We, instead of guessing them at random, perform a hybrid over all pairs. If it turns out that the pair in consideration does not end up in a a Test session, the reduction outputs a random bit (and moreover, the condition introduced for

```
Exp^{KI,F^eCK}_{Π,n}(A)
201  b ←$ {0,1}                              // Pick hidden challenge bit
202  S ← []                                  // Initialize list of session states
203  Q ← []                                  // Initialize list of queries
204  T ← ∅                                   // Initialize set of tested sessions
205  cnt ← 0                                 // Initialize session counter
206
207  for all U ∈ {1,.. ,n}:                  // Generate all long-term key pairs
208    a ←$ {1,..,p}
209    a ←$ {1,..,p} \ {sk_V : V < U}        // G_1: No long-term key collisions
210    sk_U ← a, pk_U ← g^a
211    PK[U] ← pk_U
212
213  Φ ← {b,S,Q,T,cnt,PK}                    // Global experiment state
214  b' ←$ A^O(PK)                           // Run the adversary
215  output b = b'

     // All adversary queries are "filtered" through O
O(QUERY,x)
301  Φ' ← Φ                                  // Save the current global experiment state
302  y ← QUERY(x)                            // Run the adversary's query
303  Q ←(QUERY,x,y)
304
305  if // Check if all tested sessions would remain fresh
306    ∀i ∈ T . F^eCK(Φ,i)
307    // Check if there are RO collisions
308    G_2 : ∀x,x' . T_1[x] ≡ T_1[x'] or T_2[x] ≡ T_2[x']
309         ⟹ x = x'
310    // Check if there are randomness collisions
311    G_3 : ∀i,i' . S[i].esk ≡ S[i'].esk ⟹ i = i'
312    // Check if there are secret longterm key guesses
313    G_4 : ∀U . ∃⟨H_1,(*,sk_U),*⟩ ∈ Q
314         ⟹ ∃⟨RevLTK,U,*⟩ ∈ Q
315    // Check if there are session-key guesses for non-partnered sessions
316    G_5 : ∃i . ∃⟨TEST,i,*⟩ ∈ Q
317         and ∄j ≠ i . S[i].k ≡ S[j].k
318         ⟹ ∄⟨H_2,(S[i].keymat),*⟩ ∈ Q
319    // Any session-key guesses for partnered sessions?
320    G_6 : ∃i . ∃⟨TEST,i,*⟩ ∈ Q
321         and ∃j ≠ i . S[i].k ≡ S[j].k
322         ⟹ ∄⟨H_2,(S[i].keymat),*⟩ ∈ Q :
323    return y
324  else
325    Φ ← Φ'                                 // Revert effects of bad query
326    return ◇                               // Silence response


INIT(U,role,V)
401  cnt ← cnt + 1
402  (S[cnt],m) ←$ Π.NEW(U,
                         sk_U,pk_U,role,V,PK)
403  return (cnt,m)

SEND(i,m)
501  (S[i],m') ← Π.RUN(S[i],m)
502  return (S[i].status,m')

RevSK(i)
601  return S[i].k

RevRand(i)
701  return S[i].rand

RevLTK(U)
801  return sk_U

TEST(i)
901  if i ∈ T:
902    return ⊥
903  if ∃j . S[i].k = S[j].k ∧ j ∈ T:
904    return ⊥
905  T ← i
906  k_0 ← S[i].k
907  k_1 ←$ K
908  return k_b

ISPARTNERED(i,j)
1001 return (S[i].k ≡ S[j].k)

H_1(esk,sk)
1101 if T_1[esk,sk] = ⊥:
1102   T_1[esk,sk] ←$ {0,1}^λ
1103 return T_1[esk,sk]

H_2(keymat)
1201 if T_2[keymat] = ⊥:
1202   T_2[keymat] ←$ {0,1}^λ
1203 return T_2[keymat]
```

Fig. 7. Key Exchange Experiment for NAXOS++ protocol and freshness F^{eCK}. The lines following G_ℓ are only executed in games G_m with $m \geq \ell$. Recall that $\equiv$ treats two values as equal only if they have previously been defined, see Sect. 2.2.

G_4 for this pair does not affect the game behavior, so the adversary's advantage in this hybrid step is indeed 0). For the step from G_5 to G_6, we replace guessing one party and one session by a hybrid argument over all possible combinations of a session and a party.

$$\epsilon_4 - \epsilon_5 \leq n_s^2 \cdot \left(\mathsf{Adv}^{\mathsf{CDH}}_{\mathbb{G},g}(\mathcal{B}_2(\mathcal{A})) + \frac{n_s + q_1}{2^{\lambda-1}} \right),$$

and

$$\epsilon_5 - \epsilon_6 \leq n n_s \cdot \left(\mathsf{Adv}^{\mathsf{CDH}}_{\mathbb{G},g}(\mathcal{B}_3(\mathcal{A})) + \frac{2 n_s q_1}{p} \right).$$

In game G_6, the adversary cannot make random oracle queries to the random oracle H_2 with the key material of any Test session, and thus, the adversary's advantage in G_6 is the statistical distance between uniformly random keys and actual keys, and ϵ_6 is upper bounded by $\frac{n_s^2 q_2^2}{2^\lambda}$.

B Authentication

To be useful, a key exchange protocol typically needs to provide authentication guarantees in addition to key-indistinguishability. For example, when a key is locally accepted by some session, it should be clear who else (if anyone) is in possession of the same key. One can also demand that one or both parties involved in the exchange are authenticated (mutual vs. one-way), that the guarantee holds as soon as the exchange has ended or when the key is actually used (explicit vs. implicit). Furthermore, the guarantees can be considered under a variety of trust assumptions where the adversary can corrupt long term keys of parties or not (i.e. key-compromise impersonation attacks) and can corrupt ephemeral keys.

In this section we show how authentication guarantees can be expressed as security predicates in our model. However, an exhaustive treatment of all different combinations is outside the scope of this paper, and we refer to de Saint Guilhem, Fischlin and Warinschi [65] for a thorough survey. We focus on providing definitions for some minimal set of authentication / agreement guarantees which we would normally expect to be satisfied.

B.1 Implicit Authentication

We start with a minimal agreement guarantee we would expect a good key-exchange protocol to satisfy: entity agreement, a.k.a. implicit authentication. Implicit authentication is a useful property to prove in addition to secrecy of the session key. We demand that if an accepted sessions has a partner, then that partner should be at the session's intended peer. Our formulation uses key-partnering.

$$\mathsf{ImplAuth}_F : \forall i \neq j \,.\, \Big(\big(\mathcal{S}[i].\mathsf{status} = \mathsf{accepted} \wedge \mathcal{S}[i].\mathsf{k} = \mathcal{S}[j].\mathsf{k} \wedge F(\Phi, i) \big)$$
$$\implies \mathcal{S}[i].\mathsf{pid} = \mathcal{S}[j].\mathsf{owner} \Big) \quad (8)$$

Definition 10 (Implicit authentication). *For a freshness condition F and number of parties $n \in \mathbb{N}$, a protocol Π provides ϵ-implicit authentication against an adversary $\mathcal{A}$ if*

$$\mathsf{Adv}_{\Pi,n}^{\mathsf{ImplAuth},F}(\mathcal{A}) := \Pr\left[\mathbf{Exp}_{\Pi,n}^{\mathsf{ImplAuth}_F,F}(\mathcal{A}) \Rightarrow 1\right] \leq \epsilon \;.$$

We stress that our formulation is generic in that it does not fix any particular freshness predicate. Different instantiations of the freshness lead to (substantially) different guarantees. E.g., if freshness allows the adversary to compromise the long term key of the owner of $\mathcal{S}[i]$, then the notion captures security against key-compromise impersonation (KCI) attacks. If freshness allows for the intended partner of $\mathcal{S}[i]$ to be compromised, then one captures unknown-key share attacks under this more liberal corruption model.

Furthermore, our requirement for implicit authentication is minimal. It only demands that partners agree upon the protocol participants. However, it is straightforward to extend this agreement property to cover additional variables. For instance, to ensure that the participants have different *roles* in the protocol, one can add this as an extra requirement to the ImplAuth event. In fact, agreement could be used to define a more fine-grained version of matching conversations, by demanding that partners should agree upon specific parts of their communication transcripts (and possibly leaving other parts open to manipulation). E.g., see the use of agreement related to transcripts and downgrade attacks in [14].

Additionally, the supposition of ImplAuth depends on key partnering. It would be possible to formulate ImplAuth to depend on a generic partnering mechanism, which would potentially imply subtly different authentication properties. However, as Appendix B.3 notes, our baseline theorem of key exchange partnering implies that implicit authentication under key-partnering or a generic partnering mechanism behave similarly if the partnering mechanism is sound and inverse-sound.

Finally, we note that implicit authentication does not provide any meaningful guarantees for protocols that do not satisfy key secrecy, since in such a case no meaningful authentication is achieved.

B.2   Explicit Authentication

The "implicit" aspect of implicit authentication means that a partner session satisfying the requirements is not actually guaranteed to exist. Some protocols also provide an explicit assurance that such a partner session exists: this is *explicit* entity authentication [10].

Explicit authentication demands that when a session i accepts, it is partnered with a session of the intended partner j. For stateless protocols, a minimal requirement to achieve this is that the intended peer is not corrupted before session i accepts. We capture this property via the predicate F_{PNC} below, in which the antecedent of the implication identifies the acceptance in the list of queries, and the consequent excludes any preceding long-term key reveals for the peer:

$$F_{\mathsf{PNC}}(\Phi, i)\colon \forall r < s \ . \ (\mathcal{Q}[s] = \langle \mathrm{SEND}, (i, *), (\mathsf{accepted}, *)\rangle$$
$$\implies \mathcal{Q}[r] \neq \langle \mathrm{REVLTK}, \mathcal{S}[i].\mathsf{peerID}, *\rangle) . \quad (9)$$

We can then state explicit authentication as:

$$\mathsf{ExplAuth}: \forall i \ . \ \Big((\mathcal{S}[i].\mathsf{status} = \mathsf{accepted} \wedge F_{\mathsf{PNC}}(\Phi, i)) \implies$$
$$\exists j \neq i \ . \ (\mathcal{S}[i].\mathsf{k} = \mathcal{S}[j].\mathsf{k} \wedge \mathcal{S}[i].\mathsf{pid} = \mathcal{S}[j].\mathsf{owner}) \Big) \quad (10)$$

Notice that the predicates which define implicit authentication and explicit authentication have potentially different trust assumptions: ImplAuth allows for an arbitrary freshness predicate, while ExplAuth hard-codes the requirement that the intended peer was not corrupted before the session accepted. This is because implicit agreement guarantees can make sense even if the intended partner of session $\mathcal{S}[i]$ is corrupt (for example, with eCK-type protocols), but do not make sense for explicit authentication.

The following weaker intermediate property captures just the aliveness property of authentication: when a session accepts, and the intended partner is not corrupt, a session of the peer exists.

$$\mathsf{Alive}: \forall i \ . \ ((\mathcal{S}[i].\mathsf{status} = \mathsf{accepted} \wedge F_{\mathsf{PNC}}(\Phi, i))$$
$$\implies \exists j \ . \ (\mathcal{S}[i].\mathsf{pid} = \mathcal{S}[j].\mathsf{owner})) \quad (11)$$

Relationship with Key-Confirmation. Another property which is sometimes mentioned alongside explicit authentication is *key-confirmation*. I.e., if a session accepts a key, then it is assured that some other session must also have computed the same key.[9] Intuitively, if key-confirmation is combined with a protocol that provides secrecy and implicit authentication, explicit authentication is achieved. Note that secrecy is strictly required here: a protocol that satisfies implicit authentication with an added key-confirmation step need not achieve explicit authentication.

B.3   Falsifiability and Partnering for Authentication Properties

A consequence of the baseline theorem of key exchange partnering (Theorem 1) is the following. Let Π be a protocol, let ϕ be one of the three authentication properties in this section, and let P be a sound and inverse-sound partnering mechanism. Then, Π provides ϕ under key-partnering if and only if it provides ϕ under P-partnering.[10]

One might initially think that one can prove falsifiability of some of the authentication properties relying only on one of soundness or inverse-soundness. E.g., consider implicit authentication. In the ImplAuth predicate, the key

---

[9] Modulo some technicalities regarding which session sent/received the last message of the protocol. See [39] for a more extensive treatment of key-confirmation, including these details.

[10] Strictly speaking, to apply the baseline theorem, we need to consider the adaptations of ImplAuth, ExplAuth to P-partnering rather than key-partnering, by replacing the key equality checks $\mathcal{S}[i].\mathsf{k} = \mathcal{S}[j].\mathsf{k}$ on lines (8) and (10) with a partnering check $P(\mathcal{S}[i], \mathcal{S}[j])$.

equality-partnering check is in the supposition of the predicate. So in order to argue, e.g., that, if implicit authentication holds with P-partnering, it also holds with key-partnering, one might think that it suffices to have soundness: the set of sessions satisfying the supposition of the ImplAuth predicate under key partnering would then be a subset of the set of sessions satisfying the predicate under P-partnering. However, we cannot consider the ImplAuth predicate in isolation: while the predicate itself only uses partnering in one way, there are other parts of the overall security experiment which use partnering in various ways. In particular, the IsPARTNERED oracle allows the adversary to exactly learn the partner status of every session under the partnering mechanism in use (key partnering or P-partnering), which means we must have both soundness and inverse-soundness to guarantee the whole experiment behaves identically.

References

1. Abdalla, M., Benhamouda, F., MacKenzie, P.: Security of the J-PAKE password-authenticated key exchange protocol. In: 2015 IEEE Symposium on Security and Privacy, pp. 571–587. IEEE Computer Society Press (2015)
2. Abdalla, M., Benhamouda, F., Pointcheval, D.: Public-key encryption indistinguishable under plaintext-checkable attacks. In: Katz, J. (ed.) PKC 2015. LNCS, vol. 9020, pp. 332–352. Springer, Heidelberg (2015). https://doi.org/10.1007/978-3-662-46447-2_15
3. Abdalla, M., Fouque, P.-A., Pointcheval, D.: Password-based authenticated key exchange in the three-party setting. In: Vaudenay, S. (ed.) PKC 2005. LNCS, vol. 3386, pp. 65–84. Springer, Heidelberg (2005). https://doi.org/10.1007/978-3-540-30580-4_6
4. Bader, C., Hofheinz, D., Jager, T., Kiltz, E., Li, Y.: Tightly-secure authenticated key exchange. In: Dodis, Y., Nielsen, J.B. (eds.) TCC 2015. LNCS, vol. 9014, pp. 629–658. Springer, Heidelberg (2015). https://doi.org/10.1007/978-3-662-46494-6_26
5. Becerra, J., Iovino, V., Ostrev, D., Šala, P., Škrobot, M.: Tightly-secure PAK(E). In: Capkun, S., Chow, S.S.M. (eds.) CANS 2017. LNCS, vol. 11261, pp. 27–48. Springer, Cham (2018). https://doi.org/10.1007/978-3-030-02641-7_2
6. Bellare, M.: Practice-oriented provable-security. In: Damgård, I.B. (ed.) EEF School 1998. LNCS, vol. 1561, pp. 1–15. Springer, Heidelberg (1999). https://doi.org/10.1007/3-540-48969-X_1
7. Bellare, M., Desai, A., Jokipii, E., Rogaway, P.: A concrete security treatment of symmetric encryption. In: 38th FOCS, pp. 394–403. IEEE Computer Society Press (1997)
8. Bellare, M., Hofheinz, D., Kiltz, E.: Subtleties in the definition of IND-CCA: when and how should challenge decryption be disallowed? J. Cryptol. $28(1)$, 29–48 (2015)
9. Bellare, M., Pointcheval, D., Rogaway, P.: Authenticated key exchange secure against dictionary attacks. In: Preneel, B. (ed.) EUROCRYPT 2000. LNCS, vol. 1807, pp. 139–155. Springer, Heidelberg (2000). https://doi.org/10.1007/3-540-45539-6_11
10. Bellare, M., Rogaway, P.: Entity authentication and key distribution. In: Stinson, D.R. (ed.) CRYPTO'93. LNCS, vol. 773, pp. 232–249. Springer, Heidelberg (1994). https://doi.org/10.1007/3-540-48329-2_21

11. Bellare, M., Rogaway, P.: Provably secure session key distribution: the three party case. In: 27th ACM STOC, pp. 57–66. ACM Press (1995)
12. Bellare, M., Rogaway, P.: The security of triple encryption and a framework for code-based game-playing proofs. In: Vaudenay, S. (ed.) EUROCRYPT 2006. LNCS, vol. 4004, pp. 409–426. Springer, Heidelberg (2006). https://doi.org/10.1007/11761679_25
13. Bergsma, F., Dowling, B., Kohlar, F., Schwenk, J., Stebila, D.: Multi-ciphersuite security of the Secure Shell (SSH) protocol. In: Ahn, G.J., Yung, M., Li, N. (eds.) ACM CCS 2014, pp. 369–381. ACM Press (2014)
14. Bhargavan, K., Brzuska, C., Fournet, C., Green, M., Kohlweiss, M., Zanella-Béguelin, S.: Downgrade resilience in key-exchange protocols. In: 2016 IEEE Symposium on Security and Privacy, pp. 506–525. IEEE Computer Society Press (2016)
15. Blake-Wilson, S., Menezes, A.: Entity authentication and authenticated key transport protocols employing asymmetric techniques. In: Christianson, B., Crispo, B., Lomas, M., Roe, M. (eds.) Security Protocols 1997. LNCS, vol. 1361, pp. 137–158. Springer, Heidelberg (1998). https://doi.org/10.1007/BFb0028166
16. Boyd, C., Cremers, C., Feltz, M., Paterson, K.G., Poettering, B., Stebila, D.: ASICS: authenticated key exchange security incorporating certification systems. In: Crampton, J., Jajodia, S., Mayes, K. (eds.) ESORICS 2013. LNCS, vol. 8134, pp. 381–399. Springer, Heidelberg (2013). https://doi.org/10.1007/978-3-642-40203-6_22
17. Boyd, C., Mathuria, A., Stebila, D.: Protocols for Authentication and Key Establishment. Information Security and Cryptography, 2nd edn. Springer, Heidelberg (2019). https://doi.org/10.1007/978-3-662-58146-9
18. Brzuska, C., Delignat-Lavaud, A., Fournet, C., Kohbrok, K., Kohlweiss, M.: State separation for code-based game-playing proofs. In: Peyrin, T., Galbraith, S. (eds.) ASIACRYPT 2018, Part III. LNCS, vol. 11274, pp. 222–249. Springer, Cham (2018). https://doi.org/10.1007/978-3-030-03332-3_9
19. Brzuska, C., Jacobsen, H.: A modular security analysis of EAP and IEEE 802.11. In: Fehr, S. (ed.) PKC 2017. LNCS, vol. 10175, pp. 335–365. Springer, Heidelberg (2017). https://doi.org/10.1007/978-3-662-54388-7_12
20. Brzuska, C.: On the foundations of key exchange. Ph.D. thesis, Darmstadt University of Technology, Germany (2013). http://tuprints.ulb.tu-darmstadt.de/3414/
21. Brzuska, C., Fischlin, M., Smart, N.P., Warinschi, B., Williams, S.C.: Less is more: relaxed yet composable security notions for key exchange. Int. J. Inf. Secur. 12(4), 267–297 (2013)
22. Brzuska, C., Fischlin, M., Warinschi, B., Williams, S.C.: Composability of Bellare-Rogaway key exchange protocols. In: Chen, Y., Danezis, G., Shmatikov, V. (eds.) ACM CCS 2011, pp. 51–62. ACM Press (2011)
23. Brzuska, C., Smart, N.P., Warinschi, B., Watson, G.J.: An analysis of the EMV channel establishment protocol. In: Sadeghi, A.R., Gligor, V.D., Yung, M. (eds.) ACM CCS 2013, pp. 373–386. ACM Press (2013)
24. Canetti, R., Krawczyk, H.: Analysis of key-exchange protocols and their use for building secure channels. In: Pfitzmann, B. (ed.) EUROCRYPT 2001. LNCS, vol. 2045, pp. 453–474. Springer, Heidelberg (2001). https://doi.org/10.1007/3-540-44987-6_28
25. Canetti, R., Krawczyk, H.: Security analysis of IKE's signature-based key-exchange protocol. In: Yung, M. (ed.) CRYPTO 2002. LNCS, vol. 2442, pp. 143–161. Springer, Heidelberg (2002). https://doi.org/10.1007/3-540-45708-9_10

26. Canetti, R., Krawczyk, H.: Universally composable notions of key exchange and secure channels. In: Knudsen, L.R. (ed.) EUROCRYPT 2002. LNCS, vol. 2332, pp. 337–351. Springer, Heidelberg (2002). https://doi.org/10.1007/3-540-46035-7_22

27. Chatterjee, S., Koblitz, N., Menezes, A., Sarkar, P.: Another look at tightness II: practical issues in cryptography. In: Phan, R.C.-W., Yung, M. (eds.) Mycrypt 2016. LNCS, vol. 10311, pp. 21–55. Springer, Cham (2017). https://doi.org/10.1007/978-3-319-61273-7_3

28. Chatterjee, S., Menezes, A., Sarkar, P.: Another look at tightness. In: Miri, A., Vaudenay, S. (eds.) SAC 2011. LNCS, vol. 7118, pp. 293–319. Springer, Heidelberg (2012). https://doi.org/10.1007/978-3-642-28496-0_18

29. Cohn-Gordon, K., Cremers, C., Gjøsteen, K., Jacobsen, H., Jager, T.: Highly efficient key exchange protocols with optimal tightness. In: Boldyreva, A., Micciancio, D. (eds.) CRYPTO 2019, Part III. LNCS, vol. 11694, pp. 767–797. Springer, Cham (2019). https://doi.org/10.1007/978-3-030-26954-8_25

30. Cohn-Gordon, K., Cremers, C.J.F., Garratt, L.: On post-compromise security. In: IEEE 29th Computer Security Foundations Symposium, CSF 2016, pp. 164–178. IEEE Computer Society (2016)

31. Cremers, C.: Examining indistinguishability-based security models for key exchange protocols: the case of CK, CK-HMQV, and eCK. In: Cheung, B.S.N., Hui, L.C.K., Sandhu, R.S., Wong, D.S. (eds.) ASIACCS 11, pp. 80–91. ACM Press (2011)

32. Cremers, C.J.F., Feltz, M.: Beyond eCK: perfect forward secrecy under actor compromise and ephemeral-key reveal. In: Foresti, S., Yung, M., Martinelli, F. (eds.) ESORICS 2012. LNCS, vol. 7459, pp. 734–751. Springer, Heidelberg (2012). https://doi.org/10.1007/978-3-642-33167-1_42

33. Dolev, D., Yao, A.C.: On the security of public key protocols. IEEE Trans. Inf. Theory 29(2), 198–207 (1983). https://doi.org/10.1109/TIT.1983.1056650

34. Dowling, B., Fischlin, M., Günther, F., Stebila, D.: A cryptographic analysis of the TLS 1.3 handshake protocol candidates. In: Ray, I., Li, N., Kruegel, C. (eds.) ACM CCS 2015, pp. 1197–1210. ACM Press (2015)

35. Dowling, B., Paterson, K.G.: A cryptographic analysis of the WireGuard protocol. In: Preneel, B., Vercauteren, F. (eds.) ACNS 18International Conference on Applied Cryptography and Network Security. LNCS, vol. 10892, pp. 3–21. Springer, Cham (2018). https://doi.org/10.1007/978-3-319-93387-0_1

36. Feltz, M., Cremers, C.: On the limits of authenticated key exchange security with an application to bad randomness. Cryptology ePrint Archive, Report 2014/369 (2014). https://eprint.iacr.org/2014/369

37. Feltz, M., Cremers, C.: Strengthening the security of authenticated key exchange against bad randomness. Des. Codes Cryptogr. 86(3), 481–516 (2018). https://doi.org/10.1007/s10623-017-0337-5

38. Fischlin, M., Günther, F.: Multi-stage key exchange and the case of Google's QUIC protocol. In: Ahn, G.J., Yung, M., Li, N. (eds.) ACM CCS 2014, pp. 1193–1204. ACM Press (2014)

39. Fischlin, M., Günther, F., Schmidt, B., Warinschi, B.: Key confirmation in key exchange: a formal treatment and implications for TLS 1.3. In: 2016 IEEE Symposium on Security and Privacy, pp. 452–469. IEEE Computer Society Press (2016)

40. Freire, E.S.V., Hofheinz, D., Kiltz, E., Paterson, K.G.: Non-interactive key exchange. In: Kurosawa, K., Hanaoka, G. (eds.) PKC 2013. LNCS, vol. 7778, pp. 254–271. Springer, Heidelberg (2013). https://doi.org/10.1007/978-3-642-36362-7_17

41. Gellert, K., Gjøsteen, K., Jacobsen, H., Jager, T.: On optimal tightness for key exchange with full forward secrecy via key confirmation. In: Handschuh, H., Lysyanskaya, A. (eds.) CRYPTO 2023, Part IV. LNCS, vol. 14084, pp. 297–329. Springer, Cham (2023). https://doi.org/10.1007/978-3-031-38551-3_10

42. George, W., Rackoff, C.: Rethinking definitions of security for session key agreement. Cryptology ePrint Archive, Report 2013/139 (2013). https://eprint.iacr.org/2013/139

43. Gjøsteen, K., Jager, T.: Practical and tightly-secure digital signatures and authenticated key exchange. In: Shacham, H., Boldyreva, A. (eds.) CRYPTO 2018, Part II. LNCS, vol. 10992, pp. 95–125. Springer, Cham (2018). https://doi.org/10.1007/978-3-319-96881-0_4

44. Han, S., Jager, T., Kiltz, E., Liu, S., Pan, J., Riepel, D., Schäge, S.: Authenticated key exchange and signatures with tight security in the standard model. In: Malkin, T., Peikert, C. (eds.) CRYPTO 2021, Part IV. LNCS, vol. 12828, pp. 670–700. Springer, Cham (2021). https://doi.org/10.1007/978-3-030-84259-8_23

45. Jager, T., Kohlar, F., Schäge, S., Schwenk, J.: On the security of TLS-DHE in the standard model. In: Safavi-Naini, R., Canetti, R. (eds.) CRYPTO 2012. LNCS, vol. 7417, pp. 273–293. Springer, Heidelberg (2012). https://doi.org/10.1007/978-3-642-32009-5_17

46. Jager, T., Stam, M., Stanley-Oakes, R., Warinschi, B.: Multi-key authenticated encryption with corruptions: reductions are lossy. In: Kalai, Y., Reyzin, L. (eds.) TCC 2017, Part I. LNCS, vol. 10677, pp. 409–441. Springer, Cham (2017). https://doi.org/10.1007/978-3-319-70500-2_14

47. Jeong, I.R., Katz, J., Lee, D.H.: One-round protocols for two-party authenticated key exchange. In: Jakobsson, M., Yung, M., Zhou, J. (eds.) ACNS 04International Conference on Applied Cryptography and Network Security. LNCS, vol. 3089, pp. 220–232. Springer, Heidelberg (2004). https://doi.org/10.1007/978-3-540-24852-1_16

48. Kobara, K., Shin, S., Strefler, M.: Partnership in key exchange protocols. In: Li, W., Susilo, W., Tupakula, U.K., Safavi-Naini, R., Varadharajan, V. (eds.) ASIACCS 2009, pp. 161–170. ACM Press (2009)

49. Krawczyk, H.: HMQV: a high-performance secure Diffie-Hellman protocol. In: Shoup, V. (ed.) CRYPTO 2005. LNCS, vol. 3621, pp. 546–566. Springer, Heidelberg (2005). https://doi.org/10.1007/11535218_33

50. Krawczyk, H.: Cryptographic extraction and key derivation: the HKDF scheme. In: Rabin, T. (ed.) CRYPTO 2010. LNCS, vol. 6223, pp. 631–648. Springer, Heidelberg (2010). https://doi.org/10.1007/978-3-642-14623-7_34

51. Krawczyk, H., Paterson, K.G., Wee, H.: On the security of the TLS protocol: a systematic analysis. In: Canetti, R., Garay, J.A. (eds.) CRYPTO 2013, Part I. LNCS, vol. 8042, pp. 429–448. Springer, Heidelberg (2013). https://doi.org/10.1007/978-3-642-40041-4_24

52. Kudla, C., Paterson, K.G.: Modular security proofs for key agreement protocols. In: Roy, B.K. (ed.) ASIACRYPT 2005. LNCS, vol. 3788, pp. 549–565. Springer, Heidelberg (2005). https://doi.org/10.1007/11593447_30

53. LaMacchia, B.A., Lauter, K., Mityagin, A.: Stronger security of authenticated key exchange. In: Susilo, W., Liu, J.K., Mu, Y. (eds.) ProvSec 2007. LNCS, vol. 4784, pp. 1–16. Springer, Heidelberg (2007). https://doi.org/10.1007/978-3-540-75670-5_1

54. Lauter, K., Mityagin, A.: Security analysis of KEA authenticated key exchange protocol. In: Yung, M., Dodis, Y., Kiayias, A., Malkin, T. (eds.) PKC 2006.

LNCS, vol. 3958, pp. 378–394. Springer, Heidelberg (2006). https://doi.org/10. 1007/11745853_25

55. Lee, J., Park, J.H.: Authenticated key exchange secure under the computational Diffie-Hellman assumption. Cryptology ePrint Archive, Report 2008/344 (2008). https://eprint.iacr.org/2008/344

56. Li, Y., Schäge, S.: No-match attacks and robust partnering definitions: Defining trivial attacks for security protocols is not trivial. In: Thuraisingham, B.M., Evans, D., Malkin, T., Xu, D. (eds.) ACM CCS 2017, pp. 1343–1360. ACM Press (2017)

57. Menezes, A., Ustaoglu, B.: Security arguments for the UM key agreement protocol in the NIST SP 800-56A standard. In: Abe, M., Gligor, V. (eds.) ASIACCS 2008, pp. 261–270. ACM Press (2008)

58. Pan, J., Qian, C., Ringerud, M.: Signed (group) Diffie-Hellman key exchange with tight security. J. Cryptol. **35**(4), 26 (2022)

59. Pan, J., Riepel, D., Zeng, R.: Key exchange with tight (full) forward secrecy via key confirmation. In: Joye, M., Leander, G. (eds.) EUROCRYPT 2024, Part VII. LNCS, vol. 14657, pp. 59–89. Springer, Cham (2024). https://doi.org/10.1007/978-3-031-58754-2_3

60. Pan, J., Wagner, B., Zeng, R.: Lattice-based authenticated key exchange with tight security. In: Handschuh, H., Lysyanskaya, A. (eds.) CRYPTO 2023, Part V. LNCS, vol. 14085, pp. 616–647. Springer, Cham (2023). https://doi.org/10.1007/978-3-031-38554-4_20

61. Pan, J., Wagner, B., Zeng, R.: Tighter security for generic authenticated key exchange in the QROM. In: Guo, J., Steinfeld, R. (eds.) ASIACRYPT 2023, Part IV. LNCS, vol. 14441, pp. 401–433. Springer, Singapore (2023). https://doi.org/10.1007/978-981-99-8730-6_13

62. Rogaway, P.: On the Role Definitions in and Beyond Cryptography. In: Maher, M.J. (ed.) ASIAN 2004. LNCS, vol. 3321, pp. 13–32. Springer, Heidelberg (2004). https://doi.org/10.1007/978-3-540-30502-6_2

63. Rogaway, P., Stegers, T.: Authentication without elision: partially specified protocols, associated data, and cryptographic models described by code. In: 22nd IEEE Computer Security Foundations Symposium, CSF 2009, pp. 26–39. IEEE Computer Society (2009)

64. Rogaway, P., Zhang, Y.: Simplifying game-based definitions - indistinguishability up to correctness and its application to stateful AE. In: Shacham, H., Boldyreva, A. (eds.) CRYPTO 2018, Part II. LNCS, vol. 10992, pp. 3–32. Springer, Cham (2018). https://doi.org/10.1007/978-3-319-96881-0_1

65. de Saint Guilhem, C.D., Fischlin, M., Warinschi, B.: Authentication in key-exchange: definitions, relations and composition. In: 33rd IEEE Computer Security Foundations Symposium, CSF 2020, pp. 288–303. IEEE Computer Society (2020)

66. Shoup, V., Rubin, A.D.: Session key distribution using smart cards. In: Maurer, U.M. (ed.) EUROCRYPT'96. LNCS, vol. 1070, pp. 321–331. Springer, Heidelberg (1996). https://doi.org/10.1007/3-540-68339-9_28

67. Skrobot, M., Lancrenon, J.: On composability of game-based password authenticated key exchange. In: 2018 IEEE European Symposium on Security and Privacy, EuroS&P 2018, pp. 443–457. IEEE (2018)

Socio-technical Aspects

Structuring the Chaos: Enabling Small Business Cyber-Security Risks & Assets Modelling with a UML Class Model

Tracy Tam[✉], Asha Rao, and Joanne Hall

RMIT University, 124 LaTrobe Street, Melbourne, Australia
tracy.tam@student.rmit.edu.au, {asha.rao,joanne.hall}@rmit.edu.au

Abstract. Small businesses around the world are increasingly adopting IT, thus increasing their exposure to malicious cyber activity. Small businesses struggle with implementing cyber-security, even when they are aware of the cyber-security risks around their business. Almost all modern cyber-security solutions are created and widely deployed in large enterprises. However there are fundamental differences between the characteristics of small businesses versus large ones.

Small businesses often do not have the technical expertise or the time to implement currently available cyber-security tools and standards. At the same time, cyber-security competes with other roles that small business owners take on, e.g. cleaning, sales etc. Hence, cyber security tools specific to small businesses are needed.

The most important task in cyber-security is knowing the assets that need protection, and their context. To support this information gathering phase of a small business' cyber-security journey, we propose a new UML class (Small IT Data (SITD)) model. The SITD model is designed in the UML format to ensure that it is implementable at scale. The model's structure stays relevant by using generic classes and structures that can evolve with technology and environmental changes. The SITD model keeps security decisions proportionate to the business by highlighting relationships between business strategy tasks and IT infrastructure. The SITD model's simplified non-specialist terminology and its presentation encourages sustained participation by all stakeholders, not just technical ones.

We start by constructing a set of design principles to address small business cyber-security needs. Model components are designed in response to these needs. The uses of the SITD model are then demonstrated and design principles validated by examining a case study of a real small business's operational and IT information. The SITD model's ability to illustrate breach information is also demonstrated using the NotPetya incident.

Keywords: UML Data Model · Small Business · Cyber-Security Analysis Tool

© The Author(s), under exclusive license to Springer Nature Switzerland AG 2025
C. Boyd et al. (Eds.): Ed Dawson Festschrift 2024, LNCS 15600, pp. 259–289, 2025.
https://doi.org/10.1007/978-3-031-83490-5_10

1   Introduction

Small business (0–19 employees [4]) plays a crucial role in the global economy, as measured by the number of small enterprises [20], employment statistics [10, 35] and other contributions [38,47]. The pandemic propelled small businesses globally into a new world driven by technology. Small business cyber-security has, thus, become a problem that can no longer be ignored. As the number of technically novice small businesses adopting technology (and the associated network connectivity) increases [17], so does the cyber attack surface [48] - for both the small business as well as the community. Getting small businesses to a cyber-security ready state has proved challenging, with many small business owners aware of the need for cyber-security but unsure of what to do [8,43].

Small business differs from larger enterprises in many ways, including communication style, financial resources, availability of internal expertise, and lack of immediate incentives [50]. Unlike larger enterprises, the majority of small businesses have little time and resources to study and manage IT and cyber-security. Small businesses with less than 5 employees make up nearly 90% of all businesses in Australia [11]. In these micro businesses, a business owner often takes on ancillary jobs such as cleaner, security guard and IT support, in addition to core business responsibilities. Cyber-security is only one of many competing priorities (e.g. generating sales, making products etc.) needed to keep the business alive.

Cyber-security analysis of a small business is often left up to individual implementers, using tools meant for large businesses while producing sub-optimal results for this resource-constrained cohort [50]. There is a need for an effective model to organise and analyse critical small business cyber-security information.

Cyber-security tools and processes lack focus on small business priorities and are not proportionate to the size of a small business. Fundamental to any new tools or processes is a consistent and enduring way of organising cyber-security information for subsequent analysis. Here, inspiration comes from IT where sorting and storing of information is often done via data models [28]. A data model foundation allows rapid deployment in various solution technology stacks for any potential small business security solutions.

This paper proposes a UML data model, the Small IT Data (SITD) model, and process to support the often overwhelming information-gathering phase of a small business' cyber-security journey. We first describe the rationale behind the new approach and model in Sect. 2. The target users of the model are outlined in Sect. 3. Section 4 describes the design principles. In Sect. 5, we justify the choice of UML as a modelling tool. The new class model and its components are introduced in Sect. 6, before validation via application to real-life small businesses (case study) in Sect. 7. The insights and analysis gained from the resulting models are discussed throughout. Section 8 discusses how the model aligns with the aims and design principles.

2   Problems with Existing Tools

Current cyber-security frameworks with infinite flexibility have not translated into widespread usage by small businesses [8]. Many existing cyber-security analyses and tools are designed with the flexibility to allow for use in any organisation. This flexibility requires inherent technical expertise to understand and apply appropriately. This expertise is not available within the small business space [50].

The following issues arise when a small business tries to use current tools:

- **Attack Based Lists** (e.g. OWASP [56], Mitre Att&ck [52]) – A business needs to navigate through a repository of attack techniques with no relation to business priorities. IT training is needed to understand the terminology used, as well as the implications and issues discussed.
- **Controls Based Lists** (e.g. CIS Controls [15], Essential 8 [9]) – Use of generic terms e.g. systems, applications, requires a small business to further investigate what the controls apply to. This risks some infrastructure, e.g. IoT devices, being left out altogether because they don't fall into an easily recognisable category.
- **Risk Management Based Standards** (e.g. ISO 27001 [45], NIST Cybersecurity Framework [33]) – These include broad statements that require interpretation of how controls and processes apply to a business. The results of this process often have technical consequences which are not obvious without technical training.

The vast majority of small businesses have no technical expertise [7]. With limited turnover and budget, the average small business cannot afford a cyber security professional [50]. As a non-revenue-generating task, cyber-security, in addition to needing to fit in between other business tasks in bite size amounts, needs to be understandable and usable by these non-technical small business decision makers.

Even basic advice, such as "use two factor authentication (2FA)", is not simple to implement. The business owner first needs to understand what systems and devices require 2FA, then comes the potentially overwhelming task of identifying compatible 2FA keys, determining backups and configuring compatible accounts etc. A more approachable tool, from both technical and investment perspectives, is needed to make cyber-security accessible for small businesses, making participation more attractive.

2.1   New Approach Needed

The lack of tailoring to small business undermines the effectiveness of any analytic tools or assistance. New approaches are needed to take into account the human aspects of small businesses [13,39,50]. Humans (employees and owner) are a critical part of cyber-security plans and posture [55]. When business grows, there may be resources to contract IT services. However, a good security strategy requires involvement from stakeholders at all levels in a business [51]. In particular, small business owner participation is critical in sole trader small businesses where IT is often internally managed [8].

Maintaining cyber-security ownership over the long term by a non-technical small business owner can be challenging when many cyber-security resources require some level of technical understanding. The majority of adults in developed countries do not have a high level of technical skills [36]. Expecting non-technical small business owners to gain the requisite cyber-security technical knowledge unassisted undermines a business' cyber-security self-efficacy. Lack of self-belief in the effectiveness of one's action can undermine the motivation to engage [27]. According to the EAST principle [42] of human behavioural insights (based on MINDSPACE framework [21]), making something easy also helps encourage the desired behaviour. Improving the overall ease of access for non-technical stakeholders can improve the outcome of a cyber-security solution by facilitating effective and ongoing participation.

To enable small business engagement with any new cyber-security tool, it is essential to redesign the underlying highly technical mental structure of cyber-security analysis. Any new approach has to address this gap by tailoring to small business operational and human characteristics. Essentially, a re-defining of the fundamental building blocks of how cyber-security is presented to small business is needed. Technology and cyber-risk-centric language, common in existing security frameworks, need to give way to concepts familiar to non-technical business owners.

Our new data model helps small businesses that need to undertake an initial cyber-security data gathering and analysis stage; a precursor to identifying, designing and implementing security controls. We recognised that the initial cyber-security step of recording the IT used in the business can require significant effort from small businesses, as this information is often not at the forefront of their mind [41], with many relying on informal communication [46].

In [49] we proposed an interim reusable small business cyber-security self-serve tool based on the data structures of 2 existing security processes. However, the system proposed in [49] relied on existing cyber-security structures from a cyber-security professional's perspective, which is different from that of small business owners [50]. This gap potentially undermines the ability of small business owners to independently undertake, and stay engaged with over time, cyber-security analysis. Building on the small business insights discussed above, we propose a new class model (referred to as Small IT Data (SITD) model) to extract and record small business cyber-security relevant information. This class model supports the small business self-driven cyber-security analysis process by being accessible to non-experts, and includes both technical and non-technical information.

For a small business operator, the SITD model acts as an additional guardrail to any existing cyber-security framework to document IT details. The SITD model eases cognitive load by guiding the information gathering from areas of familiarity, e.g. day-to-day tasks, before tying it back to cyber-security.

3   Target Users and Businesses of SITD Model

At a technical level, the SITD model serves as the data foundation for future small business cyber-security analysis tools and processes. There are 2 primary target stakeholders for the SITD model: the small businesses to be protected, and the cyber-professionals implementing cyber-security tools to be used by the small business.

3.1   Target Modelled Businesses

The SITD model is designed to model small businesses with 0–19 employees [4], in order to protect them. (Sole traders/single person companies are considered to have 0 employees.) In addition, our research is focused on a "most-needed" basis - businesses who do not know how to implement even with the best intentions. Thus, one exclusion to this broad scope is small businesses that offer IT-centric services and products, as they are likely to have the technical skills to use existing tools and additional security considerations (e.g. DevSecOps [29]).

3.2   Target Data Structure Users

The SITD model is created for modelling non-technical small businesses. The large number of small businesses means small business cyber-security tools need to be deployable at-scale. Technology will likely play a vital role in the tool's dissemination. Consequently, the SITD model needs to provide a structure easily implementable using technology. Hence, the more immediate users of the SITD data model are likely to be prospective cyber-security tool developers or professionals looking for a common way to structure information in a quest to protect small businesses.

The SITD model gives developers and professionals the data foundation for future security tools with a small business-centric approach. The model will help solution implementers to move away from the traditional cyber-security and technology centric approaches.

4   Model Design Principles

In addition to the small business and developer characteristics discussed in Sect. 3, the SITD model is designed with the following guiding principles to facilitate small business applications.

4.1   Focus on Business Priorities

The SITD model needs to start from the perspective of business goals, the job tasks supporting these goals, and the IT tools needed to support these job tasks. The goal of cyber-security is to facilitate secure business use of IT. To be used, IT needs to deliver value to the business. In small businesses, IT tools are often chosen because the IT solution is more convenient or efficient than its manual counterpart (e.g. digital spreadsheet for sales recording).

The re-focus towards business priorities also serves as a reminder that the business value of the IT tool needs to be preserved, even after securing it. However, business value cannot be judged from a technology-centric view alone. Another important consideration is ensuring incident response and recovery are business goals.

4.2 Capture Intangible Factors and Relationships

The SITD model needs to illustrate relationships between physical and intangible components.

Past cyber-security incidents and attack techniques have involved many factors ranging from technology and operations to people [23,25]. Social engineering attacks illustrate the need for technology to work with the less tangible aspects of an organisation such as human behaviour. The SITD model needs to capture the impacts of the non-tangible factors on the overall posture of a business, e.g. being in a highly competitive field (industrial espionage), or having disgruntled employees.

The documentation of physical and intangible factors provides opportunities for using the defence in depth security strategy [34]. This strategy allows smaller tools/solutions to be combined to form better overall security postures. The ability to combine smaller controls is advantageous to small business due to their resource constraints [50], which makes them unlikely to be able to afford large ready-made cyber-security solutions.

4.3 Allow for Incomplete Information

The threat landscape is ever-evolving [1,18] and cyber-security is never 'finalised'. Hence, the SITD model needs to support cyber-security as a continuous improvement process along with the need for it to function even in an incomplete state. In addition, businesses, particularly those in a startup phase (especially small businesses) often change on a day to day basis. As such, tools expecting linear progression or completion (e.g. waterfall methodologies) are not practicable from either a logistics or ongoing relevance perspective. Therefore, the SITD model needs to view incomplete information as an opportunity for further discussion and exploration, rather than a roadblock.

4.4 Agnostic

For maintainability into the future the SITD model should be agnostic with regards to several factors:

1. **Language** – Cyber-security crosses international borders: many cyber-crimes have transnational elements [54]. Minimising textual information provides

room for visual representations. A combination of textual and visual information has been shown to increase understanding [2] and recall [14]. Where possible the SITD model needs to prioritise visual cues over words.

2. **Technology** – Where applicable the SITD model needs to be technology agnostic to ensure continued relevance as technology or attack techniques evolve. The SITD model needs to serve as a record of the ongoing relevance of IT to the small business, and not as a static picture.

3. **Standards, Legislation and Industry** – A mobile phone used in a food service business essentially has the same technical vulnerabilities as the same one in a legal practice. However, the context of supported business goals sets these 2 phones apart as do the ramifications if the phones are breached or lost. Rather than specifically including locale-specific conditions such as HIPAA, GDPR, Reportable Breach scheme etc., the SITD model needs to capture local context and legal requirements in the business part of the model, e.g. job function, tasks, strategies.

4.5   Enable Cyber-Security Analysis

Ultimately the SITD model should aim to capture sufficient information about the small business to enable further risk analysis and discussions. Most cyber-security standards [32] emphasise the need for IT inventory recording. The SITD record, especially when linked to its users, needs to serves as input to allow planning of further security steps for the business.

The SITD model needs to capture sufficient detail to facilitate cyber-security risk analysis, including risk mitigation planning and incident analysis.

5   Choice of Modelling Tool

Our choice of the SITD model tool is driven by the needs of potential implementers of small business cyber-security solutions – IT developers and cyber-security professionals, for reasons discussed in Sect. 3.2.

Hence we focus on data model formats common within the IT industry. The following candidate approaches were identified and evaluated:

- Spreadsheets/Data Tables with New Relationship Standard.
- Entity Relationship Diagram (ERD) [16].
- Unified Modelling Language (UML) [26].

The spreadsheets/data approach is unsuitable due to lack of a standardised way for entities and relationships to be modelled in cyber-security. The table approach requires creation of a new ecosystem: with new rules needing to be created, tested and maintained. Any new relationship standard only serves to add complexity within a field already overflowing with information. Thus, UML and ERD are the options that remains.

5.1   Advantages of UML

While small business IT can technically be modelled within both ERD and UML, UML is more suitable for the following reasons:

- **Holistic nature of the UML ecosystem** – UML encompasses technical and non-technical aspects. This aligns with the aim of describing structural, intangible and dynamic aspects of small business cyber-security. For future work, UML can inherently model behaviour, business processes, timing, actions etc.
- **UML allows for different perspectives** – UML natively recognises that the same piece of data can be viewed from different perspectives (or 'views'). For example, customer information is a piece of data inside a business database, but UML can recognise that it is used by staff when a customer enquires about their account. Given that the SITD model is concerned with cyber-security in both the data itself as well as transitory events on the data, UML's view better aligns with our aims.
- **UML can be converted into ERD** – A UML class diagram can be converted to ERD, making reversion to ERD possible in the future.
- **Slimline presentation of information** – UML allows for attributes and operations to be applied to individual entities. A similar entity within ERD requires multiple objects making the entity more complex in visual appearance.
- **Use of UML within the industry** – UML has been adopted widely into the IT and business worlds, where it can be used to describe whole ecosystems of software, hardware, processes and actors involved. This focus is important given the potential developers of future small business security solutions.

In conclusion, UML design philosophy is better aligned with the SITD model goals and the possible future extensibility of small business cyber-security.

6   The SITD Model

In this section, we present details of each sub-part of the SITD model, before linking the parts together into an overall structure. Real life business operations and IT architectures are then used to illustrate the model's use. The SITD model centers on the business and branches out to the connected IT infrastructure.

The SITD model relies heavily on the class and object diagrams within UML. These diagrams operate on the concept of class and associations between these classes. All other details are defined within this construct. For a quick start guide on reading UML models and conventions, please see Appendix.

6.1   The SITD Model Classes

The classes in the SITD model reflect important small business and cyber-security entities, and as such are not restricted to physical entities. Table 1 identifies critical concepts which are treated as classes in the SITD model.

Table 1. Class areas (discussed in Sect. 6.1) covered as part of the SITD model's aim of capturing cyber and business salient information.

Class Areas	Examples
Business entity	Doe's Gardening Service
Human/group actors	Owner; Employees
Job tasks & roles	Payroll Processing; Manufacturing
Physical location	Office; Client Site
Selected hardware & software details	Mobile Phone; CAD
Remote/cloud IT systems	Client IT Systems; Cloud Data Storage
Data/information	Customer Data; Audit Records
Motivations and strategies	Stay in Business; Lifestyle; Product Quality

Note: Some concepts, described in multiple classes within IT architecture design and modelling conventions, have been simplified into a single construct. The reasons and implications are discussed in each part below. Associations (used to describe class relationships between 2 classes) contain additional information, including relationship multiplicity as well as direction. These are noted in standard UML notations.

In the next four subsections, we will look at sub-components of the SITD model. Section 6.6 connects the sub-models back into the overall model structure.

6.2   SITD Submodel: Business

To ensure security decisions are relevant and proportional, the business is central to the SITD model. The *Business Strategy* of the SITD model (Fig. 1) captures the fundamental relationships between the business, its aims and the people working in it.

The base class is centred on the business entity being protected, i.e. the business itself. Basic details of the business are captured within the attributes. The business' maturity stage and strategy [30], which affects its behaviour profile [41], are recorded for influence on business activities. The derived characteristics are placed into 3 broad categories, *Entrepreneurial, Administrative* and *Engineering*, which are then linked to individual day-to-day tasks. Entrepreneurial characteristics capture any growth ambitions e.g. partnerships, branding, while Engineering characteristics describe operational matters e.g. factory building. Administrative characteristics keep the business running, e.g. business registration, tax management, legal compliance. (For businesses with narrow business goals, the characteristics and job tasks can be combined into a single layer to streamline the SITD model.)

This view of the SITD model highlights that without the business reasons stemming from the business strategy (e.g. keeping the business alive), the tasks would not be done.

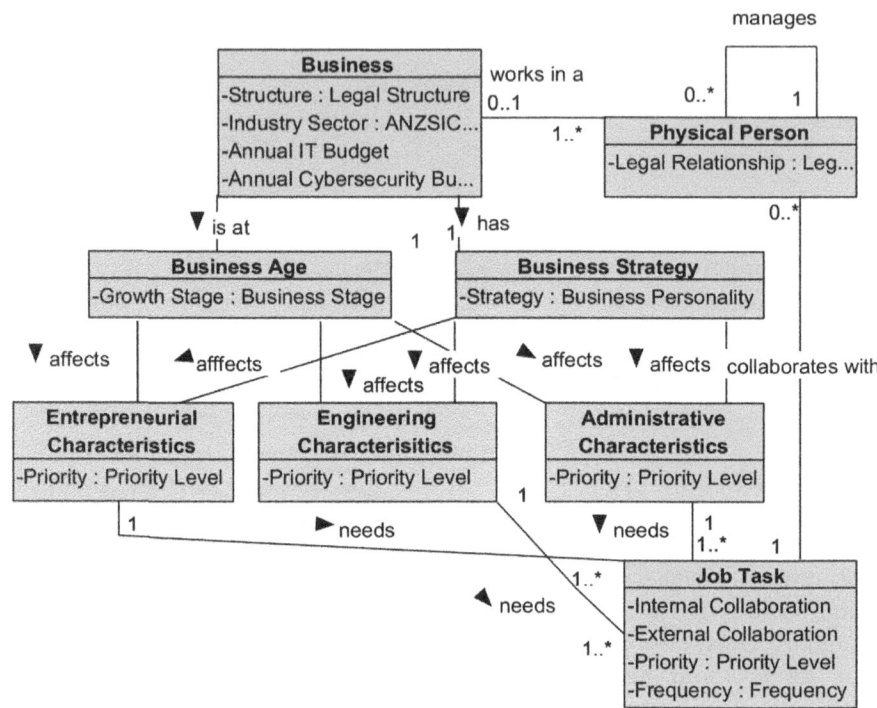

Fig. 1. UML class structure diagram showing the connections between different parts of the business. (Described in Sect. 6.2.)

The number of physical persons (and management hierarchy) working within a business is also recorded, since business is a human endeavour. In a small business, the distinction of physical people is important given the manual (and often ad hoc) processes that exist [30]. Adoption of multiple roles by small business employees leads to informal and less defined communications and processes than those in larger corporations. Since human communication forms the basis of many social engineering attacks [31], the number of employees is an important part of cyber-security strategies.

6.3   SITD Submodel: Job Function

The *Job Function* part of the SITD model describes the links between job tasks and the roles performing the tasks (Fig. 2).

The job tasks described as part of business goals are linked to the human responsible for the task. The task is performed in the context of the person's job role. The SITD model allows for more than one person to work on the same task using a collaboration link in the context of different roles (e.g. business plans being completed in collaboration between the owner and accountant).

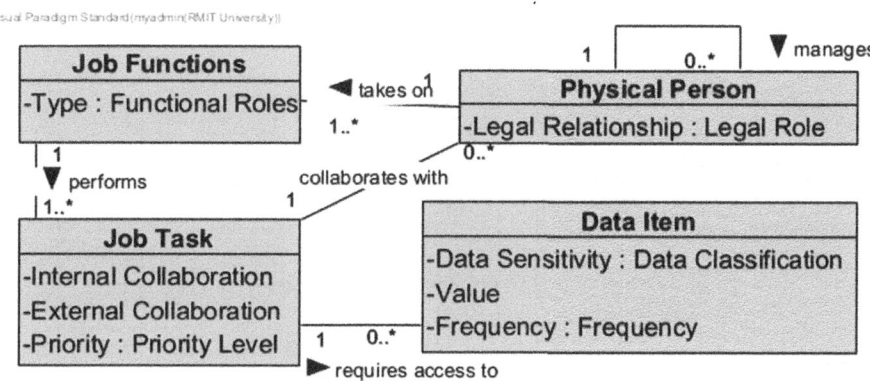

Fig. 2. The UML class structure diagram showing how job functions lead to people working together and hence needing access to specific data within the business. (Details in Sect. 6.3.)

Conversely, multiple physical people can work on the same job task via the same function roles (e.g. multiple sales assistants in a retail shop). This model allows for the same physical person to take on multiple job functions, as is common in micro-enterprises where the owner can also be the security, janitor and website administrator. In early analysis, the function role can be synonymous with a physical person; role information can be added after further analysis. This is particularly useful in sole trader/micro-companies where roles are not formally assigned or defined.

The job function model links job tasks to the data item(s) needed to perform the tasks. Every business task requires some sort of data item to be used, whether it is the product price in a sales transaction, a recipe within a manufacturing plant, or lesson plans within an education setting. Data is considered at a more fundamental level than just the electronic storage of the information.

6.4   SITD Submodel: IT Interaction

We now link data to the IT systems used to store and use this data (Fig. 3). The SITD model only includes any data stored electronically. It is assumed that any physical data stored is handled according to the existing risk management plan and outside the scope of cyber-security. Despite the SITD model's electronic focus, ISO27001 [45] does include physical access as part of risk management. Hence, any system implementing the SITD model needs to include reminders that physical security is still required.

As illustrated in Fig. 3, data items in SITD model must be stored within a destination (target) system. This is intended to be a generic container that records details of where the data is stored. The target system can range from a local drive on a laptop/phone to cloud services or records held by another business/entity. The details of the service and location are captured in the classes

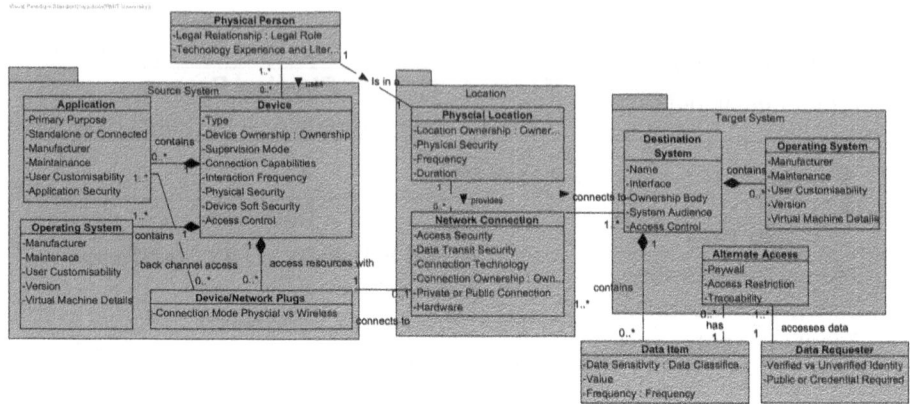

Fig. 3. UML class structure diagram showing how a person accesses specific data in target systems using their devices and network connection. (Discussed in Sect. 6.4.)

associated with the data. We recognise that data (class Alternate Access) can be retrieved by another party off the same system, e.g. business registration details can be requested by a member of the public using the registration body website. The target system classes are deliberately light on technical detail to reflect the reality that most small businesses have limited influence on the technical details of electronic data storage. For example, hosted websites only allow limited customisation from a look and feel perspective, webmail providers dictate the login process and whether multi-factor authentication mechanisms are offered, retail hardware/software manufacturers decide whether memory is encrypted by default etc.

On a physical front, the SITD model links the access to the data via a physical location (through a network connection) and device, and ultimately to a physical person. The link highlights that physical access to this device-connection pipeline plays an important part in the security posture. For example, if someone has physical access to a Wi-Fi router, then no matter how secure the target system or device, the risk of a man in the middle attack increases. This Location-Network Connection class pairing accounts for data in transit scenarios within a business, including locations outside the primary location of business.

At a physical device level, the classes are simplified from a technical viewpoint e.g. the OSI 7 layer model [19], to capture only applications, operating system (OS) and network connector classes - components the business worker interacts with. This is to ensure focus stays on the components under the worker's control on a day to day basis. An application is any software program that the business uses on a physical device, ranging from productivity suites such as Microsoft Office to browsers for access to cloud services/web pages. While the simplification does make technical vulnerability analysis more difficult, most vulnerability notifications, common vulnerabilities & exploits, as well as vendor notifications today relate impacts to applications and/or operating systems [53].

In its current version, the SITD model does not consider system to system IT events e.g. batch jobs, scheduled events. The SITD model's target audience are non-technical small businesses; the utilisation of automated events is minimal [5].

6.5 SITD Submodel: Threats

Finally, to illustrate deviations in risk between different industries and businesses, a threat model is included in the SITD model to describe any specific or general threat to the business. This section again focuses on human threat actors rather than the technical threat. Removing human motivation eliminates many reasons for exploiting a vulnerable system. This human threat actor class can describe single actors e.g. an industry competitor, or groups e.g. Advanced Persistent Threat (APT)/nation state actors.

Figure 4 illustrates the various factors of a threat. Threats are underpinned by the motivation and resources available to the threat actor (SITD model links these 2 classes to the actor class via relationships). The resource factor influences whether a threat is persistent or incidental. The motivation is directed towards a business, data item in a business or a physical person. Note that in SITD there are no restrictions on whether a data item or person strictly belongs to a small business, but rather it is the incidental relationship of the item or person to a small business that is important (e.g. where a target person's personal data maybe stored on a small business systems as a supplier.)

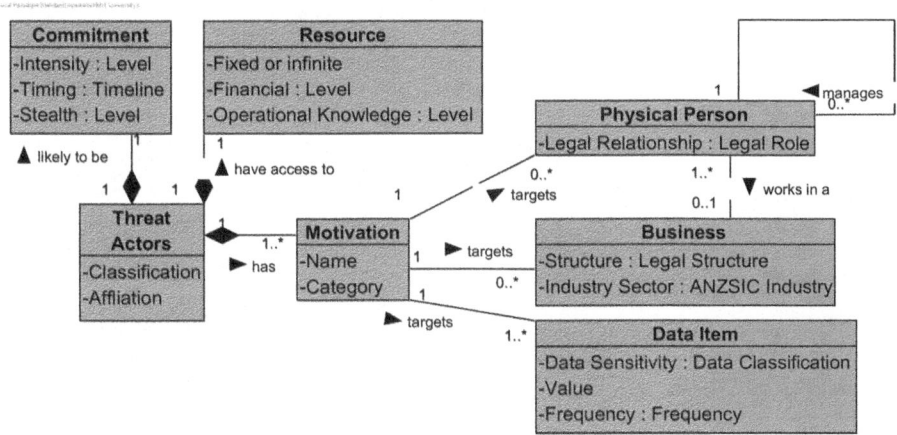

Fig. 4. UML class structure diagram showing how certain threat motivations can mean specific data (and IT system by association) can require more attention. (Discussed in Sect. 6.5.)

The majority of small businesses, before having a cyber-incident, do not perceive cyber incidents as likely [8]. The threat model is important to document motivations, especially in specialised industries (e.g. defence contractors, fiercely competitive market conditions etc.). The threat model highlights any part of the business that may require a higher level of priority to help assess adequate level of investment.

6.6 Overall SITD Model

Each subpart of the SITD model described in Sects. 6.2–6.5 can be used independently. However, when linked together with common classes, the model creates a picture of the interrelations between IT and business goals (Fig. 5). Based on the linked business goal, the business can prioritise the parts of IT needing attention from a cyber-security perspective.

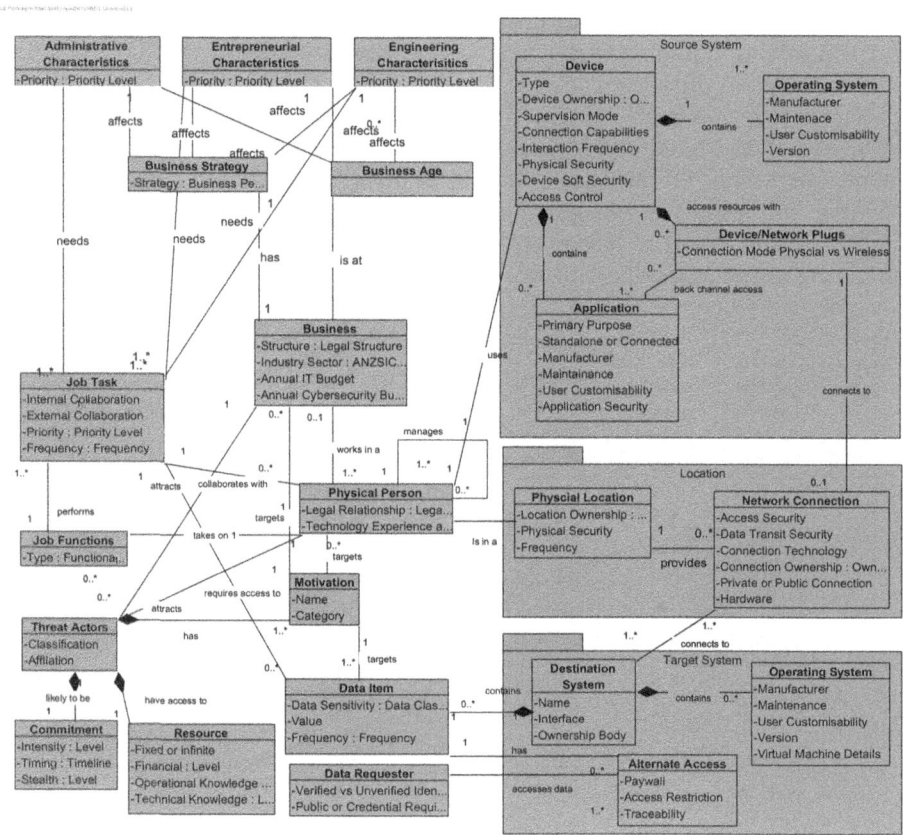

Fig. 5. UML class overview showing the relationships between various factors within a (sample) small businesses' overall cyber-security posture, discussed in Sect. 6.6.

From an analysis perspective, the relationships show how unconnected parts of the business can lead to an asset needing protection from motivated actors.

Our proposed class and relationship model highlights gaps without impeding progress. It allows for partial data to be used to trigger investigation and further discussions.

7   Applications of SITD Model

We now demonstrate the use of the SITD model by modelling a case study business. Business operation modelling of cyber-security relevant concerns is done using source data from a non-cyber-security small business case study[1] to emulate a small business owner's point of view. Technical modelling is sourced from a UK small scale IT architecture case study [37], that included small business participants. Finally, we utilise a NotPetya breach analysis to illustrate the SITD model use in incident analysis.

7.1   Modelling Business Point of View

An academic case study of an agricultural small business is used to demonstrate the SITD model. The case study was originally constructed to illustrate quality control considerations and includes details of business tasks. The small business is in the agriculture industry and manufactures products from the main crop. A labour study of another comparable region in the same country indicates that similar businesses of the same size as the agriculture business tend to operate on 1.5 FTEs (Full Time Equivalent) staff throughout the year. Seasonal workers are brought in for harvesting. For this analysis, the seasonal workers were not counted towards the employee count as they are contracted for a specific manual task (harvesting) and are unlikely to have much interaction with the business's IT infrastructure.

Entering Data Into the Model. Using NVivo software, the information for the business operation from the case study was coded to the SITD model's classes. When a piece of pertinent information (e.g. job task, person or piece of data) is discussed, it is marked with NVivo code tags of the relevant class together with a unique label (Tag of "Job Task: Harvest" is tagged in the text when harvest is mentioned). Each code tag corresponds to a single object in the object diagram (even if it is referenced/tagged multiple times). This resulted in 31 codes/objects being generated across Business, Persons, Location, Job Task and Entrepreneurial Characteristics. Two codes (Destination: Email Host and Product Competition Organiser) were reclassified to Destination System after subsequent public information research. Product Import Data was recoded to Destination System: Email Host from Data Item because the international

---

[1] As the business is currently operating, all identifying information of the small business, individuals, specific products and locations are redacted in the public version of this article to protect their privacy, including citations. Original information and citations were provided for review purposes.

product importation process relies on email. Product Competition Organiser was also given a Destination System class as some of the competitions listed in the case study allow for complete online applications.

The objects were initially placed in proximity to other instances of the same class, e.g. job tasks near other job tasks. The case study was then examined again for the relationship between objects. These relationships are drawn directly in the object diagram.

Analysing the Result. The processing of the agriculture small business case study produced Fig. 6.

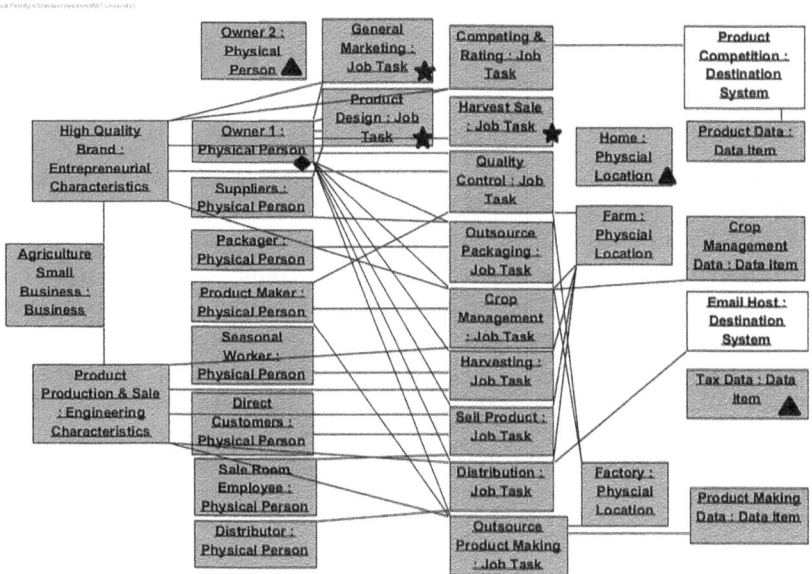

Fig. 6. Agriculture small business case study result as depicted by the SITD model. The reclassified items, Product Competition and Email Host destination systems, are unshaded. Areas of possible investigation and discussion are marked with added symbols. Discussion in Sect. Analysing the Result.

Based on Fig. 6, the following areas of hyper or lack of connectivity need discussion from a cyber-security perspective:

1. **Critical Point of Failure** - Owner 1 (marked with a diamond ◆ in Fig. 6) is involved in the majority of the tasks required to keep the small business running. Any device or system Owner 1 relies on is critical to the smooth running of the business, e.g. mobile phone, laptop or cloud services. Further examination and discussion of additional security controls, such as anti-virus and backups, needs to happen to ensure availability of their devices and systems. Owner 1 may need additional training to prevent phishing [57].

2. **Orphaned Components** - There are location (Home), person (Owner 2) and data (Tax Data) items (marked with a triangle ▲ in Fig. 6) noted in the business, but the information in the case study does not indicate relationships between these and other components.
3. **Tasks with No Details** - There are several tasks: Harvest Sale, General Marketing and Product Design, identified (marked with a star ★ in Fig. 6), noted in the case study in general, but with no information given regarding the tools/devices needed to perform them. Most tasks need information, so further exploration is required on whether there are dependencies on IT.

The lack of information in parts of Fig. 6 alone is not treated as a point of concern within the SITD model process. It is an expected by-product of the focus of small business owners, viz to keep business activities running. The purpose of this model is to help obtain the relevant details needed from a cyber-security perspective.

Task-Based Analysis. The SITD model facilitates a job task-oriented approach where each job task is laid out. From the case study, the job task of crop management is illustrated in Fig. 7 which covers looking after the crops and managing harvest time. The figure shows how issues with any elements (e.g. loss of crop management data) can ripple through the rest of the small business.

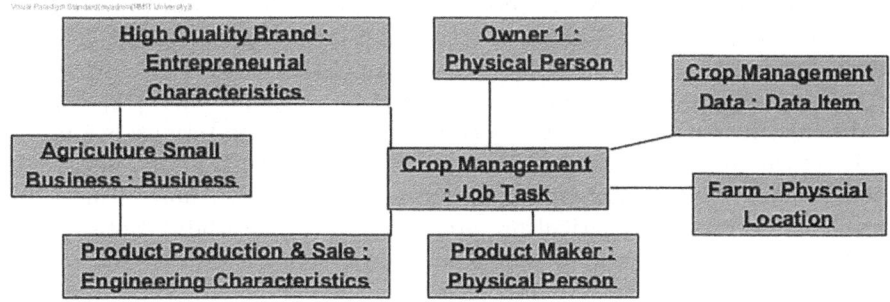

Fig. 7. Elements involved in agricultural small business crop management based on information available in the case study [37]. Discussion in Sect. Task-Based Analysis.

The case study information is inserted into the SITD model structure in Fig. 8.

The unshaded elements in Fig. 8 indicate missing information that needs further exploration in the cyber-security analysis. In the case study, crop management decisions are dependent on data like crop ripeness. Storage, management and access of data is not specified in the case study. Further information around the devices and data storage needs to be clarified. By moving through each job task, missing cyber-security context information can be further fleshed out by the cyber-security tool/professional. This information will inform further cyber-security analysis and risk mitigation.

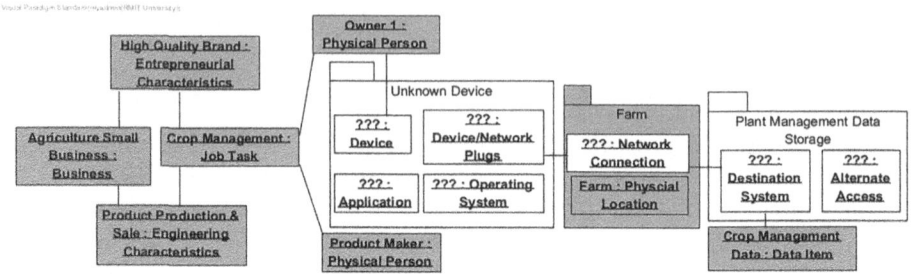

Fig. 8. Known elements from the agricultural small business crop management discovery are shaded in blue in the SITD model. Areas for discussion are unshaded. Discussion in Sect. Task-Based Analysis.

The left side of Fig. 8 clearly links the key reasons for the business to protect crop management data with the core task of crop management. This relationship information keeps at the forefront the business value protected by any potential security control. A discussion around protection of crop management data is needed as it enables the business to maintain a high-quality brand (by timing the harvest) and supports production. The context helps stakeholders assign the right level of resources and importance.

Change in Operating Environment. We now demonstrate the SITD model's ability to handle external changes to a small business, with the example of legislative change in the introduction of Australian Goods and Service Tax (GST). GST is a percentage tax that merchants collect on consumer sales [12]. The collected tax is then passed on to the government in Business Activity Statements (BAS) returns to the Australian Taxation Office (ATO). Initially, most international sellers were exempt from collection due to the low value of individual orders (such as processed agriculture products in the case study). Subsequently international merchants who achieve a substantial amount of low value sales to Australian customers [12] were also included. The GST collection requirement applies to our case study business.

To comply with the GST rule using guidance from ATO [12], the SITD model is expanded with the following class instances which were not in the case study:

- ABN: Data Item (Australian Business Number)
- Australian GST Collected: Data Item
- Lodge Tax/BAS Return: Job Task
- Pay GST: Job Task
- Customs Information: Data Item
- Customer Invoice: Data Item
- ATO: Destination System

In addition, the following existing instances are modified:

- Sell Processed Product: Job Task – Link to additional instances to comply with GST requirements.

– Production & Sale: Engineering Characteristics – Link to the need to lodge additional tax (BAS) returns to the ATO, and the payment of the GST collected using data collected during sales process.

The SITD model resulting from the external GST change is illustrated in Fig. 9, with the added instances highlighted in yellow. Note that the SITD structure does not change fundamentally despite the change in legislative environments. The SITD model is designed such that changes to specific environment factors can be handled within the confines of existing SITD model structure and items.

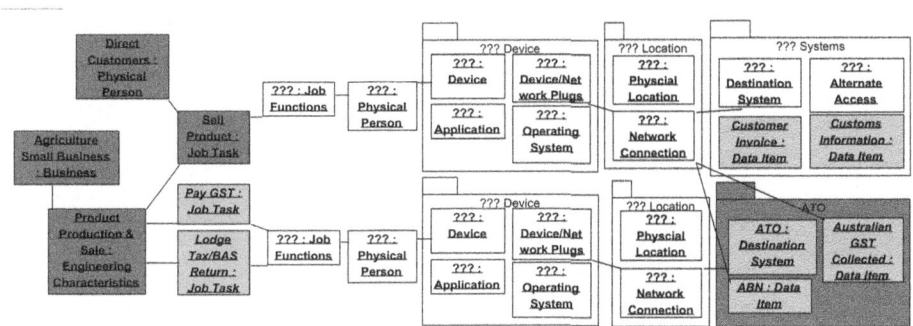

Fig. 9. GST introduction for Australian customers resulted in additional instances and links in the small business SITD model, highlighted in yellow and italic font. Missing security components are indicated by non-shaded boxes, denoting areas for further exploration to protect the product production business value. Discussion in Sect. Change in Operating Environment. (Color figure online)

Using the SITD model structure, the missing instances in Fig. 9 show up as unshaded items. These instances highlight the impact that the change has on the business in terms of cyber-security. In this GST example, the SITD diagram shows that the business needs to clarify the channels (technology, job function and person) through which the required information and tasks flow. As such, to ensure continued compliance to the product production and sale, these tools need to be protected in proportion to the business value brought by production.

7.2 Modelling IT Information

The case study used in Sect. 7.1 was written from a business operations point of view, and contains little technical information. To emulate, in general, what technical information may be discovered in a small business, we now leverage the small scale IT architectures found in the UK [37]. To be consistent with the previous business operation example of 2 FTE operators, we focus on the micro-companies (1–8 employees) described in the UK study. Figure 10 gives the overall picture.

Following the process used in the business operations analysis (Sect. 7.1), components described in the article [37] were assigned to the corresponding SITD classes (e.g. laptop/PC/phone to device class, internet to network connection). Any connected classes, according to the SITD model, to the article-identified components that were not discussed in the article were highlighted as missing information in the (unshaded) SITD structure.

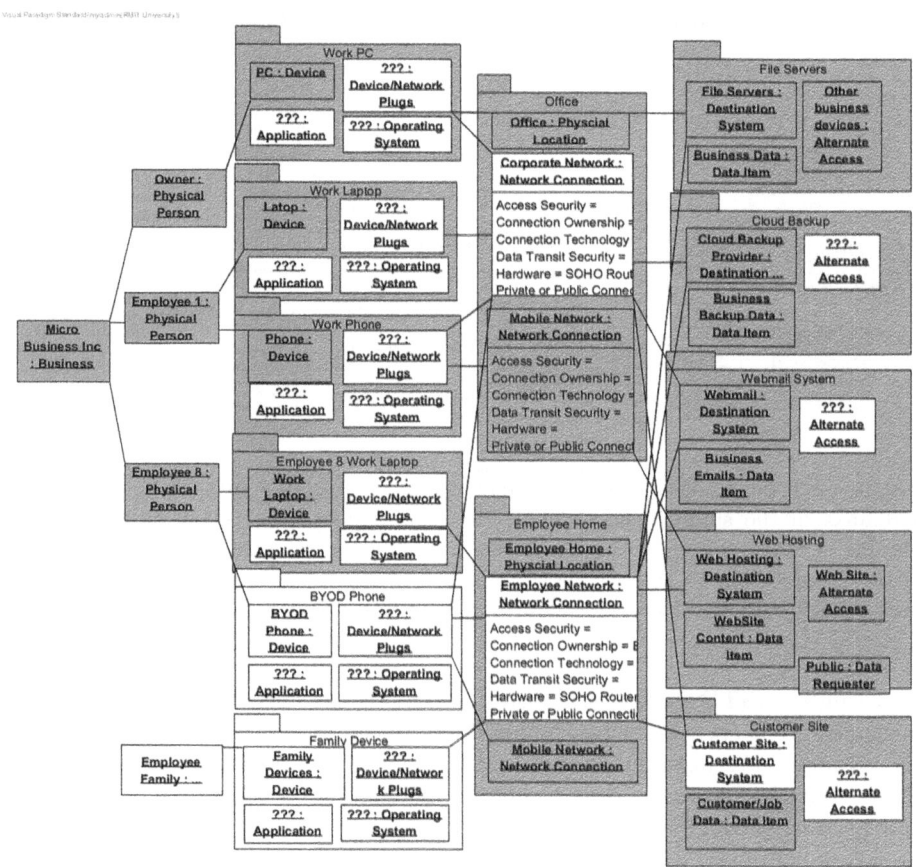

Fig. 10. Model depicting micro company (1–8 employees) architecture. Areas highlighted in blue define components discovered by the case study [37]. Any missing information/areas of concern are left unshaded. Discussion in Sect. Modelling IT Information. (Color figure online)

In Fig. 10, relationships have been assumed to facilitate ease of reading. The relationships between individual employees and their devices, while hard to present in a single page pictorially, can be stored in a data repository easily.

When the typical micro-company case study architecture is mapped onto the structure of the SITD model, the following topics are highlighted from a cyber-security perspective:

1. **Alternative Access Missing for Cloud Backup and Webmail** – Cloud backup and webmail are not mentioned in the case study [37]. The business's understanding of the configuration and the ways both systems allow third party access to the business data needs to be evaluated. The discussion needs to be from both technical (e.g. login security, sharing settings) as well as business process (e.g. terms and conditions, privacy policies) perspectives. The importance of understanding both technical and process aspects is demonstrated in past breaches of misconfigured Amazon S3 buckets [58] and Zoombombing attacks [25].

2. **Unknown device applications and operating systems** - A discussion around operating systems in use prompts thoughts around the level of support and processes needed to secure these environments. For example, updating an Android phone and applications is a different process to updating iOS phones. The architecture states that devices are used by both business and personal users. This raises a number of questions. Does the mixed use extend to applications? Are there any applications that are shared with personal use or of untrusted origins? Such cyber hygiene matters are often covered in acceptable use policies in larger enterprises [15] and need to be addressed in small businesses.

3. **Sharing the Network** – The mixed uses of networks are depicted in both the network connection as well as family members sharing that connection. The blending of personal and business use is often not addressed explicitly in cyber-analysis today. Ideal control conditions explicitly discourage shared network outside the business, which is unrealistic in a small business. By recognising a blended scenario, discussion can be held around mitigations based on the situation of the small business worker and sharer.

4. **Mobile Network** – A phone necessitates a mobile network connection. Most modern phone plans include mobile data. From the case study information, it is unclear whether this network is being used to access the business target systems. Given this network has potential as a backup data connection in the case of an incident, the mitigation strategy plan can involve the owner-operator being trained on use of mobile data to ensure business continuity.

5. **BYOD Device** – Workers are permitted to use their own devices and network connections to access business systems. Hence data transit security is another area of concern. Given that both data transit and devices are not under the small business control, measures may be warranted to secure data depending upon its sensitivity.

6. **Target Systems Security** - Given the increase in devices connected to corporate systems, the issue of lateral movement during an incident becomes much more prominent. The breach at a target system (e.g. a cloud provider) can potentially result in a higher impact as attackers can move sideways and onto other devices. A business needs to understand the nature of the connection to each site/system. This can be strengthened by exploring procedural or

technical safeguards that can be applied. The fallout of supply chain incidents were made clear with past examples such as NotPetya [23].

7. **Customer Site** - Small Office/Home Office ("SOHO") routers are not typically known for VPN, so in this scenario of connecting to customer site, any work from home employees are most likely connecting via their home network to the customer site. Clarification around any commercial and security implications around this data transit path is needed. From a commercial perspective, business needs to understand whether this path contravenes terms of agreement with customer. Alternatively from a technical mitigation perspective, whether VPN can be set up via the existing corporate network routers can influence risk management decisions.

7.3   Modelling Breach Information

To illustrate the use of the SITD model for incident analysis purposes, Maersk's experience from the NotPetya event is modelled within the SITD model structure, despite Maersk not being a small business. Breach information from small business is not well known due to a range of social and psychological reasons [50]. The NotPetya incident from Maersk's experience is chosen for the following similarities to small business characteristics:

– Maersk was "collateral damage" [59] of a wider state attack – Small businesses generally, especially micro-businesses, have insufficient resources (financial, intellectual property & data) to motivate targeted attacks. Most incidents are likely to be underpinned by an opportunistic element.
– The attack came from a Maersk's supplier – Maersk was compelled to use M.E.Doc accounting software to comply with Urkranian accounting norms [22,23]. This is reflected in small businesses often having very little negotiation power against, or sometimes in the choice of, their IT supplier relationships.
– Maersk uses IT to support the core business activity of logistics – Most small businesses are not technical [6] and employ IT as a tool to increase productivity. IT is a support function, not their core business.

The incident's information was collated using public reports of the incident [22–24], statements from Maersk's chairman [59] and accounts of employees involved [3, 44].

1. A Maersk computer in Odessa (Ukraine) received malicious code through an update from M.E.Doc, a legitimate accounting software [22,23].
2. The update contained malicious code, later named NotPetya, which included exploits Mimikatz and EternalBlue. EternalBlue leveraged an SMB version 1 vulnerability to spread the malicious code to systems across the Maersk network [22,44].
3. The malicious code, when encountering a non-patched operating system, encrypted the systems. The encryption effectively wiped the system as NotPetya did not have a built-in decryption capability [44].

4. Maersk workers started seeing computers being reset and locked throughout the corporate network [3]. Attempts to limit damage and stop the outbreak were not successful, including physical disconnections of equipment [24].
5. Workers were sent home as the extent of the computer unavailability became apparent [24].
6. The assessment and recovery process started on 45,000 PCs, 4,000 servers and 2500 applications [3,59] within Maersk globally. Most of the recoveries, including cleaning and restarting assets, involved labour-intensive processes.

The SITD model illustrates the infrastructure (Fig. 11) that enabled the breach, as well as the flow-on human and operational impacts.

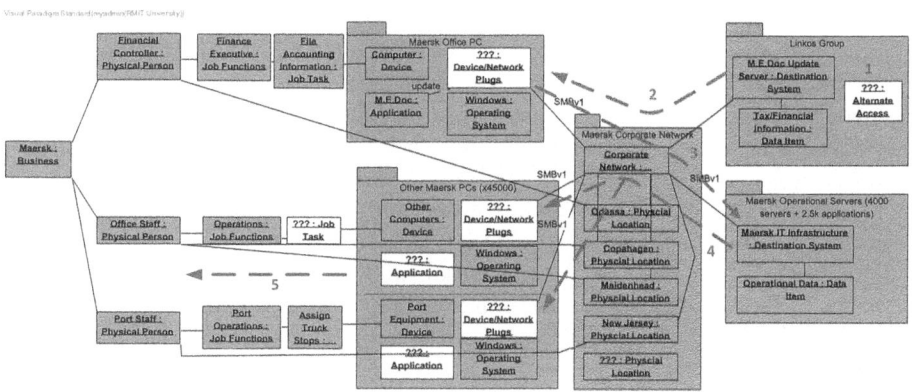

Fig. 11. The Maersk NotPetya incident mapped onto the SITD model with publicly known information, as discussed in Sect. 7.3. Unshaded areas denotes unknown components. Dashed arrow lines and numbers in green outline the steps (as listed in Sect. 7.3) and infrastructure involved in the incident. (Color figure online)

The known information around the software trojan from M.E.Docs, the initial point of infection in an office PC and subsequent impact to other Maersk PCs were widely discussed within available sources. These three aspects are recorded in the respective Applications and Devices classes. When these elements are plotted on the SITD model structure in Fig. 11, the roles that the corporate network (Network Connection class) played in disseminating the software are added. This is derived from the fact that NotPetya malware must jump from the originating Office PC to other devices through a network connection. The SITD also shows the knock-on impact to operational servers (Destination System class), which in turn led to the infection of the dock computer(s) at shipping ports.

The links between the paralysis of the corporate servers and the shutdown of dock computers, while hinted at and easily derivable by an IT worker, is not always immediately apparent to a non-technical audience. The SITD model provides a way to visually 'hop' within an often invisible IT architecture, thus laying out the severity and spread of an incident.

Missing Breach Information. In addition, the SITD model emphasises the unknown elements, (left unshaded) in-spite of the public information about the incident. The model underscores the insufficient information available about the following areas:

- The corporate network served as the central point of the outbreak. Further investigation from the incident could focus on whether there are any controls allowing ecosystem compartmentalisation. (A lack of network segmentation was raised as an existing issue for the company by an IT employee in a post-incident discussion [3].)
- Unknowns around the network connectivity mode of devices (& associated application and tasks) indicate opportunities for future incident response planning. As an example, as part of incident response planning, could key (wireless/wired) routers be identified for each physical site that can isolate an entire site from malware spread? Anecdotally, employees unsuccessfully tried to stop the spread by switching off and/or disconnecting individual workstations in an unplanned manner, not as part of a rehearsed response [23].
- The source of entry needs further investigation. How was access (legitimate or not) to Linkos (maker of M.E.Doc) group's infrastructure granted and/or managed? While this may not be resolved technically, as the malware was part of a legitimate update, the missing information can drive conversations between Maersk and Linkos as part of the supplier/customer relationship and commercial liability issues.

Examination of the above points can provide potentially valuable information for future cyber-security tightening or setup. The structure of the SITD model highlights gaps or questions that may be overlooked under the pressure of an active incident and inform post incident reviews. The SITD model structure ensures that, even under pressure, a systematic examination of available information can be conducted regardless of completeness.

8   Discussion

Section 7 shows how the SITD UML model records and maps cyber-security-relevant information for a small business. A business case study, IT architecture case study and breach incident were used to show the SITD model recording security-relevant business, and technical and incident details. Due to the socio-technical nature of cyber-security [40], all 3 types of details support the analysis of a business' cyber-security posture.

Table 2 shows, in detail, how the SITD model design and usage examples demonstrate the fulfilment of design principles set out in Sects. 3 and 4.

Table 2. Design principles (Sect. 4) versus proposed model (Sect. 6) comparison. The SITD model met the principles set out in Sect. 3.

Design Principles	Met Needs	Section(s) of This Article
Modelling Small Business (<20 employees)	✓	7.1 Modelling Business Point of View
Usable for Tool Developers	✓	5.1 Advantages of UML
Business Priorities Focused	✓	6.2 SITD Submodel: Business 6.3 SITD Submodel: Job Function 6.5 SITD Submodel: Threats 7.1 Modelling Business Point of View
Capture Intangible Factors & Relationships	✓	7.1 Task-Based Analysis
Allows Incomplete Information	✓	7.1 Task-Based Analysis 7.3 Missing Breach Information
Language Agnostic	✓	6.6 Overall SITD Model 7.1 Task-Based Analysis 7.3 Modelling Breach Information
Technology Agnostic	✓	7.2 Modelling IT Information
Standards, Legislation & Industry Agnostic	✓	7.1 Modelling Business Point of View 7.1 Change in Operating Environment
Enable Cyber-Security Analysis	✓	7.1 Analysing the Result 7.1 Task-Based Analysis 7.2 Modelling IT Information 7.3 Modelling Breach Information

The modelling of three widely-varying sources of information types demonstrated that the SITD model is capable of modelling different types of businesses, situations and information sources. The SITD model's adaptability is useful in cyber-security where small businesses have a variety of different characteristics, ranging from industry nuances to market disruption. Over the long term, this adaptability helps the SITD model stay relevant during times of change.

In the future, it is expected that SITD model will be used to underpin a small business facing cyber-security tool. Small business is expected to independently navigate and fulfil the SITD model information, through answering questions and/or other exploratory mechanisms, via the tool's mediating user interface. The output of the tool then allows the small business (and external partners) to make proportionate and critical cyber-security decisions in areas of investment, risk mitigation and incident response planning. The currency of the tool, as driven by the SITD model, will be important as small business cannot be expected to learn new tools frequently. IT in small business is a support function not core business activity. The SITD model's flexibility allows small business to continually interface with one familiar tool both at the beginning and throughout their cyber-security journey. The tool output remains relevant despite the changing cyber-security landscape.

9   Conclusion

We proposed the SITD UML data model as a way to gather and organise small business cyber-security information. Big standards, whilst flexible, lead to big knowledge requirements and resource commitments, making them difficult to adopt for resource-scarce small businesses. The SITD model provides a business friendly data structure for a future cyber-security tool where independent use by small business is desired. The SITD model's UML foundation gives a ready channel and a structured way for any prospective solution developers (technical or otherwise) to ensure relevant information is captured and organised. Furthermore, UML can readily be accommodated by technologies that allow databases, thus minimising implementation issues and effort.

The SITD model's analyses of case studies of a micro agricultural business, UK micro-businesses' architecture and NotPetya breach incident show the capability of the SITD model in capturing and organising security-relevant information. The examples demonstrated the ability of the SITD model to model businesses in varied environments. The SITD model also highlights the value of cyber-security decisions by linking the decisions to the business' operational activities, via SITD links between objects.

Future tools can use the SITD model to compile security records for further security analysis and post incident review, with the SITD model giving structure to an often qualitative, open-ended cyber-security process. The SITD model does not seek to replace existing cyber-security standards, but rather fill the existing gaps with respect to small business needs – by pivoting the cyber-security process focus from technical to small business's perspective. By facilitating a small business friendly process, the SITD model indirectly encourages sustained small business engagement with cyber-security. The SITD model lays the foundational step for enabling a new small business self-serve paradigm.

Acknowledgments. This research is supported by an Australian Government Research Training Program (RTP) Scholarship. This project was conducted under an Approval from the RMIT Human Ethics Committee (Approval Number: 23928). We would like to thank the reviewers for their helpful feedback.

Authors' Note. The business case study, in Sect. 7.1, citations and identifying information in text and figures have been anonymised to protect the privacy of the small business in publication. The original citations and information were provided to editors for review.

Appendix - Reading the Model: UML Conventions

Our model is highly reliant on UML. Here is an example to show how to interpret UML class and object diagrams.

Class (drawn as rectangles) defines independent entities or objects. From these classes, associations (drawn as lines) are used to illustrate relationships between classes. A class can exist on its own but associations must have a beginning and an ending class (which can be the same class). Classes convey structural information only (i.e. the location of the class in relation to other classes). When an instance of a class is defined, it is noted as an object.

Certain characteristics of the class are captured as attributes, primarily text fields within each class. Enumerations, which restrict the possible values in an attribute, are also defined. Despite their similarity in appearance to classes, enumerations do not play a role in the structure of the model.

Figure 12 illustrates the class diagram for a car for example.

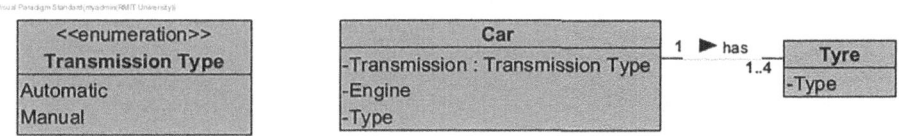

Fig. 12. Example class showing the class structure of a car in relation to its tires using UML. The '1...4' notation specifies that a car can have 1 to 4 tyres. Described in Sect. 9.

This defines that structurally a car must have a minimum of 1 tyre to a maximum of 4 as a relationship. These tyres do not need to be the same on the same car (think early bicycles with 2 different size wheels). It also states the attributes of cars and tyres (generally attributes are not mandatory unless otherwise specified). At this stage, it is not instantiated i.e. it does not describe a specific car, but rather a relationship between cars and tyres.

In describing individual cars e.g. John's car with four tyres, the object diagram is given in Fig. 13.

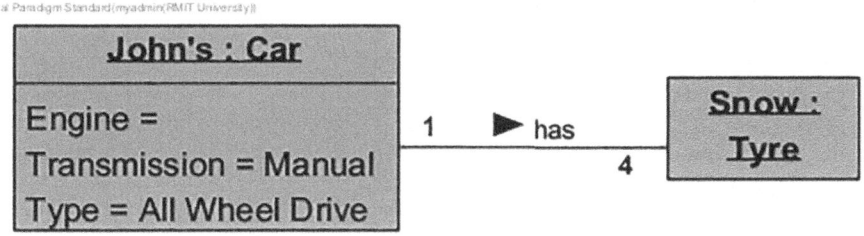

Fig. 13. Example object diagram showing how an instance of a car can be represented using UML. Described in Sect. 9.

For further information on UML, refer to UML ISO specification documentation [26].

References

1. Ande, R., Adebisi, B., Hammoudeh, M., Saleem, J.: Internet of Things: evolution and technologies from a security perspective. Sustain. Cities Soc. **54**(February 2019), 101728 (2020). https://doi.org/10.1016/j.scs.2019.101728
2. Angeli, C., Valanides, N.: Examining the effects of text-only and text-and-visual instructional materials on the achievement of field-dependent and field-independent learners during problem-solving with modeling software. Educ. Technol. Res. Dev. **52**(4), 23–36 (2004). https://doi.org/10.1007/BF02504715
3. Ashton, G.: Maersk, me & NotPetya. June 2020. https://gvnshtn.com/posts/maersk-me-notpetya/. Accessed 01 Dec 2021
4. Australian Bureau of Statistics: 1321.0 - Small Business in Australia, 2001 (2001). https://www.abs.gov.au/ausstats/abs@.nsf/mf/1321.0
5. Australian Bureau of Statistics: 8167 Selected Characteristics of Australian Business (2019). https://www.abs.gov.au/statistics/industry/technology-and-innovation/characteristics-australian-business/2017-18
6. Australian Bureau of Statistics: 8165.0 - Counts of Australian Businesses, Including Entries and Exits, June 2015 to June 2019 (2020). https://www.abs.gov.au/AUSSTATS/abs@.nsf/DetailsPage/8165.0June2015toJune2019?OpenDocument
7. Australian Bureau of Statistics: Australian Industry by Division, Australian Industry, Financial Year 2019–20, May 2021. https://www.abs.gov.au/statistics/industry/industry-overview/australian-industry/2019-20/81550DO001_201920.xls
8. Australian Cyber Security Centre, Australian Signals Directorate: Cyber Security and Australian Small Businesses (2020). https://www.cyber.gov.au/sites/default/files/2023-03/2023_ACSC_CyberSecurityandAustralianSmallBusinessesSurveyResults_D1.pdf
9. Australian Government: Essential Eight Maturity Model (2023). https://www.cyber.gov.au/sites/default/files/2023-11/PROTECTEssentialEightMaturityModel%28November2023%29.pdf
10. Australian Small Business and Family Enterprise Ombudsman: Small Business Counts (2020). https://www.asbfeo.gov.au/sites/default/files/2021-11/ASBFEOSmallBusinessCountsDec2020v2_0.pdf
11. Australian Small Business and Family Enterprise Ombudsman: Small Business Matters (2023). https://www.asbfeo.gov.au/sites/default/files/2023-10/SmallBusinessMatters_June2023.pdf
12. Australian Taxation Office: International Tax for Business (2021). https://www.ato.gov.au/businesses-and-organisations/international-tax-for-business. Accessed 28 Nov 2023
13. Bada, M., Nurse, J.: Developing cybersecurity education and awareness programmes for small- and medium-sized enterprises (SMEs). Inf. Comput. Secur. **27**(3), 393–410 (2019). https://doi.org/10.1108/ICS-07-2018-0080
14. Blanco, C.F., Sarasa, R.G., Sanclemente, C.O.: Effects of visual and textual information in online product presentations: looking for the best combination in website design. Eur. J. Inf. Syst. **19**(6), 668–686 (2010). https://doi.org/10.1057/ejis.2010.42
15. Center for Internet Security: Learn about CIS Controls v8 (2023). https://www.cisecurity.org/controls/v8. Accessed 20 Nov 2023
16. Chen, P.P.S.: The entity-relationship model - towards a unified view of data. ACM Trans. Database Syst. **1**(1), 9–36 (1976). https://doi.org/10.1145/320434.320440

17. Chiappetta, M.: Uber Eats Demand Soars Due To COVID-19 Crisis. Forbes, March 2020. https://www.forbes.com/sites/marcochiappetta/2020/03/25/uber-eats-demand-soars-due-to-covid-19-crisis

18. Colbaugh, R., Glass, K.: Proactive defense for evolving cyber threats. In: Proceedings of the 2011 IEEE International Conference on Intelligence and Security Informatics, ISI 2011, pp. 125–130 (2011). https://doi.org/10.1109/ISI.2011.5984062

19. Day, J.D., Zimmermann, H.: The OSI reference model. Proc. IEEE **71**(12), 1334–1340 (1983). http://www.inf.ufes.br/~zegonc/material/Redes_de_Computadores/TheOSIReferenceModel.pdf

20. Department for Business Energy & Industrial Strategy: Business Population Estimates for the UK and Regions 2021 (2021). https://assets.publishing.service.gov.uk/government/uploads/system/uploads/attachment_data/file/1019907/2021_Business_Population_Estimates_for_the_UK_and_regions_Statistical_Release.pdf

21. Dolan, P., Hallsworth, M., Halpern, D., King, D., Metcalfe, R., Vlaev, I.: Influencing behaviour: the MINDSPACE way. J. Econ. Psychol. **33**(1), 264–277 (2012). https://doi.org/10.1016/j.joep.2011.10.009

22. Fayi, S.Y.A.: What Petya/NotPetya ransomware is and what its remidiations are. Adv. Intell. Syst. Comput. **738**, 93–100 (2018). https://doi.org/10.1007/978-3-319-77028-4_15

23. Greenberg, A.: The untold story of NotPetya, the most devastating cyberattack in history. Wired Mag., August 2018. https://www.wired.com/story/notpetya-cyberattack-ukraine-russia-code-crashed-the-world/

24. Greenberg, A.: Sandworm: A New Era of Cyberwar and the Hunt for the Kremlin's Most Dangerous Hackers. Knopf Doubleday Publishing Group (2019)

25. Greenberg, A.: Why insider 'zoom bombs' are so hard to stop. Wired Magazine, March 2021. https://www.wired.com/story/zoombomb-inside-jobs/

26. International Organization for Standardization, International Electrotechnical Commission: Information technology - Open Distributed Processing - Unified Modeling Language (UML) Version 1.4.2 (2005). https://www.omg.org/spec/UML/ISO/19501/PDF

27. Maddux, J.E., Rogers, R.W.: Protection motivation and self-efficacy: a revised theory of fear appeals and attitude change. J. Exp. Soc. Psychol. **19**(5), 469–479 (1983). https://doi.org/10.1016/0022-1031(83)90023-9

28. Microsoft: 10 benefits of data modeling tools (2023). https://powerbi.microsoft.com/en-us/what-are-the-advantages-of-data-modeling-tools/. Accessed 09 Nov 2023

29. Microsoft: What is DevSecOps? (2023). https://www.microsoft.com/en-us/security/business/security-101/what-is-devsecops. Accessed 01 Dec 2023

30. Miles, R.E., Snow, C.C., Meyer, A.D., Jr., Coleman, H.J., Jr.: Organizational strategy, structure, and process. Acad. Manag. Rev. **3**(3), 546 (1978)

31. Mouton, F., Malan, M.M., Leenen, L., Venter, H.S.: Social engineering attack framework. In: 2014 Information Security for South Africa - Proceedings of the ISSA 2014 Conference (2014). https://doi.org/10.1109/ISSA.2014.6950510

32. National Cyber Security Centre: Asset Management, May 2021. https://www.ncsc.gov.uk/guidance/asset-management. Accessed 13 Dec 2021

33. National Institute of Standards and Technology: NIST Framework for Improving Critical Infrastructure Cybersecurity (2018). https://doi.org/10.6028/NIST.CSWP.04162018

34. National Institute of Standards and Technology: Security and Privacy Controls for Information Systems and Organizations (2020). https://doi.org/10.6028/NIST.SP. 800-53r5

35. Organisation for Economic Co-operation and Development (OECD): Small Businesses, Job Creation And Growth: Facts, Obstacles And Best Practices, June 1997. https://www.oecd.org/cfe/smes/2090740.pdf

36. Organisation for Economic Co-operation and Development (OECD): Key Facts Survey of Adult Skills (PIAAC): Full Selection of Indicator - UK, US, Australia and OECD Data Table (2018). https://gpseducation.oecd.org/IndicatorExplorer. Accessed 15 Mar 2021

37. Osborn, E., Simpson, A.: On small-scale IT users' system architectures and cyber security: a UK case study. Comput. Secur. **70**(Section 3), 27–50 (2017). https://doi.org/10.1016/j.cose.2017.05.001

38. Park, J., Campbell, J.M.: U.S. small business's philanthropic contribution to local community: stakeholder salience and social identity perspectives. J. Nonprofit Public Sect. Mark. **30**(3), 317–342 (2018). https://doi.org/10.1080/10495142.2018. 1452823

39. Renaud, K.: How smaller businesses struggle with security advice. Comput. Fraud Secur. **8**, 10–18 (2016). https://doi.org/10.1016/S1361-3723(16)30062-8

40. Schneier, B.: The importance of security engineering. IEEE Secur. Priv. **10**(5), 88 (2012). https://doi.org/10.1109/MSP.2012.132

41. Scott, M., Bruce, R.: Five stages of growth in small business. Long Range Plann. **20**(3), 45–52 (1987). https://doi.org/10.1016/0024-6301(87)90071-9

42. Service, O., et al.: EAST four simple ways to apply behavioural insights (2014). https://www.bi.team/wp-content/uploads/2015/07/BIT-Publication-EAST_ FA_WEB.pdf. Accessed 10 Dec 2021

43. Small Business Digital Taskforce: Small Business Digital Taskforce, Report to Government (2018). https://treasury.gov.au/sites/default/files/2021-07/p2018-191027-sbdt-report.pdf

44. Sood, K., Hurley, S.: NotPetya technical analysis (2017). https://www.crowdstrike. com/blog/petrwrap-ransomware-technical-analysis-triple-threat-file-encryption-mft-encryption-credential-theft/

45. Standards Australia Limited: AS ISO/IEC 27001 Australian Standard Information Technology - Security Techniques - Information Security Management Systems - Requirements. No. AS ISO/IEC 27001:2015 (2015)

46. Street, C.T., Meister, D.B.: Small business growth and internal transparency: the role of information systems. MIS Q. Manag. Inf. Syst. **28**(3), 473–506 (2004). https://doi.org/10.2307/25148647

47. Sullivan-Taylor, B., Branicki, L.: Creating resilient SMEs: why one size might not fit all. Int. J. Prod. Res. **49**(18), 5565–5579 (2011). https://doi.org/10.1080/ 00207543.2011.563837

48. Tam, T., Rao, A., Hall, J.: The invisible COVID-19 small business risks: dealing with the cyber-security aftermath. Digit. Gov. Res. Pract. **2**(2) (2020). https://doi.org/10.1145/3436807

49. Tam, T., Rao, A., Hall, J.: Rapid cybersecurity assessment system for small business' COVID move to online, **19** (2021). https://doi.org/10.14722/coronadef.2021. 23004

50. Tam, T., Rao, A., Hall, J.: The good, the bad and the missing: a narrative review of cyber-security implications for Australian small businesses. Comput. Secur. **109**, 102385 (2021). https://doi.org/10.1016/j.cose.2021.102385

51. Tan, T., Maynard, S., Ahmad, A., Ruighaver, T.: Information security governance: a case study of the strategic context of information security. In: Pacific Asia Conference on Information Systems, vol. 43. Association for Information Systems Electronic Library (AISeL), Langkawi (2017). http://aisel.aisnet.org/pacis2017/43

52. The Mitre Corporation: Mitre Att&ck (2019). https://attack.mitre.org/. Accessed 01 Mar 2021

53. The Mitre Corporation: CVE (2023). https://cve.mitre.org/. Accessed 14 Nov 2023

54. United Nations Office on Drugs and Crime: Comprehensive Study on Cybercrime (2013). http://www.unodc.org/documents/organized-crime/UNODC_CCPCJ_EG.4_2013/CYBERCRIME_STUDY_210213.pdf

55. Von Solms, R., Van Niekerk, J.: From information security to cyber security. Comput. Secur. **38**, 97–102 (2013). https://doi.org/10.1016/j.cose.2013.04.004

56. Watson, C., Zaw, T.: OWASP Automated Threat Handbook Web Applications, 1.2 edn. OWASP Foundation (2018)

57. Williams, E.J., Hinds, J., Joinson, A.N.: Exploring susceptibility to phishing in the workplace. Int. J. Hum Comput Stud. **120**(June 2017), 1–13 (2018). https://doi.org/10.1016/j.ijhcs.2018.06.004

58. WizCase Cyber Research Team: Over 80 US Municipalities' Sensitive Information, Including Resident's Personal Data, Left Vulnerable in Massive Data Breach (2021). https://www.wizcase.com/blog/us-municipality-breach-report/. Accessed 13 Jan 2021

59. World Economic Forum: Securing a Common Future in Cyberspace (2018). https://www.youtube.com/watch?v=Tqe3K3D7TnI. Accessed 05 Jan 2022

Data Processing Displacements: The Use of CHERI Fat Pointers and the GDPR

Mark Burdon[1,3](✉), Lizzie Coles-Kemp[2], Laura Shipp[2], and Lydia Blunt[3]

[1] Digital Media Research Centre/Law, Queensland University of Technology, Brisbane, Australia
m.burdon@qut.edu.au
[2] Information Security Group, Royal Holloway University, Egham, UK
[3] School of Law, Queensland University of Technology, Brisbane, Australia

Abstract. Capability Hardware Enhanced RISC (reduced instruction set computer) Instruction-set (CHERI) is a hardware-software model that potentially offers greater security capabilities through fine-grained memory protection and scalable compartmentalization. CHERI has received significant support from the UK Government as part of the Digital Security by Design program and has been implemented as a development board (Morello), by chip manufacturer, ARM. A core component of CHERI is its use of CHERI Concentrate, a new fat pointer compression scheme to enforce security properties across networked computer systems. The use of CHERI fat pointers gives rise to an important legal question about whether CHERI use involving personal data systems could be classed as data processing under the General Data Protection Regulation (GDPR). Data processing is construed broadly under the GDPR, as confirmed by multiple Council of Justice for the European Union (CJEU) decisions. However, the CJEU decisions demonstrate differences in how data processing is constructed. Some decisions focus on a singular operation that clearly corresponds to the GDPR's definition and entail data processing techniques *on* personal data. We argue other CJEU decisions have a broader construct of processing that entails the *facilitation* of data processing through a plural set of operations. Whether and how these different constructs apply to the use of CHERI fat pointers is a novel and important question. We show the limitations of the traditional approach to data processing when applied to CHERI fat pointers. We then identify three types of displacement caused by CHERI – technical, intentionality and compliance – and show how a facilitation approach to data processing is better equipped to meet displacement issues. In conclusion, rethinking CJEU jurisprudence about the nature of data processing along facilitation lines ensures that displacements caused by technological innovations, such as CHERI's fat pointer uses, are still within realistic reach of data protection law.

Keywords: CHERI · fat pointers · GDPR · data processing · data protection

© The Author(s), under exclusive license to Springer Nature Switzerland AG 2025
C. Boyd et al. (Eds.): Ed Dawson Festschrift 2024, LNCS 15600, pp. 290–308, 2025.
https://doi.org/10.1007/978-3-031-83490-5_11

1   Introduction

From a technical perspective, CHERI is a hybrid capability model [1]. It seeks to redesign the building blocks of hardware and software systems with a renewed focus on security [2]. It blends capability systems with hardware-software by making additions to conventional hardware ISA (Instruction Set Architecture) [3]. CHERI therefore allows for new security behaviors which are implemented low down in the stack and can be further manipulated within software.

New technological developments like CHERI/Morello do not exist in a legal vacuum. They are part of a historical continuum of how law and regulation apply and change in line with technical innovation. The advent of new security architectures, like CHERI/Morello consequently provides new opportunities to consider how relatively 'settled' law applies in new contexts. Data processing under the General Data Protection Regulation (GDPR) [4] is an apt example given the novel legal issues that could arise from the uncertain application of CHERI fat pointers. Considering whether, and in what conditions, the use of CHERI fat pointers is classable as data processing under the GDPR reveals underpinning tensions within data protection law and opens new ways of considering relevant CJEU decisions. In this chapter, we identify a new interpretation of relevant CJEU decisions that extends the current understanding of data processing.

The requirement for data processing under the GDPR is outlined in Article 4(2).

'processing' means any operation or set of operations which is performed on personal data or on sets of personal data, whether or not by automated means, such as collection, recording, organisation, structuring, storage, adaptation or alteration, retrieval, consultation, use, disclosure by transmission, dissemination or otherwise making available, alignment or combination, restriction, erasure or destruction

Article 4(2) provides a nested definition of processing that has different components. The first part of the definition focuses singularly on an individual operation or plurally on a set of operations. Both are performed on personal data or sets of personal data. The difference between the singular and plural application of the definition is important because it highlights the technological neutrality at the heart of the GDPR. Data protection rights extend equally to the singular actions of a paper record in a hard copy filing system and to the plural activities of data analytics involving multiple sites of data collection, storage and analysis across federated systems [5]. The examples of seemingly straightforward processing operations (e.g., collection, recording etc.) are construed expansively as either a singular operation or as a sub-process of a plural set of operations.

As our chapter contends, greater attention on the distinction between Article 4(2)'s definition and the difference between 'any operation' and 'a set of operations' reveals different judicial constructions of processing. Based on our analysis of key CJEU decisions, we argue that data processing involves the ability of a process or processes to be operated *on* personal data and one that *facilitates* data processing of personal data. The latter arises from our new interpretation of key CJEU decisions. We argue below that highlighting this distinction gives insight into the role of novel security technologies, such as CHERI, and data protection law.

Section 2 briefly outlines the CHERI/Morello architecture. Section 3 outlines the GDPR's requirement of data processing and briefly highlights the historical themes that influence its construction and application. Relevant CJEU case law is then examined and decisions are differentiated between those that entail processing on personal data in Sect. 3.1 and those that facilitate personal data processing in Sect. 3.2. Section 4 then examines how both approaches would apply in the CHERI context. We find that CHERI fat pointer usage would give rise to three types of displacement – technical, intentionality and compliance. Displacements are reflective of the disruptive nature of technological innovations which displace settled understandings of legal and regulatory application. Displacements are not obviations which intentionally seek to avoid the application of law and regulation. In conclusion, we argue for an expanded construct of data processing as a plural set of operations that facilitate data processing activities involving personal data to ensure that data protection law can deal with the types of processing displacement that arise from novel technological innovations, such as CHERI.

2 The CHERI/Morello Architecture

Computer and network security have deployed automated controls since the 1970s. However, there is now a move towards deeper embedment of digital security controls taking place on several fronts especially involving adaptive intelligent automation of security threat identification and response. These developments highlight the need for fundamental changes to the design of security controls which include embedding the protection of data still further into the core design of digital products and services to ensure whole-of-stack data assurance [6]. The move is in part motivated by a perceived resource gap where employing technologists with the relevant skills is difficult, and in part by a strong drive to threat anticipation [7]. Building on these developments, automation of security response is increasingly put forward as a possibility of reducing structural security frictions [8].

Usable security studies have long advocated for a reduction in security friction, defined by Hielscher et al. as "a problem created through a multitude of badly written security policies and measures that cost time, effort, and nerves, and are not aligned with employees routines" [9]. Growing economic and political dependency on digital technologies, including intelligent automation, also offers the promise of robust defense and protection of digital infrastructures against new and emerging threats [10, 11]. It is in this broader socio-political background that CHERI was developed as a potential far-reaching solution to ongoing security instabilities [12].

CHERI technology embeds data access control onto the computer chip itself and increases the prospects for automated data assurance. Currently available as a prototype System-on-Chip development board called Morello [12], CHERI is part of a family of technologies that seeks to provide proactive security mechanisms at the point of delivery [13]. Early CHERI prototypes were based on the 64-bit MIPS ISA, followed by 32-bit and 64-bit RISC-V, and more recently, ARM v8-A [12]. CHERI/Morello adds capabilities to an instruction set architecture [3] that allows memory to be compartmentalized within CHERI/Morello. The configuration of the technology determines what makes up each compartment of isolated memory, depending on their context. To a non-specialist, CHERI might be described as acting as a type of technological immunization layer because it isolates malware and protects data at source from unauthorized access or processing. There are two significant themes emerging from this approach: first, it automates actions to protect data previously undertaken by people (e.g., the instigation of patching, or post-hoc setting of access rights); secondly, it incorporates, through the prospect of increased automation, the processes for assuring that data is protected and compliant with legal and regulatory requirements.

Consequently, CHERI has the capacity to be a genuine disruptive influence on security provision and roles. For example, software patching currently happens post hoc and is driven by human decision making and implementation. Whereas CHERI application would obviate the need for this type of activity because it would now take place further down the hardware stack. CHERI thus uses expanded memory capability as a way of incorporating defense. A capability (or fat pointer) is an unforgeable token of authority that grants access to a region of address space [14]. Enhanced capabilities in CHERI work to extend pointers (the fat aspects) to access memory and, by doing so, act to constrain pointer use [13]. CHERI uses these capabilities, or extended pointers as a foundational way to facilitate its security implications and protection semantics [3].

Capability-based systems ensure that resources are *only* reachable via capabilities and this naturalises two security design principles. First, software should run with the minimum privileges it needs to undertake a task. Second, where software has multiple privileges, it has to select one to exercise [3]. Capabilities are thus the pointers plus extra components that allow for increased memory safety. Security is increased via secure pointer use because pointers are often the tools that get used to take control of a penetrated system by attackers [3]. CHERI works to reinforce secure pointers by providing a number of new protection mechanisms which means capability pointers become "a primary candidate to conclusively solve memory safety problems" [15]. Fat or extended pointers are consequently a pointer safety mechanism [15]. CHERI pointers with the extended information they carry about how they can be used to access a memory region, mean they can only be used in more secure ways [14]. By only using memory capabilities through fat pointers, it becomes possible to maintain higher levels of memory safety [15].

Fat pointers have the following components [3]. Firstly, there is the 64-bit virtual address which is different to other address pointers that are normally 32- or 64-bit. CHERI fat pointers also include a 1-bit tag to protect the capabilities within the memory that act to limit the range of address space accessible via the pointer [3]. There is also a set of permissions which limit the way they can be used (or dereferenced) that allows read-only as opposed to read-and-write permissions. Bounds limit the address space that are accessible via the pointer [12]. Finally, fat pointer capability is sealed therefore making it immutable [13].

The detailed format of fat pointers is outside the scope of this paper, but the interested reader may find examples in the technical specifications [3, Fig 3.1]. As shown in one example, a 128-bit fat pointer might use 64 bits for a pointer address, 16 bits to encode access permission bits, 18 bits for the object type and 27 bits that encode bounds on the memory portion that can be accessed.

The security implications of CHERI and its capabilities are fourfold [3]. First, pointer provenance validity means that only valid pointers are produced from other valid pointers.

Invalid pointers cannot therefore be generated or used. Second, the firm boundaries of fat pointer capability prevents pointer manipulation. A pointer cannot therefore be used to access a different object that is not specified in its address region. Third, CHERI prevents the escalation of pointer privilege which could, for example, allow for broadening of the bounds of pointer capabilities. Finally, permissions within a capability minimise the unintended use of pointers. CHERI pointer capabilities reduce the abuse of raw pointers and allows software to define and isolate memory regions, ensuring greater memory safety and enhanced compartmentalisation [3]. The use of CHERI fat pointers consequently reduces security vulnerabilities commonly found in software, including buffer overflows and use-after-free bugs [2]. Moreover, scalable software compartmentalisation is achievable because CHERI provides expansive forms of compartmentalisation [14]. Doing so reduces pointer abuse and ensures individual pointers are not able to provide access to the whole memory address space further reducing attack vectors.

CHERI implementation thus impacts how software applications make their memory requests throughout the architecture which means how CHERI operates could potentially change organisational practice. For example, company data will be increasingly stored and governed by memory level, pointer-based actions, which will result in increasingly compartmentalised structures developed by actors/end users implementing CHERI. This means, that to access data from the memory, the CHERI ISA will use pointers to identify a memory address space and use this to grant a legitimate memory access request, retrieving the data from the memory. Consequently, data within the memory, whether user-generated or system-generated, will have the benefit of CHERI's enhanced security principles. Despite these security benefits, CHERI use of fat pointers gives rise to questions about the nature of data processing within CHERI architectures and whether and how it would be classed under the GDPR.

3   Data Processing Under the GDPR

The definition of data processing under Article4(2) is functional in nature as it regards a non-exhaustive list of how processing can take place on personal data. Moreover, the definition aims to regulate most, if not all stages, of the data processing cycle including storage of personal data [16, p. 117]. Processing must be undertaken by a data controller and it is the controller which determines the purposes and means of processing [16]. As such, processing by itself needs to be understood in context with other data protection facets and considered holistically in relation to controller acts or intentions and the resulting outputs as part of structured filing systems. However, while we acknowledge these broader foci of application, our paper focuses on what is data processing given the novel developments arising from CHERI/Morello.

While it is technically oriented towards data processing operations, Article 4(2) is a constituent part of the GDPR's operation and thus is intended to be broadly interpreted in line with fundamental rights [16, p. 119]. Article 4(2) is similar in construction to the previous Data Protection Directive (DPD) [17]which means pre-GDPR CJEU jurisprudence remains relevant to understanding how the term is employed in the GDPR [18]. The technical construction of data processing is thus founded on the fundamental rights accorded to EU citizens from Article 8(1) of the Charter of Fundamental Rights of the

European Union [19] and Article 16 of the Treaty on the Functioning of the European Union [20]. Data processing therefore is judicially constructed in line with a fundamental right to protection of personal data [16].

Nevertheless, the rights-based framework of EU data protection is also balanced with ensuring the 'free flow of personal data between Member States' [4]. And it is here where the tension arises between the protection of fundamental rights and the potential economic value that could be derived from personal data processing. These tensions are factored into CJEU decisions which tend to privilege more weight towards data protection as a fundamental right and have resulted in case law which reinforces that data processing needs to be construed expansively. Expansive construction means that data processing of personal data remains fundamentally protected. Commentators have argued that Article 4(2) essentially covers any data processing operation and thus 'it is difficult to conceive of any operation performed on personal data which would fall outside the definition of "processing" [16]. The CJEU cases confirms this point and demonstrates the CJEU's willingness to class a wide range of activities that stretch from singular types of processing to multiple processes that make up 'a set of operations'[16].

Our examination of key CJEU case law on data processing reveals there are two separate jurisprudential tracks which can result in different application. The first track, cases involving processing on data as an operation represents the 'settled' legal position. The second track, which we identify in this chapter, provides a new interpretation of key cases that we argue considers data processing more broadly and involves facilitating processing as a set of operations. The key cases are outlined in Table 1.

Table 1. CJEU 'On' and 'Facilitation' Cases

Processing On Data as an Operation	Facilitating Processing as a Set of Operations
Puškár v Finance Office of the Slovak Republic (*Puškár*)	Fashion ID GmbH & Co. KG v Verbraucherzentrale NRW e.V. (*Fashion ID*)
Criminal proceedings against Bodil Lindqvist (*Bodil Lindqvist*)	Tietosuojavaltuutettu v Satakunnan Markkinapörssi and Satamedia (*Tietosuojavaltuutettu*)
František Ryneš v Úřad pro ochranu osobních údajů (*Rynes*)	Michael Schwarz v Stadt Bochum (*Schwarz*)
Proceedings brought by Sergejs Buivids (Buivids)	YS v Minister voor Immigratie, Integratie en Asiel and Minister voor Immigratie, Integratie en Asiel v M and S (*YS*)
European Commission v The Bavarian Lager Co. Ltd (*Bavarian Lager*)	Weltimmo s.r.o. v Nemzeti Adatvédelmi és Információszabadság Hatóság (*Weltimmo*)
Maximillian Schrems v Data Protection Commissioner (*Schrems*)	
Google Spain v AEPD (*Google Spain*)	
Camera di Commercio, Industria, Artigianato e Agricoltura di Lecce v Salvatore Manni (*Camera di Commercio*)	

We argue below that the significance of this distinction has not yet been fully realized because there has been an overt focus on matching a fact decision of individual cases with the types of singular operation contemplated in Article 4(2). As such, the fact situation of each case is important to understand the jurisprudential tracks and logics at play. The first track of cases highlights how the CJEU has matched a certain type of processing with the examples provided in Article 4(2) (e.g., collection, recording, organisation etc.).

3.1   CJEU Cases – Processing on Data as an Operation

Puškár [21] was a case decided under the DPD. The applicant sought an order to have his name removed from a list of people considered to be 'front-men' by the Slovakian Finance Directorate. Each person on the list was listed with their national identity number and tax identification number. The issue of whether the applicant's personal data had been processed was dealt with quickly by the Court. The collection of identity data directly accorded with the DPD definition of data processing and the 'drawing up of names' was an operation of data processing within the DPD's definition. Similarly, in *Bodil Lindqvist* [22], the respondent was charged with a breach of the Swedish data protection legislation because she published the personal data of work colleagues on the Internet, including family circumstances and phone numbers. The court had to decide whether the webpage publication involved the processing of personal data. The Court held that data processing took place as it was a 'disclosure by transmission, dissemination, or otherwise making data available.'

In *Ryneš* [23], the respondent installed a camera for security purposes to the outside of his home. The camera was in a fixed position, it could not turn, and it recorded the entrance to his home, the footpath, and the entrance to the house opposite. Only a visual recording could be made and 'was stored on recording equipment in the form of a continuous loop', on a hard disk drive. The images could not be studied in real time and when the disk reached full capacity, the device would record over the previous recordings and erase the pre-existing material. The Court held that processing was an operation of 'collection', 'recording', and 'storage'. The Court also decided that video surveillance stored on a continuous recording device constituted processing of personal data. *Ryneš* also confirms that processing for transient and temporary purposes can still fall within the DPD's definition. A similar fact situation arose in *Buivids* [24]. The respondent recorded a video during his attendance at a police station which he published on YouTube. The video featured captured imagery and audio of police officers. Like *Ryneš*, the Court held that processing had taken place as a recording process which was then published online as a dissemination operation.

Bavarian Lager [25] primarily concerned the right of access to personal data under the DPD. The respondent company sought access to the minutes of a meeting which contained the names of attendees. Attendee names were classed as personal data and some attendees had given consent to be identified in other documents relating to the meeting. Others had expressly refused to provide consent and others had not responded. The Court accepted that communication of such data fell within the definition of processing. Communication would have been achieved by transmission, dissemination, or otherwise making the personal data available.

The issue of data processing has also arisen in landmark CJEU cases. In *Schrems* [26], a decision involving the transfer of personal data by Facebook to the US, which could be used for national security purposes, the Court held that the transfer of personal data from a Member State to a third country 'constitutes, in itself, processing of personal data'. Specifically, the Court decided that the transfer was a 'disclosure by transmission, dissemination or otherwise' which sat squarely as classable operations under Article 4(2).

The same can also be said for *Google Spain* which recognized a right to be forgotten [27]. The applicant wanted personal data relating to him to be removed from the pages of a newspaper, as well as for Google Spain or Google Inc to remove it so that the data no longer appeared in search results. The complaint against the newspaper was rejected. However, the CJEU upheld it against Google Spain and Google Inc. *Google Spain* is a broad ranging case and we are most interested in the Court's consideration of processing. Google Spain argued that a search engine's activity cannot be considered processing of personal data which appear on a third party's web page, as a list of search results. Search engines merely process all Internet information and do not discriminate or target selected individuals. The applicant, on the other hand, argued that Google Spain determined the purposes and means of processing as part of its indexing of results. The CJEU found that Google Spain collected, retrieved, recorded and organized data 'within the framework of its indexing programmes', and stored, disclosed and made available the data as a search result [27, para. 28]. Such activities are explicitly referred to in the definition of 'processing', in the Directive and in the GDPR as singular operations.

However, processing has not always been clear cut even in cases where the CJEU has applied the singular operation assessment. In *Camera di Commercio* [28], the notion of processing was complicated because personal data was processed at different points, but it was only one set of processing that the respondent disputed [28, para. 25]. The respondent was the sole director of a construction company which became insolvent. The respondent believed properties in a previously constructed complex were not selling due to publicly available information about the liquidated company having a negative impact on prospective sales. Personal data had been processed by a company which specialized in the collection and processing of marker information and risk assessment for liquidated companies. The respondent sought to have the data erased, anonymized, or blocked by the appellant company. Notably, it was not the processing of the data by the specialized company, which was at issue, rather that the data was accessible by third parties from the register. The CJEU held that the transcription and storage of personal data in a register and its communication to requesting third parties meant that "the authority responsible for maintaining that register carries out processing of personal data" [28, para. 35].

Camera di Commercio is important to our argument because it highlights the possibilities of a more plural consideration of how one operation can fit within a broader 'set of operations' under Article 4(2) In this case, the specialized company's control and processing of the information facilitated access by third parties for further processing to occur. Doing so opens the possibility of facilitating data processing of personal data in which sub-processes that do not entail processing on personal data can still be classed as data processing because it *facilitates* the activity. The analysis of the second track of key CJEU cases outlines our novel interpretation of the facilitation approach.

3.2   CJEU Cases – Facilitating Processing as a Set of Operations

Camera di Commercio opens up the possibility of a different type of expansive approach. One in which we argue that the CJEU has been more open to find a sub-process that does not directly conduct processing on personal data. Instead, it is a constituent part of a 'set of operations' which can amount to data processing. We therefore contend that sub-processes in this jurisprudential genre *facilitate* data processing of personal data, even if the sub-process itself does not directly perform processing on personal data. Our analysis of the CJEU cases below outlines this interpretation.

Fashion ID [29] concerned Facebook social media website plugins and was decided under the DPD. Fashion ID embedded on its website the Facebook 'Like' social plugin. The key legal issue resolved in the case was whether Fashion ID and Facebook Ireland were controllers under the DPD, and if so, how was personal data processed. The processing entailed was complex and required the CJEU to undertake a detailed analysis of data collection through Facebook's plugin. The Court held that the relevant effect of the plugin meant that a website operator which embedded third party content 'cannot control what data the browser transmits or what the third-party provider does with those data'[29, para. 26]. Consequently, when a user visited Fashion ID's website, their personal data was transmitted to Facebook Ireland, whether the user was aware of it, had a Facebook profile, or clicked the Like button.

A primary issue in this case was whether Fashion ID was a controller. The Court found that Fashion ID was a controller to fulfil the Directive's aim of offering a high level of protection of fundamental rights and freedoms. Furthermore, previous case law supported the finding that a 'controller' may refer to several actors taking part in processing. Importantly for this paper, the Court held the definition of 'processing' in the DPD may

> '…consist in one or a number of operations, each of which relates to one of the different stages that the processing of personal data may involve. [29, para. 72]'

The Court held that there were several controllers who jointly determined 'the purposes and means of processing' [27, para. 73]. The key means of processing was the Facebook Like button which served as a tool 'for the collection and disclosure by transmission' of personal data [27, para. 77]. Whether the collection and disclosure of personal data by transmission was data processing was not a key factor in the case. However, Fashion ID is important because of the Court's consideration and interpretation of processing. Taking the Court's conclusion that processing 'may consist in one or a number of operations', the CJEU is construing processing expansively but in a different way to the cases above. We contend that Fashion ID opens the door for the facilitation of processing to be captured within the definition of data processing. A sub-process that may not involve processing on data itself could nonetheless be part of a 'set of operations' that is taken in its entirety, could give rise to processing on data. We contend that other cases confirm our interpretation.

In *Tietosuojavaltuutettu* [30], the Finnish Data Protection Ombudsman brought proceedings against the respondents, two related media companies that published publicly available tax information of wealthy Finnish residents in regional editions of a newspaper. The paper consisted of an alphabetical list of names that were organized according to municipality and income bracket. The respondents also signed an agreement with a telephone company to enable distribution of newspaper extracts by text message. A key issue was whether the act of transferring personal data to be published in the newspaper was processing under the DPD. Overall, the Court held that processing involved four processes: (1) collection of public domain documents (2) printed alphabetical lists (3) transfer of data to CD-ROM for commercial purposes and (4) further processing of data into text message format that could be sent direct to a customer mobile phone. The question before the Court therefore entailed whether data processing on personal data could encompass all four sub-processes.

Most of the four sub-processes were deemed to meet a singular processing operation, as outlined in the cases above. For example, the first step, the 'collection' of documents from the public domain corresponded explicitly to an operation included in the DPD definition. The second step was deemed to squarely fall under the operation of 'dissemination or otherwise making available'. The third stage, the transfer to CD-ROM, was more complex. The Court did not consider in detail why the transfer to a CD-ROM disc was considered to be processing on personal data in the same way as the other stages. Advocate General Kokott concluded

...the publication of tax data on paper constitutes a filing system and disclosure in the form of a text-messaging service presupposes the consultation of a filing system. Consequently all the abovementioned activities, including disclosure of data by means of CD-ROM, involve the processing of personal data which form part of, or are intended to form part of, a filing system [30, para. 34].

Adopting this reasoning, and acknowledging there is little explanation in the judgment as to how transferring personal data onto CD-ROM otherwise constitutes processing, it appears that this decision recognizes that a sub-process, which does not necessarily involve processing on personal data directly, can nonetheless still be classed as processing if it has a facilitation role involving a broader set of operations that are part of, or intended to be part of, a filing system. *Tietosuojavaltuutettu* is important because it can be read as reemphasizing the tacit existence of a facilitation sub-process, namely the CD-ROM transfer that indirectly involves processing on personal data.

Schwarz [31] did not specifically focus on the interpretation of processing, but the Court referred to it as part of its determination whether certain rights were at risk. The applicant applied to the city of Bochum for a passport and refused to have his fingerprints taken, as required by law. As a result, the application was rejected. Schwarz argued that the provision of fingerprint data was unnecessary and infringed certain rights in relation to the protection of personal data in the EU Charter. The Court held that the taking of fingerprints by national authorities and the storage of those fingerprints in both a database and a passport was processing of personal data. The collection of fingerprint data stored in a database is non-controversial but the storage classification in a passport gives rise to an interesting issue.

The storage of a fingerprint on a database would clearly constitute processing as a distinct operation. However, it is interesting that the Court found the storage of fingerprint data on an individual's passport also constituted processing. Fingerprint data is stored on a passport to prevent falsification of documents. Storage is expressly included as a singular operation of 'processing', yet storage within a passport for the purposes of biometric confirmation suggests that such data is required for future document falsification and confirmation uses. Storage, in this regard, is not simply the purpose of storing the fingerprint, but rather it regards the prevention of falsified documentation at some stage in the future. Consequently, the storage of fingerprint data in a passport could be construed as facilitating future processing of personal data to prevent falsified documents. Storage is not a distinct operation to fulfill a specific purpose. Instead, it is part of a plural set of operations that broadly encompass different purposes. If anything, the processing conduct on personal data as passport documentation is a latent, prospective one and one more akin to the facilitation of identity document protection, as opposed to time-bound and specific processing of personal data.

In *Weltimmo* [32] the case dealt primarily with issues of jurisdiction and applicability of the DPD. However, it required interpretation and reconciliation of the Hungarian Directive and the DPD, which provided judicial insight into interpretation of 'processing'. The applicant was a company registered in Slovakia that ran a website which advertised Hungarian properties for a fee. For one month, advertising on the website was free but thereafter, a fee was payable. Several advertisers took advantage of the free service and then requested the deletion of advertisements and personal data. The applicant charged the advertisers for these services. The advertisers refused to pay and Weltimmo sent the advertisers personal data to debt collection agencies.

The processing issue before the Court regarded whether the Hungarian implementation of data processing which translated to 'technical manipulation of data' conformed to data processing under the DPD. To use our language above, *Weltimmo* is a decision about whether the DPD definition of data processing regards a singular operation ('manipulation of data') or a plural set of operations. The Court decided that the Hungarian implementation of data processing 'must be understood as having the same meaning' as the DPD. The decision reinforces the broad interpretation of processing which needs to include for 'any set of operations.' Whether 'facilitate' or 'facilitation' can be encompassed within the interpretation of 'data processing', as 'technical manipulation of data', is unclear but the broad interpretation of processing suggests it is possible. Especially within the context of the phrase 'any set of operations' performed on personal data.

Building on from this, the final decision, *YS* [33] is closest to explicitly confirming the reach of a facilitation based 'set of operations' analysis. The decision involved two cases that were joined for judgment. In the first proceedings, YS was a third country national who applied for a residence permit in the Netherlands. In the second proceeding, M and S were also third country nationals who made the same type of application. Although the key issue of the case is about whether certain data is 'personal data' and right of access, the Court had to consider the interpretation of processing. The cases regard internal legal analysis produced by case officers which form an integral part of residence decision-making. The legal analysis may or may not be extensive. In a detailed analysis, a case officer addresses matters such as 'the credibility of statements made' and an explanation as to why the case officer would or would not consider an applicant eligible for a permit. When applicants request a copy of the minute, they receive a summary of the personal data that is contained in the document.

The applicants each requested a copy of the minute and were refused. Instead, they received a summary of personal data used in the minute. The applicants argued the minute itself should be classed as personal data and they should therefore have access to it. The Court agreed that the data which related to the applicants must be considered 'personal data'. However, the legal analysis did not constitute 'personal data', despite containing personal data. The Court stated the legal analysis 'is information about the assessment and application by the competent authority of that law to the applicant's situation.' [33, para. 40]

Regarding the processing question, it must be noted that the applicants did not argue that the legal analysis was the result of organizing, structuring, consulting, and/or using personal data, and would be considered processing. The Court was therefore not asked to consider directly what would be processing in this case. However, the Advocate General provided reasoning why the legal analysis would not be considered processing.

> The use of the words 'such as' in Article 2(b) suggests that the list of operations is non-exhaustive; ... but also indicates the type of operation that will constitute 'processing'....As I see it, all of these operations involve *an action taken with respect to* [emphasis added] personal data, but without the assessment of that data which is inevitable in legal analysis. The same applies to the concept of filing [33, para. [63–65].

The key point for our purposes is the construction of 'an action taken with respect to personal data.' The use of 'respect to', albeit decided in the negative in *YS*, suggests that the Court considers processing to be more than simply processing actions on data. A 'respect to' analysis can also give rise to considerations of facilitation as part of a broader 'set of operations.' Accordingly, there is a separation of the underpinning judicial logic which outlines the possibility of a broader, holistic interpretation and the decision in this case which declined to follow that reasoning approach. The human control over legal analysis and the assessment of personal data as part of the production of that analysis appear to be the key elements that led the Court to decide the production of legal analysis was distinct from actual data processing or facilitation of data processing. Nonetheless, we contend that *YS* clearly acknowledges the possibility of a more expansive facilitation of processing argument.

We now examine what the differentiated definition of data processing means in the context of CHERI fat pointers and GDPR application.

4   Fat Pointers as Displacements

Taking on board the above, it could be argued that the use of CHERI fat pointers would not be classed as processing *on* personal data as a singular operation even though, as discussed, most processing operations will fall under Article 4(2). Several justifications could be used to support this contention.

First, CHERI fat pointer operations are conducted so far down the hardware stack that it could be argued that no processing is conducted on data. Fat pointers do not directly process data as the type of singular operation that gives rise to Article 4(2) application. CHERI fat pointers generate the technical conditions in which compartments can be utilized for different organizational and security purposes. Data processing is not directly conducted through fat pointers. Instead, pointer use allows for conditions and capabilities to take place across the hardware and software stack. Accordingly, the use of fat pointers and compartmentalization is not the same type of singular operation envisaged by the CJEU in the cases outlined at Sect. 3.1. There is no clearly definable act of transmission, dissemination, storage or disclosure analogous to the outlined cases. In those cases, there is a clear visibility between the singular operation of processing and the personal data being processed. Consequently, it could be argued that there is a distinct separation from the conditions that CHERI fat pointers create and data processing operations. The creation of processing conditions therefore does not amount to processing on personal data.

Second, it could be argued that there is a tension between how the CJEU understands personal data in the cases at Sect. 3.1 and how data could be understood through the generation of fat-pointer conditions. The separation of condition creation and processing operations means that in CHERI implementations, data is so low down the stack that it has no semantic meaning. It is merely a stream of data that is directed by fat pointer instructions. In the case of memory protection, the fat pointers control access to the memory and in terms of compartmentalisation, fat pointers direct data into compartments and can seal off compartments that are deemed to contain malware. It is consequently not data processing that is conducted on personal data because the separation of condition creation and actual processing is such that personal data is not a relevant construct for understanding fat pointer application.

All the cases at Sect. 3.1 have a close correspondence between a processing operation and a definable set of personal data, even though there are significant ranges of fact situation. For example, the *Puškár* list and the 'drawing up of names'; the video surveillance of *Ryneš* and *Buivids;* the transmission of minutes and cross jurisdictional transfers in *Bavarian Lager* and *Schrems* respectively and the right to be forgotten by removal of Internet search index data in *Google Spain*. All cases feature a direct correspondence of process and data use that allowed the CJEU to expansively construe Article 4(2) in the context of different fact situations. Expansive construction was possible because the CJEU was able to apply a rights-based emphasis to an identifiable data processing operation correspondent to identifiable personal data. The correspondence meant that the CJEU could say with certainty that the data processed under different guises was nevertheless personal data because of how the data could be classified and used within different processing systems. The same correspondence is not directly visible in CHERI fat pointer uses and there is a greater level of uncertainty, even with an expansive juridical outlook, about whether condition generation that allows data processing equates to processing on personal data.

Finally, as highlighted in the opening discussion of Sect. 3, Article 4(2) requires an intentionality by the data controller in the operation of data processing that can result in actual processing on data itself or can manifest in an intention to process. As noted in Recital 15, the action or intention involves filing systems [4]. The purposeful context of data processing consequently regards structured forms of processing that result in outputs for automated or non-automated filing systems. As such, processing by itself needs to be understood in context with other data protection facets and considered holistically in relation to controller acts or intentions and the resulting outputs as part of structured filing systems. We note above that our focus is on data processing specifically rather than the other constituent components that would need to be holistically considered regarding Article 4(2)'s operation to CHERI. Nevertheless, for the purpose of this discussion, it is important to acknowledge that the condition creation structure of CHERI fat pointers could potentially obfuscate a controller's processing intention because it is not conducted directly and evidently through a singular processing operation.

In summary, a core security strength of CHERI is that it operates and governs structuring from deeper within the hardware stack. Everything that is then built on top of it benefits from a more secure hardware foundation. The depth of foundation is a security strength, but it could also give rise to data protection uncertainties at a foundational level. Put simply, the invisibility that naturally occurs from being so buried in the stack potentially confuses legal and juridical decision-making dependent on visible and correspondent data processes that singularly operate on personal data. The condition creation capacities of CHERI fat pointers disrupt the legal certainty of identifiable processes, processing intentions and the semantic construction of personal data. All of which could give rise to potential controller arguments that implementation of CHERI may not give rise to GDPR compliance. Such arguments would be unfortunate and unwarranted especially if it gives rise to contentions that CHERI implementation obviates GDPR compliance for controllers.

The challenges that could arise from the genuinely disruptive quality of CHERI condition creation capacities and possible impacts on constructs like GDPR data processing should not be considered as obviation. Instead, these disruptions are better considered as 'displacements' which require more nuanced legal and regulatory configurations. Obviations by their nature intentionally seek to avoid. Displacements, on the other hand, are reflective of the disruptive nature of technological innovations which displace settled understandings of legal and regulatory application. CHERI implementation is not an obviation of legal and regulatory requirement. CHERI is not intended to, and should not be understood as, a means to obviate the need for data protection compliance. Rather, as outlined immediately above in this section, it displaces the settled legal understanding that data processing only needs to be considered as a singular operation involving processing on data. If that were the case, then it could lead to the situation where future CHERI use does indeed promote data protection obviation.

Hence the need for our facilitation interpretation of processing. Judicial outcomes are flexible enough that law can find a novel interpretation along previously considered lines to better meet a displacement caused by technological disruption. The law can cover displacements, even ones that are major disruptions. Whereas obviations are more absolute. They lead to binary outcomes of whether the law applies or does not apply with the starting point being the latter. Obviations remove judicial scope to develop law and meet changing technological circumstances, as highlighted in our analysis above of how the Sect. 3.1 cases would apply to CHERI fat pointers. Instead, we argue that CHERI displacements are better met by the explicit recognition of data processing as an act of facilitation that is part of a plural set of operations. Doing so would allow the possibility that some sub-processes can facilitate data processing which is not directly undertaken on personal data and thus counter the type of CHERI fat-pointer displacements outlined above. We find justification for our argument in the CJEU cases outlined at Sect. 3.2 and we consider how they would apply to three types of displacement: technical; intentionality and compliance.

In terms of technical displacement, we note above that CHERI is located so far down that stack that it does not appear to be part of the general technological routine of data processing. Yet, the use of fat pointers is still instrumental in creating the conditions for software usage that would allow data processing to take place. As such, while CHERI fat pointers would not be involved in data processing directly, it would still be foundationally instrumental in the facilitation of data processing across CHERI architectures. The displacement occurs because data processing would be conducted through compartmentalization governed by fat pointer instructions. There is no singular operation at the CHERI level and no clear visibility between processing and data. Fat pointer use is therefore akin to file permissions in a data processing context. Once instructions/permissions are applied, they create the conditions for how operations can be conducted on a compartment or file respectively. In the CHERI fat pointer situation, processing would depend on (1) the intention of compartment use and then (2) its actual use. The process of condition creation therefore requires a fat pointer that allocates a use for a compartment and then actual processing of data based on the conditions set by fat pointer instructions. The fat pointers do not undertake processing and instead create the conditions for processing to operate.

In that sense, fat pointer use in CHERI-based systems cannot be a singular operation in the way that the CJEU has traditionally classified data processing in the Sect. 3.1 cases. Fat pointer existence is pluralistic by design. Instructions create conditions and thus enable and facilitate data processing simultaneously but at different levels of the stack. The plural nature of fat-pointer usage requires the type of flexible construction of data processing found in *Tietosuojavaltuutettu*. Remember in that case the third of four sub-processes, the transfer to CD-ROM, appears to recognize that a sub-process which does not operate to process on personal data directly can still be classed overall as data processing if it forms or is intended to form a broader filing system. Applying to CHERI, the underpinning logic of indirect application in *Tietosuojavaltuutettu* could recognize the conjoining of fat pointer intentions and actual processing operations.

The same can be said for intentionality displacements. The enhanced security capacities of CHERI require controller intention to use fat-pointer instructions on a compartment for a specified purpose. The compartment is sealed from and agnostic to other compartments until fat pointer instructions are delivered. At that point, conditions for compartment use are created and enlivened across the CHERI infrastructure. Compartmental use therefore requires intention. However, as noted above, it is not entirely clear whether this form of intention is envisaged in Article 4(2) because it may not directly relate to an intention to processing personal data as part of a filing system. The pluralistic nature of CHERI's compartment structure means intentionality is represented in the fat pointer instructions because it is those instructions that give meaning to compartmental processing. Intentionality here is removed from the directly corresponding process and personal data. These are not instructions to process personal data per se. Rather, they are instructions that allow for the facilitation of processing to take place through a compartmentalized structure.

Intentionality is displaced from a direct act or intended act to undertake processing to one that indirectly seeks to use compartments in a certain type of way, based on condition creation instructions that allow processing to take place. Again, a broader construct is needed that moves beyond the limitations of singular processing on personal data become evident. Going back to the Sect. 3.2 cases, we contend that the roots of a broader approach can be found in *YS* and *Schwartz*. The 'respect to' analysis promulgated in *YS* offers a broader facilitation construct that would better tie together the intentionality behind CHERI pointer instructions and the actual operation of data processing activities. Unlike the legal advice in *YS*, fat pointer instructions are an intrinsic input that enables processing, rather than a reasoned output, which requires determined assessment. The instruction input is integral to CHERI process operations which can be considered as part of a 'respect to', facilitative analysis. Similarly, the type of prospective processing relating to the storage of fingerprints in *Schwartz*, highlights that the nature of processing can be prospective and is not limited to a singular understanding on a given set of personal data. The fact that processing output intentions can be prospective requires that processing must be understood as a plural set of operations for it to have any sort of meaningful application.

The final displacement we consider is compliance oriented. To do so, we need to be clear about what we are arguing throughout this paper. We are not arguing that CHERI implementation means that data processing will automatically take place under Article 4(2). Rather we argue the opposite. Data controllers that use CHERI architectures cannot argue by default that data processing is obviated and therefore the GDPR does not apply. Our paper highlights that the use of CHERI fat pointers will give rise to technical and intentionality displacements for controllers. A broader construct of facilitation can ensure that different forms of CHERI-based data processing can still be covered by the GDPR. A larger issue consequently arises which goes back to our point about displacement rather than obviation. Novel security technologies, like CHERI. Data protection requirements, such as those under the GDPR, are not obviated through the displacement of security to hardware environments throughout the infrastructural stack.

The displacement of security functions to hardware means that the governance of processing operations becomes less visible and tangible. However, the lack of visibility should not lead to uncritical obviation. The opposite is in fact the case. A more critical and reasoned approach is required to address what core operational activities, such as data processing, mean in environments disrupted or displaced by new technology. Doing so, requires broader understandings of processing control and the role of multiple controllers involved in data processing, such as those entailed in *Fashion ID*. Rethinking CJEU jurisprudence about the nature of data processing along facilitation lines ensures that displacements caused by technological innovation, such as CHERI and fat-pointer uses, are still within realistic reach of data protection law.

5   Conclusion

The CJEU's approach to identify what constitutes data processing can be relatively straightforward, as highlighted in the cases at Sect. 3.1. Data processing as a singular operation is still construed expansively in line with the fundamental rights of data protection accorded to EU citizens. The breadth of singular operations in Article 4(2) gives rise to the possibility of broad judicial pronouncements of coverage in seemingly straightforward fact situations. Put together, the principles underpinning the judicial decision-making approach regards attempts to directly place the processes of individual cases squarely within definition of Article 4(2) components. In that sense, there is an attempt to directly correspond a fact situation and a GDPR processing operation.

Even though the CJEU is willing to consider data processing expansively, some technologies, such as CHERI cause displacements which means that reasoning along the lines of analogous fact situations, based on singular operation become problematic. Our paper highlights that CHERI fat pointers have a role in facilitating how the processing of data takes place. This is also true in cases where this data may include data that counts as personal under the GDPR. By facilitating compartmental data access, CHERI fat pointers also facilitate data processing. Yet, despite this situation, it is unclear whether and how the traditional construction of data processing by the CJEU would apply. The technical, intentionality and compliance displacements potentially caused by CHERI means that a facilitation approach of data processing is needed to ensure that data protection is flexible in response to new forms of disruptive technology. Doing so, reduces the prospects for data protection obviation and ensures that dealing with displacements caused by technological innovation are an intrinsic part of wide-spread implementation. Our chapter provides a new interpretation of key CJEU cases outlined in Sect. 3.2. T Our interpretation sets the foundation for an expanded construct of data processing as a plural set of operations that facilitate data processing activities involving personal data which is better suited to complex technological innovations, such as CHERI.

Disclosure of Interests.   The research was largely funded by Discribe Hub + which is part of the broader Digital Security by Design research platform. Burdon, Coles-Kemp and Shipp received funding from Discribe Hub + for the research which is related to CHERI implementation.

References

1. Woodruff, J., et al.: The CHERI capability model: revisiting RISC in an age of risk. In: Proceeding of the 41st Annual International Symposium on Computer Architecuture, in ISCA 2014. Minneapolis, Minnesota, USA: IEEE Press, pp. 457–468 (2014)
2. Slesinger, I., Coles-Kemp, L., Panteli, N., Hansen, R.R.: Designing through the stack: the case for a participatory digital security by design. In: Proceedings of the 2022 New Security Paradigms Workshop, pp. 45–59 (2022)
3. Watson, R.N.M., et al.: Capability hardware enhanced RISC instructions: CHERI In-struction-set architecture (Version 8), University of Cambridge, Computer Laboratory, 951 (2020). https://www.cl.cam.ac.uk/techreports/UCAM-CL-TR-951.pdf

 4. Regulation (EU) 2016/679 of the European parliament and of the council of 27 April 2016 on the protection of natural persons with regard to the processing of personal data and on the free movement of such data, and repealing Directive 95/46/EC (General Data Protection Regulation).
 5. Bygrave, L.A.: Data Privacy Law : An International Perspective. Oxford University Press, Oxford (2014)
 6. Anderson, R.: Why information security is hard-an economic perspective. In: Seventeenth Annual Computer Security Applications Conference, IEEE, pp. 358–365 (2001)
 7. Pfleeger, C.P., Pfleeger, S.L., Coles-Kemp, L.: Security in Computing. Pearson (2023)
 8. Heath, C.P., Crivellaro, C., Coles-Kemp, L.: Relations are more than bytes: re-thinking the benefits of smart services through people and things. In: Proceedings of the 2019 CHI Conference on Human Factors in Computing Systems, pp. 1–12 (2019)
 9. Hielscher, J., Schöps, M., Menges, U., Gutfleisch, M., Helbling, M., Sasse, M.A.: Lacking the tools and support to fix friction: results from an interview study with security managers (2023)
10. Sarker, I.H.: Multi-aspects AI-based modeling and adversarial learning for cybersecurity intelligence and robustness: a comprehensive overview. Secur. Priv. **6**, e295 (2023)
11. Sarker, I.H., Furhad, M.H., Nowrozy, R.: Ai-driven cybersecurity: an overview, security intelligence modeling and research directions. SN Comput. Sci. **2**, 1–18 (2021)
12. Watson, R.N.: UKRI digital security by design: a £190M research programme around Arm's Morello – An experimental ARMv8-A CPU, SoC, and board with CHERI support. https://www.lightbluetouchpaper.org/2019/10/18/ukri-digital-security-by-design-a-190m-research-programme-around-arms-morello-an-experimental-armv8-a-cpu-soc-and-board-with-cheri-support/
13. Watson, R.N.: et al.: CHERI: a hybrid capability-system architecture for scalable software compartmentalization. In: 2015 IEEE Symposium on Security and Privacy, pp. 20–37 (2015)
14. Mazzinghi, A.: Pointer provenance in a capability architecture. https://www.usenix.org/system/files/conference/tapp2018/tapp2018-paper-mazzinghi.pdf
15. Woodruff, J., et al.: The CHERI capability model: revisiting RISC in an age of risk. SIGARCH Comput. Archit. News **42**(3), 457–468 (2014). https://doi.org/10.1145/2678373.2665740
16. Tosoni, L., Bygrave, L.A.: Article 4(2). In: Kuner, C., Bygrave, L.A., Docksey, C., Drechsler, L. (eds.) Processing in The EU General Data Protection Regulation (GDPR): A Commentary, Oxford University Press (2020). https://doi.org/10.1093/oso/9780198826491.003.0008
17. Directive 95/46/EC of the European parliament and of the council of 24 October 1995 on the protection of individuals with regard to the processing of personal data and on the free movement of such data [1995] OJ L 281/31, art 1(1)
18. Kuner, C., Bygrave, L.A., Docksey, C., Drechsler, L. (eds.) The EU General Data Protection Regulation (GDPR): A Commentary. Oxford University Press (2020). https://doi.org/10.1093/oso/9780198826491.001.0001
19. Charter of fundamental rights of the European union [2000] OJ C 364/1, art 8(1); Consolidated version of the treaty on the functioning of the European union [2012] OJ C 326/47, art 16(1)
20. Consolidated version of the Treaty on the Functioning of the European Union OJ C 326, 26.10.2012
21. Peter Puškár v Finančné riaditeľstvo Slovenskej republiky and Kriminálny úrad finančnej správy / Case C-73/16 / 27 September 2017
22. Criminal proceedings against Bodil Lindqvist (C-101/01) [2003] ECR I-12971
23. František Ryneš v Úřad pro ochranu osobních údajů (Court of Justice of the European Union, C-212/13, ECLI:EU:C:2014:2428, 11 December 2014) (2014)
24. Proceedings brought by Sergejs Buivids (Court of Justice of the European Union, C-345/17, ECLI:EU:C:2019:122, 14 February 2019) (2019)

25. European Commission v The Bavarian Lager Co. Ltd., (C-28/08) [2010] ECR I-06055
26. Maximillian Schrems v Data Protection Commissioner (Court of Justice of the European Union, C-362/14, ECLI:EU:C:2015:650, 6 October 2015) (2015)
27. Google Spain v AEPD (Court of Justice of European Union, C-131/12, ECLI:EU:C:2014:317, 13 May 2014) (2014)
28. Camera di Commercio, Industria, Artigianato e Agricoltura di Lecce v Salvatore Manni (Court of Justice of the European Union, C-398/15, ECLI:EU:C:2017:197, 9 March 2017) (2017)
29. Fashion ID GmbH & Co. KG v Verbraucherzentrale NRW e.V. (Court of Justice of the European Union, C-40/17, ECLI:EU:C:2019:629, 29 July 2019) (2019)
30. Tietosuojavaltuutettu v Satakunnan Markkinapörssi and Satamedia (C-73/07) [2008] ECR I-09831
31. Michael Schwarz v Stadt Bochum (Court of Justice of the European Union, C-291/12, ECLI:EU:C:2013:670, 17 October 2013) (2013)
32. Weltimmo s.r.o. v Nemzeti Adatvédelmi és Információszabadság Hatóság (Court of Jus-tice of the European Union, C-230/14, ECLI:EU:C:2015:639, 1 October 2015) (2015)
33. YS v Minister voor Immigratie, Integratie en Asiel and Minister voor Immigratie, Inte-gratie en Asiel v M and S (Court of Justice of the European Union, C-141/12 and C-372/12, ECLI:EU:C:2014:2081, 17 July 2014) (2014)

The Mis/Dis-Information Problem Is *Hard* to Solve

Gregory Hagen[1], Reihaneh Safavi-Naini[1(✉)], and Moti Yung[2]

[1] University of Calgary, Calgary, Canada
rei@ucalgary.ca
[2] Google LLC and Columbia University, New York, USA

Abstract. Securing information communication dates back thousands of years ago. The meaning of *information security*, however, has evolved over time and today covers a very wide variety of goals, including identifying the source of information, the reliability of information, and ultimately whether the information is trustworthy.

In this paper, we will look at the evolution of the information security problem and the approaches that have been developed for providing information protection. We argue that the more recent problem of misinformation and disinformation has shifted the content integrity problem from the protection of message syntax to the protection of message semantics. This shift, in the age of advanced AI systems, a technology that can be used to mimic human-generated content as well as to create bots that mimic human behaviour on the Internet, poses fundamental technological challenges that evade existing technologies. It leaves social elements, including public education and a suitable legal framework, as increasingly the main pillars of effective protection, at least in the short run. It also poses an intriguing challenge to the scientific community: to design effective solutions that employ cryptography and AI, together with incentivization to engage the global community, to ensure the safety of the information ecosystem.

Keywords: Information security · misinformation · disinformation

1 Introduction

Securing information dates back thousands of years ago, primarily in the form of *secret communication*. In the time of Romans, Greeks, and Persians, generals needed to send secret messages to their allies and subordinates during wars and the message had to be hidden from the prying eyes of the enemies [1].

Steganography, the art of hiding the "existence of the message," was born. Steganography conceals a message within another cover message or object to hide its presence from anyone except the intended recipient. One of the most famous early examples of steganography dates from 500 B.C. Following the conquest of Miletus by Darius, King of Persia, Histiaeus, the tyrant of Miletus, found himself

© The Author(s), under exclusive license to Springer Nature Switzerland AG 2025
C. Boyd et al. (Eds.): Ed Dawson Festschrift 2024, LNCS 15600, pp. 309–326, 2025.
https://doi.org/10.1007/978-3-031-83490-5_12

imprisoned. To communicate with his son-in-law, Aristagoras, and incite him to rebellion, Histiaeus selected his most loyal slave, shaved his head, and inscribed a message on his scalp urging Aristagoras to revolt against Darius [2]. As the slave's hair grew back, he was sent to Aristagoras. Upon reaching Aristagoras, the slave's head was once again shaved, revealing the hidden message that ultimately led to the Ionian Revolt against Persian rule.

More recent examples of clandestine communication methods include the use of lemon juice, onion juice, or more sophisticated chemical compounds to conceal messages. Such techniques have been used by spies and agents throughout history. During World War II, agents often employed invisible ink made from various substances, such as milk, urine, or specially formulated chemicals that when applied to paper, remained invisible until activated by heat, ultraviolet light, or another chemical agent [3].

Over time, and especially with the introduction of the Internet and the World Wide Web, the security of information went beyond the need of generals and statesmen and became increasingly relevant and, in fact, crucial for everyone. Electronic commerce, heightened connectivity, and increasing integration of the physical and virtual worlds have elevated information security to a central role in the information exchange infrastructure of society. Two broad categories of techniques to protect information have emerged: cryptographic techniques and techniques that rely on data analysis and machine learning. These technologies have complementary roles: cryptography is primarily preventative and ensures that the security goals of an information system are met. Machine-learning and data analysis techniques, on the other hand, contribute primarily to the detection of misbehaviours. They may look for pre-defined combination of features or anomalous patterns of behaviour, using large data sets that are collected from the system of interest, and use them to detect signs of a breach. The two in combination aim to provide a *safe information ecosystem*: a digital environment where information is trustworthy and accessible to authorized users, while protecting individuals' privacy rights and "digital rights" that would be required in an information-driven world.

In the following, we review important elements of these two approaches as they have evolved over time, and then discuss the problem of trustworthiness of digital content, which, in a very broad sense, encompasses content integrity, veracity, and the ability to trace it to its source. We then outline the limitations of existing tools and techniques to cope with the more recent emerging problem of misinformation and disinformation. Our main observations are the following.

- Protection against mis/dis-information broadens the scope of *information security* to include protection of the *meaning of a message* in addition to the protection of its *representation* (semantics vs. syntax).
- Advancement of computing and, in particular, AI has provided tremendous power to generate content and disseminate it through the Internet, mimicking human language and interaction on the Internet.
- Protecting the semantics of messages is closely linked to identifying the *message's source*, which, in the age of generative AI, is increasingly challeng-

ing due to the difficulty of distinguishing AI-generated content from human-generated content. Technologies aiming to make this distinction face a steep uphill battle.

- Social measures, in particular, public education that emphasizes critical thinking and the evaluation of everyday information streams, as well as carefully constructed laws that define the boundaries of social interaction, form the main pillars of protection, at least in the short run.

- In the long term, combining security technologies with economic incentives could provide a promising direction for developing future technologies.

2 Technologies for Securing Information

Securing information communication systems uses a wide range of hardware and software systems. Algorithmic approaches to security can be broadly divided into cryptographic ones and data analysis/machine learning ones.

2.1 Cryptography

Cryptography started with encryption, whose goal is *hiding the message content*, but not its existence. The Caesar cipher is an elementary yet historically significant encryption algorithm that dates back to ancient Rome [1]. Named after Julius Caesar, who purportedly used it to encode his private communications, the cipher algorithm works by shifting the alphabet. Each letter in the plain-text is substituted with a letter that is a fixed number of positions down the alphabet. The Caesar cipher is an example of a *substitution cipher* which uses a permutation of the alphabet to replace each letter with another one. Another early cipher was the *transposition cipher*, which rearranges the order of letters in the plain-text to create the ciphertext. One historical example of a transposition cipher is the Scytale, an ancient Spartan cryptographic tool [1]. The Scytale involved wrapping a strip of parchment around a rod of a particular diameter and then writing the message lengthwise. When unwrapped, the message would appear scrambled and indecipherable unless the recipient possessed a rod of the same diameter, allowing for the message's reconstruction.

As cryptography evolved, cryptographers introduced a wide range of algorithms which in many cases consisted of variations and compositions of the above two approaches to increase security, while being able to analyse and predict the behaviour of the algorithm. One of the prominent examples of combining substitution and transposition ciphers to construct a powerful encryption system is in the *Enigma machine*, an intricate encryption device used extensively by the German military during World War II [4]. The Enigma machine employed a series of rotors and electrical pathways to perform letter substitutions and transpositions. The resulting ciphertext produced by the Enigma machine was highly secure, owing to the combination of substitution and transposition techniques, along with the machine's mechanical complexity and the frequent changing of rotor settings.

Cryptography and Cryptanalysis. Cryptanalysis was pioneered by ancient crypt-analysts as the art of deciphering encrypted messages without access to the encryption key. As cryptographers developed increasingly complex ciphers to protect communication, cryptanalysts devised new methods to break the ciphers. Al-Kindi, a ninth-century Arab mathematician, wrote one of the earliest known treatises on cryptanalysis [5]. Al-Kindi's treatise not only outlined methods for breaking simple substitution ciphers but also delved into the principles of frequency analysis and linguistic patterns, demonstrating a sophisticated understanding of cryptologic concepts centuries ahead of its time. Cryptography and cryptanalysis are complementary and together form the art and science of cryptology. The interplay between the two disciplines of cryptography and cryptanalysis resulted in the creation of stronger ciphers and the refinement and enhancement of cryptanalytic methods.

The *science of cryptography started with secrecy systems.* In 1949, Shannon laid the foundation of scientific cryptography by formalizing perfect secrecy and showing a system that achieves it [6]. Shannon proved that *One-Time-Pad (OTP)*, an encryption system that was invented tens of years earlier [7] and was used during World War I, achieved perfect secrecy. OTP, however, requires a random key that is as long as the message to be transmitted and must be used only once. The key must be securely shared between the two communicating parties before the system is used. OTP found limited application, mainly in highly secure military settings, such as the Moscow-Washington "hot line" during the 1940s and 50 s. During this period the main application of cryptography was the secrecy of communication.

Today, standardized encryption algorithms like AES (Advanced Encryption Standard) represent the pinnacle of cryptographic resilience. The AES algorithm has been examined and analyzed by experts around the world for over two decades, without finding any real weakness in the design. It has been adopted by governments and industries and has demonstrated remarkable resistance against advanced cryptanalytic attacks [8]. Additionally, rigorous selection processes that include scrutiny and evaluation by the worldwide community of cryptography and cryptanalysts, followed by the widespread successful deployments in real-life systems, have fostered the required trust and acceptance that are essential for modern security systems.

The Authentication Problem: Protecting Against Active Attacks. In the 1970s, the growth of the Internet brought forward two new challenges beyond hiding the message content (e.g., to provide confidentiality or privacy): the need to detect tampering with the content and the ability to trust the claimed identities of entities from whom information is received. As the digital world expanded, individuals found themselves navigating a realm where verifying the authenticity of source and content became increasingly complex. This challenge was best encapsulated in a widely circulated 1993 New Yorker cartoon featuring a dog sitting at a computer, declaring to a fellow dog: "On the Internet, no one knows you are a dog." The image perfectly captures the uncertainty surrounding identity verification in an expanding virtual world [9]. Indeed there were direct adversarial and financial gains from the mis-representation of identities and content. Malicious actors used strategies such as claiming a false identity and tampering with information for financial fraud, or impersonation of reputable organizations to deceive users into divulging their sensitive information or transfer funds.

The ground breaking invention of public key cryptography and digital signatures by Diffie and Hellman promised a conceptual solution to the problem of trusting identities and content origin in a virtual world [10]. In this paradigm, Alice has a unique pair of keys: a secret key (sk_A) known only to her and a corresponding public key (pk_A) that is public and associated with Alice's identity. Alice can securely link her identity to digital messages and documents by digitally signing them, using her secret key sk_A. The resulting signature can then be verified by anyone possessing her public key pk_A, thereby linking the document to its originator. Ensuring the integrity of messages between two trusting parties, however, uses *Message Authentication Codes (MAC)* that enable two parties who share a secret key to efficiently detect tampering of messages that are communicated between them. *"Codes which detect deception"* and can be used to authenticate messages in the presence of an adversary with unlimited computation were introduced in the pioneering work of Gilbert, MacWilliams and Sloane [11], and later formalised by Simmons [12]. It appeared that a safe information ecosystem was finally on the horizon.

The use of the term "authentication" in cryptography has many subtleties, and depends on the underlying cryptographic primitive, and possibly the context of use. A digitally signed document by Alice guarantees that the document has been generated by Alice when she is (securely) associated with the corresponding public verification key and tampering by *any other party* is detectable. A message with an attached MAC, however, can detect tampering by a *third party* who is distinct from the two trusting parties who have a shared secret key that is used for constructing the MAC. This means that either of the two trusting parties can undetectably change a document that is protected by a MAC. There are even more subtle nuances in using digital signatures to uniquely identify the sender of a message. In [13], it is argued that identification of the source of a message could be done for the purpose of assigning "responsibility" to the source or giving "credit" to them. For example, when Bob receives a signed message M from Alice to delete a file, then Bob can delete the file and gives the responsibility for deleting the file to Alice. However, when Bob receives a signed message M from Alice that shows the two previously unknown prime factors of a large integer, Bob gives "credit" to Alice for finding the primes. It is argued in [13] that the two are very different and a protocol that may work securely for one purpose, can be insecure for the other purpose. In the following we do not consider these subtleties and consider a digital signature as a cryptographic primitive that can uniquely identify the source of a message.

Cryptography Everywhere. Fast forward almost 50 years from Diffie and Hellman's groundbreaking paper and cryptography has become ubiquitous as the primary tool for ensuring security in the digital age. Today, its influence permeates every facet of our lives, from the simplest devices like garage door openers to the vast array of internet-connected devices in our homes, that we carry with us in our daily lives, and that we use in workplaces and industrial systems. Cryptography has revolutionized the way that we communicate, access services, work and interact remotely, and has become an integral component of secure functionalities across various domains. It has also played a pivotal role in innovations such as blockchain technology and other decentralized systems that have transformed traditional paradigms of trust and accountability.

2.2 Machine Learning For Security

The Prehistory of AI. The field of artificial intelligence (AI) developed around creating artificial agents that can mimic cognitive functions that are typically associated with humans, such as learning, reasoning, problem-solving, perception, and decision-making. In Greek mythology, Talos was a giant bronze automaton created by Hephaestus, the god of fire and craftsmanship, tasked with guarding the island of Crete [14]. Talos shares several characteristics of modern AI systems, including *autonomous decision-making*, *pattern recognition*, and *goal-oriented behavior*.

Early philosophers, notably Aristotle, sought to formalize deductive reasoning through symbol manipulation. Aristotle defined deduction as a discourse (logos) in which, given certain premises, a conclusion distinct from these premises logically follows because of the inherent relationship between them [15]. In his syllogistic theory, knowledge is encapsulated in the premises, and new knowledge can be deduced through logical inference. Subsequent formalizations of logic by Boole, Frege, Russell, Hilbert, and others ultimately led to the development of first-order logic [16], a cornerstone of knowledge representation and reasoning in AI [17].

The development of systems of formal reasoning was accompanied by the creation of mechanical systems for the automation of reasoning. The invention of mechanical calculators, such as Leibniz's calculating machine and Pascal's Pascaline in the 17th century, and Babbage's Analytical Engine in 19th century, were significant steps towards the development of machines capable of performing complex calculations [18]. One can also recognize the continued desire to simulate the world by building mechanical automata. These artifacts, which gradually became more sophisticated, are exemplified by Vaucanson's creations in the 18th century, including Digesting Duck [19], which, as the name suggests, was a mechanical duck that simulated the complete digestive system of a duck.

These developments, while not directly related to contemporary AI, represent important milestones in the evolution of ideas and technologies that ultimately contributed to the emergence of artificial intelligence. Mechanical calculators are precursors of todays' computers that use symbolic representation of knowledge and logical rules of deduction to infer new knowledge and mechanical self-governing automata can be seen as mechanical precursors of "bots" that we see on the Internet today. They reflect a growing interest in understanding the human mind and the potential for machines to simulate or even surpass human capabilities. However, it wasn't until the 20th century that the foundation for modern AI was truly laid.

Birth of AI. The term "artificial intelligence" was coined by McCarthy and first used in the proposal for the Dartmouth Summer Research Project on Artificial Intelligence (1956) [20]. McCarthy considered the field of AI to have its roots in Alan Turing's article "Computing Machines and Intelligence" (1950) and Shannon's paper "Programming a Computer for Playing Chess" (1950) [21]. These works, respectively, laid the groundwork for AI by proposing a criterion for machine intelligence (the Turing Test) [22] and exploring the practical application of algorithms to tackle complex problems, such as developing strategies for playing chess [23]. McCarthy's LISP programming language contributed to knowledge representation, reasoning, and common-sense reasoning that are used in many AI systems today [24].

Other AI pioneers include Minsky and Newell, who played pivotal roles in defining the field's goals and research directions [20]. Minsky, a co-founder of the MIT AI Laboratory, made significant contributions to the development of artificial neural networks (ANNs), robotics, and created the theory of the *society of mind*, according to which intelligence emerges from the interaction of many simple agents from which a mind is built [25]. All of these contributions continue to influence AI today. Newell and Simon were pioneers in cognitive science and developed ideas about the relationship between symbolic systems and intelligent action [26]. They also developed the *Logic Theorist,* the first AI program capable of proving mathematical theorems, and the *General Problem Solver* (GPS), a program designed to solve a wide range of problems using heuristic search [27].

McCulloch and Pitts' 1943 paper "A Logical Calculus of the Ideas Immanent in Nervous Activity," sparked the study of neural networks (NNs) inspired by the brain's biological structure as a system of connected neurons [17]. Basic NNs consisted of input, hidden, and output layers, and could be trained on labeled datasets (e.g., dog and cat pictures) to be able to classify future new and unseen data [17]. Despite an early promising start, a combination of unmet expectations, funding cuts, and technical limitations led to periods of stagnation known as "AI winters" in the 1970s and 1980s [17]. The late 20th and early 21st centuries witnessed a resurgence in AI, driven by advancements in machine learning and the increasing availability of data. Successes in game-playing AI, such as IBM's Deep Blue defeating the world chess champion using a brute-force approach, and DeepMind's AlphaGo, which combined deep learning with search algorithms to defeat a world champion Go player, demonstrated AI's growing ability to tackle complex problems once thought to be the exclusive domain of human intelligence [17].

Conversational agents, designed to simulate human conversation, began in 1966 with ELIZA [28], which used pattern matching and substitution to engage with users in text conversations. They evolved into more capable agents by incorporating advancements in natural language processing and machine learning. Chatbots like A.L.I.C.E. (1995) and SmarterChild (2001) in the 1990s and 2000s, respectively, offered increasingly sophisticated responses, often serving as virtual assistants or information providers [29]. Voice assistants like Siri (2011) and Alexa (2014) further blurred the lines between human and machine interaction, as these agents could understand and respond to spoken language [29].

The release of ChatGPT 3.5 in 2022 introduced an exceptionally more powerful assistant with unprecedented text-generation capabilities. Generative AI refers to AI systems that can produce new data, such as images, text, or audio, that are generated from examples it has been trained on. Today's generative AI systems, often based on deep learning techniques, generate "synthetic" content that is derived from captured knowledge and appears remarkably original and realistic. Deep generative AI models like OpenAI's ChatGPT, DALL-E, Google's PaLM, and Meta's Llama 2 are notable for their ability to generate content in audio, visual, and text formats that are increasingly difficult to distinguish from human-created content.

AI and Machine Learning in Security. The use of AI and machine learning for securing information communication dates back to the late 1980s and early 1990s. Initially, rule-based systems were employed for anomaly detection, where predefined rules were used to identify deviations from normal behavior. These early systems were limited in their ability to adapt and learn from new threats [30]. Building upon earlier work in the field of intrusion detection, the seminal work of Dorothy Denning introduced the concept of using statistical anomaly detection to identify intrusions in computer systems [31]. This laid the groundwork for the development of Intrusion Detection Expert Systems (IDES), which initially relied on rule-based systems but later incorporated machine learning techniques, such as decision trees and neural networks, to enhance their detection capabilities. Denning's work stands out as a major milestone due to its rigorous formulation of a statistical anomaly detection model and its explicit connection to intrusion detection.

The wider development of intrusion detection systems began in the early 1990s, with companies like Haystack Labs and SRI International [32] developing systems that utilized statistical anomaly detection. Today machine learning algorithms use a wide array of data including network traffic, system, device and user data, to identify unusual patterns or unexpected changes in each or combination of these data to signal a possible cyber-attack or data breach [33]. Deep learning models, like convolutional neural networks (CNNs), excel at analyzing vast and intricate datasets, enabling more accurate identification of anomalies in network traffic and other collected data that may indicate malicious activities [34].

AI-based approaches, however, face two main challenges. First, how to reliably translate a similarity score that is calculated for a potential breach and using many features, into a concrete decision, "attack" or "no attack", possibly with some indication of severity level, and balance the system's false positive and false negative. Second, how to detect new zero-day attacks for which prior information does not exist in the system. These challenges have motivated new approaches, such as unsupervised learning, to address these limitations. In practice cryptographic and machine-learning based approaches are used in concert to improve security.

3   Identifying the "Source" of a Digital Object and the Integrity of the Object

Interest in identifying the "source" of digital content, in terms of both the originator and owner, as well as verifying its authenticity and intactness, grew with the rise of electronic commerce and the distribution of digital content over the Internet.

In the early 2000s, music sharing experienced a boom, with music and media sold in smaller units, such as individual songs, and packaged in various appealing forms. Digital signatures could securely link content to its originator and be used for signing contracts. However, digital signatures could easily be stripped from the content, allowing it to be copied and redistributed. The surge in copyrighted digital content distribution over the Internet posed a new challenge: preventing illegal copying and redistribution through peer-to-peer file sharing and other forms of unauthorized reproduction or communication of works.

The new emerging technological challenge was how to authenticate the source and integrity of a digital object and trace it to its origin or owner once cryptographic protections are removed. The challenge stems from the fact that one can simply pay the required price (or fee) to access a digital object and then, since the object is in digital form, easily and perfectly copy and redistribute it, ignoring the copyrights of the content owner. New cryptographic and noncryptographic solutions in the form of innovative *fingerprinting* and *watermarking* methods were introduced to trace digital objects to their originators and/or owners and to verify the origin and/or owner of the content, thereby facilitating copyright infringement actions.

3.1   Watermarking

A watermarking system embeds imperceptible or barely perceptible data into digital objects, such as images, audio, or video, to signify properties like authenticity, integrity, or ownership, as needed. The *robustness* of watermarking systems refers to the watermark's ability to withstand various forms of manipulation, distortion, or attacks while remaining detectable [35]. A robust watermark ensures the embedded information is reliably retrievable even after the content undergoes alterations or attempts to remove or tamper with the watermark itself.

Robustness is essential for ensuring the integrity of content and authenticity of origin, but hard to achieve because of the array of tools and techniques that can be used to remove the watermark by modifying the content or creating a new copy using a different device. Techniques such as image cropping, content scaling, and lossy compression algorithms have emerged as particularly effective tools for removing or altering watermarks to make them undetectable. Creating a new recording of a song or taking a new picture of an image can heavily reduce the detectability of a watermark at the cost of reducing the quality of the digital object. Thus, watermark robustness, although essential for ensuring integrity and traceability (to the source) of the content, is hard to achieve because of the array of tools and techniques that can be used to manipulate the content and remove the watermark.

3.2 Digital Rights Management

Digital Rights Management (DRM) technology promised to securely manage access to, and the copying of, copyrighted content in accordance with copyright licenses [36]. DRM systems used watermarking and fingerprinting technologies combined with cryptography and tamperproof hardware to achieve security but introduced a plethora of new technological and legal challenges, as well as factors to be taken into account related to social dimensions.

Content origin, ownership, and tracing in practice. Today, watermarking, together with wide monitoring of Internet traffic, is used to detect copyright breaches across digital platforms. One concrete example of such a monitoring service is the Content ID system developed by YouTube [37]. Content ID employs algorithms to scan and analyze uploaded videos, comparing them against a vast database of copyrighted content provided by rights holders. When a match is detected, rights holders have the option to block the video, track its viewership metrics, or monetize it by running ads alongside the content.

A notable example of the Content ID system in action occurred when a user uploaded a music video featuring Ed Sheeran's hit song Shape of You without the necessary authorization from the copyright owner. The rights holder, alerted by Content ID, was able to identify the infringement and take appropriate action [38]. This example highlights the effectiveness of Internet traffic monitoring services in detecting and addressing copyright breaches in real-time.

Societal challenges. DRM gives rise to a myriad of citizens' rights issues, including how to implement copyright's balance in information technology. The fine line between, on the one hand, infringement and, on the other, fair use or fair dealing (or some other non-infringing use) is not easy to inscribe in code. As a result, the US Digital Millennium Copyright Act [39] and its analogues in other jurisdictions created the possibility that the copyright balance in technology and in law does not match. For instance, in Canada, the Copyright Act does not permit circumvention of an access control measure for the purposes of fair dealing, such as extracting a short excerpt of a music video for educational purposes and posting it online [40]. Arguably, forbidding such circumvention violates the right to freedom of expression as guaranteed by, e.g., the Canadian Charter of Rights and Freedoms [41]. A general conclusion that can be drawn is that regulating information technology systems runs the risk of violating the right to freedom of expression.

3.3 Fake Content

Fake content refers to any digital material that has been deliberately created, altered, manipulated, or falsified to convey misleading, deceptive, or false information. It encompasses a wide range of media, including images, videos, audio recordings, and written text, that have been tampered with to distort their original meaning or context. In the context of images and videos, fake content may use editing software to alter visual elements, such as adding or removing objects or modifying colors. Fake content includes counterfeit websites that mimic legitimate ones, with the intent to deceive users. These fake websites may closely replicate the design, layout, and branding of authentic sites, making them appear genuine at first glance.

Detecting fake content is a multifaceted exercise that may use a wide range of technologies, including forensic techniques and machine learning approaches. While detecting clumsy manipulation of media objects, for example an image, is possible for skilled users, more sophisticated cases that misrepresent the truth can become hard to detect, if possible at all. A widely discussed recent example of a clumsily modified image is a depiction of a street scene in Cuba that included a distant image of a man walking near some steps with a post coming out of his right leg [42]. After this discovery, several other images of the photographer were discovered to have been altered. The photographer admitted to using photoshop, saying that he was no longer a photo-journalist but, rather, a "visual storyteller" [43].

There are also examples of fake images that end up being used as evidence in a claim versus counter claim scenario. For example, in the "Obama skeet shooting" controversy, following debates over gun control legislation in the United States, the New Republic magazine tweeted a photograph that purported to show former President Barack Obama skeet shooting at Camp David, as he had claimed to have done [44]. The photograph was fake, however, having been inadvertently copied from a parody of *Whitehouse.gov* rather than the real website. To provide evidence for Obama's assertion, the White House later revealed another photograph that also purported to show Obama skeet shooting at Camp David, but it was derided by several conservative commentators as fake.

In the end, to be taken as evidence, there was a need to trust that the White House provided a genuine photograph of Obama skeet shooting and that it had not been tampered with.

4 The Problem of Fake Content in the Age of Generative AI

The problem of fake content in today's societies has two components: generation of fake content and its wide distribution. Advances in AI technologies have provided extremely powerful technologies for both.

Generative AI can quickly produce synthetic text, images, and audio that are increasingly difficult to distinguish from content generated through natural or human-driven processes. Although Chatbots like ChatGPT are programmed with safety guidelines to avoid generating harmful or biased content [45], they can be "tricked" to produce misleading and fake output. Determined users can exploit vulnerabilities in the system by carefully crafting prompts (queries to the chatbot) or by directly modifying small parts of the generated content. Despite efforts to employ watermarking techniques to detect and trace AI-generated content, the race between possible manipulations of AI-generated content, with the goal of removing the watermark, and fortification of watermarking techniques to be robust against possible manipulations, will be an uphill battle. Without robust automated watermarking embedding and detection mechanisms, proliferation of AI-generated fake content will be unavoidable.

The distribution of fake content can be powered by AI-enabled agents (bots) that mimic user interaction on the web and social media. Using fake or stolen credentials, bots can be registered on various platforms and programmed to interact and participate in online networks to distribute fake content as part of well-orchestrated campaigns.

Disinformation and Misinformation are both used to describe false or misleading information, but they differ in their meaning. *Misinformation*, refers to false or inaccurate information shared without the intent to deceive, while *disinformation* involves the deliberate spread of false or misleading information with the intent to deceive or manipulate others [46]. Both can have significant implications for public discourse, decision-making, and social trust.

AI significantly amplifies the ability to generate and disseminate misinformation and disinformation. AI can be used to create digitally altered or synthesized media that convincingly depict events or individuals that never occurred or existed. (When such content is generated by deep neural networks, it is referred to as a "deepfake".) The outputs of generative AI systems are becoming increasingly indistinguishable from genuine content, blurring the lines between reality and fiction. Even reputable sources, including media organizations, are susceptible to being fooled by AI-generated content. For instance, users have submitted AI-generated images purportedly depicting events such as the Israel-Gaza crisis to stock image marketplaces like Adobe Stock [47]. AI-powered bots can be used to mimic human behavior on social media platforms, creating the illusion of widespread support for, or opposition to, specific ideas, candidates, or causes. By flooding online spaces with orchestrated messages, AI-generated misinformation can distort public discourse and amplify certain narratives while suppressing others. In [48], authors have described how the convergence of technologies, including AI, social media, bots and big data analysis have created an "epistemic crisis" that endangers democracy in the US. The United Nations Policy Brief on Information Integrity on Digital Platforms considers the spread of disinformation that undermines established scientific facts to be "an existential risk to humanity" [49].

Generative AI algorithms, fueled by deep learning techniques, have democratized the creation of synthetic media, making it strikingly easy for individuals without extensive expertise, advanced technical skills or specialized knowledge, to generate highly realistic content. This accessibility has lowered the barrier to entry for malicious actors seeking to create and disseminate deceptive or misleading information.

4.1   The Challenge of Creating A Safe Information Ecosystem

Because of the ease of generating content by generative AI, a key challenge to the establishment of a safe information ecosystem is the detection of synthetic content, with the primary technique being the use of watermarking technologies. As discussed earlier, embedding robust watermarks in perceptual data is a formidable task. The task is even harder in text-based content that can be re-written in a myriad of ways. This challenge is well-recognized by experts and technology companies. It even led OpenAI, which had previously announced plans for a synthetic text detector, to retract its plan due to low accuracy [50]. Currently, there is no reliable method to discern whether text-based content was generated by AI or a human [51]. Additionally, there are many open-source generative models that can be run on personal computers and/or modified and extended to remove in-built protections and so there is no easy way to ensure that all synthetic contents will be watermarked.

Laws and Regulations. Even if synthetic content could be reliably detected, it does not guarantee that its generation or transmission could be prevented, or that it should be prevented, given our right to freedom of expression. A safe information ecosystem does not require that all misinformation and disinformation be banished. As the Special Rapporteur on Human Rights has said: "The right to freedom of opinion and expression is not part of the problem, it is the objective and the means for combating disinformation." [52]. Freedom of expression does not imply that there can be no legal restrictions on the development or use of AI systems. The communication of some deepfakes or misinformation may constitute *private law* causes of action, such as defamation, deceit and misappropriation of personality as well as a criminal offence. For an example of the latter, the recently enacted UK Online Safety Act criminalizes the transmission of deepfake pornography [53]. Similar laws exist or are proposed in the US, Canada, Australia and other countries, in all cases, dealing with harms that have occurred. In addition, the European Union regulates the development, sale and use of AI under the Artificial Intelligence Act [54], and some countries, such as Canada [55], are seeking to create similar legislation.

The Global Declaration on Information Integrity Online says that a safe information ecosystem requires information integrity [56]. The declaration defines "information integrity" as "an information ecosystem that produces accurate, trustworthy, and reliable information, meaning that people can rely on the accuracy of the information they access while being exposed to a variety of ideas" [56]. This concept of "information integrity" goes well beyond the integrity of the "presentation of information" itself that is the goal of cryptography, watermarking techniques and similar technologies. Such an ecosystem will of necessity include humans who have developed the epistemic virtues (e.g. to properly reason, doubt, and interpret) necessary to determine the trustworthiness of the source and veracity of the information provided.

4.2   What Is Possible

While efforts around the world aim to get a handle on AI safety, the focus is mostly on the safety and security of AI systems and how they are used in practice, rather than increasing public understanding of their operation and effects.

Given the limitations of both information security technology and current regulations to detect and control the spread of fake content and misinformation and to ensure the integrity of information, public education is the first and the most important step in curbing the problem of AI-generated fake content (in addition to continued efforts to find more effective technical solutions). Regulators and AI model developers need to prioritize informing the public about the capabilities, limitations, and effects of current AI models. Educational initiatives can begin by transparently demonstrating the capabilities of AI models to the public, accompanied by explanations of the underlying mechanisms and limitations of existing tracing and detection techniques, including watermarking.

Public education must also emphasize the necessity of learning how to scrutinize audio, visual, and text-based content, in order to evaluate its authenticity and the reliability of their sources. Developing these critical skills requires individuals to overcome inherent trust biases and navigate the complexities of media consumption in an age of social media and fragmented news sources.

Given the rise of generative models capable of creating synthetic media, fostering epistemic vigilance is crucial for individuals to navigate a world where differentiating between authentic and manipulated content is increasingly difficult. Automated tools that provide judgments and alerts can be helpful, and intensifying efforts to develop technical solutions is a must.

5   Concluding Remarks

The need to secure information and provide a safe information ecosystem is intertwined with our presence in the digital world. Protection against mis/disinformation requires a solution to the problem of ensuring the integrity of the *meaning* of messages, something which goes beyond traditional security technologies that largely aim to protect the integrity of *message representation* as a string of symbols. While cryptography and machine learning approaches have provided effective methods of protection for bit representations (syntax) of digital objects, they become blunt tools in ensuring the veracity of information that they carry. The protection against mis/disinformation in the age of generative AI is entangled with distinguishing between human-generated and AI-generated content. Generative AI poses a significant threat by blurring the line between authentic and fake content and interaction on the Internet as a whole. AI-powered bots can be employed as an organized army of agents in the service of a defined goal, weaponizing misinformation and disinformation to manipulate public discourse and to achieve political objectives. In the absence of effective technological countermeasures, public education and carefully constructed laws become increasingly important in restoring safety to our today's information ecosystem.

Looking ahead, while no immediate, purely technological solution is in sight, innovative solutions combining technical approaches like cryptography, watermarking, and AI (i.e., "fighting fire with fire") with incentivization mechanisms offer intriguing opportunities for researchers and technology developers.

In recent years the combination of cryptography and economic incentives has been one of the key innovations behind the success of Bitcoin and blockchain technology. Smart contract-based systems like the MakerDAO protocol on the Ethereum blockchain have further extended the use of financial incentives and *penalties* to ensure the stability and security of the system. Such combined technological solutions, when supported by a well-crafted legal framework, may prove effective in moving towards a safer information ecosystem.

References

1. Singh, S.: The Code Book: The Science of Secrecy from Ancient Egypt to Quantum Cryptography. Anchor Books, New York (1999)
2. Herodotus: The Histories. Penguin Classics (1996)
3. Macrakis, K.: Prisoners, Lovers, and Spies: The Story of Invisible Ink from Herodotus to al-Qaeda. Yale University Press, New Haven, CT (2014)
4. Greenberg, J.: The enigma machine. In: The Turing Guide. Oxford University Press (2017). https://doi.org/10.1093/oso/9780198747826.003.0018
5. Al-Kindi (841) manuscript on deciphering cryptographic messages, king faisal center for research of Islamic studies, Riyadh, Saudi Arabia, 841, manuscript
6. Shannon, C.E.: Communication theory of secrecy systems. Bell Syst. Tech. J. **28**(4), 656–715 (1949)
7. Bellovin, S.M.: Frank miller: inventor of the one-time pad. Cryptologia **35**(3), 203–222 (2011)
8. Canadian Centre for Cybersecurity: Cryptographic algorithms for UNCLASSIFIED, PROTECTED A, and PROTECTED B information, Canadian Centre for Cyber Security, ITSP.40.111 (2023). https://www.cyber.gc.ca/sites/default/files/itsp.40.111_1-e.pdf
9. Fleishman, G.: Cartoon captures spirit of the internet. The New York Times (2000)
10. Diffie, W., Hellman, M.E.: New directions in cryptography. IEEE Trans. Inf. Theory **IT-22**(6), 644–654 (1976)
11. Gilbert, E.N., MacWilliams, F.J., Sloane, N.J.A.: Codes which detect deception. Bell Syst. Tech. J. **53**(3), 405–424 (1974)
12. Simmons, G.J.: Authentication theory/coding theory. In: Blakley, G.R., Chaum, D. (eds.) CRYPTO 1984. LNCS, vol. 196, pp. 411–431. Springer, Heidelberg (1985). https://doi.org/10.1007/3-540-39568-7_32
13. Abadi, M.: Two facets of authentication. In: IEEE Symposium on Security and Privacy (1998)
14. Shashkevich, A.: Stanford researcher examines earliest concepts of artificial intelligence, robots in ancient myths. Stanford Report (2019). https://news.stanford.edu/stories/2019/02/ancient-myths-reveal-early-fantasies-artificial-life/
15. Smith, R.: Aristotle's logic. Stanford Encyclopedia of Philosophy (Winter 2022 Edition) (2000). https://plato.stanford.edu/ENTRIES/aristotle-logic/
16. Ewald, W.: The emergence of first-order logic. Stanford Encyclopedia of Philosophy (Spring 2019 Edition) (2018). https://plato.stanford.edu/archives/spr2019/entries/logic-firstorder-emergence/

17. Russell, S., Norvig, P.: Artificial Intelligence: A Modern Approach, 4th edn. Pearson (2021)
18. Goldstine, H.H.: The Computer from Pascal to von Neumann. Princeton University Press, Princeton, N.J. (1972)
19. Riskin, J.: The defecating duck, or, the ambiguous origins of artificial life. Crit. Inq. **29**(4), 599–633 (2003)
20. Moor, J.: The dartmouth college artificial intelligence conference: the next fifty years. AI Mag. **27**(4), 87 (2006)
21. McCarthy, J., Hayes, P.J.: Some philosophical problems from the standpoint of artificial intelligence. In: Webber, B.L., Nilsson, N.J. (eds.) Readings in Artificial Intelligence, pp. 431–450. Morgan Kaufmann, Burlington, Mass (1981)
22. Turing, A.M.: Computing machinery and intelligence. Mind **59**(236), 433–460 (1950)
23. Shannon, C.E.: XXII. Programming a computer for playing chess. London, Edinburgh Dublin Philosophical Mag. J. Sc. **41**(314), 256–275 (1950). https://doi.org/10.1080/14786445008521796
24. Valencia, S.: The lisp approach to AI (part 1, Medium (2017). https://medium.com/ai-society/the-lisp-approach-to-ai-part-1-a48c7385a913
25. Winston, P.H.: Marvin L. Minsky (1927–2016). Nature **530**, 282 (2016)
26. Newell, A., Simon, H.A.: Computer science as empirical inquiry: symbols and search. In: ACM Turing Award Lectures. New York, NY, USA: ACM, 1976, vol. 19, no. 3, pp. 113–126, originally published as the 1975 ACM Turing Award Lecture (1976)
27. Laird, J.E., Rosenbloom, P.S.: In pursuit of mind: the research of Allen Newell. AI Mag. **13**(4), 17–65 (1992). https://ojs.aaai.org/aimagazine/index.php/aimagazine/article/view/1019
28. Weizenbaum, J.: ELIZA–A computer program for the study of natural language communication between man and machine. Commun. ACM **9**(1), 36–45 (1966)
29. Maglogiannis, I., Iliadis, L., Pimenidis, E.: An overview of chatbot technology. Informatics **7**(3), 37 (2020)
30. Yost, J.R.: The march of IDES: early history of intrusion-detection expert Systems. IEEE Ann. Hist. Comput. **38**(4), 42–54 (2016)
31. Denning, D.: An intrusion-detection model. In: Proceedings of the IEEE Symposium Security and Privacy, pp. 118–133 (1986)
32. Bruneau, G.: The history and evolution of intrusion detection (2021). https://sansorg.egnyte.com/dl/TmT2wfl1v7
33. Halimaa, A., Sundarakantham, K.: Machine learning based intrusion detection system. 2023 3rd International Conference on Technological Advancements in Computational Sciences (ICTACS), pp. 197–205 (2019). https://api.semanticscholar.org/CorpusID:204229558
34. Lansky, J., Ali, S., Mohammadi, M., Majeed, M.K., et al.: Deep learning-based intrusion detection systems: a systematic review. IEEE Access **9**, 101574–101599 (2021)
35. van der Veen, M., Lemma, A., Celik, M., Katzenbeisser, S.: Forensic watermarking in digital rights management. In: Petković, M., Jonker, W. (eds.) Security, Privacy, and Trust in Modern Data Management. Data-Centric Systems and Applications. Springer, Heidelberg (2007). https://doi.org/10.1007/978-3-540-69861-6_19
36. Dingledy, F., Berrio Matamoros, A.: What is digital rights management? (2019)
37. Google: Copyright and rights management (2024). https://support.google.com/youtube/topic/2676339. Accessed 2 May 2024

38. Ed Sheeran wins copyright case over 'Shape of You'. https://www.bbc.com/news/entertainment-arts-61006984

39. Digital millennium copyright act. Pub. L. No. 105–304, 112 Stat. 2860 (1998) (codified in scattered sections of 17 U.S.C.) (1998)

40. Copyright Act (R.S.C., 1985, c. C-42) 1985, s. 41 (1985). https://laws-lois.justice.gc.ca/eng/acts/C-42/

41. Reynolds, G.: Step in the wrong direction: the impact of the legislative protection of technological protection measures on fair dealing and freedom of expression. CJLT **5**(3), 4 (2006). https://digitalcommons.schulichlaw.dal.ca/cjlt/vol5/iss3/4/

42. Cade, D.: Botched Steve McCurry print leads to photoshop scandal. Petapixel (2016). https://petapixel.com/2016/05/06/botched-steve-mccurry-print-leads-photoshop-scandal/

43. Sanders, L.: Ethical lapse': photoshop scandal catches up with iconic photojournalist Steve McCurry. DW (2016). https://www.dw.com/en/ethical-lapse-photoshop-scandal-catches-up-with-iconic-photojournalist-steve-mccurry/a-19296237

44. Tartar, A.: The totally serious guide to obama skeet shooting photo conspiracy theories (2013). https://nymag.com/intelligencer/2013/02/obama-skeet-shooting-photo-conspiracy-theories.html

45. OpenA: Our approach to AI safety. https://openai.com/index/our-approach-to-ai-safety/

46. Guess, A.M., Lyons, B.A.: Misinformation, disinformation, and online propaganda. In: Persily, N., Tucker, J.A. (eds.) Social Media and Democracy: The State of the Field, Prospects for Reform Cambridge: Cambridge University Press (2020)

47. Wilson, C.: Israel-Gaza: adobe accused of selling fake AI images (2023). https://www.crikey.com.au/2023/11/01/israel-gaza-adobe-artificial-intelligence-images-fake-news/

48. Benkler, Y., Faris, R., Roberts, H.: Network Propaganda: Manipulation, Disinformation, and Radicalization in American Politics. Oxford University Press (2018)

49. United Nations: Information integrity on digital platforms (2023). https://www.un.org/sites/un2.un.org/files/our-common-agenda-policy-brief-information-integrity-en.pdf

50. David, E.: OpenAI can't tell if something was written by AI after all. The Verge (2023). https://www.theverge.com/2023/7/25/23807487/openai-ai-generated-low-accuracy

51. Heikkilä, M.: Why detecting AI-generated text is so difficult (and what to do about it) plus: AI models generate copyrighted images and photos of real people. Technology Review (2023). https://www.technologyreview.com/2023/02/07/1067928/why-detecting-ai-generated-text-is-so-difficult-and-what-to-do-about-it/

52. Khan, I.: Disinformation and freedom of opinion and expression, Report of the special rapporteur on the promotion and protection of the right to freedom of opinion and expression (2021). https://digitallibrary.un.org/record/3925306?ln=en&v=pdf

53. Edwards, B.: UK seeks to criminalize creation of sexually explicit AI deepfake images without consent. Ars Technica (2024). https://arstechnica.com/information-technology/2024/04/uk-seeks-to-criminalize-creation-of-sexually-explicit-ai-deepfake-images-without-consent/

54. Regulation of the European parliament and of the council laying down harmonised rules on artificial intelligence and amending regulations (ec) no 300/2008, (eu) no 167/2013, (eu) no 168/2013, (eu) 2018/858, (eu) 2018/1139 and (eu) 2019/2144 and directives 2014/90/eu, (eu) 2016/797 and (eu) 2020/1828 (2023)

55. Bill C-27, an act to enact the consumer privacy protection act, the personal infor-
    mation and data protection tribunal act and the artificial intelligence and data
    act and to make consequential and related amendments to other acts (Canada)
    (second reading 24 April 2023) (2023)
56. Global declaration on information integrity online (Canada) (2023). https://www.
    international.gc.ca/world-monde/issues_development-enjeux_developpement/
    peace_security-paix_securite/information_integrity-integrite_information.aspx?
    lang=eng. Accessed 12 May 2024

Author Index

© The Editor(s) (if applicable) and The Author(s), under exclusive license
to Springer Nature Switzerland AG 2025
C. Boyd et al. (Eds.): Ed Dawson Festschrift 2024, LNCS 15600, p. 327, 2025.
https://doi.org/10.1007/978-3-031-83490-5

The manufacturer's authorised representative in the EU is Springer
Nature Customer Service Centre GmbH, Europaplatz 3, 69115 Heidelberg,
Germany. If you have any concerns regarding our products, please
contact ProductSafety@springernature.com

Printed and bound by CPI Group (UK) Ltd, Croydon, CR0 4YY

24/04/2026

02096365-0007